NETWARE® TROUBLESHOOTING

Micheal L. Hader

▲▼▲
Addison-Wesley Publishing Company, Inc.

Reading, Massachusetts   Menlo Park, California   New York
Don Mills, Ontario   Wokingham, England   Amsterdam   Bonn
Sydney   Singapore   Tokyo   Madrid   San Juan
Paris   Seoul   Milan   Mexico City   Taipei

To my NetWare students who push me, my friends who support me, and my family who loves me in spite of the long hours and everything else.

Many of the designations used by manufacturers and sellers to distinguish their products are claimed as trademarks. Where those designations appear in this book, and Addison-Wesley was aware of a trademark claim, the designations have been printed in initial capital letters or all capital letters.

Copyright © 1991 by Micheal L. Hader

All rights reserved. No part of this publication may be reproduced, stored in a retrieval system, or transmitted, in any form or by any means, electronic, mechanical, photocopying, recording, or otherwise, without the prior written permission of the publisher. Printed in the United States of America. Published simultaneously in Canada.

Set in 11-pt Palatino by CopyRight, Bedford, MA

Sponsoring Editor: Julie Stillman
Project Editor: Elizabeth Rogalin

ISBN 0-201-57737-2
1 2 3 4 5 6 7 8 9-MW-9594939291
First printing, June 1991

Acknowledgments

There are so many people who deserve some credit for making this book possible that it is going to be hard to mention everyone. First, I want to acknowledge the thousands of people throughout the United States and Canada who have attended my NetWare seminars. Over the past four years, over 5,000 people have brought me their NetWare problems. I am continually challenged by their questions and problems, and they have had a lot to do with my desire to develop a book in this particular format.

Many, many vendors deserve mention because of their willingness to work with someone who does not sell their products. As a seminar leader, our firm is not a reseller and some vendors won't take the time to work with us, but I really appreciate those that do. Diane Candler and Denni Conner at Thomas-Conrad have been great at getting new products to me for evaluation. Bob Behrends at Novell has helped with getting information in my hands quickly. Jeff Schwartz at TECHS International has provided a wealth of information and support through their TECHS database. Kent Sterling at Network General provides me with up-to-date information on the Sniffer protocol analyzer. I want to thank Steve Morehouse at Knozall Systems, Lori Eisenstein at Cheyenne Software, John Lomax at J.A. Lomax Associates, and Camille Marakovitz at Brightworks Development for their support in providing software for me to test.

I want to thank those who let me teach this topic in the first place. Our seminar firm, Data Tech Institute headed by John Ignozza, California State University, Fullerton and their great staff led by Dr. Ruth Truman, and California State University, Long Beach, Lynn Hendricks and the extension staff, who I've taught for ten years. Without the opportunity to teach and hear from all of those who have been in the trenches, I wouldn't know a tenth of what I know about NetWare. I want to thank the other trainers I work with, John Jackson, Vic Rezmovic, Kim Roberts, Don Evans, Jenny Minton, Debbie Sperandeo, David Howard, and Scott Foerster for their support and willingness to keep me challenged at every turn.

Acknowledgments

I owe a special thanks to a few fellow seminar leaders who challenge me to keep learning and improving. Mark Minasi and Scott Foerster have taught me much about the workings of PC hardware, disks, and printers. Mark Miller, who probably knows everything there is to know about LANs and protocols, has been great in helping me understand how LANs transport data.

Addison-Wesley has been terrific throughout the process of getting this book together. I want to thank Julie Stillman and Elizabeth Rogalin for taking on this project. Their support and professionalism made a big difference in getting everything done. As usual, I underestimated the time it would take to get some of the writing done, but their willingness to work it out is very much appreciated.

Finally, I want to thank those who are most important to me, my family. I saved their mention for last, not because it was least, but because it is the last thing one reads or hears that one remembers most. This book has seen us through a particularly difficult time due to a disastrous accident July 1990. The book became a type of therapy in that it refocused our attention away from those events onto something in the future. However, it could not have happened without the loving support of everyone: my wife Judy, whose patience never gave out even though she doesn't know a thing about NetWare, and the kids, Kristi, Jason, Bethany, Jenni, and Daniel, who asked every day if the book was done yet. They really encouraged me to keep up the work. I also want to thank my extended family, my mother who works with me every day in our office, and my friends at Family Life Ministry of the Crystal Cathedral. Your concern, support, and prayers were all felt and appreciated over the past few months while this project was taking form. I love you all, dearly.

Contents

Preface   xi

Part I   **File Server Optimization** 1

Chapter 1   **File Server Memory** 3
    1. Base Operating System 5
    2. Network Interface Card (NIC) Driver 6
    3. Disk Interface Drivers 8
    4. Dynamic RAM 9
    5. File Allocation Tables 10
    6. Operating System Options 11
    7. Communication Buffers 15
    8. Directory Hashing 16
    9. Directory Caching 17
    10. Open Files 18
    11. Indexed Files 18
    12. Shared Printers 19
    13. Value Added Programs (VAPs) 20
    14. File Caching 22
    Summary 23

Chapter 2   **Reconfiguring a NetWare 286 File Server** 25
    Linking the Operating System 26
    Installing and Configuring NetWare on the File Server 27
    Linking NetWare with Drivers 28
    Installation and Configuration 41
    Configuring Adapters 45
    Summary 55

Chapter 3   **Configuring a NetWare 386 File Server** 57
    NetWare Loadable Modules (NLMs) 57
    Console Set Commands 62
    Using Load Commands to Load LAN Drivers 73
    Using BIND Command to Link LAN Drivers 77
    Summary 79

Chapter 4 — Internal Bridges 81
Using Internal Bridges 81
Setting Up an Internal Bridge 86
Summary 86

Chapter 5 — File Attributes 87
Attribute Definitions 88
Shareable versus Non-Shareable; Read-Only versus Read-Write 92
Search Mode Attribute 103
Summary 113

Part II — Workstation Optimization 115

Chapter 6 — Configuring and Using the Network Shell 117
DOS Workstation Shells 117
The Re-director Program 124
NETBIOS Emulation 130
DOS/ODI Workstation Shells 131
Removing the Network Shell 133
Summary 135

Chapter 7 — Using the Workstation Configuration Files 137
Locating the Configuration Files 137
IPX and SPX Protocols 140
SHELL.CFG Commands and Usage 140
NET.CFG Commands and Usage 152
Summary 167

Chapter 8 — Booting the Workstation and Logging In 169
Settings for CONFIG.SYS and AUTOEXEC.BAT 169
Attaching to the File Server and Finding the LOGIN Directory 173
Solving PATH Problems 175
Login Scripts 184
Starting Up a Menu 196
Login Script Commands 196
Using MAP Commands in Login Scripts 213
Locating Configuration Files 220
Summary 223

Contents

Part III	**Third-party Software** 225	
Chapter 9	**Using Application Software with NetWare** 227	
	Data File Integrity 227	
	Configuration Files 231	
	Printing Issues 240	
	Using WordPerfect with NetWare 241	
	Summary 252	
Part IV	**Printing Problems** 253	
Chapter 10	**Setting Up Shared Printing** 255	
	Setting Up the Shared Printing Environment 256	
	Task 1—Defining Printers 258	
	Task 2—Creating the Print Server 266	
	Task 3—Creating Print Job Definitions with PRINTCON 272	
	Tasks 4 and 5—Copying Job Definitions to Other Users 277	
	Task 6—Loading and Using PSERVER 278	
	Task 7—Using RPRINTER for Remote Print Servers 278	
	Summary 280	
Chapter 11	**Printing Problems in a Network Environment** 281	
	Printing Graphics 282	
	Using Laser, LED Array, and Thermal Transfer Printers 288	
	Using Plotters as Shared Network Printers 290	
	Miscellaneous Problems 292	
	Summary 312	
Chapter 12	**Remote Printing** 313	
	Third-party Print Servers 313	
	Summary 317	
Part V	**User Accounts and Security** 319	
Chapter 13	**Controlling the LOGIN Process** 321	
	Keeping Unauthorized People Out of the Network 321	
	Controlling Valid User's Log In 326	
	Summary 332	

Chapter 14	**Solving the Rights Puzzle** 333
Rights Definition 333
Basic Rights Concepts for NetWare 286 335
Three Ways to Gain Implicit Rights 336
Clarification of Rights Gained from Multiple Sources 338
NetWare 386 Differences 340
Summary 349
Chapter 15	**Using Groups to Manage Rights** 351
Two Ways to Set Up Groups 351
Rights in Downline Directories 354
Summary 360
Part VI	**Managing the LAN** 361
Chapter 16	**NetWare Supervisors, Workgroup Managers, and User Account Managers** 363
NetWare 386 Group Managers 364
NetWare 386 User Account Managers 365
Creating Groups 366
Creating Independent File Server Domains 367
Mixed NetWare 286 and NetWare 386 Environments 369
Summary 373
Chapter 17	**Monitoring the File Server** 375
File Server Statistics Summary 375
Cache Statistics 381
Channel Statistics 387
Disk Mapping Information 390
Disk Statistics 392
File System Statistics 395
LAN I/O Statistics 398
Transaction Tracking Statistics 405
Volume Information 408
Comments on FCONSOLE 411
Diagnostic Aids 412
File Service Processes (FSP) 416
Summary 425

Contents

Chapter 18	**Documentation** 427	
	Manual Documentation Tasks 428	
	File Server Documentation 437	
	Summary 438	
Appendix A	**NetWare 286 Command Summary** 439
Appendix B	**NetWare 386 Command Additions** 481
Appendix C	**NetWare 286 Console Commands** 485
Appendix D	**NetWare 386 Console Commands** 505
Glossary	543
Index	591

Preface

This book is unique. It has a unique purpose and a unique approach. Most people don't have the time or the inclination to read another book about computers or LANs. *NetWare Troubleshooting* is not designed to replace the NetWare manuals by restating what is already there. Instead, it is designed to help you solve problems quickly and efficiently. It is designed to be a resource, a tool to be used when needed.

I have taken a collection of the most common problems that NetWare LAN administrators have and talked about how to solve them. Most of the information you will find in this book will be very practical. Many of the ideas in this book have never been documented elsewhere. This isn't a book of networking theories. Yet, it will teach you much about the inner workings of your NetWare LAN.

Much of the book is done in a scenario fashion, outlining a problem, filling in enough background to understand the problem, and then an approach for solving the problem. I think you will find this format appealing and productive. You don't have to read the entire book to get great ideas. You can tackle just the parts that are important to you now.

The diskette includes programs that help to solve particular problems, especially those in which there is a useful feature missing from NetWare. While Novell may someday incorporate these features in NetWare, many of us cannot afford to wait. We need solutions today. You will find some very useful programs on the diskette.

I believe this book can help you. If you are responsible for keeping your network up and running, you will find *NetWare Troubleshooting* a valuable resource.

In the various scenarios throughout the book, I have tackled dozens of different problems. While the book isn't designed to teach you everything there is to know about NetWare, it is designed to teach you the things that you might not know. Much of this book is derived from courses I have taught on the same subject, so I have a good feel about the types of problems people face with NetWare and how to solve them. In certain areas, we have to work around limitations of NetWare. In other situations, our application software can be a problem. As much as possible, these problems are generalized so that you will understand how to solve these problems, no matter what application software you use.

I hope that you get as much from reading this book as I did writing it. I believe you will. Good luck, and happy networking!

Micheal L. Hader
Tustin, CA

Part I
File Server Optimization

I have installed and consulted on hundreds of LANs over the past few years, and so I am aware that one of the important items of discussion is the performance of the network. Everyone wants to get every bit of performance possible from their network. Without question, the file server is an important ingredient in the recipe of factors that governs the overall performance of the LAN. Yet, the file server mystifies most people. This part explains some key issues regarding the file server and its effect on performance.

1
File Server Memory

A fundamental element of your file server and its performance is memory. Your file server's memory needs must be met for your LAN to perform to its potential. However, file server memory needs in a Novell NetWare LAN are a mystery to most because they are not documented in the manuals that come with NetWare. People have three major questions:

How much memory does the file server need?

What symptoms indicate a problem?

How do I find out how an existing file server was installed?

Keep in mind that the answer to the first question depends to some extent on the version of NetWare you are using. Also, NetWare 286 and NetWare 386 are completely different operating systems: each needs to be discussed separately.

All NetWare versions will use all the RAM your server has to offer. However, your server may not have enough RAM to do everything the way that it ought to be done to maximize performance. NetWare is designed to take advantage of the advanced features of the Intel 80286 and 80386 CPU chips. NetWare 286 supports a full complement of 16 megabytes of RAM; NetWare 386 supports 4 gigabytes. NetWare uses this RAM to maximize the server's performance.

Too little RAM in the server results in a sluggish system. Most choices made during configuration and installation of NetWare affect the system's RAM needs. Therefore, it is important that you understand both memory usage and how to change the server's configuration.

The remainder of this chapter discusses memory usage for NetWare 286. Chapter 3 contains a similar discussion for NetWare 386. Since the different versions of NetWare 286 each have unique features, I will provide an overview of memory usage options by comparing the different versions. Then I will discuss the options in detail. Table 1–1 highlights the similarities and differences among NetWare versions. In the table ELS is an acronym for Entry Level System, Novell's low-cost network products. SFT stands for System Fault Tolerant, a NetWare version with special features for error recovery.

Table 1–1. NetWare 286 memory

Memory Item	ELS I	ELS II	Advanced NetWare	SFT NetWare
1. Base Operating System	X	X	X	X
2. Network Interface Card (NIC) Drivers	X	X	X	X
3. Disk Interface Drivers	X	X	X	X
4. Dynamic RAM	X	X	X	X
5. File Allocation Tables	X	X	X	X
Mirrored Drives				X
6. Operating System Options	X	X	X	X
Dedicated Server		X	X	X
Transaction Tracking				X
7. Communication Buffers	X	X	X	X
8. Directory Hashing	X	X	X	X
9. Directory Caching	X	X	X	X
10. Open Files	X	X	X	X
11. Indexed Files	X	X	X	X
12. Shared Printers	X	X	X	X
13. Value Added Programs (VAPs)		X	X	X
14. File Caching	X	X	X	X

Table 1–1 illustrates that NetWare versions are more similar than different. However, the differences are significant and need to be understood. In the next sections I discuss each of the fourteen items in Table 1–1 in consideration of the following:

- The item's function in the file server. These discussions will help you to understand the overall file server.
- Calculations of memory requirements for each item. These discussions include general recommendations where appropriate.
- Your present file server's configuration for the item. These discussions tell you where to look to determine the configuration.

1. BASE OPERATING SYSTEM

The operating system kernel provides all basic functions of the multitasking NetWare system, including basic file and print sharing functions, security management, protocol encoding, and error recovery. These core elements may vary somewhat among the various versions of NetWare. For example, SFT's disk mirroring and disk duplexing capabilities are not part of ELS I, ELS II, or Advanced NetWare. Such differences account for differing sizes of the operating system kernel.

The basic NetWare 286 operating system is about 400K. You cannot configure this core portion of the operating system during installation. To this core, however, you can add the drivers discussed in the next two sections.

To verify the operating system's basic size, use either of the following commands.

```
DIR SYS:SYSTEM\NET$OS.EXE
NDIR SYS:SYSTEM\NET$OS.EXE
```

2. NETWORK INTERFACE CARD (NIC) DRIVERS

The interface between the operating system and the network interface card is a software driver that must be linked to the operating system during installation. Due to different protocols and different card designs, each LAN card model may have a unique driver. Unfortunately, there is very little standardization in this area. Each different Ethernet or token ring model has a different driver. ARCnet is the exception: the ARCnet card manufacturers adhere to self-imposed design standards that make these cards and their drivers practically interchangeable.

NetWare 286 can have up to four NICs installed in the file server. Novell calls this **internal bridging**. Internal bridges are useful in many situations. They allow a heavily loaded single network to be split into two or more physical networks, improving performance by reducing the overload on each network. Figures 1-1 and 1-2 show how this works. Internal bridges can also bridge two networks that use dissimilar protocols, such as Ethernet and token ring. Finally, internal bridges can extend the wiring limitations that a single network imposes. Be sure to consider including internal bridges in your overall network strategy.

Novell provides some NIC drivers; the manufacturers of the NICs provide the balance. Almost all NIC manufacturers provide drivers for their cards in a NetWare environment.

As you might expect, the sizes of NIC drivers vary from one model to another. Generally you can allocate about 20K for each NIC driver. With four NICs—the maximum allowed—this could add up to about 80K.

To determine operating system size with NICs and drivers installed, use the directory command to display the file NET$OS.EXE, in the server's SYSTEM directory. To verify which NICs are installed in the server, you have two options:

At the file server console,
Type: CONFIG.
or
Run: FCONSOLE from a workstation.
Select: LAN DRIVER INFORMATION from the menu.

Network Interface Card (NIC) Drivers

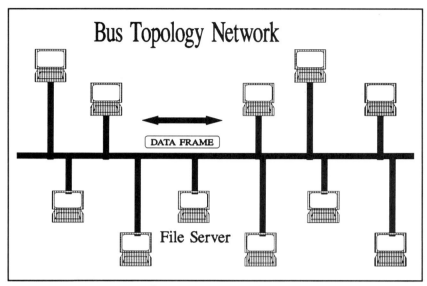

Figure 1-1. Bus LAN with no internal bridge

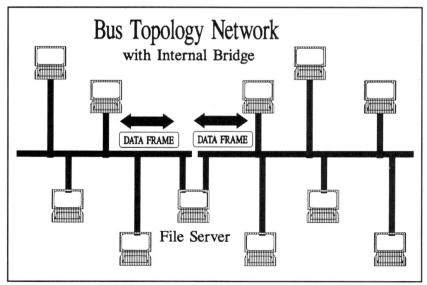

Figure 1-2. Bus LAN with internal bridge

3. DISK INTERFACE DRIVERS

The network operating system must also be linked with the appropriate driver for the disk controller(s). Novell ships NetWare with drivers for the "AT-style" or Industry Standard Architecture (ISA) ST506 type disk controller. In addition, Novell includes drivers for IBM PS/2 ESDI and MFM controllers and for the Novell Disk Coprocessor (DCB). Various disk drive and disk controller manufacturers also supply drivers for their products' use in a NetWare environment.

Up to five disk controllers can be installed in the file server. The size of the disk drivers varies from 15K to 20K, depending on disk controller type.

You can determine operating system size just as you did before, with the directory command display NET$OS.EXE in the server's SYSTEM directory. To verify which disk drivers are installed in the server, you can use the FCONSOLE program.

Type: FCONSOLE.

Select: STATISTICS from the Available Topics menu.

Select: either CHANNEL STATISTICS from the File Server Statistics menu, choose the desired disk channel, and then look at DRIVER TYPE and CHANNEL CONFIGURATION.

or

Select: DISK STATISTICS from the File Server Statistics menu and then look at CONTROLLER TYPE and DISK TYPE. If there is more than one drive, a list of available drives will be displayed.

The base operating system, the NIC Drivers, and the Disk Interface Drivers make up the size of NET$OS.EXE, the NetWare operating system. After the operating system has been linked, the only way to change these items is to rerun the setup program: NETGEN for Advanced and SFT NetWare or ELSGEN for ELS I and ELS II.

4. DYNAMIC RAM

NetWare uses file server RAM for tracking many processes that pertain to file server activities that are not readily apparent to the user. Most of these processes use memory known as the DGroup data segment. This memory segment is 64K and its size cannot be altered. Adding memory to the file server does not affect the DGroup memory allocation.

The DGroup data segment uses memory for processes known as the Global Static Data area, the Process Stack area, the Volume and Monitor Table area, the File Service Process Buffer area, and Dynamic Memory Pool 1. The Global Static Data area contains all the global variables defined in the NetWare operating system as well as those defined by NIC and disk drivers. The Process Stack area is used by NetWare as stack space for all of the NetWare operating system processes. Volume and Monitor Tables contain the data used by the file server Monitor program and the information about all of the disks that are mounted on the file server. File Service Process Buffers contain incoming file service data packets that are waiting to be processed.

Dynamic Memory Pool 1 is used by many NetWare processes. It is used for drive mappings, drive information, process control blocks, the Auto Remirror Queue, Apple MAC File support, workstations support, Spool Queue Entries, Queue Management, Queue Server information, Volume Names, VAP stacks, and semaphores. Dynamic Memory Pool 1 can range in size within the DGroup memory between 16K and 20.9K.

While the amount of RAM allocated to DGroup memory is fixed, the amount of memory used by Dynamic Memory Pool 1 can be affected by the file server and network configuration. Chapter 17 discusses DGroup memory in detail.

The size of DGroup RAM and Dynamic Memory Pool 1 can be viewed with the FCONSOLE program.

Select: STATISTICS from the Available Topics menu.
Select: SUMMARY. Near the bottom of the screen you see DYNAMIC MEMORY 1, which is the same as Dynamic Memory Pool 1, and DYNAMIC MEMORY 2, which is the same as DGROUP memory.

5. FILE ALLOCATION TABLES

Like DOS, NetWare uses a File Allocation Table (FAT) to record which blocks ("clusters" in DOS) belong to a file. To improve performance, NetWare loads the FAT into the file server's RAM. There are two reasons for doing so. First, searching through a table in RAM is faster than searching through a table on a disk. Second, it eliminates the disk reads needed to search the table on disk.

The FAT's size depends on two things.

- The drive's size affects the FAT's size. NetWare allocates 1K of RAM for each megabyte of disk. Therefore, a 300Mb disk drive requires 300K of RAM for the FAT.
- If you use SFT NetWare and its disk mirroring or duplexing feature, you must double the allocation because the mirrored drives will have different FATs.

  The FATs are equivalent in that both contain all the information for the files stored on the server disk. Differences in the FATs are due to the fact that the mirrored or duplex drives will have different sets of bad blocks. On a server with duplex or mirrored 300Mb drives, allocate 600K of RAM.

To determine your drive's size and whether it is mirrored or duplex, use the FCONSOLE program.

Select: STATISTICS from the Available Topics menu.

Select: DISK STATISTICS from the File Server Statistics menu, then select the desired drive. The line "Drive Size" shows the drive size less **hot fix area**.

The Hot Fix Redirection Table is an area of the disk that is allocated during installation and used for redirecting data when NetWare detects a bad disk block. NetWare's read–after–write verification can detect a bad block where the data cannot be written correctly. The data is then moved to the Hot Fix Redirection Table, and the bad block area is marked so that NetWare will not attempt to use it again.

To learn whether the drive is mirrored or duplex, use the FCONSOLE program.

Operating System Options

Select: STATISTICS from the Available Topics menu.

Select: Disk Mapping Information from the File Server Statistics menu. The bottom portion of the screen lists physical drives and their mirrors, if any.

6. OPERATING SYSTEM OPTIONS

Earlier in this chapter, Table 1-1, NetWare 286 Memory, illustrated that there are different choices for operating system options, depending on which version of NetWare you are using. These operating system options relate somewhat to the type of environment your LAN is to serve. Let's look at the basic differences among versions.

ELS I is the most limited version of NetWare, supporting only four workstations logged into the server. This version allows you to choose either a dedicated file server or a non-dedicated file server if you are using version 2.12 or later. In earlier versions, the file server had to be non-dedicated.

ELS II limits workstations to eight logged into the file server. With this version you can choose either a dedicated or a non-dedicated file server. See the discussion of dedicated and non-dedicated file servers at the end of this section.

Advanced NetWare supports up to 100 workstations logged into the file server. As with ELS II, the operating system options are a dedicated or a non-dedicated file server. See the next section for a discussion on the merits of dedicated and non-dedicated file servers.

SFT (System Fault Tolerant) NetWare is top-of-the-line NetWare 286 and supports up to 100 users. As its name suggests, this version is designed for better recovery from a system fault. One of its features is the drive mirroring and/or duplexing option selected during installation. The operating system option for SFT NetWare is whether or not to use the **Transaction Tracking System** (TTS).

With TTS, NetWare tracks updates or changes as they are made to data files and then records the updates or changes in a special log file. If the updating process is successful, NetWare erases the log file. If the process fails, NetWare uses the log file to reverse the changes made to the data file, restoring the file's original condition.

The operating system options add to the RAM requirements of the file server as follows.

Dedicated file server	0K
Non-dedicated file server	640K
SFT without TTS	0K
SFT with TTS	22K

You can verify which NetWare version is installed on your file server with the FCONSOLE program or the console VERSION command.

At the colon (:) prompt on the file server,

Type: VERSION.

At a workstation run FCONSOLE.

Select: VERSION INFORMATION from the Available Topics menu.

To verify the installation of the Transaction Tracking System,

Select: STATISTICS from the Available Topics menu.

Select: SUMMARY from the File Server Statistics menu. In the bottom portion of the screen, you see the line "Transactions." If TTS has been activated, this line shows a nonzero value beneath the column heading "Maximum."

If your server boots to DOS, you have a non-dedicated file server. If your file server comes up in console mode with a colon (:) prompt, you can determine if it is non-dedicated by typing DOS after the prompt. If your server is non-dedicated, it switches to workstation mode. To go back to console mode, type CONSOLE after the DOS prompt.

Operating System Options

Dedicated versus Non-dedicated File Servers

For Advanced NetWare (100-user version) and ELS II (8-user version) you can select either a dedicated or a non-dedicated file server. A dedicated file server is a personal computer (PC) that is dedicated to tasks involved in managing the network. It handles such tasks as disk sharing, file caching, printing jobs on shared printers, and security validation. It does not run any end-user applications. A non-dedicated file server does all these things, plus serves as a workstation for end-user applications.

The usual justification for a non-dedicated file server is cost. It is thought to be less expensive because a separate machine, NIC, and cable does not have to be purchased for one user. However, before deciding on a non-dedicated file server, several disadvantages need to be carefully weighed.

The biggest drawback to a non-dedicated file server is that it fosters corrupted data because a user is also using the file server machine as a workstation. Problems occur when the user turns off "his" or "her" machine before making sure that everyone else has logged off. Users who are logged on and have files open are abruptly disconnected from the server before they are able to close their files. This can either corrupt the files that were open or result in loss of data from files that were not updated. The damaged files need to be restored, using some sort of backup. Then updates made since the backup need to be recovered. The same kind of damage can also occur if the user of the workstation/file server reboots.

End-user files are not the only files at risk. If the server was turned off while updating the File Allocation Table, damage to the FAT can cause major disruption. Also, directories and bindery files are subject to no less disruptive damage. To the extent that you can train and trust the user, these problems are avoidable.

Another problem with non-dedicated file servers is that they cannot run all the programs that a user could run at a regular workstation. Two categories of software cannot run on the non-dedicated file server. The first category includes programs that *require* extended or expanded memory. The file server runs NetWare as its primary operating system. When it runs in non-dedicated mode, NetWare assigns a 640K **memory window** to the DOS application. Even though the file server has extended memory, the DOS application can only use the 640K RAM allocated to the DOS area.

The second category of programs that will not run on a non-dedicated file server includes those programs that take direct control of a hardware resource. Most DOS applications are well-behaved. That is, they access various hardware devices by issuing appropriate function calls to DOS and letting DOS handle the mechanics of the activity. However, DOS permits programs—such as those controlling a video adapter or disk drive—to bypass DOS and interface directly to the peripheral. On a non-dedicated server, NetWare, not DOS, is the primary operating system. NetWare does not permit applications to access peripherals except through NetWare. Therefore, this kind of program will not run on a non-dedicated file server. This includes many memory-resident and terminate-stay-resident programs. This is a reasonable limitation: one of the file server's primary tasks is to manage shared resources, i.e., hardware. It cannot permit programs to have uncontrolled access to the hardware.

A final problem with non-dedicated file servers is performance. A non-dedicated file server is multitasking, or able to do several things concurrently. It must manage the network while it processes the end-user's application. PCs can only do one thing at a time. They multitask using a technique called **time slicing**. Time slicing means that the PC devotes very small amounts of time to each task but appears to be doing several things at once. The issue in time slicing is how time is allocated to various activities.

When NetWare runs, approximately 60% to 70% of its time is spent on the DOS application running on the file server, and the remaining 30% to 40% is spent on other network administrative activities. This is not a configurable setting. Therefore, overall performance of the network is degraded in terms of throughput, due to the lopsided allocation of the server's time on the DOS application. To combat this problem, you must install a much faster file server, and as a result, considerably reduce the original cost savings of a non-dedicated file server.

These factors should cause you to carefully weigh the advantages and disadvantages of a dedicated versus a non-dedicated file server. You may find that the cost savings of a non-dedicated file server are not as great as they originally seem.

7. COMMUNICATION BUFFERS

Communication buffers, which Novell also calls routing buffers, are very important to your file server's overall performance. The communication buffer area in RAM is an input/output area where data packets are created and received. Because only one data packet is generally on the physical LAN channel at a time, the server uses this space to assemble packets that it is going to send to users as the channel permits. It would be very inefficient to have the file server wait until it transmitted one data packet before it could build the next. Also, as workstations send data packets to the file server, the packets are placed in the communication buffer until the server has an opportunity to work on them.

It is very important that the file server have sufficient communication buffers. If the file server runs out of communication buffers, performance suffers. It is better to have too many communication buffers than too few.

Each communication buffer requires 512 bytes of file server memory. The allowable range of communication buffer settings is from 10 to 250 (V2.15 rev. C). To calculate the communication buffers needed, use the following guide.

Each file server on the network	10
Each NIC in the file server	10
Each user logged on	1
Each user using NETBIOS emulation	10
Each shared network printer	2

Because performance is severely degraded when there are too few communication buffers, many network designers recommend using the maximum allotment of 250, regardless of the actual number required. Since each buffer is only 512 bytes, the total RAM allotment is only 125K. This is not a bad recommendation. The small portion of the 125K you are not using is unimportant considering that you must rebuild the operating system to change the quantity of communication buffers.

To determine the number of communication buffers installed on your file server, use the FCONSOLE program.

Select: STATISTICS from the Available Topics menu.
Select: SUMMARY from the File Server Statistics menu.

The lower portion of the File Server Statistics Summary has a line "Routing Buffers." Beneath the column heading "Maximum" is the number of installed communication buffers. The next column, "Peak Used," shows how many buffers you have used at one time since the file server was booted.

8. DIRECTORY HASHING

Directory hashing is a performance feature of NetWare used to solve the problem caused by having thousands of files on the file server's disk drives. Whenever a file is opened on the file server, it must first be found in the directory. For a large volume of 255Mb—the limit for NetWare 286—the default number of directory entries permitted is 17,792. Consider how long it would take to find one of these 17,792 files. If this were a database problem, you probably would not design the application to read all 17,792 records until it found the one you wanted. Instead you would design an indexing method for quickly locating the record based upon a unique key. This is what NetWare's directory hashing accomplishes. It builds a Directory Hash Table in RAM to facilitate finding files quickly on the server's drives.

NetWare creates the Directory Hash Table automatically; it is not optional. It is configurable to some extent: during file server configuration, you can establish the maximum number of directory

Directory Caching

entries permitted on the volume. Each directory entry of each volume uses four bytes in the Directory Hash Table.

To determine the number of directory entries permitted on each volume, use the FCONSOLE program.

Select: STATISTICS from the Available Topics menu.
Select: VOLUME INFORMATION from the File Server Statistics menu.
Select: a volume if you have multiple volumes.

In the middle of the display the line "Maximum Directory Entries" tells the number of files permitted in this volume.

9. DIRECTORY CACHING

Directory caching is another performance-enhancing feature that enables NetWare to read the entire directory into the file server's RAM. The server will be able to search through this directory in RAM much faster than it could search the disk. Also, directory caching eliminates a read operation to the disk. Directory caching is optional, but highly recommended if you want maximum file server performance.

The amount of file server RAM required for directory caching depends on the settings for the maximum number of directory entries permitted on the volume. Each directory entry requires 32 bytes. Therefore, for a maximum volume of 255Mb with 17,792 permitted directory entries, the amount of RAM required to cache the directory would be significant: 570K. If you did not know about this feature, you could easily underestimate your server's memory requirements.

To find out if the directory is being cached and the number of directory entries permitted on the volume, use the FCONSOLE program.

Select: STATISTICS from the Available Topics menu.
Select: VOLUME INFORMATION from the File Server Statistics menu.
Select: a volume if you have multiple volumes.

On the upper right side of the screen, the entry "Volume Cached" tells you if the volume is being cached. In the middle of the display, the line "Maximum Directory Entries" shows the number of files permitted in this volume.

10. OPEN FILES

The concept of open files should not be new to anyone who has been around PCs for a while. Just as DOS must be configured with the FILES= statement in CONFIG.SYS, NetWare must be configured for the number of open files permitted on the file server. The difference is that the file server must be set for the maximum number of files for all users who could be logged on.

The allowed range for the maximum number of open files for the file server is 10 to 1,000. Whatever the setting, each file uses 40 bytes of file server memory. In addition, about 2K of overhead are set aside to handle file and record locking. Therefore, a maximum of 1,000 open files would require roughly 42K.

Use the FCONSOLE program to determine the maximum number of open files permitted on your server.

Select: STATISTICS from the Available Topics menu.
Select: SUMMARY from the File Server Statistics menu.

The lower portion of the screen contains the line "Open Files," which tells the maximum number of open files permitted.

11. INDEXED FILES

The title of this item is not particularly well suited to helping people understand this key performance feature. I say this because people generally start thinking about their "indexed" databases

Shared Printers

and assume that this feature has to do with those files. It does, but not directly. This feature has broader application than indexed databases. This feature pertains to *any file over 2Mb,* regardless of file type.

Consider for a moment how many disk blocks (DOS clusters) a 2Mb file would occupy on the disk. In NetWare, a disk block is 4K. A 2Mb file would occupy roughly 500 blocks. This also means that the file has 500 entries in the FAT. Now, when you work with this file, you must find all of its 500 entries in the FAT. How large would the FAT be on a 255Mb drive? The answer is roughly 64,000 entries. You would have to search them all to locate the 500 you want. This is very similar to the problem described earlier for item 8, "Directory Hashing."

Indexed files in NetWare pertains to a feature enabling NetWare to build in memory an index of a file's entries in the FAT whenever that file is open on the server. The sole purpose for doing so is performance.

When configuring NetWare, you set the number of indexed files permitted open on the file server at one time. Each of these open indexed files requires 1K of file server memory.

Determining the number of indexed files permitted open on the file server is done with the FCONSOLE program.

Select: STATISTICS from the Available Topics menu.
Select: SUMMARY from the File Server Statistics menu.

The lower portion of the display contains a line "Indexed Files."

12. SHARED PRINTERS

Shared network printers may be connected to the file server. NetWare establishes a print buffer in memory for each shared printer port so that it can send a large chunk of data to the printer at once. The server is then free to do something else until the printer has printed everything in the buffer.

Each shared printer connected to the file server uses 15K of RAM. Shared printers connected to workstations by print server software do not require this RAM. A maximum of five shared printers can be configured for the file server.

This item is one of the two that I cannot verify completely because nowhere does NetWare display the printer information that was established during the file server's configuration. However, a very good clue exists: NetWare establishes a default print queue for each shared printer that was configured. These queues all have the same naming convention:

```
PRINTQ_x
```

where x represents the printer number assigned to the shared printer port. Therefore, each queue should correspond to a shared printer port.

You can view the print queue names two ways.

At the file server console,

Type: QUEUE, the console command.

Or use the workstation PCONSOLE program.

Select: PRINT QUEUE INFORMATION from the Available Options menu.

13. VALUE ADDED PROGRAMS (VAPs)

Value Added Programs, or VAPs, extend the capabilities of the basic operating system. Novell, as well as other manufacturers, develops extensions to NetWare that you can add to the environment by loading the appropriate VAP in the server. Examples of this feature are the NetWare for Macintosh VAP and the Btrieve VAP from Novell. Because these become resident programs, they require memory.

The developer of the VAP determines the amount of RAM the VAP uses. Consult the documentation provided with the VAP to determine its memory requirements.

Value Added Programs (VAPs)

Sometimes it's a little difficult to determine the amount of RAM VAPs require. The vendor's documentation is your best bet. However, you can find out a little bit of data on your own. First, you can determine the actual size of the VAPs with a directory command:

```
NDIR SYS:\SYSTEM\*.VAP
```

File size doesn't necessarily dictate memory requirements. The VAP may require memory workspace that is not part of file size. The only way to approximate this workspace is to follow the next steps when no one is logged into the file server.

1. Deactivate the VAPs by renaming them.
2. Write down their original and new names.
3. Reboot the server.
4. Check the amount of memory available for file caching through the FCONSOLE program.
5. Select STATISTICS from the Available Topics menu.
6. Select SUMMARY from the File Server Statistics menu.
7. Record the "Total Number of Cache Buffers," the number of 4K blocks in RAM available for caching.
8. Rename a VAP back to its original name.
9. Reboot the server and the VAP will reload.
10. Check the amount of memory available for file caching, following the instructions in steps 4 through 7. The difference between this number and the one obtained in step 7 represents the RAM the VAP now occupies.
11. Repeat steps 4 though 7 until you have reloaded all the VAPs.

Your list should now have the number of 4K blocks of memory each VAP requires. Multiply each by 4K to determine its RAM usage.

> **NOTE:** This is only an approximation. The actual requirements should be verified by the VAP vendor.

14. FILE CACHING

The concept of **file caching** has its roots in mainframe history. File caching began in these machines to improve throughput when the CPUs began getting much faster than their disk and tape peripherals. The basic goal is to reduce the time the CPU spends waiting for data by predicting what it is going to need next based upon what it has been using recently. The data that is thought to be needed next is fetched into memory *before* the CPU requests it. A successful prediction results in a "hit" and the disk read is eliminated. When there is a "miss," the disk read is processed normally. A companion concept to read caching is write caching, eliminating unnecessary writing when the data being written is the same as the data originally retrieved.

The NetWare server's excellent caching algorithm does a good job on both counts. Most file servers that have adequate memory will have a cache hit rate of over 90%; 90% of the time the data being requested was already in the cache or the data being written is the same as the data originally retrieved.

The amount of memory required for file caching is the answer to a two-part question. First, "How much memory will NetWare use for file caching?" and second, "How much memory does it need for file caching?"

The answer to the first question is simple. NetWare uses any memory remaining in the file server after the requirements for items 1 through 13 have been satisfied. NetWare 286 recognizes up to 16Mb of RAM.

The answer to the second question is not quite as easy—it has no definitive answer. Since the cache's purpose is to reduce reads by pre-fetching what is thought to be needed next, what should be fetched next depends somewhat on the user. In other words, some portion of this answer depends on how many users the file server services because each uses data from the server. Then, I can also assume that some portion of what should be fetched might be common to several users. Items such as program and overlay files fall into this category.

Over time, experience has helped me develop an equation which seems to work pretty well in this inexact art. First, allocate 512K to general file caching needs. Now add 512K for each group of eight users or portion thereof. This calculates to 1Mb for eight users, 1.5Mb for sixteen users, and so on. This seems to work well—you perhaps can refine the formula even more.

Finally, some have suggested putting the maximum RAM supported in the file server and forgetting the whole issue. This is not a good idea. If the amount of RAM installed dramatically exceeds the required RAM, your performance can actually *decline* because NetWare can take longer to search through the cache than it would have taken to read the needed data from the disk.

To find out how much memory your server has for file caching, use the FCONSOLE program.

Select: STATISTICS from the Available Topics menu.
Select: SUMMARY from the File Server Statistics menu.

The upper portion of the screen contains a line "Total Number of Cache Buffers." The corresponding value represents the number of 4K cache buffers available on your server for file caching.

SUMMARY

With any luck, this chapter has helped you to determine your file server's memory requirements. As I mentioned at the beginning of the chapter, one sure-fire way to slow a NetWare server is to underestimate its RAM needs. In addition, this chapter should help you understand more about NetWare design and the activities your server performs behind the scenes. This background will help you to evaluate future additions and changes to your network environment.

2
Reconfiguring a NetWare 286 File Server

Inevitably, you will have to reconfigure your file server somewhere along the way. Maybe, in the last section, you learned that your file server's configuration is not quite appropriate for your installation and you need to change a few things. Many NetWare administrators are not the same people who installed NetWare and have not been through the installation and configuration process. In this chapter, I address some "how-to's" of reconfiguring an existing file server.

The NetWare installation programs are ELSGEN for ELS I and ELS II, and NETGEN for Advanced NetWare and SFT NetWare. Your NetWare materials should include a diskette labelled either ELSGEN or NETGEN. This diskette contains the installation program. Since you cannot install or reconfigure with the original red-labelled NetWare diskettes, you must copy the originals. If your server is already installed, try to find the working copies that were used for installation.

Both ELSGEN and NETGEN programs perform two different processes during installation. The first process links the operating system with the needed drivers and creates NET$OS.EXE. The second process installs and configures NetWare on the file server.

LINKING THE OPERATING SYSTEM

This process involves selecting which NIC drivers and disk interface drivers the file server needs, and deciding how many communication buffers to establish. During this process you also assign network ID numbers to each physical network. This process actually creates the operating system, NET$OS.EXE. It also configures the NetWare utilities, COMPSURF and VREPAIR, which also must be linked with the appropriate disk interface drivers.

This process must be repeated only when a change is needed due to one or more of the following.

- A change in the NIC(s) installed in the file server.
  - A NIC is added to the file server as an internal bridge.
  - An existing NIC is reconfigured to use different settings for the IRQ, DMA, or I/O address.
  - A NIC is removed from the file server.
- A change in the disk interfaces installed in the server.
  - A change in the type of disk controller used in the server.
  - An additional disk controller is installed.
  - An existing disk controller is reconfigured to use different IRQ, DMA, or I/O address settings.
  - A disk controller is removed from the file server.
- A change is needed in the number of communication buffers.
- The operating system option needs to be changed.
  - ELS II and Advanced NetWare allow the file server to be dedicated or non-dedicated.
  - SFT NetWare allows Transaction Tracking System to be installed or not installed.

The process of linking the file server does not have to run on the file server. It can run on any PC with at least 640K of RAM and one floppy drive. As its last step, the process updates the working copies of the installation diskettes which you will use to install NetWare on the file server.

Installing and Configuring NetWare on the File Server

If you are re-linking the operating system for an existing server, you should copy the following working diskettes: NETGEN, SUPPORT, OSEXE-1, OSEXE-2, UTILEXE-1, UTILEXE-2, GENDATA, and AUXGEN. If you are adding new NIC drivers, also copy LAN_DRV_001, LAN_DRV_002, and DSK_DRV_001.

Your new version of NetWare will be made with these copies, not your original working copies. The reason for this is, if something doesn't work, you'll be able to re-load the old system while you figure out what went wrong.

INSTALLING AND CONFIGURING NETWARE ON THE FILE SERVER

You run this process after you have linked the operating system and you need to install NetWare on the file server. You also use this process to reconfigure an existing file server to change one or more of the following.

- File server name
- Partition sizes
- Hot fix redirection tables
- Volume names
- Maximum directory entries
- Maximum number of open files
- Activate or deactivate directory cache
- Maximum number of open indexed files
- Transaction tracking volume changes
- Shared printer ports
- Limit user disk space option changes

This process must be run at the file server. First boot the file server with a DOS diskette and then insert the ELSGEN or NETGEN diskette in drive A. Run ELSGEN for ELS I and ELS II or NETGEN for Advanced NetWare and SFT NetWare.

If you are changing a single option, you need only your working copies of the NETGEN or ELSGEN diskette and the diskette labelled SUPPORT. These are the only diskettes required to reconfigure an existing file server.

Custom or Default Configuration

Although the NetWare Installation manual discourages you from choosing Custom Installation, it is the choice you should make. The Default Installation makes several assumptions and decisions about your network that might be incorrect or potentially hazardous. Here are some of those assumptions.

- All NICs and disk controllers installed in the file server use the factory default settings for their IRQ, DMA, and I/O addresses, and none of these conflict with another device in the file server.
- The default 18 communication buffers for ELS I and ELS II is sufficient. The default 40 communication buffers for Advanced and SFT NetWare is sufficient.
- No other devices in the file server, such as printer ports and video adapters, use other than the IBM standard setting for the device's IRQ, DMA, and I/O addresses.
- NetWare's defaults for items such as open files and indexed files meet the network's needs.

In other words, your installation is as plain and simple as it can be and your network is pretty small. I have found that the Custom Installation options are much better for configuring NetWare. With the information I provided in the previous chapter, these options should not be confusing.

LINKING NETWARE WITH DRIVERS

Figure 2-1 illustrates the NETGEN activities required to link the operating system with the appropriate drivers. You must link three different sets of drivers to the basic NetWare operating system to make it complete: NIC (network interface card) drivers, disk drivers, and resources.

Linking NetWare with Drivers

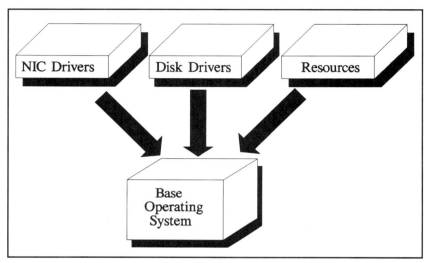

Figure 2-1. Linking NetWare with drivers

The first menu of the NETGEN or ELSGEN program asks you to select Default Configuration or Custom Configuration. In this phase of NETGEN, the major difference between these configurations is the options they offer. Since Default Configuration assumes that virtually everything is using pre-established defaults, it gives no options for setting the NIC or disk drive controller, IRQ, DMA, or I/O addresses. With Custom Configuration you can select these for the NICs and drive controllers, as well as for the other resources. The other major difference is that Default Configuration sets the communication buffers to 18 for ELS I and ELS II, and to 40 for Advanced and SFT NetWare.

After you select Custom or Default Configuration, NETGEN asks which Run Option you want to use:

Standard (Floppy disk)
RAM Disk
Hard Disk
Network Drive

Your choice depends on the machine and resources you have available for running NETGEN or ELSGEN. Standard means that you have no hard drive available. This is the most time-consuming way to run NETGEN or ELSGEN—it will probably take 45 minutes. You will have to change diskettes often during the process. The RAM Disk method is fastest, but it is not used often because it requires an 8Mb RAM disk. Not many people have 8Mb of RAM set aside. Hard Disk is the most popular method. Here again, you need 8Mb of free disk space available. NETGEN or ELSGEN copies all the needed files onto the hard disk before proceeding. Network Drive can be used on a workstation connected to a NetWare file server running NetWare 286 version 2.1 or higher. You must be a supervisor on the network to use this option since NETGEN or ELSGEN creates a subdirectory off the root directory on the server.

When you select either Hard Disk or Network Drive, NETGEN or ELSGEN creates a directory called NETWARE off the current default directory. It then creates subdirectories beneath NETWARE for each diskette used during NETGEN or ELSGEN. Then it prompts you to insert the appropriate diskette in the drive. NETGEN or ELSGEN copies all the files into the directory that matches the diskette. If you have already run NETGEN or ELSGEN and these files are already in your system, you do not have to repeat this process.

After you select a Run Option, which menu will be presented next depends on whether you have installed NetWare before. If you have already installed NetWare, you can choose from the Network Generation Options menu.

Select Network Configuration
Link/Configure NetWare Operating System
Configure NetWare Operating System
Link/Configure File Server Utilities
Configure File Server Utilities
Analyze Disk Surface
NetWare Installation
Exit NETGEN or ELSGEN

Linking NetWare with Drivers

The highlight bar will be on NetWare Installation, because the program checks the disk for the setting of a byte in the boot record indicating that NetWare can use the disk. If this byte indicates that the disk is formatted properly for NetWare, the program assumes you are installing NetWare or doing a re-install. Otherwise, the highlight bar will be on Analyze Disk Surface, which formats disks for NetWare and sets the appropriate byte in the boot record. If you want to start over to change your configuration, select the first option: Select Network Configuration.

If you choose Select Network Configuration or if you have not already installed NetWare, you can choose from the Available Options menu:

Set Operating System Options
Select Resource Sets
Select LAN Drivers
Select Disk Drivers
Select "Other" Drivers
Configure Drivers/Resources
Edit Resource List
Edit Resource Sets
Save Selections and Continue

Figure 2-2 illustrates the relationships of these menu options. Five selection activities may precede the configuration activity. The following sections discuss each option in detail. Not all options are required. You may be able to skip the Resources options as well as the Select "Other" Drivers option.

Set Operating System Options

The operating system options available depend on the version of NetWare you are installing. These options are listed in Table 2-1.

Refer to Chapter 1 for a brief discussion of these options as they pertain to the file server's memory requirements.

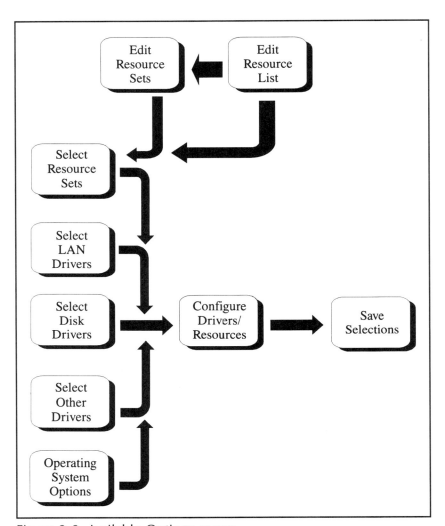

Figure 2-2. Available Options menu

Table 2-1. Operating System Options for NetWare 286 Versions

NetWare Version	Operating System Options
ELS I	Dedicated or non-dedicated file server
ELS II	Dedicated or non-dedicated file server
Advanced NetWare 286	Dedicated or non-dedicated file server
SFT NetWare 286	SFT with Transaction Tracking or SFT without Transaction Tracking

Dedicated versus Non-dedicated File Servers

A non-dedicated file server can also be used as a regular PC workstation while it is running as a file server. A dedicated file server only processes file server activities for connected users and cannot run end-user applications. The primary benefit of a non-dedicated server is that it saves the cost of purchasing and installing another workstation on the LAN. However, before deciding on a non-dedicated file server, you should be aware of the three major pitfalls of a non-dedicated file server.

Non-dedicated file servers foster data corruption. The problem here really isn't the file server's; it's the user's. Imagine the following scenario. Someone using the file server as a workstation forgets what time it is and suddenly realizes it's time for a meeting. In an unthinking, hurried moment the person forgets the PC is also the file server and just turns it off. All other users lose their connection to the file server. Their data files open on the server may be corrupted. If the server was updating the File Allocation Table (FAT), it, too, could be corrupted. Other damage could be done to the root directory and the NetWare security and bindery files. It can take days to rebuild this data on the server.

You cannot run all the programs on the server that run on a workstation. Two categories of programs cannot run on the file server.

- Programs that require extended or expanded memory. Although your server may have several megabytes of RAM, the DOS application running on the server can only access the 640K allocated by NetWare to the DOS session. The operating system uses all remaining RAM for other purposes.

- Programs that take direct control over a physical device, such as a video adapter or RAM. DOS is not a very demanding operating system. It allows programs to circumvent it and access hardware devices directly without its help. Because all file server resources are potentially shared devices, NetWare does not permit these programs to access devices except through NetWare. Attempting to run programs like this generally causes the workstation session to hang. This contributes to data corruption, because the user at the file server often reboots the server to clear the hung session, even though the server itself usually is not hung.

Non-dedicated servers tend to be too slow. Our PC-based file servers perform multitasking through a technique known as time slicing. They really do not process several tasks simultaneously, but spend a few milliseconds on each task, cycling from task to task. The important consideration is how long many time slices NetWare spends on the end-user's DOS session versus the time it spends on network activities. Unfortunately, NetWare spends about 60% to 70% of the time slices on DOS, leaving the remaining 30% to 40% for network activities. This slows performance for the rest of the LAN users.

Transaction Tracking System

SFT NetWare and NetWare 386 both have a facility called Transaction Tracking which is designed to minimize the impact of a corrupted or aborted file update process. Without Transaction Tracking, a corrupted or aborted file update process would result in partially updated data files. The usual means of recovery is to restore the original data files from a backup copy (assuming there was one) and re-start the process from the beginning. This could cause many hours of lost time and production.

Transaction Tracking System or TTS is a software feature that will create a set of log files. As updates are made to data files, the changes made are recorded in the log file. Once the update process completes successfully, the log file's information is erased. However, if the process does not complete successfully, NetWare

Linking NetWare with Drivers

can use the log file to reverse the effect of the changes that were made to the data files and restore them to the condition they were in prior to the start of the update.

The only drawback to TTS is that your software has to implement it. Novell publishes function calls that can be used with their programming libraries to activate TTS, to signal the end of an update, and to check to see if a process became corrupted and a rollback is necessary. You will need to find out if the software you are using takes advantage of these capabilities.

Select Resource Sets

This option lets you tell NETGEN or ELSGEN what kind of devices besides NICs and disk controllers you want to install in the file server. These devices include serial ports, parallel ports, and video adapters. The benefit of selecting these devices is that NETGEN or ELSGEN eliminates NIC configuration options based upon the interrupts, DMA channels, and I/O address ports used by these devices. Since multiple devices cannot share these settings, selecting the other devices here helps to avoid conflicts.

Select LAN Drivers

This menu lets you tell NETGEN or ELSGEN which NICs you want to install in the file server. On an existing installation, the LAN drivers previously selected will be displayed. The menu gives you three options:

Select Loaded Item

Load and Select Item

Deselect Item

See the boxed text for information about these choices. This menu recurs throughout the NETGEN and ELSGEN programs.

> **Select Loaded Item; Load and Select Item**
>
> Although these two options have similar names, they have different purposes. Select Loaded Item refers to selecting a driver or device that NETGEN or ELSGEN already knows. These are drivers provided by Novell or drivers that have been previously installed. When you choose this option, the program lists these "known" or "loaded" items as choices. Load and Select Item refers to devices or drivers that NETGEN or ELSGEN does not know. These are vendor-supplier drivers on a diskette. When you choose this option, the program instructs you to put the vendor's diskette in the drive, and then the program loads the drivers and adds them to the list of choices. After you load these drivers, they will be listed when the you choose Select Loaded Item.

You may select up to four NICs for one file server. Having multiple NICs in the file server is known as an internal bridge. NetWare can transmit frames across these NICs, even if the NICs are different types or use different protocols. Internal bridges reduce traffic on the physical network, interconnect dissimilar LANs, and provide a way to upgrade an existing network.

Table 2-2 lists the NIC drivers Novell supplies for various LAN adapter cards.

Table 2-2. NIC Drivers Supplied by Novell

NIC Manufacturer	Product Name
3Com	3C501 Etherlink V2.40EC
	3C503 Etherlink II V2.30EC
	3C505 Etherlink Plus V2.41EC
	3C523 Etherlink/MC V2.30EC (MicroChannel)
Gateway	G/Net V1.00

Linking NetWare with Drivers

Table 2-2, continued

NIC Manufacturer	Product Name
IBM	PC Network II V1.10
	PC Baseband V1.10
	Token Ring V2.40
Micom Interlan	NI5010 V2.30EC
Novell/Anthem	NE-1000 Ethernet V2.30EC
	NE-2000 Ethernet
	NE2 Ethernet
	NE2/32 Ethernet
	NE3200 Ethernet
	RX-Net ARCnet
	RX-Net/2 ARCnet
	S-Net V1.00
	Star Intelligent NIC V1100
Proteon	ProNet 10 P1300/P1800 V2.23
Pure Data/SMC	ARCnet

The NICs listed in Table 2-2 are not the only NICs you can use in a NetWare LAN. Other NICs generally work, if the NIC vendors have NetWare drivers for them. For example, Western Digital makes a line of NICs and supplies drivers on a diskette. You can use these drivers in place of the drivers Novell supplies.

Due to differences in NICs, NIC drivers are generally not interchangeable, even if they use the same protocol. For example, you cannot use the Novell/Anthem NE-1000 driver for a Western Digital Ethernet NIC. The exception is the ARCnet family. Usually, you can use the Pure Data/SMC ARCnet driver with any manufacturer's ARCnet NIC.

> **Standards, Compatibility and Inter-operability**
>
> IEEE and ANSI are the major groups that develop standards for data communications in the United States. Our LAN protocols are part of a group of standards known as 802.x from IEEE. Standards help to ensure compatibility of products sold by various vendors and are extremely important. Because of these standards, you can generally mix NICs from various vendors on your LAN, provided the NICs use the same set of protocols. However, each NIC may require a driver provided by its vendor.
>
> Ironically, IEEE has not adopted final standards for ARCnet. Yet most ARCnet cards are **inter-operable**. This means that vendors' NICs can be used with other vendors' NIC drivers for ARCnet. In other words, you can use the Pure Data/SMC ARCnet driver with a Tiara ARCnet NIC. This is because various ARCnet vendors have banded together to promote not only a standard, but inter-operability as a mutually beneficial goal. Therefore, almost all ARCnet NICs are completely interchangeable, unlike Ethernet or Token Ring NICs.

Each NIC must be configured before it is installed in the file server or in a workstation. During the NETGEN or ELSGEN process, you select the NIC drivers your file server needs. In addition, you select the configuration for the NIC, choosing up to seven different settings depending upon the NIC. The items that must be configured on the NIC are

- Interrupt request signal line (IRQ)
- Direct memory access channel (DMA)
- I/O address port
- Memory address
- Node address or ID
- Connector/cable type
- Remote boot ROM & RAM addresses

Linking NetWare with Drivers

Up to four NICs can be installed in a NetWare 286 file server and you must choose up to seven settings for each. The last section of this chapter goes into considerable detail about the configuration of NICs.

Select Disk Drivers

The second major component that must be linked to the operating system is the driver for each type of disk controller being used. A NetWare file server may have up to five disk controllers installed. You must select a disk driver appropriate for each controller, according to the disk channel being used. The channel is a configuration option of the disk controller itself.

Novell supplies a number of different drivers for this purpose.

IBM AT hard disk controller or compatible (ISA bus)
IBM PS/2 ESDI disk controller
IBM PS/2 MFM disk controller
IBM PS/2 Model 30 286 MFM disk controller
IBM PS/2 SCSI host adapter
Novell disk co-processor board (DCB)

These drivers suit the needs of most networks. However, always check with your vendor to make sure that these drivers suit your drive type. For example, the IBM AT Hard Disk Controller driver only works with drives that have less than 1024 cylinders and 17 sectors per track. This is not a limitation of the controller; it is a limitation of the driver Novell supplies. Many drive and PC vendors supply drivers for use in place of the drivers Novell supplies. You can install up to five disk controller/driver combinations in a NetWare 286 file server.

Select "Other" Drivers

"Other" drivers are those that NETGEN or ELSGEN does not link directly to the operating system, but to the disk drivers. These "other" drivers are rare and not usually needed. For example, the drivers used with the optical disk "jukeboxes" are usually in this category.

Configure Drivers/Resources

This menu option lets you perform three activities. First, you configure interrupt, DMA, and I/O address port settings for each NIC driver you selected. Second, because each NIC correlates to a separate physical network you must assign a unique number to each network. Third, you establish the number of communication buffers for the file server. Refer to Chapter 1 for a discussion of communication buffers.

Edit Resource List

This option lets you edit information corresponding to various resources which might be installed in a file server. Later in this chapter I discuss configuring devices that are installed in a PC. In this discussion, I explain that physical devices cannot share or use the same settings for interrupt channels, DMA channels, or I/O address ports. When configuring these devices for the file server, we can change the configuration of any conflicting device. For example, both Ethernet NICs and COM2 serial ports are commonly configured to use Interrupt 3. You can reconfigure either device to avoid conflict. If you reconfigure the COM2 device, this menu selection is used to change the configuration for the NETGEN or ELSGEN program.

Edit Resource Sets

A **resource set** is an item consisting of more than one resource item. You may combine several items into a set for convenience. When you want to use all these devices, you can select the entire set with the menu option Select Resource Sets.

After you select and configure all resources, the remainder of the process is just a matter of saving your selections and continuing, following the on-screen menu choices in the order that they appear.

Installation and Configuration

Save Selections and Continue

After your configuration choices have been made, you need to save the selections and then the NETGEN or ELSGEN program will return to the menu, Network Generation Options, shown earlier in this chapter. The remainder of the process consists of selecting each of the following menu choices in turn, while the NETGEN or ELSGEN program builds the operating system and updates several utilities:

Link/Configure NetWare Operating System
Configure NetWare Operating System
Link/Configure File Server Utilities
Configure File Server Utilities

Once these activities have been completed you will select the option to Exit NETGEN. This option will ask you if you want to download the updated data files to the working diskettes. You should answer YES to this question since you will install NetWare on the file server using your working floppies.

The next section covers the process of installing the operating system on the file server and setting various configuration options.

INSTALLATION AND CONFIGURATION

Installation or reconfiguration of NetWare occurs at the file server. You start both processes by running the NETGEN or ELSGEN program from the appropriate diskette. Figure 2-3 highlights the options affected by this process. In Figure 2-3, the dotted box around Establish a Mirror Pair signifies that this option only applies to SFT NetWare. If you are not reloading a new operating system version, the only diskettes you need to reconfigure an existing NetWare file server are those labelled SUPPORT and NETGEN. Boot the server with a DOS disk, then run either the NETGEN or ELSGEN program and follow the on-screen prompts.

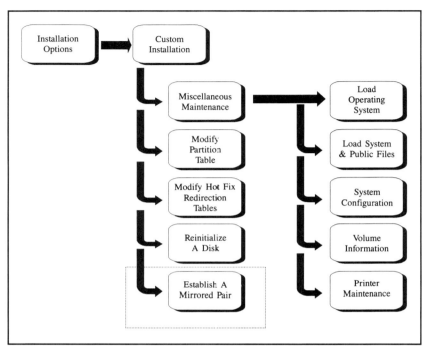

Figure 2-3. Installation options

Modify Partition Table

For a new server, you must decide how the hard disk is to be configured. This is roughly equivalent to the FDISK program in DOS. NetWare 286 must be the first partition on the disk. However, NetWare does permit you to create a DOS partition, if needed. This is useful on non-dedicated file servers. The DOS partition can be treated like a local drive C for the user who works at the file server.

NetWare partitions are limited to 255Mb. You may have up to 32 partitions in one server. If you plan to have mirrored or duplex drives (SFT only), the partitions must be the same and the entire drive must be allocated to NetWare.

Installation and Configuration

> **WARNING:** Be careful when changing existing partition data on an existing drive. You can make partitions larger at any time without a problem. However, *reducing the size of an existing partition destroys all files currently in the partition!*

Modify Hot Fix Redirection Table

An important feature of NetWare is the **Hot Fix Redirection Table**. This feature is designed to accommodate bad blocks that show up on your drive, so you do not need to back up everything and reformat the drive. The concept is simple. NetWare lets you allocate some portion of your disk space (2% by default) to the Hot Fix Redirection Table. When NetWare's automatic read-after-write verification finds a bad block on the disk, NetWare safely moves the data to the Hot Fix Redirection Table area. NetWare then updates the drive table so that the operating system will not attempt to use the bad block again. This process is completely transparent to both the user and the application that was running.

You can establish as much space as you need for the Hot Fix Redirection Table. I recommend starting with the default and changing it later, if needed. If you are going to use mirrored or duplex drives with SFT NetWare, the size of the Hot Fix Redirection Table must be the same on the mirrored or duplex drives. The values you see in the Hot Fix Redirection Tables are 4K blocks, not megabytes.

Reinitialize a Disk

Initializing a disk occurs after you first set up the NetWare partitions. It initializes the File Allocation Table and the root directory, thereby rendering any existing data useless.

> **WARNING:** Use this option with extreme caution on an existing server. It will effectively destroy all existing data!

Establish a Mirrored Pair

This SFT NetWare option lets you use the mirrored or duplex drives. With this option you can tell NetWare to treat a secondary drive as a mirror to the primary drive. If this option does not appear on the menu and you have installed multiple drives, check to be sure that the Hot Fix Redirection Tables are the same size. Mirrored drives must be the same size also.

Create Disk Volumes

In NetWare 286 each partition must have a unique volume name. By default, your first partition will have volume name SYS. Although you can change this name, it's not a good idea. Some software that runs on NetWare LANs requires a volume named SYS.

In addition to the volume names, you can establish two other parameters for the volumes. The first is the Maximum Number of Directory Entries permitted on the volume. The second is selecting whether the volume's directory will be cached. For optimal performance, choose cached.

System Configuration

Several items are established in the System Configuration area:

The name given to the file server.

Maximum number of open files.

Maximum number of open indexed files.

For SFT NetWare with Transaction Tracking, the volume to be used for the log file and the number of concurrent transactions to be tracked.

Limitations on the amount of disk space a user's files can occupy, if you want this option. If not, the option will not be present on the User Information menu in the SYSCON program.

Configuring Adapters

Shared Printer Ports

Any parallel or serial ports in the file server can be configured for shared printers. Up to five ports can be shared on a NetWare server, two serial and three parallel. NetWare assigns a printer port number to each, beginning with the first port selected as P0. The second port selected is P1, the third is P2, and so on. On serial ports, you also must establish the baud rate, the number of data bits, the number of stop bits, the parity setting, and the XON/XOFF setting. Of course, these must correspond to the setup on the printer.

Load Operating System

You may change any item discussed in the earlier sections without reloading the operating system. Set this option to NO when you are merely changing some parameters. Set it to YES when you have relinked the operating system and need to reload it. Upon continuing, the NETGEN or ELSGEN program prompts for the OSEXE-1 and OSEXE-2 diskettes.

Load System and Public Files

Changing any of the items discussed in the earlier sections does not require changing NetWare public or system files. Unless you need to reinstall these files, set this option to NO. If you set it to YES, the ELSGEN or NETGEN program prompts you to load all PUBLIC and SYSTEM diskettes.

CONFIGURING ADAPTERS

These settings can be made in different ways, depending upon the NIC. Some NICs come with software that you run to configure the NIC. Configuration data is stored in **ROM** (read only memory) on the NIC. This is the most convenient way to establish settings, because you can reconfigure a NIC without removing it. Some NICs have rows of switches which you must set to the proper configuration. Finally, you configure some NICs by placing or removing shunts on pins that protrude from the NIC. To configure the NIC, you need a copy of the documentation that comes with it. You cannot determine which method to use or the configuration options by merely looking at the NIC.

Interrupt Request Signal Line (IRQ)

Each Input/Output device in the computer occasionally needs some servicing from the CPU. However, if the CPU constantly monitored (or **polled**) every device, valuable processing time would be wasted. This is especially true for devices that are inactive for long periods and do not require CPU attention. Therefore, to avoid the CPU constantly checking the devices, the PC has internal channels called **interrupt lines**. When a device needs the CPU's attention it sends a signal down its interrupt channel to alert the CPU. These lines are physical trace wires in the PC's motherboard. There are a limited number of these lines.

The IBM PC and PC/XT architecture machines have eight interrupt channels available for adapter cards. All channels pass through each expansion slot in the PC. Potentially, two different adapter cards could transmit on the same line. However, these interrupt channels cannot be shared by multiple devices. The CPU has no way to determine which card is using the interrupt line.

> **NOTE:** IBM Micro Channel Architecture offers a significant advantage in this area. The interrupt signal includes a unique number which identifies the card to the CPU. Therefore, various adaptor cards can share interrupt lines in these machines.

Table 2-3 shows how the eight interrupt channels in the IBM PC and PC/XT architecture machines are assigned.

Configuring Adapters

Table 2-3. IBM PC and PC/XT Interrupts

IRQ #	Function
0	Timer
1	Keyboard
2	Unassigned
3	COM2
4	COM1
5	XT hard disk controller (free on ATs)
6	Floppy disk controller (PCs and XTs only)
7	LPT1

As Table 2-3 shows, Interrupt 2 is the only unassigned interrupt. This means that if I need to install both a LAN adapter card and a tape drive controller, I have a problem. The probable solution is that I will have to use an interrupt assigned to some other device. For example, I could use Interrupt 3 if I am not going to install a second serial port (COM2). The configurability of serial ports and parallel ports tends to vary greatly. Some are hard-wired and cannot be reconfigured. Others can be changed in the same way that LAN adapters are changed, with software, switches, or shunt jumpers.

The IBM PC/AT added eight more interrupts, 8 through 15. Table 2-4 shows how they are assigned.

Table 2-4. Additional IBM PC/AT Interrupts

IRQ #	Function
8	Clock
9	VGA adapter and PC network LAN adapters
10	Unassigned or Novell disk co-processor, if installed
11	Unassigned or Novell disk co-processor, if installed
12	Unassigned or Novell disk co-processor, if installed
13	Math co-processor
14	AT hard disk controller
15	Unassigned or Novell disk co-processor, if installed

Table 2–4 shows that the PC/AT has more available interrupts than the PC and PC/XT. Interrupts 8, 10, 11, 12, 13, and 15 are generally available. The Novell disk co-processor can use interrupts 10, 11, 12, or 15.

One more thing about interrupts: the lower the interrupt's number value, the higher its priority. Since LAN adapters are generally quite active, you will want to use the lowest interrupt line available.

Other adapters cards which generally have interrupts are

Secondary disk controllers
Tape drive controllers
Most internal modems (COM2 – IRQ 3)
Some mice
Digitizers and/or scanners

All NICs use an IRQ. This is complicated by the fact that most of us do not have the documentation needed to tell what other adapter cards are in our PC and which IRQs may be in use. In addition, we may have lots of PCs, all with different adapter cards installed. LAN adapter cards installed in various PCs in the LAN can be configured to use different IRQ channels, although this makes installation a little more difficult.

> **TIP:** If possible, set all your LAN adapter cards to the same IRQ and change the conflicting adapter card in the PC. This makes it easier to interchange or swap LAN adapter cards among PCs. Be sure to record the interrupt data on the Workstation Configuration Worksheet Novell provides for this purpose.

Direct Memory Access (DMA)

Another way PC designers attempted to alleviate CPU overload was to let certain memory transfers between RAM and peripheral devices occur without CPU monitoring after the transfer had been initiated. This is done through DMA channels. Like the IRQ, only

Configuring Adapters

a few channels are available to adapter cards. And, once again, two devices cannot share the same DMA. For most LAN adapters, you must set which DMA channel the LAN adapter will use. Not all LAN adapters use DMA. LAN adapter cards installed in various PCs in the LAN can be configured for different DMA channels.

Table 2-5 lists the DMA assignments for the IBM PC and PC/XT.

Table 2-5. DMA Channels

DMA	Function
0	Dynamic RAM refresh
1	Hard disk controller
2	Floppy disk controller
3	Unassigned

The IBM PC/AT and PS/2s have a second DMA controller and therefore have additional DMA channels 4 through 7 available. These may or may not be used by standard devices. Your documentation should tell you if one of these channels is in use. Due to the scarcity of DMA channels in PCs and XTs, many 8-bit NICs do not have DMA settings and, therefore, do not use the DMA feature. This results in lower performance. Given the choice, it is generally advisable to use 16-bit NICs when appropriate to gain extra configurability.

I/O Address Port

The CPU has to know where in memory to look for each device. Each device has its own address, much like you have a unique mailing address. At your address, more than one person may be receiving mail. However, PC devices are hermits. They do not share their addresses with anyone. Therefore, the LAN adapter card must be set to an I/O address that is unique within the particular PC. LAN adapter cards installed in the various PCs connected to the LAN can be configured to use different I/O addresses, although this makes installation a little more difficult.

Table 2-6 may be useful in determining current values for some of your existing devices.

Table 2-6. Common Device Settings

Device	Interrupt	DMA	I/O Address (Hex) Used for ROM and RAM	Memory Addresses
3Com 3C501	2-7 (3)	1-3 (1)	000-3F0 (300)	000-3F0
3Com 3C503	2-5 (3)	1-3 (none)	250-3F0 (300)	250-3F0
AST Clock Calendar	None	None	2C0-2C7	2C0-2C7
AT Disk Controller	14	1	1F0-1F8	1F0-1F8
AT Keyboard Controller	None	None	60-64	60-64
AT Math Co-Processor	13	None	F0-FF	F0-FF
AT Setup RAM	None	None	70-71	70-71
Bus Mouse	None	None	238-23B	238-23B
Color Graphics Adapter	None	None	3D0-3BF	3D0-3DF
COM1 Serial Port	4	None	3F8-3FF 3F8-400	3F8-3FF 3F8-400
COM2 Serial Port	3	None	2F8-2FF	2F8-2FF
DMA Controller #1	None	None	00-0F	00-0F
DMA Controller #2 (AT)	None	None	C0-DF	C0-DF
DMA Page Registers	None	None	80-8F	80-8F
EGA Adapter	None or 2	None	3C0-3CF	C0000-C3FFF
Floppy Controller	6	None	3F0-3F7	3F0-3F7
Gateway G/Net	2, 3, 5, 7 (3)	None	280-37F (2A0)	0A000-0E000
Hercules Mono Graphics	None	None	3B4-3BF	3B4-3BF
IBM PC Baseband	2-3 (2)	None	620-628 (620)	0CC00-0DC00
IBM PC Network II	2-3 (2)	None	620-628 (620)	0CC00-0DC00

Configuring Adapters

Table 2-6, continued

Device	Interrupt	DMA	I/O Address (Hex) Used for ROM and RAM	Memory Addresses
IBM Token Ring	2, 3, 7 (2)	None	A20–A24 (A20)	CC000–CFFFF
IBM SDLC Adapter	3–4	1	3A0–3AF	3A0–3AF
Interrupt Handler #1	None	None	20–21	20–21
Interrupt Handler #2	None	None	A0–A1	A0–A1
Joystick Controller	None	None	200–20F	200–20F
LPT1 Parallel Port	7	None	378–37F 3BC–3BF	378–37F 3BC–3BF
LPT2 Parallel Port	5	None	278–27F 378–37B	278–27F 378–37B
LPT3 Parallel Port	None	None	278–27A 3BC–3BE 378–37A	278–27A 3BC–3BE 378–37A
Mono Display Adapter	None	None	3B0–3BF	3B0–3BF
NMI Mask Register (XT)	None	None	A0–AF	A0–AF
Novell 286B Floppy Continued	6	2	1F0–1F8	1F0–1F8 3F0–3F7
Novell Disk Co-Processor	10, 11, 12, 15	None	320–34F	320–34F
Novell NE-1000 NIC	2, 3, 4, 5 (3)	None	300–360 (300)	300–360
Novell NE-2000 NIC	2, 3, 4, 5 (3)	None	300–360 (300)	300–360
Novell RX-Net NIC	2, 3, 4, 7 (2)	None	2E0–350 (350)	C000–DC00
Novell S-Net NIC	2	None	2B8	
Novell SCSI Controller	2, 3, 5	1, 3	340–343	340–343

Table 2-6, continued

Device	Interrupt	DMA	I/O Address (Hex) Used for ROM and RAM	Memory Addresses
Proteon P1300 NIC	2-5 (2)	1-3 (1)	300-378 (300)	300-378
Proteon P1340 NIC	2-7 (2)	1-3 (1)	A20-378 (A20)	A20-378
Proteon P1344 NIC	3-12 (12)	5-7 (5)	A20-378 (A20)	A20-378
Pure Data ARCnet NIC	2, 3, 4, 5, 7 (2)	None	2E0-300 (2E0)	C000-E000
Timer	None	None	40-43	40-43
Western Digital Floppy	6	2	3F0-3F8	
VGA Color Adapter	2 or 9	None	3C0-3DA	3C0-3DA
XT Expansion Chassis	None	None	210-217	210-217
XT Hard Disk Controller	5	None	320-32F	C8000-CBFFF
XT Peripheral Controller	None	None	60-63	60-63

*Figures in parentheses indicate default settings.

Memory Address

Many NICs and other PC adapters use a range of memory addresses for on-board ROM (read only memory). These ROM chips store programs that the NIC uses for low-level functions. Addresses for these ROMs cannot conflict with other ROM or RAM addresses. Some NICs also have some on-board RAM used for buffering I/O to the LAN channel. These addresses may not conflict either.

Node Address or Node ID

All NICs do not require this setting, although all NICs in a single network must have a unique node address. Some NICs contain a node address resident in ROM that you cannot set or change.

Configuring Adapters

Ethernet NICs are generally set this way. The rule for node addresses is that they must be unique within a physical network. The physical network number is generally assigned to a physical wiring schema connected to the NIC in the file server. Multiple wiring schemas can be connected to a file server attached to separate NICs in the file server. In a multiple wiring schema, each is considered a separate physical network. Node addresses can be duplicated on separate physical networks. Figures 2-4 and 2-5 may help you to understand this concept.

Cable or Connector Type

Different kinds of wire and cable are used by many LANs. Many NICs can be used with more than one type of wiring. In most cases, you must configure the NIC for the type of wiring and/or the connector being used. For example, most Ethernet NICs have a BNC-type connector for connecting to thin Ethernet coaxial cable and a sub-miniature-D type 15-pin connector for connecting to a transceiver cable off a thick Ethernet backbone cable. You need to check your NICs' specifications to determine whether this setting needs to be addressed for your NICs.

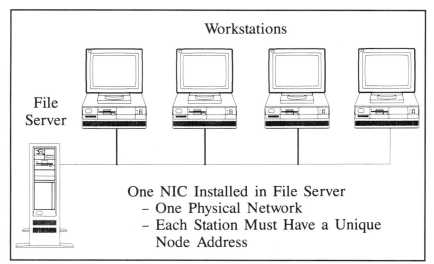

Figure 2-4. Single physical network

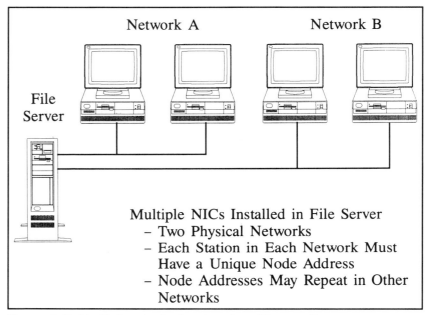

Figure 2-5. Multiple physical networks with one file server

Remote Boot ROMs

A special category of ROMs are available for most NICs. These are called **remote boot** or **remote reset ROMs** or **PROMs**. PROM stands for Programmable Read Only Memory. These devices let the workstation boot from the file server rather than finding DOS on the workstation's own disk drives. These ROMs are very popular in PCs that have only floppy drives because they eliminate the need for a boot diskette. These ROMs are required for the class of PCs known as **diskless workstations**. Diskless workstations have no drives and therefore cannot find DOS locally. When you use these ROMs, you must configure the NIC for both their presence and the memory addresses the ROM uses.

SUMMARY

In this chapter we reviewed some of the intricacies of reconfiguring an existing NetWare file server. Although there are several details about your network equipment that you have to know, the process of regenerating or reconfiguring the file server itself is not that difficult. Unfortunately, the process is not well explained in the manuals that accompany NetWare. As long as you follow my instructions of making backup copies of the eleven diskettes that are changed during the process, you are completely safe to use NETGEN or ELSGEN to regenerate NetWare. If your new version doesn't work, you can always reinstall your old working copy.

The most significant details that are imperative to know prior to using NETGEN or ELSGEN pertain to your file server hardware. It is absolutely required that you know what peripherals are installed in the file server and what settings each uses for their IRQ, DMA, I/O address, and RAM/ROM addresses. The NICs that you install in the file server cannot use any settings that conflict with any other device in the file server.

This chapter dealt mainly with configuring NetWare according to the LAN hardware being used. Throughout the remainder of this book we will be looking at software configuration issues and their impact on the network environment.

3
Configuring a NetWare 386 File Server

NetWare 386 breaks ground in many significant areas, with new concepts and procedures that affect all aspects of network administration, from installation to daily maintenance. In contrast to NetWare 286's inflexible reconfiguration procedures which require the server to be down, NetWare 386's reconfiguration procedures are dynamic. Also, some items which are not configurable at all in NetWare 286 are configurable in NetWare 386.

NETWARE LOADABLE MODULES (NLMs)

Taking advantage of the Intel 80386 CPU chip's multitasking architecture, Novell has extended NetWare 386's abilities so it can load and execute other programs while it is running. These programs are called **NetWare Loadable Modules (NLMs)**.

NLMs become part of the operating system while they are loaded and running. These programs can allocate and de-allocate memory in the file server as needed. When you unload them, they return all RAM to the operating system. They also can access the operating system as well as other NLMs. There are four kinds of NLMs:

Utilities and application modules
Network interface drivers
Disk interface drivers
Name space modules

These NetWare loadable modules add features to the basic NetWare 386 operating system. The next sections discuss the types of NLMs Novell provides.

Utilities and Application Modules

These general purpose applications run on the file server and are similar to the Value Added Processes (VAPs) of NetWare 286. Several third-party NLMs are already available to extend NetWare 386's capabilities. NetWare 386 includes several of these.

BTRIEVE.NLM — Loads database management software on the file server. (Btrieve 386 Installation and Operation Supplement.)

CLIB.NLM — Novell's C RunTime Library, used by many NLMs to access NetWare 386 function calls through the library's Application Program Interfaces (API). This library is dynamically linked with the module when the module is loaded. (NetWare System Administration—File Server Utilities.)

DISKSET.NLM — Loads information about external hard disks onto the EEPROM chip of a Novell disk co-processor board (DCB) or third-party equivalent of a DCB.

INSTALL.NLM — Installs NetWare 386 on the file server and creates the start-up files NetWare 386 requires.

IPXS.NLM — Required if you have an NLM that requires STREAMS-based IPX protocol services.

NetWare Loadable Modules (NLMs)

MATHLIB.NLM	Enhances your server's performance if your server has a math co-processor installed. It is a companion module for CLIB.NLM. You must load CLIB.NLM before loading this module.
MATHLIBC.NLM	Also a companion module for CLIB.NLM, used when your server does not have a math co-processor. You must load CLIB.NLM before loading this module.
MONITOR.NLM	Replaces the NetWare 286 monitor with a more up-to-date interface, offering many features of the NetWare 286 FCONSOLE program.
NMAGENT.NLM	Usually loads automatically when you load your LAN drivers. It enables the NetWare communication services to recognize the LAN drivers.
PSERVER.NLM	Supports remote print servers.
REMOTE.NLM	Part of NetWare 386's remote console support program which lets the supervisor review and perform console activities from a workstation.
ROUTE.NLM	Passes data frames through IBM bridges on a token ring network (source routing). You must load the TOKEN LAN driver before loading this module.
RSPX.NLM	The other half of NetWare 386's remote console program, REMOTE.NLM. RSPX.NLM loads a remote SPX driver that the server uses to communicate with the workstation that performs as a remote console. You must load REMOTE.NLM before loading RSPX.

SPXS.NLM	Required when you use an NLM that requires a STREAMS-based SPX protocol driver.
STREAMS.NLM	Required when using the CLIB.NLM.
TLI.NLM	Loaded after STREAMS.NLM and CLIB.NLM and used when a module requires Transport Level Interface communication services.
TOKENRPL.NLM	Used with token ring adapters which have remote boot capability.
UPS.NLM	Monitors the power status of a server connected to an uninterruptable power supply.
VREPAIR.NLM	Differs from the NetWare 286 VREPAIR program because it runs without downing the server. This program repairs corrupted data structures on the file server drives.

Network Interface Card

Network Interface Cards (NICs) software interfaces to NetWare 386 through NLMs rather than linking directly with the operating system as NetWare 286 does. This allows easier adaptation and upgrades. Table 3–1 lists the NetWare 386 version 3.1 NLMs for NICs.

Disk Interface Drivers

As with LAN drivers, NetWare 386 uses NLMs for the interface to the server disk drives. This, too, provides increased flexibility and upgrade ability. Table 3–2 lists the disk drivers provided with NetWare 386 version 3.1.

Table 3-1. NIC Drivers

NLM	NIC
3C503.LAN	3COM's 8-bit ISA Ethernet NIC
3C505.LAN	3COM's 16-bit ISA Ethernet NIC
3C523.LAN	3COM's 16-bit Micro-Channel Ethernet NIC
NE2.LAN	Novell's Micro-Channel Ethernet NIC
NE232.LAN	Novell's 32-bit Micro-Channel Ethernet NIC
NE1000.LAN	Novell's 8-bit ISA bus Ethernet NIC
NE2000.LAN	Novell's 16-bit ISA bus Ethernet NIC
NE3200.LAN	Novell's 32-bit EISA Ethernet NIC
TRXNET.LAN	Novell's ARCnet ISA bus NIC
TOKEN.LAN	IBM-compatible Token Ring Adapters

Table 3-2. Disk Drivers

NLM	Disk Driver
DCB.DSK	Novell's Disk Co-Processor
DCB2.DSK	Novell's Micro-Channel Disk Co-Processor
EDCB.DSK	Novell's Enhanced Disk Co-Processor
ESDI.DSK	Enhanced Small Device Interface Controllers
ISADISK.DSK	ST506/MFM AT-style Disk Controllers
PS2ESDI.DSK	IBM's Micro-Channel ESDI Disk Controller
PS2MFM.DSK	IBM's Micro-Channel MFM Disk Controller
IBMSCSI.DSK	IBM's Micro-Channel SCSI Disk Controller

Name Space Modules

In addition to supporting DOS file names, NetWare 386 supports other file naming conventions. NetWare 386 now supports Apple File Protocol (AFP) through the MAC.NAM NLM. Future plans include support for Sun's Network File Protocol (NFP).

To write NLMs, application developers must use the Novell Developer's Kit which includes modules for accessing Novell's NetWare 386 C RunTime Libraries. The programs can be written using C, 386 Protected Mode Assembly, or C++.

CONSOLE SET COMMAND

A NetWare 286 file server could only be reconfigured using NETGEN or ELSGEN, depending upon the version. These programs require the server to be down during reconfiguration. In contrast, NetWare 386 can be dynamically reconfigured at the console using the SET command. You can also place the SET command in the file server's AUTOEXEC.NCF file, so the command processes automatically when the server is booted. The SET command can configure nine different aspects of the file server, each having several options.

File Caching

Part of the server's RAM holds frequently used data in memory. Data that is being read or written is kept in the cache buffers. The space used for the cache buffers depends on the amount of RAM installed in the file server and the setting for Minimum File Cache Buffers.

Minimum File Cache Buffers

Range: 20–1000   Default: 20

This sets the minimum number of cache buffers that the file server must allocate in RAM. After all other memory requirements are met, including the Minimum File Cache Buffers, the server uses all remaining RAM for file cache buffers.

Maximum Concurrent Disk Cache Writes

Range: 10–100   Default: 50

This sets the number of cache buffers that can be written to the disk simultaneously. Increasing this number permits more writes to be made at the same time, but reduces the server's efficiency in servicing disk reads. If the number of "dirty cache buffers" exceeds 70% of the total cache buffers, increasing this setting could improve the server's performance.

Minimum File Cache Buffer Report Threshold

Range: 0–1000   Default: 20

This parameter sets a value used to determine, in part, when the file server should issue a warning of too few cache buffers. This setting's value is added to the Minimum File Cache Buffer value. When the file server has allocated the RAM it needs for all other processes, and the remaining RAM available for file caching is less than this sum, a warning message appears on the file server console.

Dirty Disk Cache Delay Time

Range: .1–10 seconds   Default: 3.3 seconds

This setting controls how long the server waits prior to writing data that is new or has changed since it was read into the cache to the disk. Decreasing this value forces the server to write more often and can reduce overall performance.

Directory Caching

In addition to caching file information, NetWare caches directory information to permit faster access to it. Increasing the buffers for directory caching decreases the amount of RAM available for file caching. The server allocates space to directory entries until it reaches its maximum directory cache buffers. If the entire directory fits in the space allocated, the directory remains resident in the file server's RAM. If a directory buffer is not accessed for a while and the server needs space, the server can allocate the buffer's space to another directory entry.

Minimum Directory Cache Buffers

Range: 10–2000   Default: 20

This parameter tells the operating system the minimum amount of RAM that *must* be set aside for the directory cache. This memory cannot be re-allocated by the operating system, even if it is not being used.

Maximum Directory Cache Buffers

Range: 20-4000   Default: 1000

This setting determines the maximum number of buffers used for directory caching. Reducing this number frees the file server RAM for other duties. Increase the value if directory searches are slow.

Directory Cache Buffer Non-referenced Delay

Range: 1 second-5 minutes   Default: 5.5 seconds

This setting determines the amount of time that a directory entry must remain in the cache when not being accessed. If an entry has been in the cache for this period and has not been accessed, the server can release this information to use the memory for another entry.

Dirty Directory Cache Delay Time

Range: 0-10 seconds   Default: .5 seconds

This parameter determines how long the file server keeps a directory write request in memory. Decreasing this value impedes file server performance, but increasing it can cause greater potential for corrupted directory information in the event of a power failure.

Directory Cache Allocation Wait Time

Range: .5 seconds-2 minutes   Default: 2.2 seconds

This setting determines how long the file server must wait before allocating an additional directory cache buffer after allocating a directory cache buffer. Decreasing this value can cause too many buffers to be allocated during a peak load situation. Increasing this value can cause the file server to perform directory searches slowly.

Maximum Concurrent Directory Cache Writes

Range: 5-50   Default: 10

This setting determines how many directory cache entries can be written to the disk at once. Increasing this number permits more writes to be made simultaneously, but reduces the server's efficiency in servicing disk reads.

Console SET Command

File System

The next sections describe the eight settings that affect how NetWare 386 works with files stored on the file server.

Volume Low Warn All Users

Values: Yes or No   Default: Yes

This setting determines whether NetWare warns users when the volume is nearly full.

Volume Low Warning Threshold

Range: 0–100,000 blocks   Default: 256 blocks

This setting, if activated, determines when NetWare issues a Volume Low warning. Block sizes in NetWare 386 can be 4096 (4K), 8192 (8K), 16384 (16K), 32768 (32K), or 65536 bytes (64K).

Volume Low Warning Reset Threshold

Range: 0–100,000 blocks   Default: 256 blocks

This setting determines how much free disk space over the Volume Low Warning Threshold Value must exist before the warning message is reset.

Immediate Purge of Deleted Files

Values: On or Off   Default: Off

When set to On, NetWare immediately purges deleted files from the server volume. This makes the SALVAGE command useless. When set to Off, you can recover deleted files with the SALVAGE command.

Minimum File Delete Wait Time

Range: 0 seconds–7 days   Default: 1 minute 5.9 seconds

This setting determines how long a deleted file can remain on the server and be recovered with the SALVAGE command. Files which have not met this minimum remain on the server, even if the volume is full.

File Delete Wait Time

Range: 0 seconds–7 days   Default: 5 minutes 29.6 seconds

This entry controls when a salvageable file can be purged from the server volume. When a volume is full, NetWare purges the oldest files first. It continues to purge files until it releases disk space equal to at least 1/32 of volume size.

Turbo FAT Reuse Wait Time

Range: .3 seconds–
1 hour 5 minutes

Default: 5 minutes
29.6 seconds

This parameter determines how long a Turbo FAT buffer remains in RAM after the file corresponding to the Turbo FAT is closed.

Maximum Subdirectory Tree Depth

Range: 10–100   Default: 25

This setting controls how many levels of subdirectory nesting the operating system permits.

Communications

Communications settings control how NetWare 386 manages communications on the network and the communication buffer area of the server's memory.

Minimum Packet Receive Buffers

Range: 10–1000   Default: 10

This option controls how many communication buffers the operating system must allocate for incoming packets. This memory cannot be reallocated even if the buffers are in use.

Maximum Packet Receive Buffers

Range: 50–2000   Default: 100

This setting determines the maximum number of buffers the file server can establish for incoming data packets.

New Packet Receive Buffer Wait Time

Range: .1–20 seconds   Default: .1 second

This setting determines how long NetWare 386 waits after receiving a request for another packet receive buffer before granting the request.

Maximum Physical Receive Packet Size

Range: 618–4202 bytes   Default: 1130 bytes

This setting controls how many bytes the data packets transmitted on the network can contain. The default size permits 1024 data bytes and 106 header bytes. Follow these guidelines to choose the appropriate setting.

- If your network uses ARCnet, use 618.
- If your network uses 1K packets, use the default.
- If your network uses Ethernet, use 1518.
- If your network uses Token Ring, use 4202.

> **TIP:** You cannot change this parameter with the console SET command. You must place the SET MAXIMUM PHYSICAL PACKET SIZE = *xxxx* command in the STARTUP.NCF file.

Console Display Watchdog Logouts

Values: On or Off   Default: Off

This command determines whether the console displays a message when the server clears a connection due to lost contact with a workstation. Lost contact can indicate a problem or that people turned off their workstations without logging off.

Memory

The next two parameters control how the NetWare 386 file server allocates memory to various processes and the size of cache blocks in memory.

Maximum Dynamic Memory

Range: 50K–16Mb   Default: 1Mb

The Dynamic Memory pool has many purposes in a NetWare 386 server.

Drive Mappings—all MAP commands that are active for all users are stored on the server

NetWare Loadable Modules (NLMs)

Service requests

Open and locked file handles

Queue Operator Tables

User connection information

Messages waiting to be sent or broadcast

Server advertising

Cache Buffer Size

Values: 4096, 8192, or 16,384   Default: 4096

This setting should correspond to the block size set for the server volume. If you have multiple volumes with different block sizes, set this entry to the smallest block size.

> **TIP:** You cannot change this parameter with the console SET command. You must place the CACHE BUFFER SIZE = *xxxx* command in the STARTUP.NCF file.

Locks

The next four sections describe the parameters that determine how NetWare 386 handles open files and record locking. There are three type of locks: file, physical, and logical. The operating system enforces a **file lock** and prevents more than one user from accessing the file. A **physical lock** locks a range of bytes on the file and permits multiple users access to the file, but protects given records during updating. The operating system enforces physical

Console SET Command

locks. **Logical locks** work by assigning names to sections of data in the file which can be locked when the application accesses the data. The application software itself, not the operating system, enforces logical locks.

Maximum File Locks

Range: 100–100,000   Default: 10,000

This setting controls the number of open and/or locked files permitted on the server.

Maximum Record Locks

Range: 100–200,000   Default: 20,000

This setting controls the number of record locks permitted on the file server at one time.

Maximum File Locks Per Connection

Range: 10–1000   Default: 250

This entry determines how many open and/or locked files a connection can have at one time. Stations that use multitasking operating systems such as OS/2 require more file locks than stations running DOS.

Maximum Record Locks Per Connection

Range: 10–10,000   Default: 500

This item sets how many record locks a connection permits simultaneously.

Transaction Tracking

Transaction tracking is a data integrity feature of NetWare 386. It ensures that updates are either made successfully and completely, or they are backed out completely in the event of a power loss, workstation failure, cable failure, or process corruption. As these updates are made to the data files, the server keeps a log file of the changes and later uses this file to reverse the changes, if needed.

Maximum Transactions

Range: 100–10,000   Default: 10,000

This parameter sets the maximum number of transaction processes that can be logged simultaneously.

TTS Unwritten Cache Wait Time

Range: 11 seconds–   Default: 1 minute
10 minutes 59 seconds   5.9 seconds

This entry determines how long an updated cache block can be held in RAM before it is written to the disk.

TTS Backout File Truncation Wait Time

Range: 1 minute–   Default: 59 minutes
1 day 2 hours 21 minutes   19 seconds

This setting determines how long the operating system holds allocated blocks for the backout file when these blocks are not currently being used.

Auto TTS Backout Flag

Values: Off or On   Default: Off

This entry determines whether the file server *automatically* backs out incomplete transactions that it finds while booting or waits for your response to the message:

Incomplete transaction(s) found. Do you wish to back them out?

> **TIP:** You cannot change this parameter with the console SET command. You must place the AUTO TTS BACKOUT FLAG = OFF/ON command in the STARTUP.NCF file.

TTS Abort Dump Flag

Values: Off or On   Default: Off

This setting determines what happens in the event of a failure on the file server during a write to a file that is marked transactional.

Console SET Command

If set to On, the backed out information is written to a file called TTS$LOG.ERR on the SYS volume. You can view this file with a text editor or print it.

If set to Off, the backed out data is not saved.

Disk

This disk parameter controls the third aspect of hot fix redirection (see the following list). Information is redirected to the Hot Fix Redirection Table under one of three conditions.

1. Write Requests. When the disk controller reports an error during a write operation, the system redirects that data to a different block and marks the original block as bad.
2. Read Requests. The disk controller reports an error during a read operation. If the drive *is not mirrored*, the data is lost and the block is marked as bad. If the drive *is mirrored*, the system retrieves the data from the mirrored drive and redirects it to the primary drive. The block on the primary drive is marked as bad.
3. Read-After-Write Verification. After a write operation, the data on the disk is read and compared to the data in the cache buffer. If the data does not match, the system redirects it to another block and marks the original block as bad.

Enable Disk Read after Write Verify
Values: On or Off   Default: On

Miscellaneous Settings

The next sections describe other settings available for NetWare 386.

Allow Unencrypted Passwords
Values: On or Off   Default: Off

NetWare 386 workstation shells encrypt the user password before sending it to the server in a packet. NetWare 286 workstation shells do not encrypt the password. However, NetWare 286 versions 2.1 and above can use the NetWare 386 shells, and public and login files.

This setting should be On when

- You use both NetWare 386 and NetWare 286 in an interconnected LAN environment, and your NetWare 286 is below version 2.1.
- You use both NetWare 386 and NetWare 286 in an interconnected LAN environment, and you do not wish to upgrade your NetWare 286 shells, and public and login files.

This setting should be Off when

- You are using only NetWare 386 on the network file servers.
- You are using both NetWare 386 and NetWare 286 file servers, and you have updated the NetWare 286 shells, and public and login files.

Maximum Outstanding NCP Searches

Range: 10–1000   Default: 51

This parameter controls the maximum number of Network Core Protocol (NCP) directory searches that can be performed simultaneously.

New Service Process Wait Time

Range: .3–20 seconds   Default: 2.2 seconds

This entry controls how long the operating system waits before responding to a request for another service process.

Maximum Service Processes

Range: 5–40   Default: 20

This setting controls how many service processes the operating system can create. You should increase the setting if the file server frequently uses the maximum file service processes.

USING LOAD COMMANDS TO LOAD LAN DRIVERS

Up to 16 different networks can be connected to a NetWare 386 file server. With NetWare 386's internal router, these networks appear to be one logical network.

The console LOAD command is used to load NetWare 386 LMs, of which LAN drivers are one category. LAN drivers for NetWare 386 all have the .LAN file name extension. The syntax for the command is:

LOAD *[path] lan_driver [options]*

The optional *path* phrase tells the server where to look for the LAN driver. Table 3–3 lists the available options for each Novell-supplied NIC driver. Definitions of parameters follow the table.

Table 3–3. LAN Driver Options

Parameter	Default Value	Supported Values	Optional
Novell NE/2 Micro-Channel Ethernet NIC—Up to 4 per Server			
FRAME	Ethernet_802.3	Ethernet_802.3　Ethernet_II　Ethernet_Snap　Ethernet_802.2	Yes
NAME	None	Any unique 17-character name	Yes
NODE	Board setting	Any 12-digit hexadecimal value[1]	Yes
RETRIES	5	0–255	Yes
SLOT	First free slot	1–8	No
Novell NE2/32 32-bit Micro-Channel Ethernet NIC—Limited by Available Slots Only			
FRAME	Ethernet_802.3	Ethernet_802.3　Ethernet_II　Ethernet_Snap　Ethernet_802.2	Yes
NAME	None	Any unique 17-character name	Yes

Configuring a NetWare 386 File Server

Table 3-3, continued

Parameter	Default Value	Supported Values	Optional
RETRIES	5	0-255	Yes
SLOT	None	Any available	No
Novell NE3200 EISA NIC—Limited to 6 per Server			
FRAME	Ethernet__802.3	Ethernet__802.3 Ethernet__II Ethernet__Snap Ethernet__802.2	Yes
NAME	None	Any unique 17-character name	Yes
RETRIES	5	0-255	Yes
SLOT	None	Any available	No
Novell NE1000 8-bit ISA Ethernet NIC—Limited to 4 per Server			
FRAME	Ethernet__802.3	Ethernet__802.3 Ethernet__II Ethernet__Snap Ethernet__802.2	Yes
INT	3	2, 3, 4, 5	No
NAME	None	Any unique 17-character name	Yes
NODE	Board setting	Any 12-digit hexadecimal value[1]	Yes
PORT	300	300, 320, 340, 360	No
RETRIES	5	0-255	Yes
Novell NE2000 16-bit ISA Ethernet NIC—Limited to 4 per Server			
FRAME	Ethernet__802.3	Ethernet__802.3 Ethernet__II Ethernet__Snap Ethernet__802.2	Yes
INT	3	2, 3, 4, 5	No
NAME	None	Any unique 17-character name	Yes
NODE	Board setting	Any 12-digit hexadecimal value[1]	Yes

Using LOAD Commands to Load LAN Drivers

Table 3-3, continued

Parameter	Default Value	Supported Values	Optional
PORT	300	300, 320, 340, 360	No
RETRIES	5	0-255	Yes
Novell TRXNET 8-bit ISA or Micro-Channel ARCnet NIC—Limited to 4 for ISA, 6 for Micro-Channel			
INT	2	2, 3, 4, 5, 7	No
MEM	D0000	C0000, CC000, D0000, DC000, E000	No
NAME	None	Any unique 17-character name	Yes
PORT	2E0	2E0, 2F0, 300, 310, 350	No
RETRIES	100	0-255	Yes
3COM 3C503 Ethernet NIC—Limited to 4 per Server			
FRAME	Ethernet_802.3	Ethernet_802.3 Ethernet_II Ethernet_Snap Ethernet_802.2	Yes
INT	3	2, 3, 4, 5	No
MEM	C8000	C8000, CC000, D8000, DC000	No
NAME	None	Any unique 17-character name	Yes
NODE	Board value	Any 12-digit hexadecimal value except 0, a broadcast address, or multicast address	Yes
PORT	300	300, 310, 330, 350, 250, 280, 2A0, 2E0	No
RETRIES	5	0-255	Yes
3COM 3C505 16-bit NIC—Limited to 3 per Server			
DMA	5	1, 3, 5, 6, 7	No
FRAME	Ethernet_802.3	Ethernet_802.3 Ethernet_II Ethernet_Snap Ethernet_802.2	Yes

Table 3-3, continued

Parameter	Default Value	Supported Values	Optional
INT	9	3, 4, 5, 7, 9	No
NAME	None	Any unique 17-character name	Yes
NODE	Board value	Any 12-digit hexadecimal value[1]	Yes
PORT	300	300, 310, 320	No
RETRIES	5	0-255	Yes
3COM 3C523 Micro-Channel NIC—Limited to 4 per Server			
FRAME	Ethernet__802.3	Ethernet__802.3 Ethernet__II Ethernet__Snap Ethernet__802.2	Yes
NAME	None	Any unique 17-character name	Yes
NODE	Board value	Any 12-digit hexadecimal value[1]	Yes
RETRIES	10	0-255	Yes
SLOT	None	Any available	No
IBM Token Ring—Limited to 2 per Server			
LS	0	0-255	Yes
MEM	0	A0000-F0000	Yes
NAME	None	Any unique 17-character name	Yes
NODE	Board setting	Any 8-digit hexadecimal value	Yes
PORT	A20	A20, A24	Yes
SLOT	None	Any available	Yes
SAPS	0	0-255	Yes
TBC	2	0-2	Yes
TBZ	0	96-65535	Yes

[1] The node address cannot be 0, a broadcast address (FFFFFFFFFFFF), or a multicast address.

Using the BIND Command to Link LAN Drivers

Parameter	Definition
DMA	Determines the DMA channel the driver should use for the NIC.
FRAME	Instructs Ethernet and Token Ring NICs which packet header type to use. All file servers and workstations on the same wiring network must use the same frame type.
PORT	Sets the I/O address the NIC uses.
SLOT	A Micro-Channel option only that tells the CPU which expansion slot the NIC occupies.
INT	Sets the interrupt the NIC uses.
RETRIES	Instructs the driver how many times to re-try when a packet transmission fails.
NAME	Establishes a logical name assigned to the NIC to be used as an alternate reference.
NODE	Overrides the node address set on the NIC for some NIC types.
LS	Sets the number of 802.2 link stations.
MEM	Sets the memory address for the LAN driver.
SAPS	Sets the number of 802.2 service access points.
TBC	Sets the transmit buffer count.
TBZ	Sets the transmit buffer size. The default uses the maximum packet size that either the operating system or the NIC allows.

USING THE BIND COMMAND TO LINK LAN DRIVERS

The console BIND command is essential to NetWare 386. This command links a communication protocol driver to a loaded LAN driver, which in turn is bound to a specific NIC in the file server. The syntax for this command is

```
BIND protocol TO lan_driver
[driver options] [protocol options]
```

Configuring a NetWare 386 File Server

The meanings of the elements in the command line are described next.

protocol Right now, the only protocol shipped with NetWare 386 is IPX. Your Novell reseller and other third-party vendors supply other protocol drivers such as TCP/IP.

lan_driver The drivers available for NetWare 386 version 3.1 are

NE2	NE1000	NE2000
NE232	TRXNET	TOKEN
3C503	3C505	3C523
NE3200		

driver options The driver options available are

DMA=*number* Corresponds to the setting for the DMA channel on the NIC

INT=*number* Corresponds to the setting for the interrupt (IRQ) used on the NIC

MEM=*number* Memory address of any ROM resident on the NIC

PORT=*number* Identifies the I/O port (usually called the I/O address) used for the NIC

SLOT=*number* Identifies the slot where a Micro-Channel NIC is installed

protocol options NetWare's IPX protocol now has only one option: NET=*number*. This option establishes the physical or IPX internal network number.

1. The network address assigned to an existing network.
2. The network number assigned to a new network.
3. The IPX internal network number assigned when multiple copies of the LAN driver have been loaded using different frame types and bound to the same NIC.

SUMMARY

You can reconfigure NetWare 386 while the file server is up and running by issuing console SET commands and loading different LMs. Unlike NetWare 286, the NetWare 386 server is dynamic. It allocates and de-allocates memory as needed. After you have fine-tuned your server to your environment, the necessary SET commands can be placed in the STARTUP.NCF and AUTOEXEC.NCF files.

4
Internal Bridges

Internal bridges are an important concept in NetWare. An internal bridge is created when more than one NIC is installed in a file server attached to separate physical networks. The bridge provides a route for frames from one network to be transferred to another network. It is "internal" because bridging is done within the file server by installing multiple NICs. NetWare 286 supports up to four NICs per file server, while NetWare 386 supports up to sixteen NICs per file server. In this chapter, I discuss the merits of internal bridges and make recommendations for their use.

USING INTERNAL BRIDGES

You can use internal bridges to accomplish three major goals:

- Reduce LAN channel load
- Interconnect dissimilar LANs
- Provide upgrade path

Reducing LAN Channel Load

Presently, most LAN protocols allow only one data frame to be transmitted at a time on the physical network. The IEEE 802.x standards provide considerable detail about how to mediate the physical channel so that data frames arrive safely at their destination. When more than one data frame is on the channel, collisions can occur. The result: data frames have to be retransmitted. Excessive collisions can severely degrade overall throughput. This one-frame-at-a-time transmission method can be a major factor in a LAN's performance. Regardless of the protocol or topology used, as you add more stations to the LAN, increased channel loads decrease performance.

One task of a network manager is to find the source of decreased performance and take whatever steps are available to increase it. This includes monitoring the load on the data channel. Unfortunately, NetWare does not provide any solid statistics for monitoring channel loads accurately. NetWare 286 has a supervisory program FCONSOLE which displays statistics but does not provide enough detail to measure channel loads accurately. All FCONSOLE tells you is the number of packets or frames transmitted since the server was booted. You roughly estimate this data by using average packet sizes for each protocol. Table 4–1 lists the average packet size and the capacity of each protocol.

Table 4–1. Packet Size and Capacity

Protocol	Average Packet Size	Capacity
Ethernet	1518 bytes	10M bits per second
ARCnet	618 bytes	2.5M bits per second
Token Ring	1130 bytes	4Mb or 16M bits per second

Multiply these frame sizes times the number of packets transmitted for the total number of bytes transmitted. Multiply the bytes times eight to get the total bits. To determine utilization, divide this number by the number of seconds in which the data was gathered. Of course, this is a very rough estimate. It does not consider such issues as peak and off-peak load changes or variable packet sizes. Third-party monitoring packages, such as Thomas Conrad's TXD, Cheyenne Software's Monitrix, and Network General's Watchdog and Sniffer, give much more accurate information.

The rule of thumb is whenever the overall load exceeds 60% to 70% of capacity, divide the network using an internal bridge.

Using Internal Bridges

The concept of using an internal bridge is simple. You segment the network into separate, smaller physical networks, each attached to the file server with its own NIC. Figure 4-1 illustrates a star topology network with two hubs connected to one file server.

Setting up a bridge like the one in Figure 4-1 has no impact on end-users. All users will be displayed when you run the SLIST program. However, each LAN A user has a network address different from the LAN B users. Each LAN may now have a data packet in the channel, potentially doubling the network's throughput.

It is unfortunate that more people are not aware of this concept. Some companies have purchased faster file servers hoping to improve performance only to discover that all computers wait at the same speed. Buying a faster file server does not help performance very much if degradation is being caused by channel load.

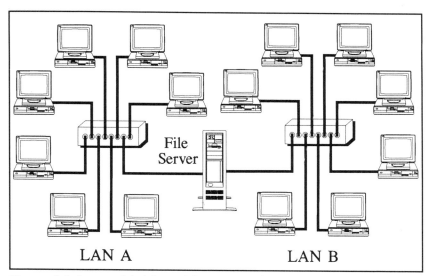

Figure 4-1. Internal bridge with star topology

Bridging Existing Dissimilar LANs

Another popular use of internal bridges is to connect dissimilar LAN types. A typical scenario is when two different departments each install a LAN independently. One department chooses one protocol suite and topology while the other installs something else. Sooner or later, someone wants to link these LANs. Figure 4-2 shows the result.

In Figure 4-2, an existing file server has become the bridge server and has two different kinds of NICs installed. There can be an active frame on each physical network. Because different protocols use different frame formats, the server performs a protocol conversion for transmitting frames from one network to the next. In addition to the difference in data frame format or layout, the data frames' actual size can vary, so the server may have to build two or more frames for one protocol for a single frame from another protocol. For example, the maximum size of an Ethernet data packet is 1024 bytes, while ARCnet's maximum is 512 bytes. This means that an Ethernet packet that is to be retransmitted on ARCnet will be sent in two frames. NetWare performs this task.

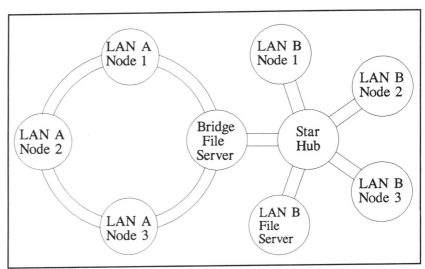

Figure 4-2. Bridging a star topology and a ring topology LAN

Using Internal Bridges as an Upgrade Technique

The third common use of internal bridges is similar to bridging dissimilar LANs. LAN technology is rapidly changing, and protocols are being enhanced. Transmission techniques under development will permit huge increases in data transmission speeds. Already, **Fiber Distributed Data Interface** (FDDI) has a foothold in LANs. Developed for fiber-optic media, FDDI permits data rates of 100M bits per second. Sooner or later, you will want to upgrade your LAN to take advantage of newer technology. The problem is that new technology may mean more investment in hardware NICs and cable. Most organizations cannot afford to toss everything they have done and buy into a new technology.

The transition can be made easier and less expensive up-front by phasing in new technology over time. This lets you get started without abandoning the investment you've already made. You can install an NIC for a newer technology in the server with the existing NIC. As your time and budget permits, you can move existing workstations to the new network. Figure 4-3 shows two different networks serviced by a single file server.

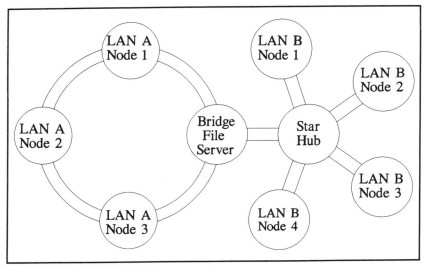

Figure 4-3. Bridging networks with one server

SETTING UP AN INTERNAL BRIDGE

The process of installing an internal bridge in a NetWare server is actually quite straightforward. You will have to relink the operating system with the drivers for each NIC installed. You must also assign a unique network address to each physical network. Then you install the new version of the operating system on the file server. That's all there is to it.

You perform these tasks with the ELSGEN or NETGEN program. Refer to Chapter 2 for detailed information on these programs.

SUMMARY

This short chapter introduces concepts that are very significant in planning and maintaining your network. Internal bridging—a new concept to many—should not be overlooked. Internal bridges can solve LAN channel overload, interconnect dissimilar LANs, and provide an easier path for upgrading an existing network. As you plan your network's growth and development, consider using internal bridges.

5
File Attributes

Files stored on the NetWare server have attributes that control their use. These attributes are assigned file-by-file, using NetWare's FLAG command or FILER utility. Part of the file's directory information, file attributes do not change when the server is down or rebooted. In the same manner that rights govern access to directories, file attributes govern access to individual files. In a LAN, not all files are treated equally. Some need to be shared and accessible to many users. Sharing can have a couple of definitions. If we say a file is shared, do we mean that multiple users can have *simultaneous access* to the file? Or, do we mean that multiple users can access the file, *one at a time*? I think that you can readily see the significant difference between these two. One means that many users all use the same file at the same time, hence it is shared. The second also means that the file is shared: others have a right to use the file, but only when no one else is using it. Which of these files is shared?

In addition, what would the consequences be if this file is a data file which routinely needs updating? What kind of access do we need now? Is the file a shared file? How is it shared? Do multiple users make changes simultaneously or serially? All these questions provide insights into the problems and nature of shared multi-user computer systems. These problems are the same for all classes of multi-user systems, from mainframes to PC LANs.

In addition to rights and Trustee Assignments, there must be a method for regulating access to individual files stored on the network. The major issues confronting us are type of access—simultaneous or serial—and data integrity. In this chapter, I raise issues and propose solutions for using Novell's Advanced NetWare as a true, multi-user local area network system. Most of the discussion focuses on file attributes.

A **file attribute** is a piece of information, kept at the file level, that governs how users can access a given file. All files have file attributes, not only in NetWare, but even in the stand-alone PC environment. However, Novell NetWare offers more options than DOS, due to the LAN's multi-user nature.

ATTRIBUTE DEFINITIONS

There are ten different attributes in Novell's SFT NetWare (nine in Advanced and ELS NetWare) that a file might possess. A file might have a single attribute or a combination of many. Of the seven attributes, five relate to access. The other two are specialty attributes. A list of the ten attributes follows. If you can change an attribute with the NetWare FLAG command, an attribute letter follows its name on the list. You can only change the other attributes with the FILER utility.

1. Normal (N)
2. Shareable (S)
3. Read Only (RO)
4. Read-Write (RW)
5. Execute Only
6. System File
7. Hidden File
8. Indexed (I)
9. Transaction Tracked (T) (SFT only)
10. Modified Since Last Backup

These attributes govern the file use privileges in the NetWare environment. An attribute is the same for all users who have access to the file through their Effective Rights.

Attribute Definitions

> **TIP:** To change an attribute, users must have the Modify Right in their Effective Rights.

Normal (N)

Normal is the default attribute NetWare assigns when a user adds a new file to the file server. Normal files are not shareable and have read-write access.

Shareable (S)

When On, this attribute lets multiple users access a file *concurrently*. When this attribute is Off, a user may only access a file *serially*, that is, when no one else is using it. You can alter this attribute directly with various application software packages. The HOLDON and HOLDOFF commands and the HOLD parameter in SHELL.CFG also affect this attribute. The default is Off.

Read Only (RO)

When this attribute is On, users can only read the file. They cannot update it. Program files are generally marked this way. When this attribute is Off, NetWare permits read-write access to the file. The default is Off.

Read-Write (RW)

A read-write file is one that users can update. Normal (N) files are read-write, because this is a default attribute for new files.

Execute Only

This attribute defines a special situation and applies only to files with a .COM or .EXE file name extension. When On, this attribute protects a file: users cannot change the file by writing to it, deleting it, or renaming it, nor can they copy it. This attribute prevents others from making unauthorized copies of our application programs.

System File

Files marked as system files are special files the NetWare operating system uses to function. Do not tamper with these files! They do not appear in a normal directory list.

Hidden File

A hidden file does not appear in a directory list obtained using the DIR or NDIR command. The FILER utility does not list it unless the FILER options are set to find hidden files. Usually, applications use hidden files as a form of copy protection. However, users can hide their own files, if needed. Some NetWare system files possess both the System File attribute and the Hidden File attribute.

> **WARNING:** Do not change this attribute for files hidden by the application software. Chances are that the application requires that these files be hidden to run.

Indexed (I)

When turned On, this attribute causes the server to build an index of a file's clusters from the File Allocation Table. By indexing the File Allocation Table clusters for the file, NetWare can access the various clusters much more quickly. This option uses 1K of server memory for each indexed file. See Chapter 1 for more information on file server memory use. The maximum number of indexed files allowed is configured when NetWare is installed. Only a supervisor can set this attribute. This attribute is intended for use with large data files—those over 2Mb. Since each cluster only holds 4096 bytes, a file of over 2Mb would have over 500 clusters in the File Allocation Table. Using the Indexed file attribute dramatically reduces the time NetWare takes to search for the needed cluster.

Attribute Definitions

Transaction Tracked (T) (SFT Only)

This attribute marks a file as a tracked file. Transaction tracking facilitates restoring data files to their original state when a catastrophic failure happens. For example, what if you are processing a month-end task that resets the month-to-date totals to zero and also adds the month-to-date figures to the year-to-date figures, and the server goes down in the middle of this process? How could you restart the process where it stopped? You probably couldn't. However, some of your data file was updated and some wasn't. What do you do? Without transaction tracking, you would have to restore your data from your backup source and start the process over again, *if* you had backed up immediately prior to this process. If you didn't, the problem is even more severe. You would have to retrace your steps from when you last backed up until this procedure began. With transaction tracking, NetWare keeps a log file of all changes made to data files. If a severe problem prevents the process from completing, NetWare can restore your data files' original condition, using the log file to reverse any entries made.

Usually software packages, such as accounting systems, have to be designed to take advantage of Novell's Transaction Tracking System. You must be a supervisor to mark a file for transaction tracking.

Modified Since Last Backup

The system automatically sets this attribute, but a user can change it. Any time a file is added to the server's disk or an existing file is modified in any way, this attribute is set to On. When the file is backed up using LARCHIVE, NARCHIVE, or any NetWare compatible software, this attribute is set to Off. One option of most back-up systems is to back up only those files which are new to the system or have been modified since the previous back-up. This is **incremental back-up**. Of course, incremental back-up does not take as long as a full back-up and is, therefore, quite popular. Incremental back-up software looks for this attribute to determine whether to include the file in the back-up.

SHAREABLE VERSUS NON-SHAREABLE; READ-ONLY VERSUS READ-WRITE

Recognizing that the Maximum Rights Mask and the user's or group's Trustee Assignments govern overall access to a directory and its files, file attributes are an additional vehicle for regulating access file-by-file. One of the most important of these is the Shareable attribute. The default for this attribute is Off, meaning that the file is non-shareable. Another attribute governs whether users can open the file for read-write access or read-only access. To fully understand NetWare, you need to understand fully the definition and impact of both attributes.

A file marked read only can only be opened for read access. It cannot be opened for write access. The default setting of this attribute for new files is read-write. Of course, to write to the file, a user needs a Trustee Assignment that allows writing to files in that directory. Most data files are flagged for read-write access, while program files are generally flagged read only.

The Shareable Attribute and Network Performance
Keywords: FLAG, shareable, cache, attributes

Scenario The Shareable attribute can dramatically impact the LAN's performance, especially when the marked file is a shareable program file. If you are using the CACHE BUFFERS statement in your SHELL.CFG configuration file to enhance the performance of NetWare and you flag a file as shareable, the attribute disables the cache. The **cache** is a memory area at the workstation, where the NetWare file server automatically sends data that NetWare "thinks" the workstation is going to want next. A **hit** occurs when NetWare has guessed correctly: the data requested is already in the workstation's memory and therefore no further read is required by the file server. When the cache is disabled, it takes more read requests to get the same amount of data from the file server.

The reason for this is not readily apparent but makes sense. Whenever NetWare detects a file marked shareable, it assumes that the file is a data file. Because the data file is shared, many users may be updating different sections of it concurrently. If caching were taking place, the section of the file in one workstation's memory might be the section that someone is updating at another workstation. This could lead to one workstation "seeing" different values for the same data that another station is using. This could be disastrous in a LAN environment. Therefore, NetWare disables the workstation's cache when the file is flagged shareable. NetWare will not send data that the workstation has not requested and it will send requested data in much smaller increments. This means more packets will be sent on the LAN, decreasing its performance. The bottom line is that program files and any other read-only file should be marked non-shareable, read only. Generally, overlays for programs have to be flagged as shareable files.

Solution Be very selective about setting file attributes, especially attributes of executable files and program overlays. Do not blindly accept the software vendor's recommendation to flag all these files SRO. In fact, you should flag as many of these files as possible NRO. The deciding criteria for whether a program file should be SRO or NRO is the file's status when in use by a user. If the file is opened on the file server, read into the workstation's RAM, and then closed immediately on the file server, you should flag the file NRO. If the file remains open on the file server, you will have to flag it SRO. You can tell how the file behaves either by monitoring it at the file server using the MONITOR program, or you can use FCONSOLE.

Protecting Program Files
Keywords: FLAG, attributes, programs, execute only

Scenario

One problem many organizations face is that users of their computer systems make illegal copies of software. The software industry attempted to minimize this problem using sophisticated copy-protection schemes. Unfortunately, copy-protection had two major flaws. First, clever programs or hardware successfully beat most schemes. Some programs simply copied copy-protected programs. Others completely removed copy-protection. Second, copy-protection schemes imposed often annoying and sometimes dangerous constraints on the end-user community.

An example is the scheme that required a key diskette. To run the software, you needed the manufacturer's copy-protected key diskette. This annoyed hard disk users. In addition, when something happened to the key diskette, it would have to be returned to the manufacturer for replacement. This could take several days and, in the meantime, the software could not be used. Another approach required users to enter information, somewhat randomly chosen, from the manual that came with the software. The assumption was that only the real owner would have the manual—quite an assumption—and therefore copies would be useless. If the real owners ever lost their manuals, they were out of luck. So instead of locking up the software, they locked up the manual, after making a copy.

Copy-protection schemes make life in a LAN environment miserable because these schemes were designed for single-user machines. Key diskettes don't work because not all workstations need floppy drives. Other schemes are equally poor. Novell NetWare offers some good solutions. Remember that users cannot even "see" programs in directories for which they have no Search Right. They cannot copy files if they do not have Open and Read Rights. So some protection already exists within the normal NetWare directory access privilege system. The issues regarding software protection in a NetWare environment are

- Preventing unauthorized duplication and distribution of programs.
- Limiting the number of users to the number licensed by the software vendor and the client-user.

Solution

NetWare has a file attribute that only applies to executable programs (.COM and .EXE), called Execute Only. This flag must be set through the FILER program on a file-by-file basis by a supervisor-level user. After a file is marked execute only, this attribute cannot be removed. This attribute prevents unauthorized duplication of program files. After a program file has been marked execute only, you cannot copy it with COPY, NCOPY, or any other copy utility. You cannot back it up or rename it, because these are merely other forms of copying. Marking the file execute only effectively prevents users from copying program files. Execute-only files cannot be renamed. Because program updates generally have the same name as the previous version, this could be a problem except that a supervisor-level user can delete the file.

Solving the second problem effectively and safely involves the use of semaphores by the application. This feature, now available in the NetWare environment, has to be implemented by the application software developer. When a program opens a semaphore, NetWare checks the open semaphore count to see if any are available. If fewer semaphores are open than the maximum allowed, the program continues. Otherwise, the program will not be allowed to continue.

Some third-party software products such as Brightwork Development's Sitelock, Saber Software's Saber Meter, and LAN System's LAN Shell provide software tracking and metering for LAN software.

Using Hidden Files for Sensitive Data
Keywords: FLAG, attributes, hidden files

Scenario   Another method of protecting sensitive files is to use the Hidden File attribute, again from the FILER utility. This attribute makes the file invisible to the user. When this attribute is set, the file does not appear in DIR or NDIR directory lists or in the Files window of the FILER utility. When a file is hidden, no users can access it. This means that if an executable program file is hidden, you cannot run it.

> **TIP:** Record the names of hidden files. It is difficult to change this attribute if you do not know the file name.

NetWare Error Messages
Keywords: FLAG, HIDEFILE, RIGHTS, PATH, memory, attributes

Scenario

These error messages appear in many network utilities such as FLAG, HIDEFILE, or RIGHTS.

```
"Error Getting Drive Information From Network"
"Error Getting Temp Path Handle From Network"
"Error Getting User Rights Information From Network"
```

If the operating system returns an error code when requested to get the drive mapping of an established internetwork handle, likely causes include

1. The server running out of available DGroup memory workspace
2. A corrupted directory
3. Corrupted bindery files

Solution

Since there are three possible causes, I'll address each solution separately.

1. The only steps that can be taken to get more memory allocated to DGroup are:

   a. Reduce the number of directory entries permitted for the disk volumes. This is done with the NETGEN or ELSGEN program. You can safely reduce this setting to any value that exceeds the present number of files stored on the file server volume. To check an existing volume's maximum setting and the number of files on the volume, use the VOLINFO program.

   b. Reduce the number of VAPs (Value Added Processes) loaded on the file server. Each VAP uses DGroup memory for its internal variables. This may not be an option for you if the VAP provides some network facility that you have to have.

NetWare Error Messages

    c. Reduce the number of allocated drive MAPs. Drive mappings are used to create logical assignments of directories and to create search routes to program directories. MAP commands are often placed in the login script which means they are allocated even if the user is not using them. Every MAP is stored on the file server in DGroup memory. Reduce these by placing the MAP commands in the user's menu script or batch files used to launch the application. The essential idea is to eliminate all mappings except those that the user has to have at all times. Issue the appropriate MAP commands when the user selects an application. When the user finishes the application, delete the associated drive mappings.

2. Repair corrupted directories with the VREPAIR utility located on the UTILEXE diskette. Boot your server with a DOS diskette. Then run VREPAIR.
3. Rebuild the bindery files with BINDFIX, a program in the \SYSTEM directory of the SYS volume. It should be run when no other users are logged on. It creates new bindery files, NET$BVAL.SYS and NET$BIND.SYS, and renames bindery files with .OLD extensions.

Local Drives May Not Have File Attributes
Keywords: FLAG, attributes

Scenario   The FLAG error message

"Local Drives May Not Have File Attributes"

appears when a user specifies a local drive in the command, that is, attempts to FLAG files on a local drive.

Solution   FLAG works only for files stored on internetwork disks. Files located on local drives do not have the same attributes and directory structure as files stored on a file server. Therefore, the FLAG command does not work on local files.

Specified Volume Not Found
Keywords: FLAG, attributes

Scenario The FLAG error message

"Specified Volume Not Found"

appears when you specify a complete directory and the volume specified is not on the internetwork's mounted volume list.

Solution Make sure that the volume was mounted and that you typed the volume name correctly in the FLAG command.

Specified Drive Not Mapped to Network
Keywords: FLAG, attributes

Scenario The FLAG error

"Specified Drive Not Mapped to Network"

appears when the user specifies a drive that is not mapped to the internetwork, for example, FLAG H:FILENAME.EXT where drive H: is not mapped to an internetwork directory.

Solution Issue an appropriate MAP command to create the logical drive assignment or change the drive specified in the FLAG command.

SEARCH MODE ATTRIBUTE

This file attribute is not one of the normal ten NetWare attributes, because you cannot view it with NDIR or FILER or change it with FLAG or FILER. However, the search mode setting for each file is an attribute that is part of the file's directory information.

The Search Mode attribute determines how an executable program searches for related files that are part of the application. The Search Mode attribute only applies to executable files, that is, files with .EXE or .COM extensions. Normally, programs running under NetWare behave just as they do running under DOS. NetWare searches for programs according to the path, like DOS, and searches for data files according to the way the application is set up. The Search Mode attribute can change this.

SMODE is an important option in Novell NetWare. It is related to the DOS PATH or the NetWare MAP SEARCH function. Normally, PATH and MAP SEARCH instruct the system to search directories other than the current default directory to locate executable files (.COM or .EXE) or batch files (.BAT). The system looks for the file with the .COM extension in the current directory first. If it doesn't find it, then the system searches the current directory for an .EXE file. If the .EXE file is not found, the system checks the current directory for a .BAT file. If all these searches fail, the system moves to the first directory specified in the PATH statement and repeats the process. This continues until the program or batch file is either found and executed or the system notifies the user that the command or file name is incorrect.

SMODE expands on the default method of searching for files. One reason for this is that the normal procedure only searches for either executable files (.COM or .EXE) or batch files (.BAT). It ignores data files and other files, such as program overlays. SMODE sets options that increase or change the default means of searching for files. The SMODE parameter determines how the system acts. You can use only one parameter with the SMODE command. If you omit the parameter, SMODE displays the current setting.

The seven parameters for the Search Mode attribute are listed next.

Parameter	Usage
0	This is the default mode. It uses the standard procedure described earlier for locating files and only searches for executable or batch files.
1	If a path was specified to start an executable file, then the system searches that directory for data files. If the data file is not found, the system searches the directories specified in the PATH statement, for example,

        `F>SYS:\APPS\DBASE\DBASE`

This command tells the system to run a program called DBASE. This program is in the SYS volume and in a directory with the path name \APPS\DBASE. When it looks for a data file, the system searches the current default directory. Then it searches the SYS:\APPS\DBASE directory. If the file is not here, the system searches according to the PATH statement in effect.

2	Only the current default directory will be searched.
3	If a path was specified to start an executable file, then the system searches that directory for data files. It does not search the other directories unless the data file is to be opened in read-only mode. If the data file is not found and it is to be opened as a read-only file, then the system searches the directories specified in the PATH statement.
5	The system searches the specified directory path where the program was found. Then the system searches the current default directory and all directories in the PATH statement for data files.
7	If files opened by the executable program are read only, the system searches the default directory and all directories in the search path.

Search Mode Attribute

The syntax for the SMODE command is

```
SMODE [directory path] [parameter]
SMODE [filespec] [parameter]
```

Here are examples using the SMODE command.

```
SMODE ATRIUM/SYS:/MFG 2
```

Changes all executable files in the MFG directory to search mode 2.

```
SMODE ACCTG.COM 5
```

Changes only ACCTG.COM in the current default directory.

Files not changed with the SMODE command have the default SMODE 0.

Using SMODE

You can use the SMODE command to solve a variety of problems common to LANs. You'll see a good example later in Chapter 11. Four NetWare programs, CAPTURE, NPRINT, PCONSOLE, and PRINTCON, use a print job database called PRINTCON.DAT. The problem is that these programs look for the PRINTCON.DAT file in the user's mail directory. This means that if each user does not have a copy of the file, the programs do not work properly. To simplify maintenance, most network administrators would prefer to have a single copy of PRINTCON.DAT accessible to all users.

They can accomplish this by copying the PRINTCON.DAT file into the PUBLIC directory of the file server, changing the four programs' Search Mode attributes to 5 or 7, and establishing a search path to PUBLIC. Then the four programs will look in the PUBLIC directory when they do not find PRINTCON.DAT in the user's mail directory.

This command is one of the most important, yet most overlooked, commands in NetWare. You can use it to solve many configuration problems that cannot be handled any other way.

Solving Software Configuration File Problems
Keywords: SMODE, configuration, PATH, search

Scenario

Almost all software uses some sort of set-up file to configure the software for the type of PC, display, and printer being used. In a LAN environment, this configuration file needs to be sensitive to which particular workstation is using the application. Most software applications do not properly address this problem. Most address it by tying a configuration file to the particular user. This approach doesn't work if the user uses different PCs with different configurations.

For example, Lotus 1-2-3 uses a configuration file called 123.SET. When 1-2-3 is run, the program looks for 123.SET in the current default directory. If it does not find the program there, it looks in the directory where the program resides. Neither approach works adequately when users start up the application using different PCs.

The problem with most configuration files is that their manufacturers have not addressed the issues of working in a LAN environment with various hardware configurations very well, if at all. Configuration files have three primary purposes:

- To load the appropriate drivers for the user's hardware. These include drivers for the video adapter and printer, as well as other user-specific hardware such as a mouse or scanner.
- To direct the software where to look for the application's related files, data, or program.
- To establish the user's preferred settings for the software itself. These include items such as monitor colors, menu options, and macros.

When you think about it, these three things can vary quite a bit. Having only one configuration file for everyone probably won't work. The hardware drivers a user needs depend on the machine that the user sits down at. Users probably have the same

Solving Software Configuration File Problems

preferences, no matter which machine they use. Default directories might be based upon the user or upon groups that the user belongs to.

Actually, I advocate that software vendors put these items in three separate configuration files so that LAN administrators can set up networks according to their users' needs.

Solution

To solve this problem, you need to determine which PC is being used and find the correct configuration file for that machine's hardware, regardless of its user.

You can accomplish this by using the System Login Script to set a search path to a directory that is determined by the PC's node ID from the LAN adapter card. Then you set up a program that uses the configuration file to search this directory.

1. List all your node IDs. Be sure to include leading zeros. You can do this by logging in all PCs and typing USERLIST/A. Alternatively, you can place the following command in the System Login Script to place the node ID in a DOS environment variable:

   ```
   DOS SET NODE = "%P_STATION"
   ```

   After the machine has been logged in, you can view the node ID by typing SET.

2. Create a directory called STATIONS off the root directory:

   ```
   MD \STATIONS
   ```

3. Beneath the \STATIONS directory, create directories that correspond to each node ID. If your node IDs are eight characters or less, type

   ```
   MD \STATIONS\node_ID
   ```

   If your node IDs are longer than eight characters, use FILER to create the directories:

   ```
   CD \STATIONS
   FILER
   ```

Select Subdirectory Information.

Press the INS key to add each directory using the full node ID.

4. Create the necessary configuration files for each hardware configuration needed. Use FILER to copy these files into the appropriate \STATIONS*node_id* directory.

5. Make sure that there are no copies of the configuration file in any other directories (usually the program directory or the data directory).

6. Add the configuration directory to the user's environment as a search drive with a MAP command in the System Login Script:

    `MAP INS S2:=SYS:STATIONS\%P_STATION`

7. Use the SMODE command to change the search behavior of the software programs. You can do this to the individual program files or to the entire directory:

    `SMODE server/vol:\directory\program.ext 5`

    or

    `SMODE server/vol:\directory 5`

Speeding Up Applications by Moving Overlay Files
Keywords: overlays, programs, attributes, SMODE

Scenario Many software applications are so large that the program code has been broken into overlay files which the application loads as needed. These overlays can be performance thieves in a LAN environment. Much of the traffic on the LAN channel can result from the workstation having to continually load different overlays from the file server.

Most software applications search for their overlay files in the directory where the executable file was found. In a LAN environment, most programs reside on the file server. It would be much better for performance to load the overlays from the workstation, if the workstation has either a local hard disk or a large enough RAM disk. It's easy to copy the files to the user's disk. The trick is to make the executable file look for the overlays in a directory other than the one used for the executable file.

Solution You can solve this problem with the SMODE command, which changes the Search attribute of executable files. The technique is to move the overlays to the user's local source and delete them from the program's home directory on the server. Add a search path in the user's environment that points to the user's local drive and the directory where the overlays are stored. Change the original program's executable files, which are still on the server, so their Search attribute is 5 or 7.

The following example might be used for a dBASE application.

1. Copy the appropriate dBASE files from the server to the user's local drive:

    ```
    MD C:\APPS\DBASE
    NCOPY SYS:PROGRAMS/DBASE/*.OV* C:\APPS\DBASE
    ```

2. Remove the same files from the file server:

   `DEL SYS:PROGRAMS/DBASE/*.OV*`

3. Add the local directory to the user's search path:

   `MAP INS S3:=C:\APPS\DBASE`

4. Change the executable file's Search attribute:

   `SMODE SYS:PROGRAMS/DBASE 5`

NetWare 386 SMODE Bug
Keywords: SMODE, NetWare 386

Scenario   A bug in NetWare 386 versions 3.00 and 3.10 prevents you from using the SMODE command with files that have file names longer than five characters. You can tell if your NetWare has this bug by using the SMODE command with an executable file with a name longer than five characters.

Solution   Work around this bug by renaming the file with a file name of less than six characters. Then, you can use SMODE to change the file's Search attribute. After you change the attribute, rename the file with its original name. The attribute will stay set. To use this process, you must have Modify Rights in the directory where the executable file resides, and you must flag the file as a read-write file to rename.

Shareable Files Reverting Back to Normal
Keywords: attributes, FLAG

Scenario A user data file was flagged as a shareable, read-write file (SRW). However, after running the application that uses this file, the attributes are set back to normal or non-shareable, read-write (NRW), which prevents multiple users from having access to the file at the same time. The file then has to be reflagged SRW and this process keeps happening over and over.

The problem lies with the application software not being written properly for a network environment. Typically, this occurs when a data file is getting updated. Many applications create a new, updated version of the file and then delete the original file. As a default, NetWare flags new files as NRW, unless the application software sets the attributes to SRW. If the application does not set the attributes to SRW, this problem occurs.

Solution Since this is an application problem, the correct solution is for the software vendor to correct the program. However, until this is done there is a public-domain program included on the diskette that comes with this book. The program is called SRW.COM. It is a memory-resident program you can load prior to running the application. Fortunately, it is a small program. It will flag any files that are created as SRW.

SUMMARY

Setting file attributes is one of the essential tasks of a network administrator. Most experienced PC users are familiar with the attributes that DOS uses. NetWare expands upon these attributes in ways that are important for networks. While most attribute settings are straightforward, a few situations require special attention. One of the duties of the network administrator will be to determine what attribute settings should be used for all of the files stored on the file server that are shared by multiple users.

This chapter also discussed the Search Mode attribute, which is often overlooked because it isn't changed with the FLAG command or with the FILER program. The SMODE program changes the Search Mode attribute. This attribute only applies to executable program files and is used to determine how these files search for related data and program files. This setting gives the network administrator much more flexibility than DOS in determining how programs will be installed and run.

Since problems caused by incorrect attribute settings show up immediately, most NetWare users quickly become familiar with setting the file attributes. Fortunately, most attribute changes are done only once.

Part II
Workstation Optimization

This part of the book focuses on the workstations connected to the LAN. Because most end-user processing is performed at the workstation, the set up and configuration of these PCs greatly impacts overall network performance. The next three chapters deal with setting up the user's workstation for the NetWare environment. Chapter 6 explores the components and functions of the network shell. Chapter 7 discusses an important configuration file called SHELL.CFG. Chapter 8 focuses on setting up the user's environment during the login process.

6
Configuring and Using the Network Shell

There are two different sets of **network shell programs**. A network shell set consists of programs that provide the interface between the user's workstation PC and the rest of the network. The set's various components perform different tasks while a workstation communicates with the file server or other workstations in the network. Some parts of the shell are configurable; others are not. It is very important that you understand the configuration options of the network shell and their impact on the network.

The more common set is the files that NetWare has used for the past several years, commonly called the **DOS workstation shells**. NetWare 386 has a new set of workstation shell programs, **DOS/ODI workstation shells**. ODI stands for **Open Data-Link Interface**. These shells differ from their earlier counterparts in that they can support multiple protocols without having to reboot the computer.

DOS WORKSTATION SHELLS

The DOS workstation shell programs consist of the following components:

Configuring and Using the Network Shell

Function	Hardware Interface	Re-director	NETBIOS Emulator	Configuration File
File name	IPX.COM	NET2.COM NET3.COM NET4.COM XMSNET3.EXE XMSNET4.EXE EMSNET3.EXE EMSNET4.EXE	NETBIOS.EXE	SHELL.CFG

All executable components of the shell (files with the extension .COM or .EXE) are memory-resident programs that are loaded before you log into the network. Generally, these programs must be loaded before other memory-resident programs, especially if the other memory-resident programs are terminate-stay-resident (TSR) programs. In most cases, the shell programs are loaded during the processing of AUTOEXEC.BAT.

IPX.COM

This shell component provides the hardware interface between the NIC, the PC, and the network. **IPX** (**I**nternetwork **P**acket **EX**change) is part of a protocol set for network communication management that Novell licensed from Xerox Corporation. IPX is the portion of the shell responsible for creating data packets in the correct format and inserting them in the LAN channel. IPX also disassembles packets the workstation receives, passing the data portion of the packet to the other shell components, the operating system, and the application software.

Because the IPX.COM program interfaces physically with the network, the IPX program varies, depending on the type of network used. Therefore, the IPX.COM program must be generated using the NetWare SHGEN program. Different NICs and even different configurations of the same NIC require different IPX.COM programs. The NetWare manuals explain how to generate the IPX.COM program file. You need the NetWare diskettes labelled SHGEN-1, SHGEN-1, LAN-DRV-001, and LAN-DRV-002. You may not have SHGEN-2 and LAN-DRV-002 if you received NetWare on 3.5 inch diskettes. Attempting to load an improperly configured IPX.COM program on the workstation usually results in an error message or a "hung" workstation which you will have to reboot.

IPX.COM Will Not Load
Keywords: shell, workstation, IPX, interrupts, DMA, memory address

Scenario

You try to load the IPX.COM program, and the loading process fails. You may see an error message indicating that the IPX.COM is not appropriate for the NIC in use or the workstation may just hang, requiring you to reboot the machine.

Because the IPX program is the low-level interface between the physical components of the network cabling, the NIC, and the PC, it is unique to each configuration. Different NICs require different drivers to be linked with the NetWare shell object files. In addition, the IPX.COM program's configuration option must match the physical configuration of the NIC itself. NetWare 286 includes the NIC drivers listed next.

Vendor	Network Adapter Model
3Com	3C501 Etherlink V2.40EC
	3C503 Etherlink II V2.30EC
	3C505 Etherlink Plus V2.41EC
	3C523 Etherlink/MC V2.30EC (Micro Channel)
Gateway	G/NET V1.00
IBM	Asynchronous (COM1/COM2) V1.00
	PC Network II V1.10
	PC Baseband V1.10
	Token Ring V2.40
Micom Interlan	NI5010 V2.30EC
Novell	Ethernet NE-1000 V2.30EC
	Ethernet NE-2000
	Ethernet NE/2
	RX-Net V1.00
	RX-Net/2 SMC PS110
	S-Net V1.00
	Star Intelligent NIC V1100
	Star Intelligent NIC—No Interrupts

Proteon	ProNet 10 P1300/P1800 V2.23 with checksum
Standard Microsystems	ARCnet
Pure Data	ARCnet V1.00

You can use other NICs in NetWare workstations, if the NIC vendors provide the drivers needed to create the IPX.COM program for the NIC. Almost all NIC vendors provide drivers for NetWare.

To create the IPX.COM program, you need the appropriate driver and you need to configure the driver to match the configuration of the NIC itself. You must configure up to four items on the NIC to configure IPX.COM:

Interrupt request signal line (IRQ)

Direct memory address channel (DMA)

I/O address port

ROM/RAM addresses

There may be other settings on the NIC, such as the node number or cable type, which are not used to generate IPX.COM.

The basic rule for configuring these four items is that none of the settings can conflict with corresponding settings for any other device installed in the PC. Table 6-1 may be useful for configuring the NIC and IPX.COM.

Table 6-1. Common Device Configuration Options

Device Name	IRQ	DMA	I/O Address	ROM Address	ROM Address Length
3COM 3C501	2, (3), 4, 5, 6, 7	(1), 3	(300), 310	(CC000-CFFFF), EC000-EFFFF	16K
3COM 3C503	2, (3), 4, 5	(1), 3	250, 280, 2A0, 2E0, (300), 310, 330, 350	C8000-CBFFF, (CC000-CFFFF), D8000-DBFFF, DC000-DFFFF	16K
3COM 3C505	2, (3), 4, 5, 7	1, 3, (5), 6, 7	(300), 310, 320, 330	(CC000-CFFFF), EC000-EFFFF	16K
AST Clock Calendar	None	None	2C0 - 2C7	None	None

IPX.COM Will Not Load

Table 6-1, continued

Device Name	IRQ	DMA	I/O Address	ROM Address	ROM Address Length
AT Hard Disk Controller	(14)	(1)	1F0 – 1F8	E000-EFFF	4K
CGA Adapter	None	None	3D0 – 3BF	B800-BBFF	1K
COM1 Serial Port	(4), None	None	3F8 – 3FF	None	None
COM2 Serial Port	(3), None	None	2F8 – 2FF	None	None
EGA Adapter	(2), None	None	3C0 – 3CF	A000-AFFF B800-BFFF	4K 2K
Floppy Controller	6	None	3F0 – 3F7	NA	NA
Gateway G/Net NIC	(3)	None	280, 2A0, (2E0), 300	A000-A3FF, C000-C3FF, (D000-D3FF), E000-E3FF	1K
Hercules Monochrome	None	None	3B0 – 3B9	None	None
IBM SDLC Adapter	3, (4)	1	3A0 – 3AF	None	None
IBM PC Network II	(2), 3	None	620	(CC000-CFFFF), CE000-D1FFF, D6000-D9FFF, DC000-DF000, DE000-E1FFF	16K
IBM Token Ring	(2), 3, 7, 10, 11	None	(A20), A24	(CC000-CDFFF), (D8000-DBFFF), CE000-CFFFF, D4000-D7FFF, C4000-C5FFF, C0000-C3FFF, D0000-D1FFF, D8000-DBFFF, D2000-D3FFF, DC000-DFFFF	8K ROM, 16K RAM
LPT1 Parallel Port	(7)	None	(378-37F), 3BC-3BF	None	None
LPT2 Parallel Port	(5)	None	(278-27F), 378-37B	None	None
LPT3 Parallel Port	None	None	(278-27A)	None	None
Monochrome Display Adapter	None	None	(3B0-3BF)	B000 – B100	256 bytes

Table 6-1, continued

Device Name	IRQ	DMA	I/O Address	ROM Address	ROM Address Length
Novell 286B Floppy Controller	(6)	(2)	1F0-1F8 & 3F0-3F7	None	None
Novell Disk Co-Processor	10, (11), 12, 15	None	(340-347), 348-34F, 320-327, 328-32F	None	None
Novell NE1000 NIC	2, (3), 4, 5	None	(300), 320, 340, 360	C800-E800, CC00-EC000, D000-F000	8K
Novell NE2000 NIC	2, (3), 4, 5	None	(300), 320, 340, 360	C800-E800, CC00-EC000, D000-F000	8K
Novell NE/2 NIC	(3), 4, 5, 9	None	(1000-102F), 2020-204F, 8020-804F, A0A0-A0CF, B0B0-B0DF, C0C0-C0EF, C3D0-C3FFF	(C8000-C9FFF), CA000-CBFFF, CC000-CDFFF, CE000-CFFFF, D0000-D1FFF, D2000-D3FFF, D4000-D5FFF	8K
Novell RX-NET	(2), 3, 4, 7	None	(2E0), 2F0, 300, 350	(D000-F000), C000-E000, CC00-EC000, DC000-DE000	8K
Proteon P1300	(2), 3, 4, 5	(1), 2, 3	(300), 308, 310, 340	None	None
Proteon P1340	(2), 3, 4, 5, 6, 7	(1), 2, 3	(A20), 300, 308, 310, 340	None	None
Proteon P1344	3, 4, 5, 6, 7, 9, 10, 11, (12)	(5), 6, 7	(A20), 300, 308, 310, 340	None	None
Std. Micro ARCnet	(2), 3, 4, 5, 7	None	(2E0), 2F0, 300	C000-FFFF, (D000-10FFF), E000-11FFF	16K
Thomas Conrad ARCnet	2, 3, 4, 5, 6, 7, 9, 10, 11, 12, 14	None	(2E0), 2F0, 300, 350	C000-FFFF, C400-103FF, C800-107FF, CC00-106FF, (D000-10FFF), D400-113FF, D800-117FF, DC00-116FF	16K
VGA Adapter	(2), 9	None	3C0	(C0000-C4FFF)	20K

IPX.COM Will Not Load

Table 6-1, continued

Device Name	IRQ	DMA	I/O Address	ROM Address	ROM Address Length
Western Digital Floppy Controller	6	2	3F0, 3F8	None	None
XT Hard Disk Controller	5	None	320	None	None

The workstation may hang when you try to load IPX.COM. This may occur because

- When IPX.COM loads, it tries to initialize the NIC according to the configuration used when the IPX.COM program was generated. If the IPX settings do not match those of the physical NIC itself, the machine usually hangs.
- A conflicting I/O address port or RAM/ROM address between the NIC and another device installed in the workstation causes the PC to hang.
- Conflicting IRQ and DMA channels generally do not cause the workstation to hang when IPX loads, but may cause the workstation to hang afterwards.

Solution First verify that the IPX.COM configuration matches the NIC configuration. To determine the IPX configuration, change to the directory or drive where IPX resides and type

    IPX I

This displays the configuration of the IPX.COM program. Now, inspect the NIC to verify that the setting shown matches the NIC configuration. If not, you need to change the NIC configuration, or regenerate IPX.COM using the correct configuration.

If IPX.COM and the NIC configuration are configured properly, then the conflict is between the NIC and the other peripherals installed in the PC. This situation is more difficult to resolve because you must know what other peripherals are installed and how each is configured. You need the manufacturer's documentation to determine the configuration of most devices.

> Consider software programs such as Touchstone Software Corporation's Checkit, Digasoft's QAPlus, and SuperSoft's Service Diagnostics for your system support toolbox. While none gives 100 percent accurate information about every type of device that you can install in a PC, these programs do provide a great deal of information about what has been installed, as well as the IRQ, DMA, and memory setting being used by the devices detected.

THE RE-DIRECTOR PROGRAM

The next component of the workstation shell, the **re-director program**, gets this name from the function it performs. This program intercepts all commands and function calls the user or the application issues and then decides how to process the command. If the command or function requires a resource within the workstation, the re-director passes it to DOS. If the command or function requires network resources, the re-director passes it to IPX.COM which bundles it into a packet for the file server. In most cases, the decision is based upon the software interrupt used. Figure 6-1, the re-director program, illustrates this basic concept.

Seven different re-director programs are furnished with NetWare. The one you use depends on two things:

- The version of DOS you are using.
- Where in RAM you want to load the re-director.

Table 6-2 lists your choices.

Table 6-2. Re-director program choices

DOS Version	Base RAM (640K)	Expanded Memory (EMS)	Extended Memory
2.xx	NET2.COM	N/A	N/A
3.xx	NET3.COM	EMSNET3.EXE	XMSNET3.EXE
4.xx	NET4.COM	EMSNET4.EXE	XMSNET4.EXE

The Re-director Program

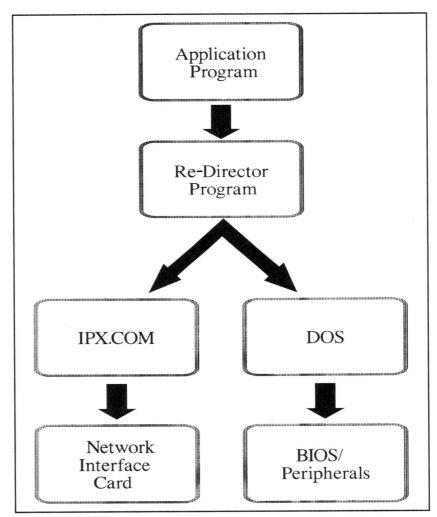

Figure 6-1. The re-director program

As application programs get larger, DOS grows in size, and more device drivers become available, users are scrounging for every byte in the 640K base RAM area that they can get their hands on. The XMSNET and EMSNET versions of the re-director program let you put most of the re-director program in extended or expanded memory. Even though these programs do load into these higher memory regions, they also require about 7K of conventional memory. Novell released these versions of the re-director program in the summer of 1990.

The re-director program loads immediately after the IPX.COM program. A feature of the latest re-director programs lets you unload them when you are not logged onto the network. To do so, type the program name followed by the U parameter. Here are some examples.

```
NET3 U
EMSNET4 U
XMSNET4 U
```

If you are not logged off the network, unloading the re-director *will* log you off.

Re-director Program Will Not Load
Keywords: shell, IPX, re-director program, login

Scenario   The re-director program does not load properly.

Solution   If the re-director program does not load successfully, there can be several causes.

- The re-director program you are trying to use is not correct for the DOS version you are using. Use the DOS VER command to verify your DOS version.
- You are trying to use the XMSNETx or the EMSNETx version of the re-director program, but you do not have this type of memory available.
- You are trying to use the EMSNETx version of the re-director program, but the DOS device driver for EMS memory management is not loaded.
- If none of these has caused the problem, there may be an incompatible or defective BIOS chip(s) in the PC itself. Check with your vendor to insure that the BIOS in your machine is the most current available. If not, replace it with the current version. This is most common in machines manufactured prior to 1986.

File Server Could Not Be Found
Keywords: IPX, re-director program, login, shell

Scenario   This message is displayed immediately after the re-director portion of the shell is loaded and the user cannot log on.

When the re-director program is loaded, it attempts to connect with a file server on the network by transmitting a **broadcast packet**. This packet is addressed to all PCs on the network rather than a specific PC. This first broadcast packet asks, "Are any file servers present?" Any file servers that are running respond by sending a packet back to the sending PC. Then, the re-director program sends another broadcast packet which says, "I want to connect to a file server. Can I?" Any file servers which have an available connection respond by sending their node and network identification back to the workstation. When the workstation receives none of these packets, the error message is displayed.

Solution   The most common cause of this error message is a faulty connection or cable. Nine times out of ten, the cause of this error is a loose network cable, an unterminated end or connector, or another problem related to the network's wiring. Rarely is the problem with the IPX or re-director program. Therefore, the first thing to determine is the wiring connections' integrity, according to the type of topology you're using.

BUS Topology

Check:	all T-connectors for loose connections.
Check:	for missing or damaged terminators at each end of the cable.
Make sure:	any required grounds are intact.
Check:	any transceiver cables for loose connections.
Check:	power to any repeaters.
Run:	NIC diagnostics, if available.

File Server Could Not Be Found

Star Topology

Check:	for unterminated passive hub connections and damaged terminators.
Check:	the power supply to active hubs.
Check:	for loose connections at the PC and the hub.
Run:	NIC and hub diagnostics, if available.

Ring Topology

Check:	for loose connections.
Check:	the MAU's ports for in-ring or out-of-ring status, if applicable.
Test:	the ports on the MAU with the initialization tool, if applicable.
Check:	the power supply to the MAU, if applicable.
Run:	NIC and MAU diagnostics, if available.

A good question to always ask is, "What has changed recently?" Most of the time, these problems crop up right after something has been moved or rearranged. I have seen cables crushed by filing cabinets and desks, and cables pulled out of their connectors when someone stepped or tripped on them. Whenever PCs, cables, or hubs are moved, there is a possibility that something will come loose or be unplugged.

Finally, check the network for duplicate node addresses. Duplicate node addresses can also cause "File server cannot be found" errors. Ethernet networks should not have this problem since the node address is not configurable. On Ethernet, the node address is a 12-character hex value where the first four characters are a Xerox-assigned value unique to the vendor of the NIC. The remaining eight characters are established by the vendor, giving over 2 billion combinations per vendor. ARCnet, some non-IBM token-ring NICs, and other types of NICs may use configurable node addresses. These node addresses must be checked to make sure that no duplicates are used within a network. Usually, a duplicate address is the result of a network card being installed using the factor-default address which may already exist elsewhere in the network.

NETBIOS EMULATION

The third component of the workstation shell is the NetWare **NETBIOS emulation program**, NETBIOS.EXE. This component is not always required. If it is used, it is loaded immediately after the re-director program. The key question here is whether or not you need this program.

The easy answer is that you need the program if your application software requires a NETBIOS-compatible network. However, this answer does not explain much, so I'll briefly discuss what NETBIOS is about so that you better understand its role in networks.

To manage network communications, NetWare uses a set of protocols known as XNS (Xerox Network Services). Xerox Corporation developed this set of transport protocols for their minicomputer networks. The NetWare IPX and SPX protocols are part of the XNS protocols. Novell has used these protocols since 1983, before IBM entered the PC networking industry in 1985. At that time, there were no major market-leading vendors of network operating systems. Therefore, there was little need for IBM's network products to conform to anyone else's protocols. IBM developed its own set of network protocols called NETBIOS, an acronym for **NET**work **B**asic **I**nput **O**utput **S**ystem.

Since IBM's entry into the LAN business in 1985, NetWare has become the market leader. However, application software developers have to make choices when developing their software. NETBIOS and XNS are two separate ways of accomplishing much the same thing. An application software company has to decide which protocol the software will use. Some applications run only in an XNS environment. This means that their software will not run under IBM's PC Network software. Nor will it run under OS/2 LAN Server or OS/2 LAN Manager. This may mean taking quite a risk, ignoring the "IBM solution." Some applications run only in a NETBIOS environment. This means their vendor has adopted IBM's ways and ignored market-leading NetWare. Other vendors have taken time to develop separate drivers for either environment, not wanting to close any doors.

NetWare's shell program, NETBIOS.EXE, is designed to allow software written to run under NETBIOS protocols to run on a NetWare XNS-protocol LAN. The NETBIOS.EXE program provides NETBIOS functions to an application running in NetWare's XNS environment. If the application software requires NETBIOS compatibility, this portion of the shell provides that compatibility. The only real drawback is the loss of additional RAM at the workstation to support NETBIOS applications. Unfortunately, the NETBIOS.EXE program loads into the base 640K RAM memory area.

You can unload the NETBIOS program when you are not logged onto the network by running the program with a U parameter:

```
NETBIOS U
```

DOS/ODI WORKSTATION SHELLS

These shells are currently available for NetWare 386 only. One problem area in networking is **internetworks**. An internetwork is a network of several subnetworks. A companion term to internetworks is **WAN**, or wide area network. In a WAN, the individual networks in the internet are not at the same site. Computer networks, internetworks, and WANs are not new. Some corporations with large data processing needs have been networking their computers together for the purpose of sharing information for years. What is new is the entry of the PC into this environment.

After you begin to investigate combining several different kinds of computer systems in a single network or internetwork, you soon discover that all do not share a set of rules for communicating with each other. Various computer systems have different sets of protocols that manage information passing between systems. These protocols fall into three major categories: media protocols, transport protocols, and client-server protocols. Ethernet, ARCnet, and Token-Ring are all **media protocols**: they govern the type of physical connection made on the network. **Transport protocols** provide rules for moving data packets from one network node to another. **Client-server protocols** govern how a node requests data from a server and how the server responds.

All these protocols work together to move data around the network; however, there are many competing standards for each type of protocol. This makes the network manager's task difficult in an internetwork or WAN environment. The International Standards Organization (ISO) is working to resolve these problems based upon the Open Systems Interconnection (OSI) Reference Model, but the standard is still at least several years away.

Novell is tackling these problems on several fronts. First, NetWare supports all major media protocols. These include Ethernet running on coaxial cable, unshielded twisted pair wire and fiber optic cable, Token-Ring, and ARCnet. Second, in the past, NetWare has supported its own transport protocol, Internetwork Packet Exchange/Sequenced Packet Exchange (IPX/SPX derived from Xerox's Network Systems), IBM's NetBEUI/DLC, and Apple's AppleTalk. Other transport protocols such as TCP/IP, DECnet, and LU6.2 are also popular in the internetwork community.

The new NetWare Open Data-Link Interface (ODI) provides a standard interface by which a single NIC can support multiple transport protocols without conflict. ODI provides a consistent interface to the NIC drivers and transport protocols, allowing them to operate independently of the hardware being connected. Vendors can develop drivers for their protocol stacks according to this interface and feel confident they will run on any NIC that is using an ODI driver. Novell plans to write their IPX/SPX, AppleTalk, NetBEUI, and TCP/IP protocols to conform to this standard. Under TCP/IP, NetWare will support Telnet, FTP, SMPT, and other TCP/IP applications.

The first major development in this area is NetWare 386's DOS/ODI workstation shells. The DOS/ODI shells replace the older DOS workstation shells. Initially, Novell provided support for IPX/SPX protocols with the DOS/ODI workstation shells, and has pledged other support in the near future. The components of the DOS/ODI workstation shells are:

Removing the Network Shell

Program Name	Function
LSL.COM	Link Support Layer
driver.COM	NIC driver
IPXODI.COM	Protocol Manager
XETx.COM EMSNETx.COM XMSNETx.COM	Re-director
NET.CFG	Configuration File

Because this book was written in the early stages of development of the DOS/ODI drivers, many specifics of multiple protocol support were not available. With NetWare 386 v3.1 Novell delivered only the IPXODI protocol manager which supports the NetWare IPX/SPX protocol. Novell also delivered DOS/ODI-compliant NIC drivers for the Novell OEM-NICs: NE-1000, NE-2000, NE2/32, NE3200, and RXNet. The re-director programs are the same as those used for the DOS workstation shells. None of these programs are configurable, nor do they need to be generated like the DOS IPX.COM program. All configuration, including NIC configuration, is done through the NET.CFG file. This file is described in Chapter 7.

REMOVING THE NETWORK SHELL

As mentioned earlier in this chapter, you can remove the latest versions of the re-director programs—NETx, EMSNETx, and XMSNETx—from RAM after you have logged off of the network by reissuing the command followed by the letter U (unload). Here are some examples.

NET3 U	Unloads the conventional RAM re-director program for a workstation using DOS 3.xx.
EMSNET4 U	Unloads the expanded RAM re-director program for a workstation using DOS 4.xx.
XMSNET4 U	Unloads the extended RAM re-director program for a workstation using DOS 4.xx.

In addition, you can unload the current versions of the NETBIOS emulation program, NETBIOS.EXE, the same way. The NETBIOS.EXE program loads into conventional RAM only, so this is very useful. Because all applications may not need NETBIOS emulation, you can now load the program when you need it and remove it when you don't. For example:

NETBIOS U   Unloads the NETBIOS emulation program

If you cannot unload your re-director program or NETBIOS programs with the U parameter, you have older versions of these programs. You should obtain new versions from Novell or your Novell dealer, or you can download them from the NetWare NOVA Forum on Compuserve.

Unfortunately, you cannot unload the IPX program in the same manner. This program resides in conventional RAM, using valuable space (19K to 41K) that most people would like to reclaim when they are not using the network. On the utility disk, you will find TSRNET.ZIP, a file you can use to unload the IPX program (or any other memory-resident program). The TSR utilities are a set of public domain programs developed by Kim Kokkonen. You can reach Kim at TurboPower Software, P.O. Box 66747, Scotts Valley, CA 95066-0747.

This utility, when uncompressed, contains the programs MARKNET and RELNET which unload a memory-resident program used on a networked PC. The documentation file TSR.DOC tells you exactly what procedures to follow to use this utility.

Unloading Memory-resident Programs

When you unload memory-resident programs to regain memory, consider the importance of the order in which the programs are loaded and how it affects the unloading procedure. The sole purpose for unloading memory-resident software is to free memory. However, if you don't follow the proper procedures, you won't achieve this objective.

For example, here is a list of the contents of conventional RAM in a machine in my office that is logged into our LAN:

Removing the Network Shell

Memory Area	Size	Description
1630 – 163C	.2K	Available
163D – 18B4	9.9K	FASTOPEN
18B5 – 1A3F	6.2K	SHARE
1A40 – 1BA4	5.6K	COMMAND
1BA5 – 1BE5	1K	COMMAND environment
1BE6 – 1BF1	.2K	Available
1BF2 – 2154	21K	IPX
2155 – 230D	6.9K	XMSNET4
230E – 9FFF	499K	Available

You can see that both IPX and XMSNET4 are memory-resident. To reclaim space, I need to unload both IPX and XMSNET4. If I use the TSRNET utility to unload only IPX, the result would be a "hole" in the PC's usable memory. New programs would still start to load at address 230E, and the space once occupied by IPX would not be available.

Therefore, when unloading memory-resident software, you must unload all memory-resident programs down to the one that you want to eliminate and then reload those you still want to use. The TSRNET utilities make this pretty easy to do.

SUMMARY

This chapter examined the task of establishing a connection between a workstation and the network through the software loaded at the workstation, commonly referred to as the workstation shell. The workstation shell consists of various programs that have specific tasks to perform in maintaining a connection between the workstations and the NetWare file server. In troubleshooting a NetWare LAN, it is critical that the LAN administrator understand the role of these programs and their options. The next chapter will discuss the configuration files that can be used to configure the workstation shell: SHELL.CFG and NET.CFG.

7
Using the Workstation Configuration Files

An important component of NetWare's workstation shell is the configuration file. This file is analogous to CONFIG.SYS, a file used to configure DOS according to a user's specific hardware and software needs. The workstation shell configuration file configures the workstation shell and determines how it interacts with the network according to user needs.

The name of this file depends on which version of the workstation shell files you use. Workstations using the traditional NetWare workstation shell programs, IPX and NETx, use SHELL.CFG. The new DOS/ODI workstation shell files use NET.CFG. For more information about these other workstation shell files, see Chapter 6.

LOCATING THE CONFIGURATION FILE

The workstation shell programs read the configuration file when they are loaded. In the case of the DOS workstation shell programs, both IPX.COM and the re-director program read SHELL.CFG. These programs look for SHELL.CFG in the current default directory.

Configuration File Not Found
Keywords: configuration files, SHELL.CFG, workstation

Scenario

A common mistake in locating the configuration file is that the batch file used to load the workstation shell programs does not reference the appropriate directory. On a workstation with a local hard disk, workstation shell files are generally placed in a separate directory. If these files are located via a DOS path, the configuration file is not going to be found. Consider the following example.

A batch file called LAN.BAT loads the workstation shell and starts the log-on process. This batch file might look like this:

LAN.BAT	Comments
`@ECHO OFF`	Turn off echo of batch commands.
`IPX`	Load the IPX program.
`NET4`	Load the re-director program.
`F:LOGIN`	Run the Login program. This assumes that the CONFIG.SYS file has either a LASTDRIVE = E statement or no LASTDRIVE statement.

The workstation shell files are in the directory NET off the root directory of drive C. The directory contains the files IPX.COM, NET4.COM, and SHELL.CFG.

The DOS path references the NET directory:

`PATH C:\DOS;C:\;C:\NET`

If the LAN.BAT file resides in the root directory, then you would normally execute it from that directory:

`C:\>LAN`

The DOS path allows you to find and load the IPX and NET4 programs. However, the current default directory is the root directory. You cannot read SHELL.CFG because IPX and NET4 look for it in the current default directory, not the directory where IPX and NET4 are located.

Locating the Configuration File

Solution

Modify the NET.BAT file in the example.

LAN.BAT	Comments
@ECHO OFF	Turn off echo of batch commands.
CD \NET	Change the default directory to the directory where the shell programs are located.
IPX	Load the IPX program. It reads SHELL.CFG for relevant statements.
NET4	Load the re-director program. It reads SHELL.CFG for relevant statements.
CD \	Return to the root directory.
F:LOGIN	Run the Login program. This assumes that the CONFIG.SYS file has either a LASTDRIVE = E statement or no LASTDRIVE statement.

This same concept applies to the DOS/ODI shell programs and their configuration file NET.CFG. The DOS/ODI programs only search the current default directory for the configuration file.

IPX AND SPX PROTOCOLS

IPX (Internetwork Packet Exchange) and SPX (Sequenced Packet Exchange) are the basic protocols Novell NetWare uses for communication on the network. The major difference between IPX and SPX is how the recipient of a data packet responds. The protocols translate into different types of data packets. IPX packets are **connectionless packets**: a workstation that sends data to the file server does not require that a connection be established, nor verification of the packet's receipt. Each IPX packet is an individual entity, unrelated to any other IPX packet. IPX packets are used for addressing, routing, and switching information to move packets from one location to another.

SPX is a **connection-oriented protocol** requiring that each packet be verified by its recipient. Each SPX process establishes a virtual connection between the file server and the workstation before sending packets. SPX tasks are guaranteeing delivery, sequencing packets, detecting and correcting errors, and suppressing duplicate packets.

IPX advantages are low overhead and speed. It does not require that a packet travel a predetermined route. SPX advantages are guaranteed delivery, guaranteed packet sequencing, and suppressing duplicate packets. Software developers decide which of the protocols best suit their applications. In SHELL.CFG and NET.CFG, Novell provides configurable parameters that can affect the behavior of each packet type.

SHELL.CFG COMMANDS AND USAGE

The SHELL.CFG commands are grouped according to various shell functions: IPX options, EMSNETx options, NETx options, and NETBIOS options.

IPX Options

IPX options govern parameters that NetWare uses when transmitting and receiving IPX and SPX packets over the network. These options affect how the IPX.COM shell file makes connections with the file server and how retries are handled.

SHELL.CFG Commands and Usage

CONFIG OPTION = x
Default = none

This option allows the IPX program to be loaded with a specific configuration. The configuration options are the same number you see after you type the command

    IPX D

With this command the network supervisor can reconfigure a NIC without generating a matching IPX.COM program.

IPX PACKET SIZE LIMIT = number
Range = 576 to 6500   Default = 4160

This option limits a packet's maximum size. The LAN adapter normally sets this limit. 4160 is optimal for Token Ring, even though the driver can transmit packets of up to 16K. 1536 is optimal for Ethernet.

IPX RETRY COUNT = number
Default = 20

Status: sometimes may need a higher value

This option determines how many times the workstation resends a packet when the sending station does not receive verification of receipt. The IPX protocol uses the NetWare network drivers to communicate with other stations. This protocol does not dictate that the receiving station send back verification. However, because most IPX packets initiate some sort of activity, the workstation does wait for this type of response. Increasing the value for this option causes more resend operations if the workstation receives no response. Network performance may slow down as a result.

I have occasionally increased this value when many packets have been lost or when the packets must cross several bridges before reaching their destination. Lost packets, however, are symptoms of other network problems such as faulty wiring or bad LAN adapter cards.

IPX SOCKETS = number

Default = 20

Status: no change generally needed

This option determines the number of sockets available at the workstation. An IPX **socket** is a buffer where the workstation can receive packets from the LAN. Generally, a process occurring between the file server and a workstation requires a socket. The more processes, the more sockets required. For example, a workstation sharing its printer in a non-dedicated fashion might be transmitting print data while running some other program. Separate sockets would be required for printing and for the application. Software manufacturers can provide answers to specific questions about the number of sockets.

SPX ABORT TIMEOUT = number

Default = 540

Status: sometimes increased for LANs of over 50 workstations

This option determines how long SPX waits for the workstation to receive an acknowledgment packet when an SPX connection has been requested. If the workstation receives no packet within the time limit, the session terminates. The default of 540 is about 30 seconds. In a LAN, packets are continuously sent around the network, so 540 should suffice. Each increment is a clock tick and the clock ticks about 19 times per second.

SPX CONNECTIONS = number

Default = 15

Status: no change generally needed

This option sets the maximum number of SPX connections that the workstation can make concurrently. The software used on the network determines the number of SPX connections required. If the workstation uses multitasking software, such as Microsoft Windows, multiple processes will require more SPX connections.

SHELL.CFG Commands and Usage

SPX LISTEN TIMEOUT = number
Default = 108

Status: no change generally needed

This option determines how long SPX waits before requesting the other station to send a packet verifying that the connection is still valid. This parameter also uses clock ticks. The default of 108 is about 6 seconds.

SPX VERIFY TIMEOUT = number
Default = 54

Status: sometimes increased for LANs of over 50 workstations

This option determines how long the station waits to send a packet informing the other side of the connection that it is still connected. This option is also in clock ticks. The default of 54 ticks is about 3 seconds.

EMSNETx Options

The EMSNETx re-director program loads into expanded memory supported by a LIM 4.0 expanded memory driver. About 7K of the EMSNETx program resides in conventional RAM, the remainder loads into expanded memory. The option below permits you to increase the size of the code page so that it will be detected by other programs using expanded memory. All NETx options can be used with EMSNETx re-director programs.

ENTRY STACK SIZE = number
Range = 5 to 40   Default = 10

This option allocates more expanded memory to the EMSNET driver. Relatively small in size, the EMSNET driver might not be detected by other TSR programs and become corrupted. If you experience difficulty with other TSRs while trying to use the EMSNET driver, try increasing this setting.

NETx Options

CACHE BUFFERS = number

Default = 5

Status: increasing this parameter generally improves performance of the workstation and the LAN

This option allows the workstation to establish a cache for working with program files or other files that are not shareable. Each increment uses 512 bytes of the workstation's memory. Shared files or files tracked by the Transaction Tracking System SFT NetWare or Netware 386 cannot use this cache. Because the file server memory cache block size is 4096 bytes (except in NetWare 386), I recommend a multiple of 8 as the value for this entry.

Establishing a cache buffer at the workstation allows the file server to send data to the workstation which the file server has cached for the workstation, before receiving a packet from the workstation requesting it. This allows the file server to spread its traffic load somewhat. The advantage to the workstation is better performance: data needed next may be at the workstation before the application requests it.

EOJ = On or Off

Default = On

Status: no change generally needed

When On, NetWare automatically closes open files and releases file and record locks when an application program finishes.

FILE HANDLES = number

Default = 40

Status: select this setting according to the software applications in use

This option determines how many files the workstation can have open on the file server concurrently. It keeps track of pointers that indicate where the application is in the file. Many newer

SHELL.CFG Commands and Usage

database applications allow up to 255 open files, predicating an increase in the default. This setting is independent of the FILES= statement in the workstation's CONFIG.SYS file, which applies only to files open on the workstation's local drives. If you use multitasking software, such as Microsoft Windows, at the workstation you need to increase this value.

HOLD = On or Off

Default = Off

Status: no change generally needed

When this setting is On, after the workstation has accessed a file, other users cannot write to that file until the program finishes. Although other users cannot update the file, they may still read it. If other users could write to the file, their changes would be overwritten when you save the file. Normally most LAN-oriented software programs do this automatically. On may be required for using software that was not designed for LANs.

LOCAL PRINTERS = number

Default = None

Status: implement this if the workstation does not have a local printer

Normally, the BIOS start-up routine of the PC checks for local printing ports installed on the PC. However, it does not know if any printers are attached to these ports. In the network environment, not all workstations have attached local printers. A workstation may do all its printing on shared printers attached to the file server. This feature is activated normally by the CAPTURE or NPRINT NetWare commands. However, if a user does not issue the CAPTURE command before trying to print, the workstation may hang and need to be rebooted. This can cause data loss and other data corruption problems. Setting this parameter to 0 solves this problem and still allows a local printer to be attached to the workstation. This setting is very useful for eliminating problems that occur when a user hits SHIFT-PRTSC when not using a shared printer.

LOCK DELAY = number

Default = 1

Status: no change generally needed

This option determines how long the workstation waits before trying to lock a network resource after an unsuccessful lock attempt. This setting is in clock ticks.

LOCK RETRIES = number

Default = 3

Status: no change generally needed

This option determines how many times the workstation tries to lock a network resource. The application software normally handles this so it does not need to be set at the workstation.

LONG MACHINE TYPE = name

Default = IBM_PC

Status: use this if DOS files are kept on the file server and multiple versions of MS-DOS are used

This option sets the variable that the LOGIN Script keyword %MACHINE accesses. It allows the LOGIN process to determine the machine type of the workstation. The name assigned can be any value, unless specific software applications require specific machine names. This is an effective way to load multiple DOS versions on the file server (in separate directories, of course) and map the workstations to the correct one.

MAX PATH LENGTH = number

Default = 255

Status: no change generally needed

This setting allows the PATH to exceed the DOS string limit of 128 bytes. The default of 255 bytes is the maximum value.

SHELL.CFG Commands and Usage

MAXIMUM TASKS = number

Range = 8 to 50   Default = 31

Status: no change generally needed

This parameter establishes the maximum number of tasks that can be active concurrently on the workstation.

PREFERRED SERVER = name

Default = no preferred server

With this very helpful new setting, you can specify a file server to attach to during boot-up on the network. You don't need the server name in the LOGIN command.

PRINT HEADER = number

Default = 64 bytes

Status: no change generally needed. If you use Apple Laser-Writers from DOS workstations, set this to 255

The workstation uses this area to hold special escape-code sequences that must be sent to the printer before a print job starts.

PRINT TAIL = number

Default = 16 bytes

Status: no change generally needed

The workstation uses this area to hold special escape-code sequences that must be sent to the printer when a print job ends.

READ ONLY COMPATIBILITY = On or Off

Default = Off

Status: depends on your environment

This option controls what happens when the workstation attempts to write to a file flagged as read only. When set to Off, read-only files cannot be opened for write access: the open request fails. When set to On, a read-only file can be successfully opened for write access without failing. However, the first attempt to write to the file produces an error. The On setting is compatible with how NetWare versions 1.x through 2.0x behave.

SEARCH MODE = number

Range = 1 to 7   Default = 1

Status: depends on your environment

This option determines what happens when a program file (with a .COM or .EXE extension) is not found in the user's current default directory, based on the series of preconfigured options described next. Use the option that fits the majority of your applications. That will be the default setting. Then use the SMODE command for individual files on the LAN. This parameter is very useful when programs cannot find overlay files or data files—a particularly prevalent problem with older software applications.

Mode	Activity
1	If the command issued specified a file path, search only the specified directory. If the path was not specified, search the default directory and then search any directories specified by the MAP SEARCH segments.
2	Search the default directory only for data files.
3	If the command issued specified a file path, search only the specified directory. If a path was not specified *and* the program opens data files for read-only access, the program file searches for data files in the current default directory and then searches any directories specified by the MAP SEARCH segments.
4	Reserved for future use.
5	Search the default directory and all other directories specified by any MAP SEARCH segments, regardless of whether the command issued specified the path.
6	Reserved for future use.

SHELL.CFG Commands and Usage

> 7   If the program file opens data files for read-only access, search for data files in the default directory and all other directories specified by any MAP SEARCH segments, regardless of whether the command issued specified the path.

SHARE = On or Off

Default = On

Status: no change generally needed

When On, this option allows a called program (a program run by another program) to maintain the same open file handles and pointers as the calling program.

SHORT MACHINE TYPE = name

Default = IBM

Status: use if DOS files are kept on the file server and multiple MS-DOS versions are used

This option sets the variable that the %SMACHINE keyword in the LOGIN Script command accesses. When you use the Short Machine Name parameter, take care of these details:

- If you plan to use the EXIT command in the system or user's login script, you must add the LOGIN Script command PCCOMPATIBLE to the login script. Otherwise, the EXIT command will not be supported.

- The NetWare menu programs, such as SYSCON, FILER, and SESSION, use an overlay file for color palettes called IBM$RUN.OVL. You must create a version of this overlay using your Short Machine Type as the first characters of the file name. For example:

```
SHORT MACHINE TYPE = CMPQ
```

Copy the IBM$RUN.OVL file to create one for this Short Machine Type:

```
NCOPY SYS:PUBLIC\IBM$RUN.OVL
SYS:PUBLIC\CMPQ$RUN.OVL
```

TASK MODE = 0 or 1
Default = 1

Status: no change needed unless the workstation uses Microsoft's Windows 386

When set to 1, NetWare handles Windows 386 virtual tasks correctly. When set to 0, NetWare destroys Windows 386 tasks when switching from task to task.

NETBIOS Options

The following SHELL.CFG options only apply to those using NETBIOS emulation.

NETBIOS ABORT TIMEOUT = number
Default = 540

Status: sometimes increased for LANs of over 50 workstations

This option determines how long NETBIOS waits to receive a packet from the workstation it is connected to. If it does not receive a packet, the session terminates. The default of 540 is about 30 seconds. In a LAN, packets are continuously sent around the network, so 540 should suffice. Each increment is a clock tick, and the clock ticks 18.21 times per second.

NETBIOS BROADCAST COUNT = number
Range = 2 to 65535   Default = 2 or 4

This parameter may be required when you use interconnected networks and NETBIOS emulation. The setting reflects the time taken to broadcast a name resolution packet across the network. Multiply this value by the setting for NETBIOS BROADCAST DELAY to determine the time. The default is 2 if NETBIOS internet = Off; otherwise the default is 4.

SHELL.CFG Commands and Usage

NETBIOS BROADCAST DELAY = number

Default = 36 if NETBIOS INTERNET = On, otherwise 18

You may need to increase this value for internetworks, when many packets are lost, or when network traffic is heavy.

NETBIOS INTERNET = On or Off

Default = On

To increase performance, set the value to Off when you run a single network with a dedicated file server and NETBIOS applications. If you are running an internetwork, multiple LAN segments, or a non-dedicated server, you must leave this setting On.

NETBIOS LISTEN TIMEOUT = number

Default = 108

Status: no change generally needed

This setting determines how long NETBIOS waits to hear from the other station before it requests that the other station send it a packet to indicate that it is still active. This parameter also uses clock ticks. The default of 108 is about 6 seconds.

NETBIOS RECEIVE BUFFERS = number

Range = 4 to 20   Default = 6

Status: no change generally needed

This parameter establishes the number of send buffers created at the workstation for inbound packets.

NETBIOS RETRY DELAY = number

Default = 10

Status: no change generally needed

This parameter works with the IPX RETRY COUNT parameter. It determines how long the station waits between sending packets when trying to establish a connection. The default of 10 is about 1/2 second.

NETBIOS SEND BUFFERS = number

Range = 4 to 20   Default = 6

Status: no change generally needed

This parameter establishes the number of send buffers created at the workstation for outbound packets.

NETBIOS SESSIONS = number

Range = 4 to 100   Default = 10

Status: no change generally needed

This parameter sets the maximum number of sessions that NETBIOS supports concurrently.

NETBIOS VERIFY TIMEOUT = number

Default = 54

Status: sometimes increased for LANs of over 50 workstations

This setting determines how long the workstation waits to send a packet informing the other side of the connection that it is still connected. This option is also in clock ticks. The default of 54 is about 3 seconds.

NET.CFG COMMANDS AND USAGE

NET.CFG is the configuration file used with the new NetWare DOS/ODI workstation shell programs. As of this writing, these shells are only available with NetWare 386. The NET.CFG commands are grouped according to various shell functions: protocol options, LANSUP driver options, IPX options, EMSNET options, NETx options, and NETBIOS options.

Protocol Options

The following option is used to decide which network board will be bound to the IPXODI driver. If this option is omitted, IPXODI will bind to the first network board it finds.

NET.CFG Commands and Usage

BIND name

Default = none

This command binds the IPXODI.COM program to the NIC driver. The drivers presently shipped with NetWare 386 version 3.1 are listed next.

TRXNET	Novell RX-Net NIC
NE2	Novell 16-bit MicroChannel Ethernet
NE2-32	Novell 32-bit MicroChannel Ethernet
NE3200	Novell 32-bit EISA Ethernet
NE1000	Novell 8-bit ISA Ethernet
NE2000	Novell 16-bit ISA Ethernet
3C503	3Com ISA Ethernet
3C523	3Com MicroChannel Ethernet
LANSUP	IBM LAN Support Program

LINK DRIVER drivername

Default = channel #1

DMA [#1 | #2] channel
INT [#1 | #2] hex_interrupt_value
MEM [#1 | #2] hex_starting_address [hex_length]
PORT [#1 | #2] hex_starting_address [hex_length]
PS/2 SLOT number

This NET.CFG statement tells the workstation shell how the NIC is configured. It contains optional phrases which correspond to various NIC options. The DMA, INT, MEM, and PORT options allow for the configuration of either of two channels (#1 or #2). The driver names are those listed previously for the protocol option BIND.

FRAME frame type

Default = Ethernet_802.3 for Ethernet LANs
= Token-Ring for Token Ring LANs

This command specifies the type of frame format used with the NIC. Valid frame types are listed next.

Frame Type	Protocol
Ethernet_802.3	IPX
Ethernet_II	IPX, TCP/IP, DEC, AppleTalk, XNS
Ethernet_802.2	OSI, IPX
Ethernet_Snap	TCP/IP, IPX
Token-Ring	IBM, IPX, OSI
Token-Ring_Snap	TCP/IP, IPX, DEC

LOOK AHEAD SIZE number

Default = 18

This option sets the number of bytes in the packet that the LAN driver sends to the Link Support Layer to determine how to route the packet. IPX and SPX protocols both contain the destination address for the packet as part of the packet's first 18 bytes. Other protocols may require more bytes.

PROTOCOL name hex_protocol_ID frame_type

Default = None

This option provides support for protocols other than IPX/SPX. The name is the new protocol's name, followed by a protocol ID number and frame type. As of this writing, Novell only supports the IPX/SPX protocols. Third-party vendors may develop support for other protocols.

SEND RETRIES number

This parameter specifies the number of times the NIC driver tries to resend a packet following a communications error.

NET.CFG Commands and Usage

LANSUP Driver Options

SAPS number

Default = 1

You need this option for the IBM LAN Support driver (LANSUP). You must allow SAPs (Service Access Points) for all applications that use the IBM LAN Support program.

LINK STATIONS number

Default = 1

You use this option with the IBM LAN Support program. It sets the number of link stations LANSUP allows.

MAX PACKET number

Default = 1128

This parameter sets the maximum packet size the LANSUP driver allows.

IPX Options

IPX options govern how network communications are handled by the IPX/SPX NetWare protocols. These options configure the workstation shell to permit flexibility in handling how data packets are sent and verified.

CONFIG OPTION = x

Default = None

This option allows the IPX program to be loaded with a specific configuration. The configuration options are the same number you see after you type the command

```
IPX D
```

With this command the network supervisor can reconfigure a NIC without regenerating a matching IPX.COM program.

IPX PACKET SIZE LIMIT = number

Range = 576 to 6500   Default = 4160

This option limits a packet's maximum size. The LAN adapter normally sets this limit. 4160 is optimal for Token Ring, even though the driver can transmit packets of up to 16K. 1536 is optimal for Ethernet networks.

IPX RETRY COUNT = number

Default = 20

Status: sometimes may need to be increased

This option determines how many times the workstation resends a packet when the sending station does not receive verification of receipt. The IPX protocol uses the NetWare network drivers to communicate with other stations. This protocol does not dictate that the receiving station send back verification. However, because most IPX packets initiate some sort of activity, the workstation does wait for this type of response. Increasing the value for this option causes more resend operations if the workstation receives no response. Network performance may slow down as a result.

I have occasionally increased this value when many packets have been lost or when the packets must cross several bridges before reaching their destination. Lost packets, however, are symptoms of other network problems such as faulty wiring or bad LAN adapter cards.

IPX SOCKETS = number

Default = 20

Status: no change generally needed

This option determines the number of sockets available at the workstation. An IPX socket is a buffer where the workstation can receive packets from the LAN. Generally, a process occurring between the file server and a workstation requires a socket. The more processes, the more sockets required. For example, a workstation sharing its printer in a non-dedicated fashion might be transmitting print data while running some other program.

NET.CFG Commands and Usage

Separate sockets would be required for printing and for the application. Software manufacturers can provide answers to specific questions about the number of sockets.

SPX ABORT TIMEOUT = number

Default = 540

Status: sometimes increased for LANs of over 50 workstations

This option determines how long SPX waits for the workstation to receive an acknowledgement packet when an SPX connection has been requested. If the workstation receives no packet within the time limit, the session terminates. The default of 540 is about 30 seconds. In a LAN, packets are continuously sent around the network, so 540 should suffice. Each increment is a clock tick, and the clock ticks about 19 times per second.

SPX CONNECTIONS = number

Default = 15

Status: no change generally required

This option sets the maximum number of SPX connections that the workstation can make concurrently. The software used on the network determines the number of SPX connections required. If the workstation uses multitasking software, such as Microsoft Windows, multiple processes will require more SPX connections.

SPX LISTEN TIMEOUT = number

Default = 108

Status: no change generally required

This option determines how long SPX waits before requesting the other station to send a packet verifying that the connection is still valid. This parameter also uses clock ticks. The default of 108 is about 6 seconds.

SPX VERIFY TIMEOUT = number

Default = 54

Status: sometimes increased for LANs of over 50 workstations

This option determines how long the station waits to send a packet informing the other side of the connection that it is still connected. This option is also in clock ticks. The default of 54 ticks is about 3 seconds.

EMSNETx Options

The EMSNETx re-director program loads into expanded memory supported by a LIM 4.0 expanded memory driver. About 7K of the EMSNETx program resides in conventional RAM, the remainder loads into expanded memory. The option below permits you to increase the size of the code page so that it will be detected by other programs using expanded memory. All NETx options can be used with the EMSNETx re-director programs.

ENTRY STACK SIZE = number

Range = 5 to 40   Default = 10

This option allocates more expanded memory to the EMSNET driver. Relatively small in size, the EMSNET driver might not be detected by other TSR programs and become corrupted. If you experience difficulty with other TSRs while trying to use the EMSNET driver, try increasing this setting.

NETx Options

The network re-director programs, NETx, EMSNETx, and XMSNETx, can be configured to suit the needs of individual users or workstations connected to the network. The following options are used to determine how the re-director program, DOS, and the file server will interact with each other.

NET.CFG Commands and Usage

CACHE BUFFERS = number
Default = 5

Status: increasing this parameter generally improves performance of the workstation and the LAN

This option allows the workstation to establish a cache for working with program files or other files that are not shareable. Each increment uses 512 bytes of the workstation's memory. Shared files or files being tracked by the Transaction Tracking System SFT NetWare or Netware 386 cannot use this cache. Because the file server memory cache block size is 4096 bytes (except in NetWare 386), I recommend a multiple of 8 as the value for this entry.

Establishing a cache buffer at the workstation allows the file server to send data to the workstation which the file server has cached for the workstation, before receiving a packet from the workstation requesting it. This allows the file server to spread its traffic load somewhat. The advantage to the workstation is better performance: data needed next may be at the workstation before the application requests it.

EOJ = On or Off
Default = On

Status: no change generally needed

When On, NetWare automatically closes open files and releases file and record locks when an application program finishes.

FILE HANDLES = number
Default = 40

Status: select this setting according to the software applications in use

This option determines how many files the workstation can have open on the file server concurrently. It keeps track of pointers that indicate where the application is in the file. Many newer database applications allow up to 255 open files, predicating an increase in the default. This setting is independent of the FILES=

statement in the workstation's CONFIG.SYS file, which applies only to files open on the workstation's local drives. If you use multitasking software, such as Microsoft Windows, at the workstation you need to increase this value.

HOLD = On or Off
Default = Off

Status: no change generally needed

When this setting is On, after the workstation has accessed a file, other users cannot write to that file until the program finishes. Although other users cannot update the file, they may still read it. If other users could write to the file, their changes would be overwritten when you save the file. Normally, most LAN-oriented software programs do this automatically. On may be required for using software that was not designed for LANs.

LOCAL PRINTERS = number
Default = None

Status: implement this if the workstation does not have a local printer

Normally, the BIOS start-up routine of the PC checks for local printing ports installed on the PC. However, it does not know if any printers are attached to these ports. In the network environment, not all workstations have attached local printers. A workstation may do all its printing on shared printers attached to the file server. This feature is activated normally by the CAPTURE or NPRINT NetWare commands. However, if a user does not issue the CAPTURE command before trying to print, the workstation may hang and need to be rebooted. This can cause data loss and other data corruption problems. Setting this parameter to 0 solves this problem and still allows a local printer to be attached to the workstation. This setting is very useful for eliminating problems that occur when a user hits SHIFT-PRTSC when not using a shared printer.

NET.CFG Commands and Usage

LOCK DELAY = number

Default = 1

Status: no change generally needed

This option determines how long the workstation waits before trying to lock a network resource after an unsuccessful lock attempt. This setting is in clock ticks.

LOCK RETRIES = number

Default = 3

Status: no change generally needed

This option determines how many times the workstation tries to lock a network resource. The application software normally handles this, so it does not need to be set at the workstation.

LONG MACHINE TYPE = name

Default = IBM_PC

Status: use this if DOS files are kept on the file server and multiple MS-DOS versions are used

This option sets the variable that the LOGIN Script keyword %MACHINE accesses. It allows the LOGIN process to determine the machine type of the workstation. The name assigned can be any value, unless specific software applications require specific machine names. This is an effective way to load multiple DOS versions on the file server (in separate directories, of course) and map the workstations to the correct one.

MAX PATH LENGTH = number

Default = 255

Status: no change generally needed

This setting allows the PATH to exceed the DOS limit of 128 bytes. The default of 255 bytes is the maximum value.

MAXIMUM TASKS = number
Range = 8 to 50   Default = 31

Status: no change generally needed

This parameter establishes the maximum number of tasks that can be active concurrently on the workstation.

PREFERRED SERVER = name
Default = no preferred server

With this very helpful new setting you can specify a file server to attach to during boot-up on the network. You don't need the server name in the LOGIN command.

PRINT HEADER = number
Default = 64 bytes

Status: no change generally needed. If you use Apple LaserWriters from DOS workstations, set this to 255

The workstation uses this area to hold special escape-code sequences that must be sent to the printer before a print job starts.

PRINT TAIL = number
Default = 16 bytes

Status: no change generally needed

The workstation uses this area to hold any special escape-code sequences that must be sent to the printer when a print job ends.

READ ONLY COMPATIBILITY = On or Off
Default = Off

Status: depends on your environment

This option controls what happens when the workstation attempts to write to a file flagged read only. When set to Off, read-only files cannot be opened for write access: the open request fails. When set to On, a read-only file can be successfully opened for

NET.CFG Commands and Usage

write access. However, the first attempt to write to the file produces an error. The On setting is compatible with how NetWare versions 1.x through 2.0x behave.

SEARCH MODE = number

Default = 1

Status: depends on your environment

This option determines what happens when a program file (with a .COM or .EXE extension) is not found in the user's current default directory, based on the series of preconfigured options described next. Use the option that fits the majority of your applications. That will be the default setting. Then use the SMODE command for individual files on the LAN. This parameter is very useful when programs cannot find overlay files or data files—a particularly prevalent problem with older software applications.

Mode	Activity
1	If the command issued specified a file path, search only the specified directory. If the path was not specified, search the default directory and then search any directories specified by the MAP SEARCH segments.
2	Search the default directory only for data files.
3	If the command issued specified a file path, search only the specified directory. If a path was not specified *and* the program opens data files for read-only access, the program file searches for data files in the current default directory and then searches any directories specified by the MAP SEARCH segments.
4	Reserved for future use.
5	Search the default directory and all other directories specified by any MAP SEARCH segments, regardless of whether the command issued specified the path.
6	Reserved for future use.

7   If the program file opens data files for read-only access, search for data files in the default directory and all other directories specified by any MAP SEARCH segments, regardless of whether the command issued specified the path.

SHARE = On or Off
Default = On

Status: no change generally needed

When On, this option allows a called program (a program run by another program) to maintain the same open file handles and pointers as the calling program.

SHORT MACHINE TYPE = name
Default = IBM

Status: use if DOS files are kept on the file server and multiple MS-DOS versions are used

This option sets the variable that the %SMACHINE keyword in the LOGIN Script command accesses. When you use the Short Machine Name parameter, take care of these details:

- If you plan to use the EXIT command in the system or user's login script, you must add the LOGIN Script command PCCOMPATIBLE to the login script. Otherwise, the EXIT command will not be supported.
- The NetWare menu programs, such as SYSCON, FILER, and SESSION, use an overlay file for color palettes called IBM$RUN.OVL. You must create a version of this overlay using your Short Machine Type as the first characters of the file name. For example:

    SHORT MACHINE TYPE = CMPQ

Copy the IBM$RUN.OVL file to create one for this Short Machine Type:

    NCOPY SYS:PUBLIC\IBM$RUN.OVL CMPQ$RUN.OVL

NET.CFG Commands and Usage

TASK MODE = 0 or 1
Default = 1

Status: no change needed unless the workstation uses Microsoft's Windows 386

When set to 1, NetWare handles Windows 386 virtual tasks correctly. When set to 0, NetWare destroys Windows 386 tasks when switching from task to task.

NETBIOS Options

The following SHELL.CFG options only apply to those using NETBIOS emulation.

NETBIOS ABORT TIMEOUT = number
Default = 540

Status: sometimes increased for LANs of over 50 workstations

This option determines how long NETBIOS waits to receive a packet from the workstation it is connected to. If it does not receive a packet, the session terminates. The default of 540 is about 30 seconds. In a LAN, packets are continuously sent around the network, so 540 should suffice. Each increment is a clock tick, and the clock ticks about 19 times per second.

NETBIOS BROADCAST COUNT = number
Range = 2 to 65535   Default = 2

This parameter may be required when you use interconnected networks and NETBIOS emulation. The setting reflects the time taken to broadcast a name resolution packet across the network. Multiply this value by the setting for NETBIOS BROADCAST DELAY to determine the time.

NETBIOS BROADCAST DELAY = number
Default = 36 if NETBIOS INTERNET = On, otherwise 18

You may need to increase this value for internetworks, when many packets are lost, or when network traffic is heavy.

NETBIOS INTERNET = On or Off

Default = On

To increase performance, set this value to Off when you run a single network with a dedicated file server and NETBIOS applications. If you are running an internetwork, multiple LAN segments, or a non-dedicated server, you must leave this setting On.

NETBIOS LISTEN TIMEOUT = number

Default = 108

Status: no change generally needed

This setting determines how long NETBIOS waits to hear from the other station before it requests that the other station send it a packet to indicate that it is still active. This parameter also uses clock ticks. The default of 108 is about 6 seconds.

NETBIOS RECEIVE BUFFERS = number

Range = 4 to 20   Default = 6

Status: no change generally needed

This parameter establishes the number of send buffers created at the workstation for inbound packets.

NETBIOS RETRY DELAY = number

Default = 10

Status: no change generally needed

This parameter works with the IPX RETRY COUNT parameter. It determines how long the station waits between sending packets when trying to establish a connection. The default of 10 is about 1/2 second.

NETBIOS SEND BUFFERS = number

Range = 4 to 20   Default = 6

Status: no change generally needed

This parameter establishes the number of send buffers created at the workstation for outbound packets.

NETBIOS SESSIONS = number

Range = 4 to 100   Default = 10

Status: no change generally needed

This parameter sets the maximum number of sessions that NETBIOS supports concurrently.

NETBIOS VERIFY TIMEOUT = number

Default = 54

Status: sometimes increased for LANs of over 50 workstations

This setting determines how long the station waits to send a packet informing the other side of the connection that it is still connected. This option is also in clock ticks. The default of 54 is about 3 seconds.

SUMMARY

This chapter covered one of the more obscure details about the workstations' shell file configuration. Many NetWare supervisors and users do not know about the workstation configuration files, SHELL.CFG (NetWare 286 and NetWare 386 DOS shells) and NET.CFG (NetWare 386 DOS/ODI shell). These files can be tremendously useful in solving various network problems. They are as important to the workstation as CONFIG.SYS is to DOS. Network supervisors should take time to study these files and their options to configure their workstations for optimal network performance.

8
Booting the Workstation and Logging In

Chapters 6 and 7 covered the components of workstation software required to connect to the NetWare file server. This chapter explores the other facets of connecting to, and logging into, the network.

SETTINGS FOR CONFIG.SYS AND AUTOEXEC.BAT

All PC users are familiar with these two DOS files and their importance. In NetWare these files are still important, even though most NetWare shell configuration is done with SHELL.CFG or NET.CFG. These files were covered in detail in Chapter 7.

Due to individual user's needs, I can provide few specifics about setting up these files. However, let's consider a couple of general settings that might differ from those used for a stand-alone PC.

CONFIG.SYS

You should check two statements in the CONFIG.SYS file that affect a user connected to a NetWare LAN: FILES = *number* and LASTDRIVE = *letter*.

FILES = *number*

This is the statement for settings files. It establishes how many open file handles DOS can track at once. It is likely that you will need to increase the setting's value for a workstation connected to a LAN. The user logged into the file server may need the capacity for more open files than DOS alone requires. The exact setting depends on the software applications used on the workstation.

LASTDRIVE = *letter*

This statement allocates drive letters to local devices. Its default value E means that local drives are lettered A through E. These drives do not have to exist physically. In the LAN environment, NetWare also uses drive letters for the assignment of directory paths. NetWare can use only the single character drive letters A through Z.

AUTOEXEC.BAT

Whether to put the commands that load the network shell files upon booting up the PC into the AUTOEXEC.BAT file is a decision based on the user's circumstances. If the user is always going to log into the network, then you might as well load these programs from the user's AUTOEXEC.BAT file. Also consider the use of NetWare print server software or another vendor's print server software. Most print server software packages allow workstation printers to be shared network printers. However, to share the printer, the workstation shell programs must be loaded at the workstation, along with a program that permits sharing the printer. If you plan to share workstation printers, then you will probably load the shell files from the user's AUTOEXEC.BAT file.

Invalid Drive Specified
Keywords: login, drives, IPX, re-director, LASTDRIVE

Scenario

Based upon the setting for LASTDRIVE, NetWare assigns the SYS:LOGIN directory to the next available drive letter when the network shell files are loaded at the workstation. If LASTDRIVE = E, then NetWare assigns the login directory to logical drive F:. The SYS:LOGIN directory is the only file server directory that the user can access before logging into the network. This directory contains the LOGIN.EXE and SLIST.EXE programs; two NetWare programs can be run without logging into the network.

If a user changes the LASTDRIVE statement in the CONFIG.SYS file, the file server assigns SYS:LOGIN to the drive letter following the one assigned with LASTDRIVE. If the user has a batch file for connecting to the network, the batch file is incorrect immediately after the change as this example shows.

NET.BAT	**Old CONFIG.SYS**	**New CONFIG.SYS**
@ECHO OFF	LASTDRIVE = E	LASTDRIVE = G
IPX	FILES = 40	FILES = 40
NET4	BUFFERS = 24	BUFFERS = 24
F:		
LOGIN		

The batch file no longer works with the new CONFIG.SYS, since the SYS:LOGIN directory will be assigned to logical drive H.

You also see this error message when you log out of the network from a logical drive other than the one assigned to the SYS:LOGIN directory. When you log out from a logical drive, NetWare assigns the SYS:LOGIN directory to that drive, unless it's a local drive. For example, if you assign logical drive M to a directory on the file server and M is also the current default drive when you log out, SYS:LOGIN will be assigned to drive M. If the batch file that logs you into the network uses a different drive, such as F, you see the error message because logical drive F does not exist.

Solution

There are two possible solutions for this problem. One is to change the batch file to correspond to the updated CONFIG.SYS:

NET.BAT
```
@ECHO OFF
IPX
NET4
H:
LOGIN
```

The second is to replace the logical drive letter in the batch file with a command to run a small program that automatically finds the last active drive letter and make it the current default drive. This program is appropriately named LASTDRIV.EXE. It's in the file on your diskette called LASTDRIV.ZIP. This public-domain program written by Mike Watkins eliminates the need to change the batch file every time someone changes CONFIG.SYS or logs out from an inappropriate logical drive. If you log out from logical drive M as in the earlier example, the LASTDRIV program would find drive M and make it the current default drive. Then you could run the LOGIN program. A sample batch file including this program might look like this:

NET.BAT
```
@ECHO OFF
IPX
NET4
LASTDRIV
LOGIN
```

ATTACHING TO THE FILE SERVER AND FINDING THE LOGIN DIRECTORY

When you load the workstation shell programs, the following events happen.

1. The workstation sends a broadcast packet that asks if any file servers are present. Broadcast packets are addressed to all workstations.
2. Any file servers on-line respond that they are there.
3. The workstation sends another broadcast packet requesting a connection to a file server. This is an indiscriminate request addressed to all workstations.
4. Each file server with an available connection sends a packet which informs the workstation of an available connection and the file server's network and node address.
5. The workstation sends a connection request to the file server first to respond to the workstation's request for a connection.
6. The file server grants a connection to the workstation and maps the SYS:LOGIN directory to the first available drive letter at the workstation. The workstation displays a message similar to this one:

```
Attached to server ATRIUM1
Thursday, January 17, 1991    9:34:11 am
```

Due to the broadcast nature of the first two workstation requests and the fact that the workstation sends a connection request to the *first* file server to respond, it is difficult to predict which file server a workstation attaches to in a multiple file server environment. This is not a problem because part of the LOGIN program syntax includes the name of the file server that you wish to log on to:

```
LOGIN servername/username
```

If you want to ensure that the user connects to a specific file server, the SHELL.CFG and NET.CFG configuration files can include the statement:

```
Preferred server = servername
```

This statement instructs the workstation to try to connect to the specified server, rather than the one that responds first. If no connection is available on the specified server, the workstation then attempts to connect another file server.

When the file server grants a connection to the workstation, the file server makes the SYS:LOGIN directory available by mapping the directory to the workstation's next available drive letter. This drive letter is determined by the workstation's drive table, which is set by the existence of physical and logical drives and the LASTDRIVE statement in the user's CONFIG.SYS file. Any change in the user's PC configuration or CONFIG.SYS assigns a different drive letter to the SYS:LOGIN directory.

When you log out of the file server, the file server again assigns the SYS:LOGIN directory to a logical drive letter, depending on one of the following conditions:

- The user's current default directory is a local drive, either physical or logical. The SYS:LOGIN directory is assigned to the next available drive letter as determined by the workstation's drive table.

OR

- The user's current default directory is a logical drive letter mapped to a directory on the file server. The SYS:LOGIN directory is assigned to the current drive letter. This implies that upon logout, the SYS:LOGIN directory is not necessarily assigned to the same drive letter assigned when the workstation initially connected to the file server.

    For example, if a user's CONFIG.SYS contained the statement LASTDRIVE = E, the SYS:LOGIN directory is assigned to drive F when the connection is established. However, when a user logs out and the current directory is M: because logical drive M was mapped to a file server directory (MAP M:=SYS:USERS), the SYS:LOGIN directory is mapped to logical drive M.

SOLVING PATH PROBLEMS

PC users are accustomed to the DOS PATH command, which establishes the search path DOS uses when trying to locate executable programs and batch files. In the NetWare environment, PATH performs the same function. However, NetWare augments the DOS PATH with the logical drives assigned as NetWare search drives. You establish NetWare search drives with the NetWare MAP command:

```
MAP [INS[ERT]] S[EARCH]n:=
servername/volume:directory path
```

In the command, n is a number from 1 to 16.

In the next several sections, I will explain and explore the implications of NetWare and the DOS path. I have included several scenarios that will help you work with NetWare and the DOS path.

Logging in and the DOS PATH

The user workstation is still using DOS as its operating system. Therefore, NetWare is affected by DOS commands and DOS is affected by NetWare commands. Obviously, they must work together in a coordinated fashion. One of the critical areas in this cooperation is the DOS path and NetWare search drives, both of which perform the function of allowing the operating system to locate executable programs and batch files. This section will clarify how the DOS path and NetWare search paths work together.

Disappearing DOS PATH Segments
Keywords: path, map, login, search

Scenario

It is important to know what happens to an existing DOS PATH when a user logs into the network. For this example, let's assume that no login scripts exist. Suppose the user's existing DOS PATH is:

```
PATH C:\DOS;C:\;C:\WP;C:\UTILS
```

This DOS PATH searches four directories if an executable program or batch file is not found in the user's current default directory. When the user logs into the file server, NetWare does two things.

First NetWare maps the user's DOS PATH to NetWare search drives in the order that they appear in the PATH. The result is an environment that looks like this:

```
SEARCH1:= C:\DOS
SEARCH2:= C:\
SEARCH3:= C:\WP
SEARCH4:= C:\UTILS
```

Then NetWare uses a set of default search and drive assignments. The result is that NetWare maps the first search to the SYS:PUBLIC directory, replacing the first search directory:

```
SEARCH1:= Z:. [ATRIUM1/SYS:PUBLIC]
SEARCH2:= Y: [ATRIUM1/SYS:]
SEARCH3:= C:\
SEARCH4:= C:\WP
SEARCH5:= C:\UTILS
```

Notice that the first directory of the DOS PATH is gone. When you log out, NetWare doesn't put that first directory back. As you log in and then log out during the day, the DOS PATH slowly disappears, one directory at a time. This common problem has a simple solution.

Disappearing DOS PATH Segments

Solution Add the search drive for the SYS:PUBLIC directory to the System Login Script, using this command as the first statement in the Script:

    MAP INSERT SEARCH1:=SYS:PUBLIC

INSERT instructs the LOGIN program to insert this search segment as the first search directory before the directories listed in the DOS PATH statement.

Long DOS PATH Statements
Keywords: path, map, login, search

Scenario Sometimes users have extremely long DOS PATHs because they want to be able to start any program from any directory on their local drives. This presents a problem for NetWare which only supports 26 search segments. (Even though the limit for the MAP SEARCH command is 16 search drives, NetWare can search a maximum of 26 directories.) NetWare truncates any portion of the DOS PATH that exceeds this limit.

Solution The only solution to this problem is to store the user's DOS PATH using a utility, set PATH to only the needed directories, and then log into the network. After the user logs out of the network, you can restore the original DOS PATH. The programs DPATH, STORPATH, and LASTDIR on the diskette offer similar approaches for solving this problem and minimize the changes users must make to their batch files when they decide to update or change their DOS PATH. All three store the users' current DOS PATH in a DOS environment variable. They allow the user to restore the original path when needed. All three have .DOC files explaining their use.

Solving PATH Problems

Mapping Search Drives

When creating a search directory for NetWare to use to locate executable programs and batch files, consider what search number to use and where to put the programs.

Choosing a Search Number
Keywords: map, login, search

Scenario

Since the length of the users' DOS PATHs are unknown when you set up the LAN, you should either insert NetWare search directories at the top of an existing search list or add them to the bottom of the list. This can be complicated because users can change their DOS PATHs at any time, temporarily by typing a new one or more permanently by changing a batch file.

Solution

To map a NetWare directory at the top of the search list, use INSERT as part of the MAP command:

```
MAP INSERT SEARCH1:=ATRIUM1/SYS:PROGRAMS/WP
```

Adding the NetWare directory to the end of the existing search list is complicated because you cannot automatically determine where the end of the list falls. One user might have five directories in their search list, while another might have eight or ten. A MAP command rule might be useful in this regard: gaps between search numbers are prohibited. For example, a user's current search list may look like this:

```
SEARCH1:= Y:. [ATRIUM1/SYS:PUBLIC]
SEARCH2:= C:\
SEARCH3:= C:\WP
SEARCH4:= C:\UTILS
```

If you issue this MAP command:

```
MAP SEARCH16:=SYS:PROGRAMS/WP
```

the resulting search directories would be

```
SEARCH1:= Y:. [ATRIUM1/SYS:PUBLIC]
SEARCH2:= C:\
SEARCH3:= C:\WP
SEARCH4:= C:\UTILS
SEARCH5:= W:. [ATRIUM1/SYS:PROGRAMS/WP]
```

Choosing a Search Number

The MAP SEARCH16 would be revised to reflect that the directory mapped is assigned to search segment 5. This example illustrates that you do not need to know the length of a user's DOS PATH to add a directory to the end of the list. There is a drawback, however. The command to delete a search drive is the MAP DELETE command, which *does not* delete and renumber like the MAP SEARCH. The command

```
MAP DELETE SEARCH16:
```

results in the error message:

```
No mapping for SEARCH16: has been defined
```

Therefore, there is no easy or convenient way to remove the search directory at the end of a search directory list.

Program Locations
Keywords: search, path, programs, map

Scenario The main question for consideration is the location of the application programs. Obviously, if the application programs are stored only on the file server, then inserting a search directory near the top of the search list is most appropriate. However, the question becomes more complicated if the user has versions of the same application programs residing on a local drive. Now the question is, "Which copy of the program do you use—the local one or the one on the file server?"

There is no correct answer to this question. Under some circumstances you might want to find the copy of the program on the user's local disk. It is somewhat common for users to have versions of applications specifically set up for their hardware configurations. Also, local versions of applications can be used when the user is not logged in or when the network is down. However, just as common is the concept that if you are logged into the network, then you use the network version of the program. These situations create a need for using different versions of the MAP SEARCH.

Solution You might map the example given in the previous scenario as follows:

```
MAP SEARCH16:=SYS:DATABASE
```

This adds the network directory to the end of the current list. If the user already has a local directory in the PATH, then that version would be found first. The network version would be used if the user does not have a local directory with the programs in the PATH.

In the second example, the MAP command might be issued as follows:

```
MAP INSERT SEARCH1:=SYS:DATABASE
```

Program Locations

This command inserts the file server's directory at the top of the list, so it would be used when loading the program. In this case, it does not matter if the user has a local directory in their existing PATH; the file server's directory is searched first.

Finally, I have seen many situations where the only way to address this issue is to set up the user's menu or batch files so the user can choose which version to use, network or local. Based upon the user's choice, the appropriate MAP command is issued.

LOGIN SCRIPTS

NetWare uses Login Scripts much like DOS uses the AUTOEXEC.BAT file. Login Scripts are executed when the user initially logs into the network. These Login Scripts set up the user's working environment and execute any necessary initial processes when the user logs in. Login Scripts are divided into two types: System Login Scripts and User Login Scripts.

System and User Login Scripts

There is only one System Login Script per file server. The network supervisor creates and maintains the System Login Script through the NetWare SYSCON program. This Login Script is processed for all users immediately after NetWare has qualified the user's security parameters and permitted the user to log in. The System Login Script is in a file called NET$LOG.DAT residing in the SYS:PUBLIC directory on the file server.

NetWare also has an optional Login Script that can be established for each user through the SYSCON program. The User Login Script is processed immediately after the System Login Script, if a User Login Script exists for the user. The file containing the User Login Script is called LOGIN. It resides in the directory created beneath SYS:MAIL that corresponds to the NetWare-assigned user ID number.

From a functional viewpoint, it is up to the network supervisor to create and maintain the Login Scripts, System and User. Even though NetWare allows users to edit and maintain their own Login Scripts, this is not common practice. The reason is that the user usually doesn't know the ins-and-outs of network organization. In addition, many users really don't care to know about the network's organization or details of the Login Script commands.

From a practical viewpoint, I prefer not using User Login Scripts at all. There are two reasons for this. First, it is much easier to maintain one, all-inclusive Login Script than many individual Login Scripts. There is no capability in the User Login Script that does not exist in the System Login Script. Second, the only way

Login Scripts

way the supervisor can maintain control over each User Login Script is to make sure the user cannot change it. This is accomplished by changing the user's rights to their mail directory, removing the Write right from the user's Trustee Assignment in that directory.

Using IF in Login Scripts

Probably the most significant Login Script command is the IF command which allows the Login Script to perform commands based upon a condition. If you have never used the IF Login Script command, make sure you review it in the section "Login Script Commands" later in this chapter. Using the IF command, you can perform tasks based on who the user is, what groups the user belongs to, and other pertinent criteria. This is the command that allows a supervisor to build a single System Login Script instead of individual User Login Scripts.

Using # in Login Scripts

The Login Script processor uses the # (EXTERNAL PROGRAM EXECUTE) command to *suspend* Login Script processing and execute an external program. The external program must be an executable program, that is, a file with a .COM or .EXE file extension. After the external program finishes or is terminated, control passes back to the Login Script for processing any remaining Login Script commands. Although this can be a very useful capability, there are four important items to keep in mind when using this command.

- When the Login Script processor passes control to the external program, the processor remains resident in the PC's RAM. On one of my PCs, I ran a program called RAMFREE which reports how many bytes are available. From the DOS prompt, I had 571,312 bytes free. I then ran the same program from within a Login Script using the # command. This time the program reported only 494,368 bytes free, a difference of nearly 77K. This large amount of memory occupied by the Login Script processor may limit the programs you can run using the # command. It also can create problems if you use the # command to start a menu system, because the Login Script processor again stays resident.

- You cannot use the # command to load memory-resident programs. These programs, often called TSRs (Terminate-Stay-Resident programs), load into the PC's RAM and stay there, even when they are not in use. The workstation shell programs, IPX and NET4, are memory-resident programs. (Don't worry about these—they must be loaded prior to logging in.) The problem with loading memory-resident programs is that they cause a "hole" in RAM when the LOGIN program finishes. Figure 8-1 illustrates the problem.

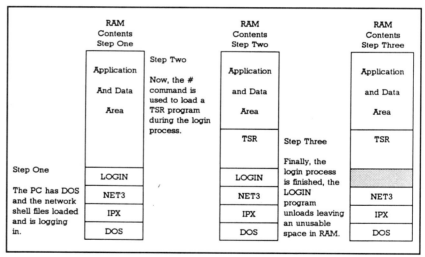

Figure 8-1. Loading TSR programs during login

Login Scripts

- The # command can only pass control to an executable file ending with .COM or .EXE. This prevents you from using the # command to run a batch file. On the utility diskette is a program called GO-COM, an executable file you can use to run a batch file. The syntax for the Login Script command would be similar to

    `#[d:][path]GO-COM y:COMMAND.COM myfile.bat`

`[d;]`	Logical drive where GO-COM resides
`[path]`	Directory where GO-COM resides
`y:`	Drive letter where COMMAND.COM resides
`myfile.bat`	Name of the batch file you want to run

- Because this command runs an external program, the user must have appropriate rights to the directory where the program resides and the proper search path or directory reference must be included in the command which will allow the program to be located.

Eliminating Default Drive Mappings
Keywords: map, logical drives, defaults

Scenario

The Login Script processor's logical drive assignments are a nuisance. NetWare allows you to assign a logical drive letter to any directory on the file server with the MAP command. Logical drives are used as a form of network shorthand so that directories are easier to manipulate. Instead of specifying the file server name, the volume name, and the directory path, you can assign the entire reference to a single drive letter. After you have done this, you can refer to the area simply by using the drive letter reference.

Without a User Login Script, however, the Login Script processor creates its own default logical drive assignments. The problem is that you may not want these default drive mappings that NetWare creates. For example, I logged in with no System Login Script or User Login Script and the result looked like this:

```
Drive A     Maps to a local disk.
Drive B     Maps to a local disk.
Drive D     Maps to a local disk.
Drive E     Maps to a local disk.
Drive F := ATRIUM1/SYS:
Drive X := ATRIUM1/SYS:PUBLIC
Drive Z := ATRIUM1/SYS:PUBLIC
     -----
SEARCH1 :=Y:. [ATRIUM1/SYS:PUBLIC]
SEARCH2:= C:\
SEARCH3:= C:\WP
SEARCH4:= C:\UTILS
```

Eliminating Default Drive Mappings

Solution Notice how the LOGIN program assigned logical drives F, X, and Z in the example. To prevent this from happening, many network supervisors create User Login Scripts with only a REMARK command in them. There is an easier answer, however. To avoid NetWare's default logical drive assignments, use the Login Script EXIT command to terminate the Login Script. Defaults are assigned only when there is no User Login Script and the System Login Script finishes by processing with a command other than the EXIT command. Because the EXIT command terminates the Login Script processing, you can use it to pass control to an external program or batch file.

Finding DOS and Setting COMSPEC

In this discussion, my intent is not to ignore the fact that some users use operating systems other than DOS. However, DOS remains the overwhelmingly dominant operating system for the PC. After users connect to the network, their need to access DOS does not diminish. The user's workstation still uses DOS to run applications. The user still needs access to DOS utility programs such as FORMAT, DISKCOPY, and so on.

The DOS SET COMSPEC command instructs DOS where to look to reload the COMMAND.COM program, if the last program happened to unload the transient portion of DOS. A couple of factors can make finding DOS and locating COMMAND.COM complicated in a network environment.

- Some users may not have DOS on a local drive, because they use either a diskless workstation or a workstation that has only floppy drives.
- Everyone does not necessarily use the same DOS version or even the same release number, due to hardware differences and individual needs. Hardware differences have led to all the various vendor-specific versions of MS-DOS and IBM's PC-DOS. Also, some users tend to not keep up with the most current release levels for a variety of reasons, particularly the increased RAM each DOS version has required.

I will deal with the issue of locating the correct version of DOS first and then the issue of the COMSPEC setting.

Locating the Correct DOS Utilities
Keywords: DOS, map, search

Scenario

Locating the correct DOS utilities hinges largely on the type of PC used. If the PC has a local hard disk, this problem should be minimal. I would guess that virtually all hard disk PCs have the DOS utilities directory in the PATH statement in the AUTOEXEC.BAT or another .BAT file executed during boot up. If this so, the users should still have a search path to locate the DOS utilities in the directory on the users' local drives after they log into the file server. This eliminates the problem of finding the DOS utilities.

The problem is more serious with floppy disk PCs and diskless workstations (PCs with no disk drives). Users of these machines must find the DOS utilities on the file server. This means they must have an active search path to a directory containing the DOS programs. Because different PC brands use different DOS versions, multiple versions of the DOS programs must be copied into separate directories.

Solution

I recommend a directory structure similar to the one illustrated in Figure 8–2.

In this example three types of PCs are in use, as represented by the directories labelled IBM, CMPQ (Compaq), and HP (Hewlett Packard). Assume that for each machine type different DOS releases may be in use. As a result, in this simple scenario, we need eight versions of DOS on the file server. The tricky problem to solve is: a search path is needed to access the correct DOS version.

The correct version depends on the machine in use, not the user at the machine. Therefore, you must place the appropriate MAP SEARCH command in the System Login Script. As simple as it sounds, doing so is complicated because there is no way to determine automatically which machine uses which version and release of DOS.

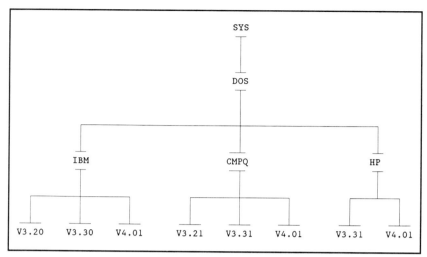

Figure 8-2. Network DOS directory structure

To solve the problem, you need to use one of two commands that are available for your SHELL.CFG or NET.CFG shell configuration file. Table 8-1 summarizes these commands.

Table 8-1. SHELL.CFG/NET.CFG Commands

Command	Maximum Value	Default Value	Login Script Identifier
Short Machine Type =	4 characters	IBM	SMACHINE
Long Machine Type =	14 characters	IBM_PC	MACHINE

NetWare uses default values if the statement does not exist in the user's SHELL.CFG or NET.CFG, or if the user's PC does not have a SHELL.CFG or NET.CFG configuration file. Because these two commands have Login Script identifiers, you can use them to set up a command in the Login Script based upon their value. In addition, with another Login Script identifier, OS_VERSION, the Login Script processor can identify which release of DOS the PC used to boot up. Therefore, the SHELL.CFG or NET.CFG file and a corresponding Login Script MAP command could be established.

Locating the Correct DOS Utilities

SHELL.CFG or NET.CFG Statement	Login Script MAP Command
Short Machine Type = CMPQ	MAP SEARCH16:= SYS:DOS/%SMACHINE/%OS_VERSION
Long Machine Type = HP	MAP SEARCH16:= SYS:DOS/%MACHINE/%OS_VERSION

> **NOTE:** Although Login Script commands can be typed in uppercase, lowercase, and mixed case, Login Script identifiers (MACHINE, SMACHINE, and OS_VERSION in the example) must be typed in uppercase.

This command should be the second command in the System Login Script, immediately following the command to create a search path to the SYS:PUBLIC directory. The percent symbol (%) preceding a value in a Login Script command instructs the Login Script processor that a Login Script identifier follows; use the value of the identifier here rather than a literal value. Choosing between Short Machine Type or the Long Machine Type is largely a matter of preference and availability, but one consideration is that choosing the Short Machine Type forces you to do two other tasks which are not addressed well in the NetWare documentation.

The first is minor. Whenever Long Machine Type is set to a value other than IBM-PC, you must add the Login Script command PCCOMPATIBLE to the Login Script. Otherwise, the Login Script EXIT command will not work.

Second, the NetWare menu utilities such as SYSCON, FILER, and SESSION normally use IBM$RUN.OVL, the file containing color palette settings. When Short Machine Type is set to something other than IBM-PC, these menu utility programs search for a file that begins with the value of Short Machine Type followed by $RUN.OVL. In the previous example, these utilities would look for a file called CMPQ$RUN.OVL or HP$RUN.OVL. You can create these files by copying the IBM$RUN.OVL file.

I will conclude this discussion by explaining why the example uses SEARCH16 as the location for the new search directory and why this command is second in the System Login Script. To understand this fully, you must remember that some users have local hard disks and some do not. Users with local hard disks already have a PATH statement which probably includes their DOS directory, but users of diskless workstations or floppy disk PCs do not. The hard disk PC users already have a search drive mapped to their local DOS directory by their PATH statement when they log in. If a DOS path exists when the user logs in, the MAP command in the example adds a file server directory to the end of their search directory list. This directory will not be used unless the user attempts to run a DOS program that is not in their local DOS directory. However, floppy disk PC and diskless workstation users have no DOS PATH, so this MAP command will be renumbered to the next search directory, following any search directories the Login Script has already established. If the only search drive created is one to the SYS:PUBLIC directory, then this becomes SEARCH2.

Login Scripts

Setting COMSPEC

After you are able to locate the rest of the DOS utilities, it's pretty easy to set COMSPEC correctly. The Login Script processor uses the COMSPEC command to establish where the system searches for COMMAND.COM. NetWare's syntax for this command is

```
COMSPEC = *n:COMMAND.COM
```

or

```
COMSPEC = drive:COMMAND.COM
```

or

```
COMSPEC = Sn:COMMAND.COM
```

    n   Number from 1 through 16 corresponding to the drive number

    drive Drive letter assigned, A through Z

The third syntax is the most practical.

If you created a search directory to the DOS directory as the previous section recommended, you can create one COMSPEC command that works for everyone. Your only other concern is to have hard disk users make sure that their DOS directory is the first directory in their PATH statement, for example:

```
PATH C:\DOS;C:\;C:\WP;C:\UTILS
```

When the user logs in, the System Login Script maps SEARCH1 to SYS:PUBLIC. The hard disk user's DOS PATH causes their local DOS directory to become SEARCH2. If the user has a floppy disk PC or a diskless workstation, and a search directory to DOS established as the preceding section recommended, then MAP SEARCH16 would have become SEARCH2 for that user. Therefore, the COMSPEC could be established for all users:

```
COMSPEC = S2:COMMAND.COM
```

STARTING UP A MENU

Usually users log into the network and see a menu for choosing their activities on the network. This is done at the end of the Login Script by issuing an EXIT command with the syntax:

    EXIT ["[d:][path][filename]"]

The file specified may be an executable file with a .COM or .EXE extension or a batch file. NetWare is not particular about what menu system you use. NetWare comes with its own menu system which you can use to create NetWare-style menus that look and feel like the NetWare menu utility programs. You can also use practically any other system, from simple batch file menus to sophisticated NetWare-specific third-party menu systems.

I think a third-party product deserves consideration because it links into NetWare and extends the capabilities of the LOGIN process beyond those of NetWare's Login Script commands and identifiers. The product is Batch Console.

This product allows the network supervisor to create and control the LOGIN process, check for changes made to the user's CONFIG.SYS and AUTOEXEC.BAT files, download new workstation shell files automatically, extend the LOGIN process capabilities beyond NetWare's Login Script commands and identifiers, run programs on idle PCs from other workstations, as well as manage a point-and-shoot, user-sensitive menu system. It deserves a look from any network supervisor who is trying to maintain a coherent user interface and control system. For more information, write or call Knozall Systems, Inc., 375 East Elliot Road, Suite 10, Chandler, AZ 85225, (602) 545-0006.

LOGIN SCRIPT COMMANDS

Table 8-2 lists the Login Script commands and summarizes their use. Table 8-3 lists Login Script keywords or identifiers. The sections following the tables describe the commands in more detail.

Login Script Commands

Table 8-2. Login Script Commands

Command	Use
#	Processes an external program during Login Script processing.
ATTACH	Allows connection to other file servers during LOGIN.
BREAK	Enables or disables CTRL C or CTRL BREAK which will abort the Login Script processing.
COMSPEC	Specifies where the operating system should look to find COMMAND.COM.
DISPLAY	Displays a text file during LOGIN.
DOS BREAK	Enables or disables CTRL BREAK for interrupting programs.
DOS SET	Allows setting of a DOS environment variable during the LOGIN process.
DOS VERIFY	Enables or disables read after write verification when copying files to a local disk drive.
DRIVE	Sets the current default drive.
EXIT	Terminates the Login Script and passes control to another program if desired.
FDISPLAY	Displays a word processing file during LOGIN.
FIRE PHASERS	Generates a noise to alert the user.
GOTO	Branches the Login Script to a preset label in the Login Script for further processing.
IF...THEN	Allows decisionmaking Login Scripts that can vary their process dependent upon various conditions.
INCLUDE	Allows a text file containing Login Script commands to be processed with the Login Script.
MACHINE NAME	Allows setting a DOS variable called MACHINE.
MAP	Performs logical and search drive mapping.
PAUSE	Temporarily suspends Login Script execution.
PCCOMPATIBLE	Informs LOGIN that the machine is a PC compatible.
REMARK	Used to enter remarks for documentation into the Login Script file.
SHIFT	Used to shift inbound parameters on location (same as SHIFT in DOS batch).
WRITE	Displays information on the monitor during LOGIN.

Booting the Workstation and Logging In

Table 8-3. Login Script Keywords or Identifiers

Keyword	Use
AM_PM	Returns am if morning, pm if after 12:00 pm. Example: IF AM_PM = "am" or IF AM_PM = "pm"
BEGIN	Starts a section of Login Script commands.
DAY	Returns calendar day of month 1 through 31. Example: IF DAY = "1"
DAY_OF_WEEK	Returns day of the week, i.e., "Monday," "Tuesday," etc.
END	Ends a section of Login Script commands.
ERROR_LEVEL	A value. 0 = No errors. Any other value = Error.
FILE_SERVER	Name of the file server.
FULL_NAME	Returns the user's full name. Example: IF FULL_NAME = "John Q. Public"
GREETING_TIME	Returns "morning" if LOGIN time is before noon, "afternoon" if it is past noon but before 6:00 pm, and "evening" if it is past 6:00 pm.
HOUR	Returns "1" - "12" for hour of the day. Example: IF HOUR = "2" AND AM_PM = "pm"
HOUR24	Returns "00" through "23" for 24 hour format. Example: IF HOUR24 = "14"
LOGIN_NAME	Returns the user's account name. Example: IF LOGIN_NAME = "GUEST"
MACHINE	Returns the value of LONG MACHINE TYPE established by SHELL.CFG.
MEMBER OF	Evaluates if user is a member of the group specified. Example: IF MEMBER OF "PRODUCTION"
MINUTE	Returns "00" through "59" corresponding to current clock time.
MONTH	Returns numeric value of month "01" through "12." Example: IF MONTH = "06"

Login Script Commands

Table 8-3, continued

Keyword	Use
MONTH_NAME	Returns literal month name, i.e., "January," "February," etc.
NDAY_OF_WEEK	Returns "1" through "7" starting with Sunday = "1".
NETWORK_ADDRESS	Returns the internal network number of the file server.
NEW_MAIL	Returns "YES" or "NO" dependent upon new files residing in user's MAIL\ID subdirectory.
OS	Returns "PCDOS" or "MSDOS" for which was used to boot up the workstation.
OS_VERSION	Returns the DOS version number in the format "VX.XX" dependent upon the version used to boot up the workstation.
P_STATION	Returns the hexadecimal value of the physical station as determined by the LAN adapter card installed at the workstation.
SECOND	Returns "00" - "59" depending on the seconds on the workstation's clock.
SHORT_YEAR	Returns the last two digits of the current year, i.e., "89," "12," etc.
SMACHINE	Returns the value established for SHORT MACHINE TYPE in SHELL.CFG.
STATION	Returns the station number where the user logged in.
USER_ID	The identifier number assigned to the user by NetWare.
YEAR	Returns the full 4-digit year, i.e., "1989," "2012," etc.

(EXTERNAL PROGRAM EXECUTION)

Syntax   #[server[/volume:[\directory\]]
          filename[parameters]

Defaults Current server, volume, and directory; no parameters

Use   This command executes an external program *without terminating the Login Script*. It only works with programs with a .COM or .EXE file name extension. You cannot use it to run Terminate-Stay-Resident (TSR) programs. After the called program terminates, control passes back to the Login Script.

Example   Run CHKDSK on the user's local hard drive when logging in:

          # \DOS\CHKDSK C: /F

ATTACH

Syntax   ATTACH [servername[/username[;password]]]

Default   None

Use   This command allows the user to "attach" to multiple file servers during LOGIN. If the servername, username, and password are specified, NetWare attempts to log the user into the file server specified.

> **NOTE:** The username and password must be valid on the file server that is being "attached" to. If they are not, ATTACH fails.

If the servername is not specified, NetWare prompts:

    Enter the server name:

If the username is not specified, NetWare prompts:

    Enter login name for server servername:

If the password is not specified, NetWare prompts:

    Enter password for server servername:

Login Script Commands

Examples Attach to other servers without specifying which one:

```
ATTACH
```

Attach to file server ATRIUM2 without specifying username or password:

```
ATTACH ATRIUM2
```

Attach to file server ATRIUM2 specifying username and password:

```
ATTACH ATRIUM2/JOHN;GREAT-TIME
```

> **NOTE:** A problem area in NetWare is attaching to multiple file servers. Each user must exist on each file server. In addition, if passwords are required, the user must supply the password for both. If you enforce periodic changes to passwords, you cannot keep the Login Script ATTACH command up to date without changing the Login Script each time users change passwords. Therefore, I don't recommend putting the password in the ATTACH command in the Login Script.

BREAK

Syntax   `BREAK ON | OFF`

Default `BREAK OFF`

Use   If set to On, the user can abort Login Script processing by pressing CTRL C or CTRL BREAK during Login Script execution. In addition, no keystrokes are saved in the keyboard buffer while the Login Script is being processed because NetWare is watching for the user to abort the Login Script. If a user aborts Login Script processing, the user cannot restart the process without performing a LOGIN and starting over.

When set to Off, the user cannot abort the Login Script process.

This command has no impact on the DOS BREAK command, a separate command with different implications.

Example	Disable the user's ability to abort the Login Script processing: BREAK OFF Enable the user to abort the Login Script processing: BREAK ON

COMSPEC

Syntax	COMSPEC = [*servername*/[*volume*:]] [*directory*\\]*filename.ext* COMSPEC = *drive*:*filename.ext* COMSPEC = SEARCH*x*:*filename.ext*
Default	Current server, volume, and directory
Use	This command tells NetWare where to look to find the DOS COMMAND.COM program or any other DOS shell that might be used. COMMAND.COM files differ for different versions of MS-DOS and PC-DOS, so the system needs to know where to look to reload this file. If the system cannot find COMMAND.COM, the workstation hangs and NetWare sends the message: Bad or missing COMMAND.COM System halted To restart this workstation, you must reboot it. Usually you use this command to tell NetWare to go back to where it found the original COMMAND.COM in the first place, usually a local drive at the workstation. If you are going to reload COMMAND.COM from the file server, then you must create separate directories for each version of PC-DOS and each version of MS-DOS in use. In SHELL.CFG and NET.CFG, the important parameters are LONG MACHINE TYPE and/or SHORT MACHINE TYPE. These correspond to Login Script keywords %MACHINE and %SMACHINE, respectively. SHELL.CFG resides with your other NetWare boot files.

Login Script Commands

Examples
Search for COMMAND.COM on the floppy boot disk:
```
COMSPEC = A:\COMMAND.COM
```
Search the local hard disk's DOS directory:
```
COMSPEC = C:\DOS\COMMAND.COM
```
Search the file server's DOS directory:
```
COMSPEC = ATRIUM/SYS:DOS\COMMAND.COM
```
Reload COMMAND.COM from the second SEARCH area:
```
COMSPEC = SEARCH2:COMMAND.COM
```
Reload COMMAND.COM from logical drive G:
```
COMSPEC = G:COMMAND.COM
```

DISPLAY

Syntax
```
DISPLAY [server[/volume:[\directory\]]] filename.ext
```

Default
Current server, volume, and directory

Use
This command displays the contents of a text file during the Login Script process. This file must be a "normal ASCII" file, one that does not contain special characters a word processor uses for formatting. You can create this kind of file with the DOS EDLIN utility or from the command prompt using COPY CON: *filename.ext*. The entire file will be displayed. DISPLAY does not have any user PAUSE options, other than CTRL S (pause) and CTRL Q (resume). To use the PAUSE statement to pause a large file, you must split it into separate files.

To display a file created with your word processor, use the FDISPLAY command described later in this chapter.

Example
Display a message file called MESSAGE.TXT from the PUBLIC directory:
```
DISPLAY \PUBLIC\MESSAGE.TXT
```

DOS BREAK

Syntax	DOS BREAK ON ¦ OFF
Default	DOS BREAK OFF
Use	When set to Off, this command prevents the user from aborting a DOS program in process by pressing CTRL C or CTRL BREAK. If DOS BREAK is set to On, the user may interrupt DOS programs by pressing CTRL BREAK. If the user presses CTRL BREAK during Login Script processing and BREAK is set to Off, the interrupt occurs after the Login Script has been processed.
Example	Disable the user's ability to abort a DOS program by pressing CTRL C or CTRL BREAK:

DOS BREAK OFF

Allow the user to abort a DOS program by pressing CTRL C or CTRL BREAK:

DOS BREAK ON

DOS SET

Syntax	DOS SET *name* = "*expression*"
Default	None
Use	This command sets DOS Environment variables from the Login Script. The two most common DOS Environment variables are PATH and PROMPT. PATH is not set using this command, but PROMPT might be. The expression used is the expression required for the particular DOS variable. Some DOS batch files use Environment Variable Names to pass parameters. (For more about this, see the sections on Batch Files and the CONFIG.SYS–SHELL command in your DOS manual.) You can set DOS Environment Variable Names with the DOS SET command.
Examples	Set the DOS Prompt to display the current default drive, directory, and > symbol:

DOS SET PROMPT = "PG"

Login Script Commands

Set a DOS Environment variable named PCONFIG to HPLASER.CFG:

```
DOS SET PCONFIG = "HPLASER.CFG"
```

Set a DOS variable for identifying the user:

```
DOS SET USER = "%LOGIN_NAME"
```

Set a DOS variable to identify the physical station:

```
DOS SET STATION = "%P_STATION"
```

DOS VERIFY

Syntax   DOS VERIFY ON ¦ OFF

Default   DOS VERIFY OFF

Use   The DOS COPY command does not automatically verify that what it has written matches the contents of the original file. (The NetWare NCOPY command does, however.) When set to On, this command forces DOS to verify the COPY command.

DRIVE

Syntax   DRIVE n:

Default   None

Use   Used in a Login Script, this command changes the current default drive to either a logical drive established by the MAP command or a physical drive. To change the default to a logical drive letter, the logical drive assignment must have been established using the MAP command earlier in the Login Script. The variable *n*: can have a value from A through Z.

Examples   Change the user's current default drive to local physical drive C:

```
DRIVE C:
```

Change the user's default drive to logical drive G: created with a MAP command:

```
DRIVE G:
```

EXIT

Syntax
    `EXIT`
    `EXIT "filename"`
    `EXIT "command"`

Default
    None

Use
    The EXIT command terminates the Login Script file process. If used without a parameter, it returns the user to the command prompt in the current default drive and directory. When used with a filename parameter, it terminates the Login Script but starts the program specified if the program is found in the current default directory or in a SEARCH path specification. The file name can refer to a file ending with .COM, .EXE, or .BAT.

    If used with a command parameter, EXIT terminates the Login Script and executes the internal DOS command specified. You cannot use the EXIT command to start Terminate-Stay-Resident (TSRs) software, such as SideKick or SuperKey, because the LOGIN.EXE file is already loaded in the workstation's memory. You must start TSR programs from the command prompt or a batch file.

Examples
    Terminate the Login Script process:

    `EXIT`

    Terminate the Login Script and start a word processor with the command "WORD":

    `EXIT "WORD"`

    Terminate the Login Script and list the files in the current directory:

    `EXIT "DIR/P"`

    Terminate the Login Script and start up a batch menu system called BMENU.BAT:

    `EXIT "BMENU"`

FDISPLAY

Syntax
: `FDISPLAY [server[/volume:[\directory\]]] filename.ext`

Default
: Current server, volume, and directory

Use
: This command displays the contents of a text file during the Login Script process. Like DISPLAY, FDISPLAY can display a "normal ASCII" file. Unlike DISPLAY, FDISPLAY can also display text files containing special characters a word processor uses for formatting. FDISPLAY strips the special formatting characters from the file and displays the entire text. FDISPLAY does not have any user PAUSE options, other than CTRL S (pause) and CTRL Q (resume). To use the PAUSE statement to pause a large file, you must split it into separate files.

Example
: Display a message file called MESSAGE.TXT from the PUBLIC directory:

    `FDISPLAY \PUBLIC\MESSAGE.TXT`

FIRE PHASERS

Syntax
: `FIRE PHASERS [n TIMES]`

Default
: $n = 1$

Use
: This command is fun! It makes an interesting sound similar to an arcade noise. Its primary purpose is to alert the user of some event occurring during the Login Script process.

GOTO

Syntax
: `GOTO label`

Default
: None

Use
: This command can be used to branch processing to a label contained elsewhere in the Login Script. The label, followed by a colon (:), must be on a line by itself. As of this writing, this command was only available for NetWare 386, but I suspect it will be added to NetWare 286 soon.

Example GOTO DONE
.
.
.
DONE:

IF...THEN

Syntax   IF [not] *condition* THEN *command*

Default None

Use   This command gives your Login Script decisionmaking capability. It can be used to test many different elements of the environment and act upon the result. To use this command effectively, you must be familiar with the Login Script keywords or identifiers. These are listed and summarized in Table 8–3 near the beginning of this section.

Each keyword can be used in a Login Script IF statement. Keywords must be preceded with a percent symbol (%).

Examples Set a search path so the user can find the correct DOS files on the file server. Cancel the LOGIN process if the user's machine type is not resident on the file server:

```
IF SMACHINE = "IBM" BEGIN
    MAP INSERT SEARCH2:=\%SMACHINE\%OS_VERSION
    EXIT
END
IF SMACHINE = "CMPQ" BEGIN
    MAP INSERT SEARCH2:=\%SMACHINE\%OS_VERSION
    EXIT
END
WRITE %SMACHINE;"is not installed. Please notify
your supervisor"
PAUSE
LOGOUT
```

Login Script Commands

Notify users when they are late logging into the system:

```
IF MEMBER OF "PROD" AND %HOUR24 >="08"
AND %MINUTE > "00"
THEN WRITE "The time is
";%HOUR24;":";%MINUTE;" and you are late!"
```

INCLUDE

Syntax   INCLUDE [*server*[*/volume*:[*directory*\]]] *filename.ext*

Default   Default server, volume, and directory

Use   With this command you can include Login Script file commands that have been typed into a text file to be processed as part of the Login Script. It is used to include standard Login Script files as part of the LOGIN process.

> **NOTE:** This is one of the most useful, yet underutilized, Login Script commands in NetWare!

Remember that the key to managing the NetWare environment effectively is using groups. We grant Trustee Assignments on the basis of group membership. In addition, we generally need to set up MAP SEARCH segments based on the same group needs. Without this command, we would have to type the MAP SEARCH commands, plus any other Login Script commands that applied to this group, in each member's Login Script file. In addition, if something has to be changed, we have to change it in each user's Login Script. Using the INCLUDE command minimizes this redundancy.

To use this feature, you type Login Script commands into a "normal ASCII" text file. You can put as many commands as needed in this one file. Specify the file as part of the INCLUDE command in the user's Login Script and the commands in it are executed as if they were resident in the Login Script.

Example Set up a default LOGIN where PUBLIC gets mapped to SEARCH1, DOS gets mapped to SEARCH2, and a text file called MESSAGE.TXT is displayed using DISPLAY command. The text file might look like

```
MAP INSERT SEARCH1:=\PUBLIC
MAP INSERT SEARCH2:=\DOS
DISPLAY \PUBLIC\MESSAGE.TXT
PAUSE
```

The entry in the user's Login Script would be:

```
INCLUDE \PUBLIC\LOGIN.TXT
```

This one line would be required in the Login Script of each user who plans to use this particular configuration.

MACHINE NAME

Syntax `MACHINE NAME = "literal"`

Default None

Use This Login Script command sets a DOS environment variable called MACHINE NAME. Some software applications require it. It differs from the LONG MACHINE TYPE or the SHORT MACHINE TYPE set by SHELL.CFG.

Example Create a DOS environment variable for a Compaq PC for later use in a batch file or DOS program:

```
MACHINE NAME = "COMPAQ"
```

MAP

Syntax `MAP drive:=[server[/volume:]]directory`
`MAP [INSERT] SEARCHx:=[server[/volume:]]directory`

Default Current server and volume

Login Script Commands

Use | The Login Script can contain any valid MAP command. Generally, as part of the user's Login Script, we want to establish that user's environment by mapping any needed logical drives and setting up the search segments required for the user to execute the software applications needed. You can enter as many MAP commands in the Login Script as you need to accomplish this. Usually we do not want users to spend time learning the MAP command syntax or using the SESSION utility to set up their environment every time they log into NetWare.

PAUSE

Syntax PAUSE

Default None

Use This command suspends Login Script execution, generally so that the user can read information being displayed on the monitor. It is often used after the DISPLAY or FDISPLAY command. The system displays this message after executing the PAUSE command:

```
Strike a key when ready...
```

After you press a key, the Login Script continues its processing cycle. You can use multiple PAUSE commands in a Login Script.

Example Run the USERLIST program during the Login Script processing and pause so the user can read it:

```
.
. (Login script commands)
.
# USERLIST
PAUSE
.
. (Login script commands)
.
```

PCCOMPATIBLE

Syntax	PCCOMPATIBLE ¦ COMPATIBLE
Default	None
Use	This command tells the Login Script processor that your machine is a PC compatible when you have used the LONG MACHINE TYPE parameter in the SHELL.CFG. If the LONG MACHINE TYPE exists in the SHELL.CFG, NetWare does not always process the EXIT *filename* command properly. PCCOMPATIBLE cures the problem. If you use a SHELL.CFG file to tell NetWare about other machine types and have difficulty EXITing to an application, try this command in your Login Script.

REMARK

Syntax	REMARK *text*
	REM *text*
	* *text*
	; *text*
Default	None
Use	With this command you can enter statements in a Login Script file that are not Login Script commands and, therefore, should not be processed. A very useful tool for putting documentation in your Login Scripts, it is also helpful when you make changes or test your Login Script. You can make a Login Script command into a comment without deleting it by inserting REMARK before the command. The Login Script processor ignores any information following the REMARK command on the same line.

WRITE

Syntax	WRITE "*text*"
	WRITE *keyword*
	WRITE "*text*";*keyword*;"*text*"
Default	None

Use | This command displays or "writes" information to the user's monitor during the LOGIN process. Text information must be enclosed in quotation marks ("). These reserved characters can also be part of a text string:

\r   Carriage return; go to the next line
\n   New line
\"   Embedded quotation mark
\7   Make a beep sound

Examples | Display a message to the user that welcomes them to the system, using their name:

```
WRITE "Welcome to the network,
";LOGIN_NAME;". Have a nice day."
```

or

```
WRITE "Welcome to the network,
%LOGIN_NAME. Have a nice day."
```

Display a message that instructs users where to call for help:

```
WRITE "If you need assistance,
call extension 2280."
```

Display the user's network address, station number, and their login date and time:

```
WRITE "Network: %NETWORK_ADDRESS
Station Number: %P_STATION"
WRITE "%DAY_OF_WEEK, %MONTH_NAME %DAY,
%YEAR - %HOUR: %MINUTE %AM_PM"
```

USING MAP COMMANDS IN LOGIN SCRIPTS

Probably one of the most important commands in the Login Script is MAP. The MAP command allows for easier referencing of directories on the network disk. Because network disk drives and volumes tend to be larger than their DOS counterparts due to the number of users sharing data on the network, Novell's NetWare uses names for servers, volumes, and directories. Typing the entire reference every time you need to refer to a file or directory can be quite tedious:

server/volume:/directory path/filename.ext

As usual, the longer the data string a user types, the more chances there are for error. Retyping these references is very annoying. The MAP command simplifies this problem.

The MAP command has four uses:

- Allows the substitution of a logical drive letter for referencing a server/volume:/directory path.
- Creates a search path for NetWare to use when files having the .COM, .EXE, or .BAT extension are not in the user's current default directory.
- Removes logical drive letter assignments and search paths.
- Displays information about the current assignments of logical drive letters and search paths.

In the remainder of this chapter, we will take a close look at the MAP command. We will explore how it works in establishing logical drive letters to disk areas. We will also have a considerable discussion of the search routing mechanism, especially as compared to the DOS PATH command.

Mapping Directories to Logical Drives

NetWare uses a naming structure to reference the shared network disk areas. Since a single LAN can include multiple file servers, each file server must be named when NetWare is installed. The name differentiates the file server a particular user wants to reference. In addition, a single file server may have more than one physical or logical hard disk. The maximum size of a NetWare 286 hard disk volume is 250Mb; the size can be 4Gb for NetWare 386. Any file server with a larger hard disk must be split into volumes when the disk is formatted for NetWare 286. Separate physical drives are always separate volumes in the file server running NetWare 286. NetWare 386 does support combining multiple partitions and multiple physical drives in one volume. When installing NetWare on the file server, each volume in a single file server is given a unique three-letter volume name. The same volume name may be used in different file servers serving the same LAN.

Using MAP Commands in Login Scripts

In addition to the server name and the volume name, Novell's NetWare uses directories on the volumes to organize data in the same fashion as PC-DOS and MS-DOS. NetWare directory names follow the same naming conventions as their DOS counterparts. A directory can have an eight-character directory name and a three-character extension. (Most people do not use the extension because it requires more typing.) The same reserved characters that cannot be used in DOS file names cannot be used in NetWare directory names.

It is much more convenient to use the MAP command to assign a specific server, volume, and directory reference to a single *logical* drive letter. Here is the MAP command syntax for assigning *logical* drive letters:

```
MAP d:=[server/][volume:]\directory path
```

You might use the MAP command this way:

```
MAP G:=ATRIUM/SYS:\WORD   or   MAP G:=\WORD
```

The square brackets [ ] in the command syntax enclose optional parts of the command. If you have only one server and one volume, NetWare automatically references them. In the example just given, we have shown both ways. In the example, I created a logical drive, G:, and assigned it to a directory called WORD. In this context, the word *logical* describes an abstract area: no *physical* drive G: exists. However, now I can use G: to refer to the disk area ATRIUM:SYS:\WORD. This logical assignment is a shorthand way to refer to network disk directories.

With the MAP command, NetWare can assign all twenty-six letters, A to Z, to logical drives. Drive letters A to E are assumed to be local physical drives on the user's workstation. If you use the MAP command to assign these drive letters, NetWare asks you if you wish to assign these letters:

```
Drive D: currently maps to a local disk
Do you want to assign it as a network drive? (Y/N) Y
```

Drive D: would be whatever drive, A to E, you specified in the MAP command. If you respond Y, NetWare performs the MAP specified. This can be a problem. If the drive letter, A to E, corresponds to a real physical drive, NetWare asks the same question. If you respond Y again, NetWare performs the MAP command as specified. Now the user's physical drive D: is not available until logical drive D: is removed!

> **WARNING:** Be careful when MAPping local physical drives: they become inaccessible until you remove the MAPping.

Usually this version of the MAP command is used to create logical drive letters for the data directories where the user's work is to be kept. Logical drive mappings are not permanent. They terminate when the user logs out of the network. When the user logs into the network, any needed logical drive mapping must be redone unless the MAP command is part of the user's Login Script or part of a batch file which is processed when the user logs in.

> **WARNING:** When a user logs out from a logical drive, the server's LOGIN directory is assigned to the logical drive that the user logged out from. If this drive differs from the one that the user normally logs from, this can cause the error message Invalid drive specified.

Creating Search Routes to Find Programs

The MAP command also creates a search path NetWare uses to locate programs or batch files. Program files have a .COM or .EXE file name extension. Batch files, often used to start programs, have the file name extension .BAT. When you type a command after the system prompt, the operating system uses a preset sequence to decide what to do next.

First the operating system checks to see if the command is an **internal command**, built into the resident operating system program files. Commands like COPY, DIR, DEL, CHDIR, MKDIR, and RMDIR are examples of internal DOS commands. NetWare does not have its own internal commands. NetWare uses the DOS commands, however, when connected to the LAN.

Then, if the command is not an internal command, the operating system checks to see if the command is an external binary image program, ending with the extension of .COM. A .COM program is an **image program**: It uses the same addresses when loaded as appear in the program when viewed on the disk. This concept is not important to our discussion. NetWare and DOS look in the current directory for this program file.

If a .COM program cannot be found in the current directory, NetWare searches the current directory for a "relocatable" or external binary program that has an .EXE extension. .EXE and .COM files are similar, except that the addresses used in an .EXE file are offset by the address where the program is loaded. Right now, this distinction is not important for our discussion either.

Finally, NetWare will search the current directory for a batch file that has a .BAT extension.

If none of the three steps succeeds in locating a file, then one of two events occurs. First, NetWare looks for a PATH statement in the environment area of DOS memory. The PATH statement sets a search path that the operating system uses to locate either a .COM or .EXE file. If no PATH statement exists, the operating system displays the message:

```
Bad command or file name
```

If a PATH statement does exist, NetWare searches each directory specified looking for the .COM or .EXE file. If the path statement specifies multiple directories, NetWare searches the one listed first for the .COM file and then the .EXE file. If this search fails, NetWare searches the second directory listed for the .COM or .EXE file and so on, until the operating system either finds the file or runs out of directories to search. If the search succeeds, NetWare loads the file into memory and executes it. If NetWare doesn't find the file, it sends the message:

```
Bad command or file name
```

PATH statements can occur two ways. First, the DOS PATH command can be executed before you log into the LAN. Almost all users who have a local hard disk have a PATH statement in their AUTOEXEC.BAT file or another batch file that is executed whenever they boot up their PC. The format for the DOS PATH command is

```
PATH [drive:]\directory;[drive:]\directory...
```

A semi-colon (;) separates successive directories. If you do not specify a drive, the operating system uses the current default drive.

The second way to set the PATH is to use the NetWare MAP command. This command can set up search routes to both local and network directories. The syntax for using the MAP command this way is

```
MAP [INSERT] SEARCHx:=server/volume:\directory path
```

The letter x above sets the priority or sequence number for this MAP SEARCH command. x can have a value from 1 through 16. In both the DOS PATH command and the NetWare MAP SEARCH command, the search path specified only applies to the named directory. Any directories beneath the one indicated are not searched.

> **NOTE:** To search a subordinate directory, you must create a separate PATH segment or use another MAP SEARCH command.

There are several rules for using the MAP SEARCH command.

- No more than 26 MAP SEARCH routes can be active, SEARCH1: through SEARCH26:.
- Gaps between successive search priority numbers are prohibited. NetWare automatically renumbers search priorities to close gaps. For example, if the user issues the following two MAP SEARCH commands:

Using MAP Commands in Login Scripts

```
MAP SEARCH1:=SERVER/VOL:PUBLIC
MAP SEARCH5:=SERVER/VOL:DATABASE
```

and no other MAP SEARCH commands have been issued, NetWare *automatically* transforms the second MAP SEARCH command to

```
MAP SEARCH2:=SERVER/VOL:DATABASE
```

- NetWare assigns MAP SEARCH segments a logical drive letter starting with letter Z and working toward the beginning of the alphabet.
- If a DOS PATH statement exists, the DOS segments are mapped to SEARCH segments in the order that they were in the DOS PATH statement. The first segment becomes SEARCH1, the second becomes SEARCH2, and so on. The NetWare MAP SEARCH command *replaces* the segment of the DOS PATH statement with the corresponding MAP SEARCH drive letter assignment. This replacement is done on an equivalence basis. That is, SEARCH1 would replace the first segment, SEARCH3 would replace the third segment, SEARCH5 would replace the fifth segment, and so on.
- You can use the optional INSERT parameter to place a SEARCH segment before existing segments. SEARCH segment priorities would shift up one number, starting from the insert. For example, assume the following MAP SEARCH segments already exist:

```
MAP SEARCH1:=SERVER/VOL:\PUBLIC
MAP SEARCH2:=SERVER/VOL:\DOS
MAP SEARCH3:=SERVER/VOL:\DATABASE
```

Now you issue a new MAP SEARCH command:

```
MAP INSERT SEARCH2:=SERVER/VOL:\WORDPROC
```

The MAP SEARCH segments would now be

```
MAP SEARCH1:=SERVER/VOL:\PUBLIC
MAP SEARCH2:=SERVER/VOL:\WORDPROC
MAP SEARCH3:=SERVER/VOL:\DOS
MAP SEARCH4:=SERVER/VOL:\DATABASE
```

A MAP INSERT SEARCH *does not* replace DOS PATH segments.

- When you log out, NetWare releases the network segments of the PATH automatically, leaving only local drive segments in the DOS PATH statement.
- Unless you specify otherwise, NetWare *automatically* performs the following MAP commands:

    MAP SEARCH1:=SERVER/VOL:\PUBLIC
    MAP Y:=SERVER/VOL:\PUBLIC
    MAP F:=SERVER/VOL:*username*

In other words, NetWare sets up the first search segment to the directory containing the NetWare utilities and assigns it to logical drive Z:. It also sets up logical drive letter Y:, mapped to this same area. It looks in the root directory for a directory corresponding to the user's name and if one exists, maps this area to logical drive F:. *To prevent NetWare from performing these default mappings, terminate the Login Script with an EXIT command.*

Setting up search routes for NetWare to use to locate files is a normal LAN activity; however, not understanding the rules causes a great deal of confusion and frustration. Unfortunately, the NetWare manuals do not spell out these rules.

LOCATING CONFIGURATION FILES

A significant problem in networks is that the software industry seems to lag behind the needs of network users. One area where this shows up is configuration files. Most software programs have configuration files that are used for three purposes: determining hardware configurations such as monitor types and printers, rodents, etc; determining where the data directories are for the data files; and saving user-defined preferences that relate to the software.

Since software companies haven't dealt very well with these issues in a network environment, let's look at how we can solve the problem from the LAN administration end. If the software uses separate files for these three purposes, we're in good shape. If all three are in one file, there's not much we can do.

Locating Configuration Files

Hardware configuration is a problem because users do not always use the same machine. Whenever a user sits down at a PC and uses the software, we need to locate the correct configuration file for the hardware being used. This problem can be solved pretty well if the hardware configuration is kept in a separate file.

Hardware Configuration and Lotus 1-2-3
Keywords: configuration files, hardware, SMODE, machine type

Scenario

Lotus 1-2-3 uses a file called 123.SET for hardware configuration. The software looks in the user's current default directory for 123.SET and, if it does not find it, looks in the directory where the program was installed. If it doesn't find 123.SET there, Lotus 1-2-3 won't start.

Solution

Putting 123.SET in a user directory doesn't work when the user can sit down and use other machines which require different hardware configurations. Here are the steps we can take to solve the problem.

Create: configuration files for each hardware combination we have. Because these all have the same name (123.SET), we will create a directory structure just for these files:

```
SYS:CONFIG
SYS:CONFIG/MONO
SYS:CONFIG/VGA
SYS:CONFIG/EGA
```

Copy: the configuration files for each software package according to the configuration into these directories.

Delete: the configuration files from the default directory or program directories. We do not want the application to find them there.

Create: a search path to the correct configuration directory based on the machine that the user uses. This requires

- A statement in the user's SHELL.CFG file on the workstation which identifies the machine. We could use LONG MACHINE TYPE = for this.
- A search map to this directory in the System Login Script:

```
MAP INS S2:=SYS:CONFIG/%MACHINE
```

Summary

Change: the way 1-2-3 searches for its data files with the SMODE command:

```
SMODE SYS:APPS/123 5
```

Parameter 5 instructs the 1-2-3 program to search the user's path to find data files.

This technique of forcing a program to look elsewhere for files is a powerful and underutilized feature of NetWare. You can use it to solve a myriad of problems like the one described here. The SMODE parameter is like a file attribute. It stays set once it is changed because it is part of the file's directory information.

SUMMARY

This chapter focused on the process of logging into the network and setting up the user's environment. We have covered some of the more challenging aspects of this process that can pose problems in NetWare. While it is difficult to address every conceivable problem or user environment, this chapter has laid a foundation of solid concepts that can be used to create a solid and reliable user environment that is easy to maintain.

Part III
Third-party Software

The sole purpose of installing NetWare is to allow a network to run. After the network is running, its users work with other software applications. This part is about using third-party software programs. Because it's impossible to cover all applications that you could install and run on a NetWare LAN, this part focuses on some general principles and then presents a few scenarios involving popular programs.

9
Using Application Software with NetWare

Because this topic is so broad, I divided the chapter into several sections. Many different issues need to be discussed when talking about software that is installed on a LAN. I will discuss these issues one by one and try to draw a complete picture of what has to happen to make software run the way we want on the LAN. The following sections correspond to the various issues you must address for each software package. These issues are data file integrity, configuration files, and printing.

Each topic has various subtopics. Each topic is also affected by a pervasive problem: software vendors are sometimes less knowledgeable about NetWare features than you or I. As a result, software is sometimes poorly designed for a NetWare environment.

DATA FILE INTEGRITY

Perhaps the most important issue concerning software use in a LAN environment is data file integrity. Of course, no one wants to corrupt data files, so when erroneous data is on the LAN, this issue is paramount. Simply installing an application on a LAN does not make the application safe.

With respect to data file integrity, I want you to clearly understand that the central issue is how concurrent or simultaneous access by multiple users to a data file is handled. In the LAN environment multiple users can access the same software at the same time. You need to know how this affects the data files the software uses.

First, you must recognize that installing software does not magically make the software able to handle concurrent access to the data files by multiple users. Software that was not designed for LANs knows nothing about file locking and/or record locking. Yet locking is absolutely essential if multiple users can access a file simultaneously. NetWare cannot provide locks for an application that was not designed for the NetWare environment.

> **WARNING:** Without file or record locking, data files will be corrupted if multiple users access them simultaneously. Therefore, you must restrict access to these data files to one user at a time to safeguard the file's integrity. The exception is software designed specifically to allow concurrent access.

How NetWare accesses files depends on the file's attribute settings. Four settings affect data files. You can change these settings with the FLAG command or the FILER program.

- N   Normal file, a non-shareable, read-write file that can only be opened by one user at a time.
- S   Shareable file that can be opened simultaneously by multiple users.
- RO   Read-only file that can only be read. It cannot be updated or written to. This is the normal setting for program files.
- RW   Read-write file that can be updated. This is the normal setting for data files.

You can readily assume that the data files from a non-LAN application are RW (read-write). Because the application cannot handle record or file locking, you can also assume that the data files must have the N (non-shareable) setting as well, limiting access to one user at a time.

Data File Integrity

However, the LAN's not safe yet. The N attribute only permits one user to open the file at a time, but let's look more closely at what actually happens on the file server.

You generally use two kinds of applications on the LAN. I'll call them RAM-based applications and file-based applications. The setting for the N attribute works differently for these application types.

File-based Applications

A file-based application accesses data from the file a piece at a time. While the application is processing, it holds the data file open and reads or writes to it as needed. As records are needed, the application reads them from the data file. As changes are made, the application writes data back to the data file. This is common for most database applications, accounting applications, and transaction processing applications. The N attribute makes the file-based application safe for a LAN, because while the user runs the application, the data files are held open, but cannot be opened by any other user.

RAM-based Applications

The RAM-based applications work differently. Spreadsheets, word processors, and graphics packages tend to be this type of application. I call these applications RAM-based because when a data file is opened—let's say a spreadsheet—the server opens the file and then transmits the entire file to the workstation that opened it. After this is done, the workstation has the file in memory or RAM. However, now the server closes the file on the file server while the user's application works with the file in memory.

This is how non-LAN software was designed to work. Because the developer was concerned that the stand-alone user might just turn the machine off without properly exiting from the application, the software was written so that after the file was loaded into memory, the disk file would be closed to ensure data integrity.

On the LAN, the server responds just like the user's local hard disk used to respond. After the file has been completely transmitted to the workstation's memory, the server closes the data file. Because the data file is closed, it becomes available for another user because it's not open and, therefore, not shared. This can lead to two users working on the same file without knowing it. Even worse, when users finish their work and save the file, the server opens the data file, writes the changes back to the data file, and then closes the file. This happens when the first user finishes and again when the second user finishes. The version of the file on the disk is the version created by the last user to save the file—that version overwrote the previous one.

You can easily see the potential for disaster in a LAN environment. This problem is not easy to fix because the server merely responds to the software as the software told it to respond. To a certain extent, Novell attempted to help us with this problem with the HOLDON command. This command "holds" a file from being updated by another user, if the original user issues the HOLDON command before entering the application. For example, a spreadsheet user issues a HOLDON command before starting the spreadsheet software. After the spreadsheet data file is retrieved, it is held so that no other user can write to it until the original user exits the application and issues a HOLDOFF command.

The problem is that although the file is held so that other users cannot write to it, it is not held so that other users cannot read it. The second user can still retrieve the file from within the spreadsheet application. The HOLDON condition initiated by the first user does not warn the second user that the file is held. Both users think that they are the only one using the file and that they can safely update it. The second user gets a network error message when attempting to save the file because it is held by the first user. The second user can save the file under a different name, however.

The bottom line is that you must be extremely careful when adding applications to your LAN. If an application is a "network" version, it should have provisions for locking and protecting shared data files. If the application is not a network version, you must make sure the file is non-shareable and that multiple users do not try to access a shared file simultaneously.

CONFIGURATION FILES

Almost all software comes with configuration files used by the application for three general purposes:

- Hardware drivers. There is no standard PC. Right now, there are no less than seven different types of video interfaces, from text-only monochrome to the recently announced eXtended Graphics Array (XGA). There are probably hundreds of different printers. Then there are keyboards, mice, and many other goodies. How does an application know what equipment it runs on? One use of configuration files is to configure the application to use the hardware drivers required for the workstation using the software. The settings for this file depend upon a user's machine.
- File locations. Another common task of the configuration file is to establish the location of files, both data and software. Many applications have settings that permit various files to be located in different directories. The settings for this element depend on who the user is or what group the user belongs to.
- User preferences. Some applications allow the user to select various options such as screen colors, type of menus, or help level. These user-defined settings are stored in a configuration file for the user.

How Many Configuration Files Do You Need? Where Do You Put Them?

Keywords: configuration, software, hardware, files

Scenario The problem with software in a LAN environment is setting up the application so that all users have the correct configuration file for their needs. This can be especially challenging when one user uses different machines with different configurations.

Another question you must investigate is, "In which directory does the software expect to find the configuration files?" Some applications look in the user's current directory; others look in the software's **home directory** (that is, the directory where the software resides).

In this scenario and the next three, I address these configuration file issues from a general viewpoint. However, to make the principles clear, I am using a popular application as an example: 1-2-3 by Lotus Development Corporation. This product has configuration files for hardware drivers (123.SET) and directory locations (123.CNF), but not user preferences.

Solution If your organization uses many different monitor and printer types, you need a different configuration file for each combination. Many applications hang when you attempt to use the wrong configuration file for the type of monitor you are using.

The goal is to decide how many different combinations exist in your LAN. This determines how many variations of the configuration file you need to create. I work this out with a chart similar to the one in Table 9-1. Across the top row, I list the various styles of monitors we have. Down the left side, I list the types of printers we use. Then I name each combination of monitor and printer in the LAN.

How Many Configuration Files Do You Need? Where Do You Put Them?

Table 9-1. Hardware Matrix

	MDS	CGA	HGA	EGA	VGA	8514	SVGA	XGA
HP LaserJet				EGA_LJ	VGA_LJ			
HP DeskJet							SVGA_DJ	
Epson FX-80	MDA_FX							
Apple LaserWriter						8514_LW		
IBM Proprinter II		CGA_PR						
IBM Page Printer								XGA_PP
NEC P7			HGA_P7					
Toshiba P341				EGA_341				

The matrix determines how many different versions of the hardware configuration file, 123.SET, I need to create.

The next problem to solve is where to put all the files. I recommend a separate set of directories for each. Your directory structure might look similar to the one shown in Figure 9-1.

Copy the appropriate 123.SET file into each subdirectory. One reason for separate directories is that configuration files from other software applications can use these same directories for their configuration files, as long as the names of each application's configuration file is different.

After you copy the various versions of 123.SET into its corresponding directory, make sure that no copies of 123.SET exist in the 1-2-3 home directory or in any default directory where the user runs 1-2-3.

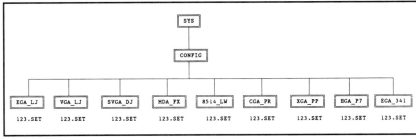

Figure 9-1. Configuration directories

Changing the Application's Behavior
Keywords: SMODE, PATH, search, programs, data files

Scenario The last problem is that Lotus 1-2-3 looks for 123.SET in the user's current default directory or in the software's home directory. This is not acceptable. The same user may always have the same current default directory when starting 1-2-3, even though the user actually uses different PCs with different configurations and needs a different 123.SET.

Solution To solve this problem, let's investigate a NetWare command most network administrators often overlook—the SMODE command.

    Syntax   SMODE [*directory path*] [*parameter*]
                 SMODE [*filespec*] [*parameter*]

    Examples SMODE ATRIUM/SYS:/MFG 2
                 SMODE ACCTG.COM 5

    Default   Files not changed with the SMODE command have the default SMODE 0.

SMODE is an important NetWare command. It is related to the DOS PATH and the NetWare MAP SEARCH commands. Normally, PATH and MAP SEARCH instruct the system to search directories other than the current default directory to locate executable files (with the file name extension .COM or .EXE) or batch files (with the file name extension .BAT). The system looks for the file with the .COM extension in the current directory first. If the search fails, the system then searches the current directory for an .EXE file. If this search fails, the system checks the current directory for a .BAT file. If all three searches fail, the system moves to the first directory specified in the PATH statement and repeats the process. This continues until the system either finds and executes the program or batch file or the system notifies the user that the command or file name is incorrect.

Changing the Application's Behavior

SMODE goes beyond the default method of searching for files. The default procedure only searches for either executable files (.COM or .EXE) or batch files (.BAT), totally ignoring data files and other files such as program overlays. SMODE sets options that expand or change the default method of searching for files. The SMODE parameter determines how the system locates files. You can use only one parameter with the SMODE command. If you omit the parameter, SMODE displays the current setting.

A major feature of SMODE is that it affects the executable file by assigning an SMODE parameter to the file itself. This means that an SMODE setting is a fixed parameter stored in the NetWare directory along with other pertinent file information. Because the SMODE setting is an extended NetWare attribute, you only need to issue the SMODE command once. However, you can use the SMODE command again to change the parameter after you have set it for a given file. Parameters and their uses are listed next.

Parameter	Use
0	The default mode uses the standard PATH and MAP SEARCH procedures described earlier for locating files; that is, it only searches for executable or batch files.
1	If you specify a path to start an executable file, then the system searches that directory for data files. If the system does not find the data file, then the system searches the directories specified in the PATH statement, for example,

                F>SYS:\APPS\DBASE\DBASE

This command tells the system to run a program called DBASE. This program is in the SYS volume in the directory \APPS\DBASE. When it looks for a data file, the system searches the current default directory. Then it searches the SYS:\APPS\DBASE directory. If it does not find the file, the system continues to search according to the PATH statement in effect.

2	The system searches only the current default directory.

3   If you specify a path to start an executable file, the system searches that directory for data files. It does not search other directories unless the data file is to be opened in Read-Only mode. If the search fails and the data file is to be opened as a read-only file, the system searches the directories specified in the PATH statement.

5   The system searches the specified directory path where the program was found. Then the system searches the current default directory and all directories in the PATH statement for data files.

7   If files opened by the executable program are read-only, the system searches the default directory and all directories in the search path.

To alter the way 1-2-3 searches for related files, I use a command similar to

```
SMODE SYS:APPS\123 5
```

This command sets the search mode attribute on all executable files in the SYS:APPS\123 directory to 5, causing 1-2-3 to search the user's path for data files like 123.SET.

Putting the Configuration Directory in the User's Path
Keywords: SHELL.CFG, machine name, NET.CFG

Scenario The final step in setting up the configuration files for 123.SET is to add a MAP SEARCH to the user's environment that puts the appropriate directory in the user's path so that 1-2-3 can find the 123.SET file. The question is, "How do you issue a standard MAP command when you don't know which machine the user is using?"

Solution In response to this question, you place an entry in the user's SHELL.CFG or NET.CFG file. Because this file resides on the workstation, locating and using it does not depend on your knowing who the user is. Add this command to the file:

```
LONG MACHINE TYPE = configuration name
```

The configuration name corresponds to the name assigned in Table 9-1 and the directory assigned in Figure 9-1. This SHELL.CFG or NET.CFG command corresponds to the Login Script variable MACHINE used to create a MAP SEARCH to the appropriate directory.

You can now modify the User Login Script or the System Login Script by adding the configuration reference to the path. The next example suggests command lines that you could add to the Login Script.

```
MAP INSERT SEARCH3:=SYS:CONFIG/%MACHINE
PCCOMPATIBLE
```

The login command, PCCOMPATIBLE, is required whenever you use the LONG MACHINE TYPE setting in SHELL.CFG or NET.CFG. Without it, the EXIT and # Login Script commands do not work properly. Novell has never given me a satisfactory answer as to why this is required; nevertheless we must include this command in the Login Script.

Now, when the user tries to run Lotus 1-2-3, the system looks in the user's current directory for 123.SET, then looks in the application's home directory for 123.SET. When it does not find 123.SET in either place, it searches the directories in the user's path and finds 123.SET in the configuration directory.

Configuration File Summary
Keywords: configuration, software, hardware, files

Scenario 123.CNF is the file that 1-2-3 uses to determine where the user's data files reside. Using the same techniques discussed in the preceding three scenarios, you can also handle issues related to 123.CNF.

Solution Since you have set the SMODE attribute for 1-2-3's executable file to parameter 5, 1-2-3 also uses the user's path to search for 123.CNF. This means you can put this file wherever you want, as long as you create a search path for it. 1-2-3 does not have a user preferences configuration file, but if it did, you could use the same technique.

This technique is likely to present a new way of thinking about setting up applications to run on the network. It's not discussed in any application installation instructions I have seen. Using it effectively takes both planning and understanding how your application uses configuration files. The payoff is that it makes your network much easier to manage and maintain over the long run.

> **WARNING:** This technique does not work for every application. Specifically, it does not work when the application uses a single configuration file for hardware drivers, file locations, and user preferences. Hardware settings depend on the machine used; directory settings usually depend on the user or the group; user preferences are user specific. There is no easy way to solve the configuration file problem when one file determines all these settings.

PRINTING ISSUES

Many applications are not designed for LAN printing. Sometimes it seems even LAN applications are not designed for LAN printing because their options for printer, job, and queue selection are few. At the most basic level, many applications never send an end-of-file character to the printer to signify that printing is complete and allow NetWare to close the print file. Of course, usually the Timeout or the Auto Endcap NetWare print option eventually gets the job to print. It's inconvenient to exit the application just to release a print job; however, in some cases this is the only way to release the job.

Obviously, non-LAN applications don't know anything about the network printing environment. Your ability to print to the network printers depends on your understanding of the NPRINT and CAPTURE commands. Of course, you must issue the CAPTURE command *before* you start the application.

Even applications that advertise LAN and/or NetWare compatibility rarely allow you to conveniently select the queues or print jobs that you created for your environment. I think that these problems have two sources. First, many software developers do not take time to learn how to program for Novell's APIs (Application Program Interfaces), even though this would simplify and enhance how their products work with NetWare's queues and print management features. Second, software developers are always wary about tying their software too closely to a specific product like NetWare. This is unfortunate. With NetWare's huge installed base and corresponding market share, developers ought to expend extra effort to make their products run smoothly on NetWare.

For the most part, the CAPTURE command is the vehicle for getting jobs to shared network printers. Because the job definition varies due to different Timeout parameters, different queues, and other application needs, you may need to issue different CAPTURE commands for different applications. Some network administrators even add user menu choices that let the user select the printer options needed for the application the user intends to run. For more information on printing in a NetWare environment, see Chapters 10, 11, and 12.

USING WORDPERFECT WITH NETWARE

Perhaps the most popular PC word processor is WordPerfect Corporation's WordPerfect. From surveys of those attending my seminars, I have learned that over 50 percent use WordPerfect. I have used it myself after abandoning my first word processor in 1985 after using it for four years. In six years, I have written two books, about eighteen courses, a few articles, and hundreds of miscellaneous pieces. As much as I like and depend on WordPerfect, it is not LAN perfect. In this section, I discuss some details of installing and using WordPerfect in a NetWare LAN. My goal is not to teach WordPerfect, but to illustrate specific nuances and problems with using it in a NetWare environment.

Installing WordPerfect on a NetWare LAN

You must install WordPerfect 5.1 with the WordPerfect installation program. Various files on the WordPerfect diskettes have been compressed electronically and are not in usable formats. The instructions in the next sections will help you install WordPerfect on your LAN.

Logging In

You should log in as a supervisor or as someone who has full rights in the directory where you want WordPerfect installed. The installation program can create a new directory for you, if you have the appropriate NetWare rights.

Mapped Drives

The installation program asks on which logical drive you want to install WordPerfect. The options shown correlate to the drives you have mapped.

WordPerfect Directory

The installation program displays a directory called WP51 which it creates beneath the current default directory. If you want to change the directory's name or location, type the name and location you prefer.

Modifying CONFIG.SYS

WordPerfect needs to have a FILES= statement in the user's CONFIG.SYS file. The installation program queries if you want to update the CONFIG.SYS file on the machine you are using. If you do, the installation program places the statement FILES=20 in your CONFIG.SYS.

> **WARNING:** You need to verify that your WordPerfect users have a FILES= statement allocating at least 20 open files in their CONFIG.SYS file.

The installation program only modifies the CONFIG.SYS of the user running the installation program.

Modifying AUTOEXEC.BAT

WordPerfect's installation program queries if you want to update the AUTOEXEC.BAT file. Respond No to this query. The installation program changes AUTOEXEC.BAT by adding the drive and directory where WordPerfect is installed. Because drive letters depend on the user's mapped drives, you do not want the installation program to make this change. Your users will locate WordPerfect with a MAP SEARCH command in the Login Script or a menu script.

The WordPerfect Environment File WP{WP}.ENV

The installation creates a default configuration file for WordPerfect called WP{WP}.ENV. It puts two parameters in this file based on responses to the next queries. The first asks what type of network you have. The second asks which directory you want to use for user set-up files. Your responses add the parameters listed next to WP{WP}.ENV.

/NT=x Corresponds to the network number (x) selected. Possible values are

  0   Other
  1   Novell NetWare

	2	Banyan Vines
	3	TOPS Network
	4	IBM LAN Network
	5	NOKIA PC-Net
	6	3Com 3+
	7	10Net
	8	Artisoft LANtastic
	9	AT&T StarGROUP
	A	DEC PCSA
	B	3Com 3+ Open
	*	No Network

/PS=*d*:*path*\   Instructs WordPerfect to use .SET files for each user and tells where these .SET files will be located. When users change their WordPerfect configuration, their .SET file is modified. Therefore, the user needs ROSW rights in this directory. For this reason, you may not want .SET files to reside in the WordPerfect home directory.

Selecting Printers

Your next task is to select the types of printers that you use with WordPerfect. You must select all printer types, shared or not, that your users use. After you select the printers, follow the on-screen prompts, inserting the various diskettes that the installation program needs.

Creating the WordPerfect Default Set-up File
Keywords: WordPerfect, configuration

Scenario WordPerfect uses two set-up files, WP{WP}.SET and WPxxx}.SET. WP{WP}.SET is WordPerfect's default set-up file. WPxxx}.SET is a user set-up file that overrides the default set-up file. The characters xxx correspond to the ID assigned to the user. Unfortunately, WordPerfect cannot use the NetWare account names to identify users. I'll talk more about this a little later.

Solution Having finished the basic installation, you need to establish system defaults. You start WordPerfect with a special user ID and the command:

```
WP /U={WP
```

The user designation {WP is an assigned ID the WordPerfect administrator uses when updating system defaults. The items that you establish default settings for include:

Mouse driver	SHIFT F1 1
Display options	SHIFT F1 2
Back-up options	SHIFT F1 3 1
Beep options	SHIFT F1 3 2
Cursor speed	SHIFT F1 3 3
Document summary	SHIFT F1 3 4
Fast save	SHIFT F1 3 5
Back-up file locations	SHIFT F1 6 1
Thesaurus and Dictionary locations	SHIFT F1 6 3
Printer file location	SHIFT F1 6 4
Graphic images location	SHIFT F1 6 6
Page format	SHIFT F8 2
Line format	SHIFT F8 1

Creating the WordPerfect Default Set-up File

        Printer selection   SHIFT F7 S

        Font selection   CTRL F8 4

After you choose all the settings you want to use as defaults,

Press: F7 to exit WordPerfect.

Type: N after the save file prompt.

Type: Y after the exit prompt.

You have updated the file WP{WP}.SET.

Creating WordPerfect User Set-up Files
Keywords: WordPerfect, user, configuration

Scenario Establishing user set-up files is one of the most difficult tasks in installing WordPerfect on a NetWare LAN. WordPerfect uses a three-letter designation for each user corresponding to the user's initials. The problem is that more than one user may have the same initials. I think the only way to handle this reliably is for the network administrator to assign the three-letter codes and use the User Login Scripts to set them up for WordPerfect. If you do not do so, users may end up using someone else's initials or not using the same initials every time.

Solution After you assign each user a three-letter code, you can tackle the user set-up file two ways. One is to let WordPerfect set up the file automatically when the user first logs in. Then it is up to the user to correctly choose printer set-up and data file locations. This is a risk: users who make the wrong choices may not get set up properly. However, in the short run, this means less work for the network administrator.

The other way to address the problem is for the network supervisor to create each of the user files. To create files for each user that correspond to the user initials, you can either copy WP{WP}.SET or just run WordPerfect using the users' codes:

```
NCOPY WP{WP}.SET WPxxx}.SET
```

Or just run WordPerfect using the user's initials:

```
WP /U=xxx
```

xxx corresponds to the user initials you want to use. I prefer this method because I usually have to set up the user options for the user. The items you must select for each user are:

Creating WordPerfect User Set-up Files

Mouse driver	SHIFT F1 1
Display options	SHIFT F1 2
Back-up options	SHIFT F1 3 1
Beep options	SHIFT F1 3 2
Cursor speed	SHIFT F1 3 3
Document summary	SHIFT F1 3 4
Fast save	SHIFT F1 3 5
Back-up file locations	SHIFT F1 6 1
Printer file location	SHIFT F1 6 4
Printer selection	SHIFT F7 S
Printer queue selection (network printer)	SHIFT F7 S E P *queuename*
Printer port selection (local printer)	SHIFT F7 S E P *port*
Font selection	CTRL F8 4

After you set these items appropriately for the user's preferences and hardware,

Press: F7 to exit WordPerfect.
Type: N after the save file prompt.
Type: Y after the exit prompt.

Establishing the WordPerfect User ID in a Login Script
Keywords: WordPerfect, user, initials

Scenario   The best way to handle the user initials for WordPerfect is in the Login Script. If you use User Login Scripts, add this command line to their Login Script:

```
DOS SET WPC="/U-xxx"
```

xxx corresponds to the user initials you set up for the user. If you use just a System Login Script, you must add a command line for each user similar to the

```
IF LOGIN_NAME = username THEN DOS SET WPC="/U-xxx"
```

This may be tedious, but you only need to do it once and then update it when you add users to or remove users from the network.

While you do this task, you may want to set other WordPerfect start-up parameters corresponding to the user's environment. The WordPerfect start-up parameters I find useful are:

/D-*drive*:*directory*   Instructs WordPerfect where to put overflow and temporary files. Sometimes it's useful to put these on the user's local hard disk to improve performance and reduce disk requirements on the file server. Changing this option also lets you omit Create, Write, and Delete (NetWare 386 Erase) rights from the WordPerfect directory. You can redirect the temporary files to the user's home directory.

/M-*macro*   Instructs WordPerfect to execute a macro immediately upon start up. I use this option to load a style sheet automatically for a user who always uses the same styles.

Establishing the WordPerfect User ID in a Login Script

/R   If the user has LIM 3.2 or LIM 4.0 compatible expanded memory, this option loads menus, overlays, and messages into this memory, speeding up WordPerfect substantially.

/X   Tells WordPerfect to restore the defaults from the user's .SET file. This option causes WordPerfect not to update the user's .SET file with any changes the user made during the session. The changes are active for the session; they are not permanent.

For a complete discussion of WordPerfect start-up options, read Appendix N of the WordPerfect manual.

Using a Network Printer

The final aspect of setting up WordPerfect on the LAN is using the printer itself. The user can select the type of printer with the Print menu (SHIFT F7 S). If the user presses 3 or E from the Select Printer menu, the Edit menu comes up. From this menu the user can choose option P to select a port or choose option 2 to select a shared print queue. To select a queue, the user then chooses option 8 or O (other). Otherwise, users can select which port their printer is attached to.

The problem with those menus is that they allow the user to select a printer type that is not assigned to the selected queue. WordPerfect does not know how the NetWare queues are assigned to various printers. You must teach your users which queues correspond to which printers.

Another aspect of shared printer use concerns print job definitions. (These are covered in Chapter 10.) Because NetWare uses print job definitions, you must make sure that the File Contents setting for the job definition used is set to Byte Stream, not Text. The printer drivers that WordPerfect uses send control characters to manage the printer. Also make sure that users do not include the TABS parameter in their CAPTURE or NPRINT commands.

Another point worth considering is multiple copies of a print job. WordPerfect has an option that allows the user to select multiple copies of the document, as does NetWare's CAPTURE and NPRINT commands. Also, once the print job is in the queue, you can change the number of copies desired with the PCONSOLE program prior to the job printing. Altogether, there are four different ways to specify the number of copies to print. You may wonder which is best.

The answer depends on your needs. If convenience is your most important criterion, selecting the number of copies in WordPerfect will be best. WordPerfect will reprocess the document for each copy. This might be quite time-consuming if the document is lengthy and includes graphics.

If speed is your most important criterion, then selecting the number of copies through a NetWare program option is best. Indicating multiple copies to NetWare and one copy for WordPerfect results in much faster printing from WordPerfect, since it only processes the file once. NetWare merely rewinds the print file for each copy. The end result is the same. Use the C= parameter for either CAPTURE or NPRINT. In PCONSOLE, you will have to select the proper queue and print job to change the number of copies.

In addition, if speed is important to you, you will find that you get better throughput by printing a file in WordPerfect and then using NetWare's NPRINT command to print the file. You can set up WordPerfect to do this by selecting "Other" during the printer port selection (SHIFT F7 S E). You will find substantial improvement when using graphics or soft fonts in your documents.

Printing Lotus 1-2-3 Files

The most widely installed spreadsheet is Lotus Development Corporation's 1-2-3. The first section of this chapter covered potential problems using this product in considerable detail. The topic of the earlier section was handling 1-2-3's configuration files, 123.SET and 123.CNF. If you have problems with 1-2-3 hardware configurations, review that section.

The 1-2-3 topic I will discuss in this section is data files and printing. 1-2-3 is a LAN product—it can run on a network. The question is, "How LAN aware is 1-2-3?" The answer, unfortunately, is "Not very!" 1-2-3 does not support NetWare's shared printer/queue arrangement. You must issue a CAPTURE command before entering 1-2-3 to tell it to print to the network printer, not a local printer. The 1-2-3 installation program only permits you to select four text printers and 23 graphics printers. The 23 graphics printers are adequate for most LANs, but the four text printers fall quite short.

You encounter the same problem with 1-2-3 that you run into with so many other LAN applications. It is entirely possible and very likely that a user will select a printer type inappropriate for the queue that the user's job is going to use. This frustrates the user a great deal.

Another problem is "shared" spreadsheet files that more than one user can access. Lotus 1-2-3 is a RAM-based application: after the spreadsheet is retrieved into the workstation's RAM, it is closed on the file server. This potentially allows other users to load the same spreadsheet into their RAM. This can result in one user's changes overwriting the changes made by the user who saved the file first. The file attributes shareable and non-shareable have no impact on this problem. Shareable only affects the ability to have the file "open" by more than one user. After a spreadsheet is retrieved into RAM, it is no longer open.

Lotus 1-2-3 has adequate protection for this. Before retrieving the spreadsheet, the user places a reservation on the spreadsheet. The user can reserve several files at once. This is important because 1-2-3 can link cells from several spreadsheets.

SUMMARY

This chapter might be the most important in the book in terms of helping you better understand how some applications behave in a NetWare environment. You must understand and apply the concepts presented in this chapter to any software that you install. By pointing out both general and specific problems, I have tried to show you how to approach this topic systematically.

It is clear to me that the job of a network administrator is much like a detective's when it comes to applications running on the LAN. The vendor's documentation generally does not clearly explain how software interacts with the network. I always follow the manufacturer's guidelines first, then modify them to suit the needs of a particular network. I hope that this chapter has provided clues to where to look to solve certain types of application problems. The next part of the book covers the task of setting up shared printers, a very important aspect of setting up the LAN.

Part IV
Printing Problems

Printing is an integral part of any PC application. Networks offer the benefit of increased flexibility by allowing users to have access to printers that are not necessarily attached to their PC, but located elsewhere on the network. As is usually the case, increased flexibility comes at the cost of additional complexity. Unfortunately, the complexities of network printing are not easy to unravel. This section will discuss printing in a NetWare environment and offer guidelines for solving specific problems.

10
Setting up Shared Printing

Novell provides print server software with NetWare 286 version 2.15 rev. C and above and with NetWare 386. This product was released in the summer of 1990. With a single copy of the NetWare print server, you may share up to 16 printers. Multiple licenses of the print server software are available for larger networks.

The print server manages printing jobs on various printers. The print server may be either the file server or a workstation that is configured to be a dedicated print server. The print server software for Netware 286 contains two versions of the print server program:

> PSERVER.VAP   For NetWare 286 file servers that will be print servers
>
> PSERVER.EXE   For workstations that will be print servers

The print server software for Netware 386 contains two versions of the print server program:

> PSERVER.NLM   For NetWare 386 file servers that will be print servers
>
> PSERVER.EXE   For workstations that will be print servers

You can attach shared printers to the print server using a COM or LPT port, or attach them to any workstation on the network. For workstations that are going to share their printer, files that come with the print server are:

RPRINTER.EXE	Workstation resident module
RPRINTER.HLP	Help file
RPRINT$$.EXE	Workstation transient code

In addition, the remote workstation must have access to the files SYS$HELP.DAT, SYS$MSG.HLP, and ???$RUN.OVL.

The workstation that is sharing its printer does not have to be logged into the network, but the workstation shell files must be loaded. Therefore, I recommend that you copy these workstation files into the SYS:LOGIN directory, rather than the SYS:PUBLIC directory where the installation program copies them.

SETTING UP THE SHARED PRINTING ENVIRONMENT

Novell's documentation does not provide very good instructions for all the tasks needed to correctly set up the shared printing environment. In my experience, over 90 percent of the problems that people experience when trying to use shared printers are related to set-up. Table 10-1 outlines the tasks you must complete to create the proper environment for shared printing using the NetWare programs.

As you see, seven different tasks and seven different programs are required to get the job done. None of the tasks is particularly difficult.

Setting up the Shared Printing Environment

Table 10-1. Setting up Shared Printers

Task	Program Used	Objective	Reason
1	PRINTDEF	Define the type of printers used and how they work.	NetWare can put the printer into various modes at the start of a print job. This is used with software that does not include printer drivers.
2	PCONSOLE	Define the print server, shared printers, queue names, queue users, queue operators, queue assignments, queue priority, printer notification list, form change option.	This is the step where the basic implementation of your printing environment is made.
3	PRINTCON	Define print job set-up information.	NetWare uses the print job definitions to decide what setting to put the printer into at the start of the print job.
4	NCOPY	Copy the PRINTCON.DAT file to a directory that users can access.	Separate PRINTCON.DAT files for each user does not work in most environments.
5	SMODE	Change the programs that access the PRINTCON.DAT file so that those programs search the user's path.	PCONSOLE, CAPTURE, NPRINT, and PRINTCON look for the PRINTCON.DAT file in each user's SYS:MAIL\userid directory.
6	PSERVER	Load the print server software on the file server or a dedicated workstation.	The print server software manages the printing tasks.
7	RPRINTER	Load the remote workstation resident software.	Workstations with shared printers attached must have this software loaded.

TASK 1—DEFINING PRINTERS

The task of defining print devices is done with the NetWare PRINTDEF program. Printers have to be defined so that NetWare will be able to reset the printer and initiate printer modes for various print jobs.

Who's Controlling the Printer?

Anyone who has ever purchased a new printer and spent several hours reinstalling or reconfiguring dozens of software application packages is acutely aware of a major shortcoming of the PC-DOS/MS-DOS computing world. That shortcoming is that DOS knows very little about printers and how to activate and deactivate their various features. Therefore, each software application that wants to use the features of the printer must be capable of sending the appropriate control information to the printer itself.

The technical term for this problem is **device dependence**. In most applications, the software vendor supplies special software programs called *printer drivers* which work with the main application programs to use the features of the printer. Since each software vendor does this for its own software, the printer drivers must be installed and changed for each software package for the installed printer and then changed again if a different printer is installed later.

However, not all software applications use printer drivers because they don't generally access the special features of the printer. Many database programs, accounting, and management reporting systems offer only the type style and spacing of a very standard printer. This software can't use any other printer features.

This is the current state of affairs in the DOS printing world. Sometimes the application controls printing; sometimes the default or most recent printer settings control printing.

However, users want to use different fonts, line spacing, pitch, or orientation with software that offers no printer drivers. Novell NetWare has attempted to bridge this gap. NetWare can initiate various printer features by sending the appropriate printer

Task 1—Defining Printers

commands to the printer. *You can only issue these printer commands at the start of a print job. Therefore, any features activated apply to the entire print job: you cannot turn them on and off during the print job.*

Creating Printer Definitions with PRINTDEF

With this program, you create Printer Definition Files (.PDF) that NetWare uses to control the printer and define the forms that you can assign to various print jobs. NetWare v2.15 comes with an installation diskette labelled PUBLIC-9 which has sample PDF files that you can use as a starting point for many printer definition files.

During this process, you need the manual that comes with your printer. You will enter the control codes used to activate various printer functions into the PDF file. The next sections describe the three steps in creating a printer definition file. They are assigning a name that identifies the printer, entering control codes for the functions that your printer can perform, and combining functions to create printer modes.

Assigning a Printer Name

Figure 10-1 shows the first screen of the PRINTDEF program, a menu that you use to choose to define either a print device or a form.

After you select Print Device, you see the menu shown in Figure 10-2. You can choose to edit an existing device, import a device from an existing PDF file, or export a device you have defined to its own PDF file.

> **NOTE:** The PDF files from version 2.15 are in the PUBLIC directory or on the PUBLIC-9 diskette. You can import them directly from one of these sources.

After you select Edit Print Devices, the screen shown in Figure 10-3 appears. It lists any pre-existing print devices. To add a new printer to the list, press INS. Type the printer's name and then press ENTER. The name appears on the list of printers.

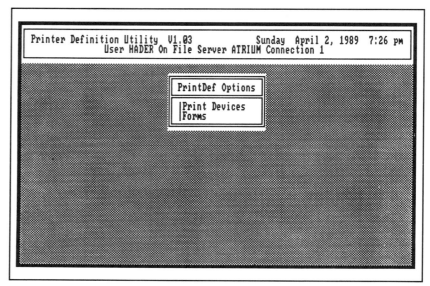

Figure 10-1. PrintDef Options menu

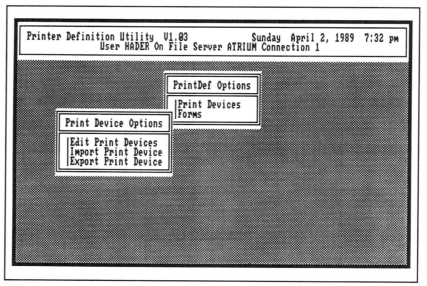

Figure 10-2. Print Device Options menu

Task 1—Defining Printers

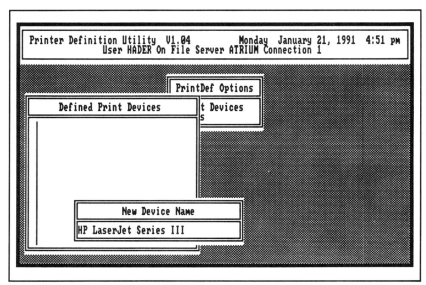

Figure 10-3. New device name

After you have defined the name of the print device you must complete two tasks. The PrintDef Options screen shown in Figure 10-4 presents two selections. *Choose the second selection Device Functions first*.

Device Functions

Device functions define all types of special capabilities that an output device can use at the beginning of a print job. To complete this task, you need the manual that comes with your printer. You do not need to define all functions in your printer manual, only those that you want NetWare to use at the beginning of a print job. For example, it is unlikely that you need to define the *underline* function, unless you plan to underline everything in the entire print job.

> **NOTE:** The function you must define in all cases is the function for resetting the printer to its default settings. If you do not define this function, jobs are printed using the last settings activated in the printer.

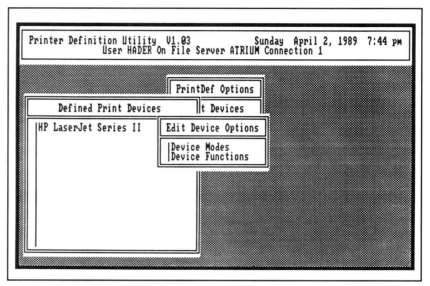

Figure 10-4. Edit Device Options menu

Control codes look like technological gibberish to most new PC users and, to a large extent, they are. But to get our print device to work, we have to enter them on the Function Definition Form shown in Figure 10-5. To get started, we need to define the features we want that a software application package does not already offer.

The device manual for your printer lists control codes in one of three formats: decimal, hexadecimal, or ASCII. Better manuals list all three. Decimal codes are sets of numbers, usually two or three digits per number and two to four numbers per set. Hexadecimal codes are two-character numeric or alphanumeric codes. The highest alphabetic character is F. ASCII characters usually start with ESC or ^[(which represents the Escape character) or CTRL or ^ (which represents the Control character). A series of standard keyboard characters follows the Escape or Control character. Here are examples of all three types of control codes from the Hewlett Packard LaserJet Series II Printer User's Manual:

Task 1—Defining Printers

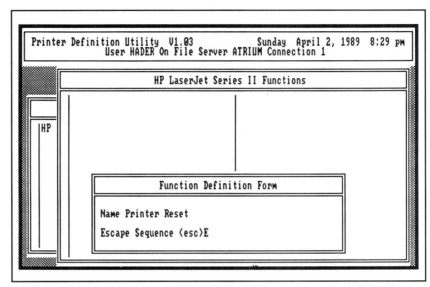

Figure 10-5. Function Definition Form

Function	Decimal	Hex	ASCII
Printer Reset	027 069	1B 45	Esc E
8 Lines per Inch	027 038 108 056 068	1B 26 6C 38 44	Esc &l8D
16.66 Characters per Inch	027 038 107 050 083	1B 26 6B 32 53	Esc &k2S

Fortunately, the PRINTDEF program can use ASCII codes, which are the easiest. If your printer manual doesn't have ASCII codes, you need a conversion table. (There is one in the back of the IBM Basic manual and most software manuals.)

Device Modes

The next process is to build **modes** from the functions that you define. A mode is a combination of functions that produces a desired setting for the print device. For example, you may wish to print a report on the laser printer that uses landscape (horizontal) orientation and 16.66 characters per inch.

NOTE: You must define Re-initialize mode for all printers. NetWare uses this mode to reset the printer for the next print job. The Re-initialize mode is usually made up of one function, Reset. The Re-initialize mode will be used whenever no job definition is specified.

Use the Printer Mode list illustrated in Figure 10-6 to assign a mode name. Then press ENTER. The window shown in Figure 10-7 appears, listing the functions used to create the particular mode.

To add new functions from the list of functions already created, press INS. The list of existing functions shown in Figure 10-8 appears. Repeat this process until you have chosen all the functions needed for the particular mode.

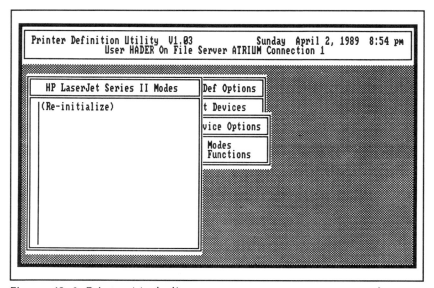

Figure 10-6. Printer Mode list

Task 1—Defining Printers

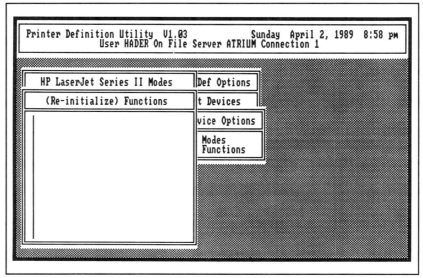

Figure 10-7. Printer modes and functions

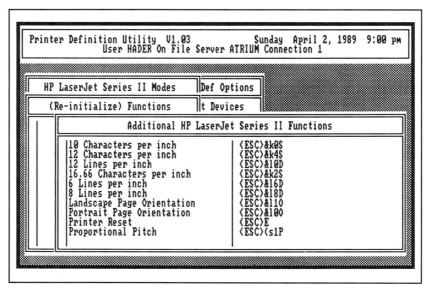

Figure 10-8. Printer Function list

> **NOTE:** Always begin modes with the Reset function. This assures that the printer's previous settings are released before the print job.

The number of modes you create depends on the number of different settings that you need NetWare to initiate, as opposed to those features that your application software initiates. Each printer installed should have its own list of functions and modes.

TASK 2—CREATING THE PRINT SERVER

The print server software comes with a completely revised version of the PCONSOLE program. This new version does most of the required set-up work for the print server. However, before using PCONSOLE, you need to design your shared printing environment on paper by answering these questions:

- Where are the shared printers located? What kind of printers are they? What port on the PC do they use?
- What queues are going to be needed? Who can use each queue? Who are the queue operators?
- To which printer(s) will each queue be assigned? At what priority?
- Which form change option do you want to use for each printer?
- Who do you want notified when the printer is out of paper or off line?
- Which users or groups will be print server operators?

Figure 10-9 illustrates a network where the print server software runs on the file server. Two shared printers are attached to the print server (file server) and two printers are attached to local workstations. Each printer was assigned a printer number during the print server definition. In addition, queues were assigned to each printer. Multiple queues assigned to the same printer may be given different priorities.

Task 2—Creating the Print Server

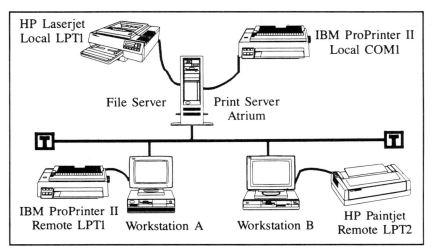

Figure 10-9. Network print server and printers

Table 10-2 outlines the various components of the NetWare PCONSOLE program that you use to create the queues and print servers. Each column in the table represents a menu level; each row represents an option that you select from a menu.

Printer Configuration

A print server can service up to 16 printers, each of which must be defined according to the items listed in Table 10-3.

Creating Queues, Queue Users, and Queue Operators

When you install NetWare with NETGEN, you also select any printer ports that are going to be used for network printers. You assign each port a printer number from 0 through 4. In addition, NetWare creates queues for each printer: PRINTQ__0, PRINTQ__1, PRINTQ__2, etc. NetWare also assumes that you will assign PRINTQ__0 to printer P0, PRINTQ__1 to P1, and so on.

With NetWare, you can create as many additional queues as you need, and you can assign queues to printers in whatever fashion you need. For instance, in NetWare, the same printer can service

Table 10-2. PCONSOLE Program

Primary Option	Menu Option		Menu/Display		
Change Current File Server	Select Server from list				
Print Queue Information	Select Queue from List				
		Current Print Job Entries	Select Print Job from List		
		Current Queue Status	Displays Status Enable/Disable New Entries		
		Currently Attached Servers	Displays List		
		Print Queue ID	Displays Queue's ID		
		Queue Operators	Displays List	<INS> Select Operators from Users & Groups List	
		Queue Servers	Displays List	<INS> Select Servers from List	
		Queue Users	Displays List	<INS> Select Users from Users & Groups List	
Print Server Information	Select Server from List				
		Change Password	Enter New Password		
		Full Name	Assign Name		
		Print Server Configuration			
		File Servers Serviced	Displays List	<INS> Select Servers from List	
		Notify List for Printer	Displays Installed Printers	Displays List	<INS> Select from Users & Group List
		Printer Configuration	Select Printer to Install	Define Printer Information	
		Queues Serviced by Printer	Displays Installed Printers	Displays Queues Attached	<INS> Select Queue

Task 2—Creating the Print Server

Table 10-3. Printer Configuration Items

Name	Setting/Explanation
Printer Name	Optional. The default is PRINTER x. This is a name to describe the type of printer.
Type	Type of printer connection:
	Parallel, LPT1 Remote Parallel, LPT1
	Parallel, LPT2 Remote Parallel, LPT2
	Parallel, LPT3 Remote Parallel, LPT3
	Serial, COM1 Remote Serial, COM1
	Serial, COM2 Remote Serial, COM2
	Serial, COM3 Remote Serial, COM3
	Serial, COM4 Remote Serial, COM4
	Defined Elsewhere
	Defined elsewhere applies when the printer has been defined on another server.
Use Interrupts	This setting should be Yes if the printer port is configured to use interrupts. If set to No, the CPU must poll the port periodically for activity which wastes CPU time and slows down the computer.
IRQ	The interrupt setting for the printer port.
Buffer Size	This is the amount of RAM you want to establish at the print server as a printer buffer. Larger buffers may help on print servers servicing graphics files.
Starting Form	This setting determines which form the print server assumes is loaded when each time the print server is initialized. This is the form number established in PRINTDEF.
Queue Service Mode	Change Forms As Needed—This mode requires form changes whenever the next job is set to a different form.
	Minimize Forms Changes—This mode causes the print server to print all jobs in the highest priority queue requiring the current form first before requesting a form change.
	Minimize Forms Changes Across Queues—This mode causes all jobs using the same form in all of the attached queues to be printed before requiring a form change.
	Never Change Forms—This mode causes the print server to never request a form change.
Baud Data Bits Stop Bits Parity XON/XOFF	Serial printers must have these elements of serial communications defined for the printer.

two queues. This is useful when you need queues that have different priorities. You can assign a queue to a printer with a stated priority. On the other hand, more than one printer can service a single queue. This is useful when you have many print jobs and two or more identical printers. Figure 10-10 illustrates these concepts.

Use the PCONSOLE program and its Available Options menu (Figure 10-11) to create queues, queue users, and queue operators. This task takes but a few moments. Only queue users are allowed to place print jobs in the queue. Queue operators can manage the jobs in the queue, resequencing and deleting them or placing them on hold.

You add and maintain print queues by selecting the Print Queue Information option. This opens the window illustrated in Figure 10-12, displaying a list of existing queues. To create a new queue, press INS, type a name for the queue, and then press ENTER.

After you add the queue, select it, and the menu of queue-related options shown in Figure 10-13 appears.

With the choices, Queue Users and Queue Operators, you can add or change the users who can place print jobs in the queue and who can manage print jobs in the queue. Queue users and queue operators can be any combination of valid users or groups.

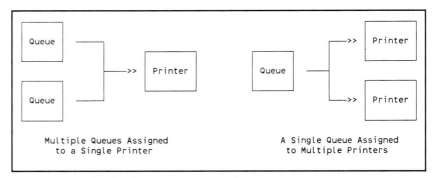

Figure 10-10. Assigning queues to printers

Task 2—Creating the Print Server

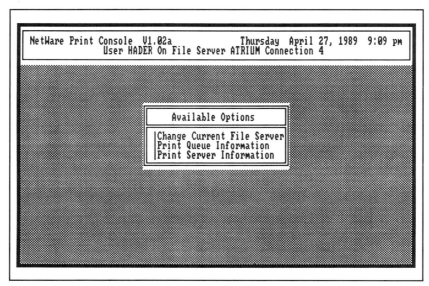

Figure 10-11. PCONSOLE Available Options menu

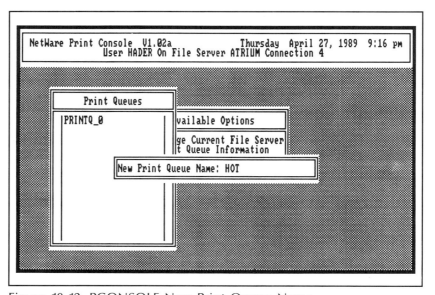

Figure 10-12. PCONSOLE New Print Queue Name

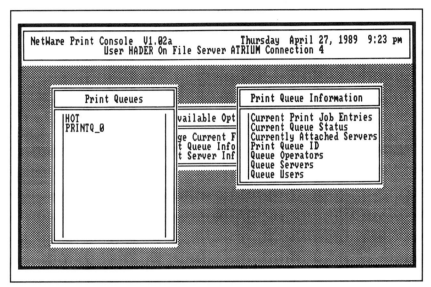

Figure 10-13. PCONSOLE Print Queue Information menu

> **NOTE:** Many organizations set up queues for each department and then make one or two users the queue operator for a department. This tends to decentralize some of the management of print jobs.

TASK 3—CREATING PRINT JOB DEFINITIONS WITH PRINTCON

To explain this step, I must digress a little. You access shared printers in NetWare by using the CAPTURE or NPRINT commands. Both have a myriad of parameters. *However, none of these parameters lets you select either a printer or a printer mode. Therefore, to use the printer modes created with the PRINTDEF program, you must create a corresponding print job definition with PRINTCON.* The J= parameter corresponds to the print job.

If your software controls the printer adequately, then all you need to do is define a standard print job as the default print job. This default print job should require no special printing modes, except

Task 3—Creating Print Job Definitions with PRINTCON

the one required to initialize the printer. Furthermore, you need to define a default print job for each different type of shared printer. This takes care of most routine printing when the application software has printer drivers and knows how to control the printer.

For other printing, when NetWare controls the printer using the printer's special modes that the application software does not offer, you need to define a print job for each special mode you want NetWare to use on each shared printer.

NetWare can initiate printer modes at the beginning of a print job. It cannot, however, change modes during a print job. For example, at the start of a print job, NetWare can use a previously defined mode so that a laser printer prints landscape orientation and condensed print. This mode would have been defined earlier using the PRINTDEF program. However, NetWare cannot change modes while the job is printing to underline the heading and then print non-underlined text during the same job.

> **NOTE:** At least one print job should correspond to each printer mode created in PRINTDEF; otherwise, the mode will never be able to be used.
>
> If no print job definitions exist, NetWare uses a set of default settings which do not print graphics and downloadable fonts properly!

The opening PRINTCON menu is similar to the one shown in Figure 10-14.

Select Edit Print Job Configurations to see a window displaying currently defined print jobs. The first print job you must create is the one used when no specific job name is issued with the CAPTURE or NPRINT commands. The print job definition screen looks like the one shown in Figure 10-15.

Several items on this form concern us. I have listed them according to the printing area they affect.

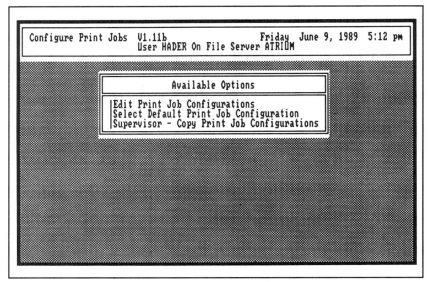

Figure 10-14. PRINTCON Available Options menu

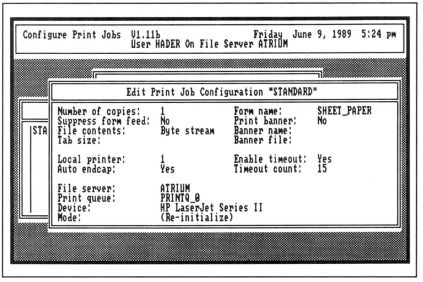

Figure 10-15. PRINTCON Job Definition form

Task 3—Creating Print Job Definitions with PRINTCON

File Types	Software Type	Printer and Mode
File Contents	Auto Endcap	Device
Tab Size	Enable Timeout	Mode
		Print Queue

File Contents

The File Contents setting has two options: Text and Byte Stream. The default setting is Text. Text type causes NetWare to attempt to interpret any control codes into printable characters. Byte Stream causes NetWare to pass control characters directly to the printer without interpretation. To print graphics correctly or use downloadable fonts, the correct setting for File Contents is Byte Stream. The correct setting for any print job where you are using a printer mode established in PRINTDEF is Text. There are probably no control codes in the file if you are using a NetWare printer mode to activate printing features. Text files print faster than Byte Stream files.

Tab Size

The Tab Size option only applies to text file contents. Any tab character expands to the number of spaces indicated. This is another source of problems when you do not specify the correct file contents type. In a byte stream file, a tab character passes directly to the printer without change.

Auto Endcap

NetWare knows a print job is complete when it receives an end-of-file character from the application creating the print job. If Auto Endcap is On and NetWare receives no end-of-file character, NetWare closes the print job when the application finishes and the user exits the program. If Auto Endcap is Off and NetWare receives no end-of-file character, NetWare discards the print job if the application finishes.

Enable Timeout

When the user exits the program, the setting for Auto Endcap determines the print job's status. Many older PC programs do not send an end-of-file character; therefore, the job never prints until the user exits the program. If Enable Timeout if set to Off (the default) and NetWare receives no end-of-file character, NetWare keeps the print job open even when the application is finished sending data. If Enable Timeout is set to On, NetWare waits a specified number of seconds for more data. If it receives no additional data, the print job is closed and ready to print.

Set the number of seconds generously, especially for printing databases and graphics. Often, extensive calculations are required to print these and if the timeout period is too short, the print job may be closed prematurely.

Device

With the Device option, you can select a previously defined print device for a particular print job.

Mode

Use the Mode option to select the appropriate mode for the printer you want to use. For the default job, the mode should be Re-initialize. If you want NetWare to set up the printer for a job, select a mode from the list created earlier in PRINTDEF.

Print Queue

Finally, select the queue that this job will be placed in. Obviously, the queue chosen should be assigned to the printer that you selected.

TASKS 4 AND 5—COPYING JOB DEFINITIONS TO OTHER USERS

The last item that must be done in PRINTCON is to copy the print job definitions to other users. The file that contains the print job definitions is called PRINTCON.DAT. It is located in the \MAIL\userid directory of the user who created the print job definitions. (If the Supervisor account was used, the userid for Supervisor is 1.) This file needs to be in each user's \MAIL\userid directory. You can use the PRINTCON menu selection, Supervisor—Copy Print Job Configurations, to do this. Unfortunately, this option does not allow you to copy into several users' directories at once.

Actually, here's a good idea that has gone amiss. NetWare wants these PRINTCON.DAT files in each user's MAIL directory on the premise that users want to define their own custom print jobs. Experience has taught me that this doesn't work. First, most users don't know enough about the print job definitions to use them correctly. Second, if users change their own PRINTCON.DAT files, the supervisor can never change them unless the supervisor logs in as each user.

What is needed is one universal print job database, PRINTCON.DAT, accessible to everyone. Before you create it, you must solve two problems:

- Where to locate PRINTCON.DAT so that everyone can access it. A good candidate is the PUBLIC directory.
- How to change the behavior of CAPTURE.EXE, NPRINT.EXE, and PCONSOLE.EXE, which look for a PRINTCON.DAT in the user's own MAIL directory.

You can solve this problem with the SMODE command, changing these programs' search modes to value 5, so they search the user's path for PRINTCON.DAT.

Now the shared printer environment is complete. Now users can send jobs to the shared printers with the CAPTURE or NPRINT commands and the J=*jobname* parameter specifying which print job setting to use. If the J= parameter is omitted, NetWare uses the default job established in PRINTCON.

TASK 6—LOADING AND USING PSERVER

There are three varieties of PSERVER: PSERVER.NLM, PSERVER.VAP, and PSERVER.EXE. The next three sections describe them.

PSERVER.NLM

PSERVER.NLM is a NetWare loadable module for establishing a print server at the file server. It loads on the file server running NetWare 386 and provides basic management functions for print servers. It displays the current status of the 16 possible shared printers. Once you have loaded this file, you can use the ALT-ESC combination to return to the colon prompt. From the colon prompt, you can unload PSERVER with the command UNLOAD PSERVER printserver.

PSERVER.VAP

PSERVER.VAP is a NetWare 286 version of PSERVER.NLM for providing a print server on a NetWare 286 file server. It provides basic management functions for the print servers. From the colon prompt, you can unload PSERVER with the command PSERVER STOP. You can restart it with PSERVER START.

PSERVER.EXE

PSERVER.EXE is an executable module that loads at a dedicated workstation to provide print server services. This version's display looks like PSERVER.NLM's display. It reports the status of up to 16 printers in the network. Only the PCONSOLE program can unload it.

TASK 7—USING RPRINTER FOR REMOTE PRINT SERVERS

RPRINTER is the program you use to share a workstation printer in non-dedicated mode. The syntax for RPRINTER is

```
RPRINTER print_server printer number
```

Task 7—Using RPRINTER for Remote Print Servers

For RPRINTER to work, a version of PSERVER must be running on either the file server or a dedicated print server.

RPRINTER becomes a memory-resident program on the workstation and requires about 9K of RAM. *It is loaded after IPX and NET but the workstation does not have to be logged in.* The workstation needs access to the files:

RPRINTER.EXE	SYS$MSG.DAT
RPRINT$$.EXE	IBM$RUN.OVL
RPRINTER.HLP	SYS$HELP.DAT

If you are using the SHELL.CFG Short Machine Type, you need a copy of xxxx$RUN.OVL corresponding to the Short Machine Type. These files can be either on the local workstation or you can copy them into the LOGIN directory on the server.

RPRINTER can be removed from the workstation's RAM by typing:

RPRINTER *printserver printer number -r*.

> **WARNING:** The RPRINTER program presents a potential problem. Even though RPRINTER has been loaded at the workstation to make the workstation's printer a shared network printer, the workstation's user can still print directly to the printer with the NetWare CAPTURE or NPRINT commands. Unfortunately, if this happens while another job is printing on the printer, the result is garbled print with the output from two different jobs mixed together. Therefore, the workstation's user should always use the CAPTURE or NPRINT command to send jobs to the printer.

SUMMARY

This chapter has covered the details of setting up the printing environment for NetWare in a concise manner. With this information you should be equipped to set up and maintain shared printers. You should review the NetWare CAPTURE and NPRINT commands, which send jobs to the shared printers. In the following chapter, I will discuss specific problems that occur in using shared printers.

11
Printing Problems in a Network Environment

No other problem causes users more disillusionment with a network than improperly printed jobs. Most people's computer work results in a finished, hard copy document of some sort. Naturally we want to see our work in its final form, neatly printed, and ready to impress. Printing problems are unsettling to users. When jobs do not print properly, users' confidence in the computer, the software, and the network rapidly erodes. It's even more frustrating when users' jobs print just fine on their local printer, but do not print the same way on the network's printers.

Two areas that cause problems for NetWare users are printing graphics and using laser printers. Usually, these problems occur when users attempt to print graphics on a shared network printer, not when users print to their locally connected printer. You can overcome most problems if you understand how to set up the users' environment for these activities.

In this chapter, I'll explore many printing problems commonly encountered in the network environment, particularly problems with printing images on a shared printer. My goal is to inform you of known problems and, whenever possible, provide step-by-step solutions.

PRINTING GRAPHICS

Several circumstances can make the task of printing graphic images on a network printer problematic:

- The application software's configuration and setup.
- The settings for the print job definition being used.
- The parameters issued with the user's CAPTURE command.

You must consider each item when you try to solve problems associated with printing graphic images on a shared printer. In the next few scenarios, I'll discuss each item and make specific recommendations for setting up the users' environment correctly.

Improperly Configured Applications
Keywords: printing, configuration files, application

Scenario

A commonly overlooked problem with printing graphics in a network environment is configuring the application for the correct printing device. Due to a lack of standards, different printers have different software interfaces (i.e., control character sequences) that are used to invoke various printer functions. To print graphics, you need a software program called a **driver** that sends the correct control characters to invoke a function to the printer. Therefore, the application must be configured for the printer being used. This can be complicated in a network.

In a network environment with shared printers available to users, the application software must know which printer the user intends to use. Users can generally access shared printers and printers attached to their workstation. If the application software does not permit the selection of the printer type within the program itself, printing on shared printers of different types is cumbersome at best.

Consider Lotus 1-2-3. It uses a configuration file called 123.SET to figure out the type of printer being used. The software reads this file when the application starts. After the application is running, it's impossible to change the printer defined in 123.SET.

This causes two problems. First, you need different versions of the configuration file, depending on the printer. Chapter 8 discusses how to configure NetWare so that the configuration files are in directories other than the user's default directory or the directory where the application was installed. This permits you to configure the application for the correct configuration file based upon which machine the user is using.

Second, many users can access various types of printers that are configured to be shared network printers. An application like Lotus 1-2-3 that uses a configuration file at start up provides no way for the user to select a different printer from within the application. In these cases, the user must exit the software, perform some task to change the configuration file being used, and then start the application again. This is hardly convenient or user friendly, but if the user does not complete these tasks, the probable result is a garbled print job or even a hung printer.

Solution

The most common problem with using application software on a network is not having the correct printer driver in effect for the printer that the user is using. It's developing procedures for users to follow when they have the opportunity to use different types of printers. The network's complexity and software's inflexibility combined with the users' limited understanding of these problems spell printing trouble unless you do the following:

Create: a configuration file scheme similar to the one outlined in Chapter 8 to locate the correct configuration files automatically, based on the user's workstation configuration.

Create: menu selections that permit the user to choose a printer.

Make sure: the proper configuration files will be available for the user and the printer chosen.

Teach: the user how to make selections (if the software permits printer selection) and how the network is configured in relation to these selections.

Improper Print Job Definitions
Keywords: printing, print jobs, timeout, CAPTURE

Scenario

When a job is printed on a shared network printer, NetWare uses the print job definition parameters established by the job name specified in the CAPTURE or NPRINT command (J=*jobname*), or the parameters set for the default job if no job parameter was given. Any job definition used for printing graphics should include the following settings:

File contents:	Byte stream
Tabs:	None

Graphic files typically print slowly due to the complexities of calculating a bit-mapped image. Therefore, the job definition's setting for Enable Timeout and Timeout Count must be carefully set. If the application does not send an end-of-file character after the job, use Enable Timeout. The Timeout Count setting must allocate enough time for the job to complete. If it is too short, the NetWare print spooler closes the file prematurely, and parts of the image print on separate pages. You can also establish the Timeout Count setting with the CAPTURE command's TI= parameter.

Printing a graphic image with an incorrect job definition results in garbled data and partial images printed on each page. These problems can also result in the printer hanging up or being knocked off-line.

Solution

Make sure that the print job definitions used with graphic print jobs have the File Contents parameter set to Byte Stream and the Timeout Count is long enough so that the print file doesn't close prematurely.

Problem Using the CAPTURE Command
Keywords: printing, CAPTURE, timeout, queues

Scenario

Used at the workstation, the CAPTURE command redirects the output of a printing task from the user's local printer to a shared network printer. This command can cause problems that stem from a few different situations implied in the last scenario. In this scenario, I'll discuss each in more detail.

Incorrect use of the CAPTURE command can cause three major problems:

- Users can redirect printing from their local printer to a shared network printer. If the application they are using is configured for their local printer and the network printer is a different type, users must reconfigure their software before printing. Users often forget to do this or don't know how.

- Users can specify the TI= parameter that governs how long the print spooler waits for more data before automatically closing the print job's queue file. Impatient users often set this parameter to a value insufficient for the job, as evidenced by partially printed pages.

- Perhaps the most severe problem with user-issued CAPTURE commands is misuse of the Q= parameter. This parameter lets a user send a job to any queue that the user is entitled to use and also overrides the queue specified in the job definition. The problem is that during print server configuration, queues are assigned to specific printers. The user may not understand these assignments. Obviously, if the user takes a print job that the software is configuring to print on a laser printer and sends it to a queue assigned to a dot matrix printer, garbled printing results. Unfortunately, NetWare does not catch this problem because it assumes that the user knows how to use the Q= parameter of the CAPTURE command.

Problem Using the CAPTURE Command

Solution These CAPTURE command problems are minimized when the CAPTURE command is issued for the user through a batch file of menu script created by the network administrator, who understands the implications of these conditions. The problems usually occur when users are permitted to issue these commands independently but do not understand either the command or the configuration of shared printers and queues on the network.

USING LASER, LED ARRAY, AND THERMAL TRANSFER PRINTERS

I suspect that laser printers make up the fastest growing segment of the high quality printing market. LED array printers are similar to laser printers, but use a different technology for emitting light onto the photosensitive drum. Thermal transfer printers are top-of-the-line color printers for applications demanding high resolution color graphics. These three types of printers have capabilities unparalleled in dot matrix and character printers. Their capabilities include multiple fonts and point sizes that can be internal, downloadable, or cartridge based, text and image rotation, duplex printing, multiple paper trays, and more.

Improperly Printing Laser Printers
Keywords: printing, laser printer, control codes

Scenario

The increased flexibility that laser, LED array, and thermal transfer printers offer requires a more complex printer control language to manage all the features available. Usually, drivers that must be installed for each software application control these printers. Many software applications supply a wide range of printer drivers for these printers. Usually, the application software controls the printer in the NetWare environment, as in DOS.

For applications that do not have printer drivers, see Chapter 8. It discusses how to create printer and print job definitions that put the job in a given mode when it starts a print job. Even with the proper configurations in PRINTDEF (defining the printers and how they work) and PRINTCON (defining the print job configurations), another problem can appear: the buffer space NetWare uses to contain the control codes for the printer can be exhausted. The default size of the buffer for initial codes is only 64 bytes. The size of the buffer for the reset functions is only 16 bytes.

Solution

If buffer space is exhausted, the job prints improperly. Exactly what happens depends on the circumstances. The job may be garbled or the printer may hang. You can expand these buffers by adding a couple of commands to the workstation's SHELL.CFG or NET.CFG file:

```
PRINT HEADER =
PRINT TAIL =
```

The allowable range for the print header is 64 to 255 bytes. The range for the print tail is 16 to 64 bytes. Increasing buffer size generally solves problems with downloadable fonts and Postscript printing.

USING PLOTTERS AS SHARED NETWORK PRINTERS

The other type of print device commonly used to print graphics is the plotter. Plotters print using a pen-like device to draw the image. Most plotters can print four to sixteen colors. The print control mechanism uses the appropriate pen for each color.

Printing to a Shared Plotter
Keywords: printing, plotter, queue

Scenario

The problem with shared plotters is that many software applications interact directly with the plotter during the printing process. In other words, not only does the software send control characters and data to the plotter, but the application awaits responses from the plotter itself. Although this is not true of all software that prints to a plotter, it is the norm for applications such as CAD (computer aided design), CAE (computer aided engineering), and other graphic design software.

In a shared environment, output from the application does not go directly to the print device (i.e., the plotter). It is placed in a disk file on the file server. This is the source of the problem. The application "thinks" that it is sending data directly to the plotter but it is actually sending it to a disk file. When the application pauses for a response from the plotter, the file server does not respond as the plotter would. As a result, printing to the plotter via the network does not work.

Solution

Most plotters must be directly attached to a workstation that is running the application that requires the plotter. Another available solution involves more hardware. A new category of specialized print server has a small box attached directly to the LAN cabling. Shared printers can be attached to this device, without being attached to a workstation. Users establish a virtual connection between their PC and this device. This connection lets the plotter communicate back and forth to the application as if the plotter were attached locally to the PC. Presently, a couple of vendors make these devices:

NetPort	**LanPort**
Intel Corporation	Microtest
(800) 538-3373	(800) 526-9675

MISCELLANEOUS PROBLEMS

This section covers a variety of problems that are difficult to categorize into general sections because they are specific to a given situation. Of course, in one way or another, they all affect the task of printing in a network environment.

RPRINTER Not Loading Properly at the Workstation
Keywords: printing, remote workstations, RPRINTER, print server

Scenario   The NetWare print server allows shared printers to be attached to workstations on the network. These printers are called **remote printers**. The workstation that has a remote printer attached must run a program called RPRINTER that notifies the print server of the remote printer and its printer number as established in the print server set-up done with the PCONSOLE program. The problem occurs when the RPRINTER program is run while the print server is still performing some internal checking immediately after the print server is loaded at either the file server or a dedicated print server PC. The error message is

```
Unable to attach to print server SERVERNAME. Error(66)
Unable to complete initialization process.
```

Solution   This is mostly a timing problem caused by the workstation attempting to load RPRINTER too soon after the PSERVER program is loaded. This happens frequently in small offices when computers are all turned on at the same time in the morning. If a couple of minutes are allowed to pass, this error should not occur.

If you load RPRINTER via a batch file such as AUTOEXEC.BAT, consider modifying the batch file using commands similar to those in the following example.

> **WARNING:** In the example, it's assumed that the PSERVER program will be loaded and, therefore, the print server will exist. If loading the print server is discretionary, do not make similar modifications. There is no way to break out of the loop without the print server being loaded and RPRINTER loading successfully.

```
.
.
.
:P-LOOP
RPRINTER printerserver printer#
IF errorlevel 1 GOTO :P-LOOP
ECHO Remote Printer Installed
.
.
.
```

In the example, printerserver is the name of the print server as defined with the PCONSOLE program. Printer# corresponds to the printer number (0 to 15) established for this remote printer during the print server configuration with the PCONSOLE program.

Warning—Cannot Create Spool File
Keywords: printing, spool, disk space

Scenario

You see this error message on the file server console when someone attempts to print to a shared printer. As I explained earlier, print jobs do not go directly to the printer in a shared environment. Instead, NetWare opens a disk file on the file server to hold the print job. These disk files are kept in a directory beneath the SYS:SYSTEM directory. The directory's name corresponds to the NetWare ID number assigned to the print queue when it was created.

This error occurs when free disk space on the file server's SYS: volume drops below 2Mb to 3Mb or only 20 to 30 directory entries are available on the SYS: volume.

Although this error is not fatal, it causes jobs to print improperly because NetWare does not open disk files for print jobs on the server. This problem can appear to be intermittent if users constantly create and delete files on the file server.

Solution

The first step is to check the amount of free disk space and the number of free directory entries. The NetWare VOLINFO program provides this information for all volumes on the file server. If the free disk space is less than 2Mb to 3Mb, you have two options: remove files from the file server or move some files from the SYS: volume to another volume on the server. If no other volumes have enough free space, you must add more disk space to the file server and then move the files. This requires running the NETGEN or ELSGEN installation programs for NetWare 286 or the INSTALL NLM (NetWare Loadable Module) for NetWare 386.

If you have ample free disk space but not many free directory entries, then you must reconfigure the file server using the NETGEN program on the file server if you are using NetWare 286. (NetWare 386 does not run out of free directory entries.) To begin, you need your working copies of the installation diskettes labelled NETGEN and SUPPORT and a bootable DOS diskette. Then follow these steps to reconfigure the number of directory entries on the file server. (You must be a network supervisor to undertake this procedure.)

Make sure: everyone is logged off the file server.

Shut down: the file server.

Issue the DOWN command at the server console or run the FCONSOLE program from a workstation.

Turn off: the file server.

Insert: a bootable DOS diskette in the server's floppy drive.

Turn on: the file server.

The file server should boot up. You will see the DOS A> prompt.

Insert: the diskette labelled NETGEN in drive A.

Type: NETGEN and press ENTER.

Insert: the SUPPORT diskette when prompted.

Select: Custom Configuration from the menu.

To select a menu item, highlight it and press ENTER.

Select: Installation Option.

The next menu lists four ways you can run the NETGEN program; Standard (floppy disk), RAM Disk, Hard Disk, and Network Drive.

Select: Standard.

You must select Standard because you use only the NETGEN and SUPPORT floppy diskettes for this procedure.

Select: Install NetWare from the NetWare Installation menu.

This option should already be highlighted if you are using your working copies of the NetWare installation diskettes. If it is not, you are not using the right diskettes. After you select this option, you will swap the diskettes about four times, following the prompts.

Confirm: the Disk Drive list.

After you swap the diskettes as prompted, a window appears. It lists the type of disk drive interface installed when your version of NetWare was initially configured. No changes should be

Warning—Cannot Create Spool File

needed. Respond to the prompts by pressing ESCAPE and then select the option Drive List Is Correct from the following menu.

Select: Custom Configuration from the System Configuration menu.

This necessary but redundant step reflects poor programming by Novell. Although you have already chosen Custom, the parameter is not passed to this point, so select Custom again.

Select: Miscellaneous Maintenance from the Installation menu.

This is the only selection you make from this menu. Volume information is accessed through the Miscellaneous Maintenance menu.

Select: Volume Information from the Miscellaneous Maintenance menu.

NETGEN lists the volumes installed on the file server.

Select: the SYS volume.

Increase: the number of directory entries.

The current number is probably the default value that NETGEN established during installation. Increasing this value permits more entries in the directory. There is no optimal value for this entry, but it's a good idea to use a multiple of 128. NetWare directories contain 128 files per directory block.

Press: ESCAPE twice to return to the Miscellaneous Maintenance menu.

Change: the Load Operating System option to No.

At the top of the Miscellaneous Maintenance menu is the choice Load Operating System. Changing the number of directory entries does not affect the operating system, so set this option to No. The default is Yes.

Change: the Load System and Public Files option to No.

The second choice on the Miscellaneous Maintenance menu is Load System and Public Files. Changing the number of directory entries does not affect the files loaded in the SYSTEM or PUBLIC directories, so set this option to No. The default is Yes.

Select: Return to Previous Menu from the Miscellaneous Maintenance menu.

Select:	Return to Previous Menu from the Installation Options menu.
Select:	Continue Installation from the Configuration Options menu.
Select:	Yes from the Install Networking Software on File Server menu.

This may be the most misleading, misnamed option in the entire NETGEN/ELSGEN program. It really means, "Do you want to save your changes?" Of course, the answer is Yes. The system prompts for the NETGEN and SUPPORT diskettes and then returns to the NetWare Installation menu.

Select:	Exit NETGEN from the Installation menu.
Reboot:	the file server.

Postscript Jobs Not Printing Properly
Keywords: printing, Postscript, CAPTURE, NPRINT

Scenario Postscript by Adobe Systems Inc. is a page description language for graphic printers that's very popular for its high quality graphics and font capabilities. The interpreter of this language is contained in ROM in the printer itself; therefore, only Postscript-compatible printers can print jobs that contain this language. Postscript-compatible printers will not print properly if the print job contains anything that they do not understand. This is usually why Postscript print jobs fail to print properly or the printer hangs.

Solution The first step to solve Postscript printer problems is to make sure the user has installed and configured the proper printer driver for the Postscript printer and the application. If so, investigate the setting for the Print Job Definition's File Contents, the parameters for the CAPTURE or NPRINT commands, and the control code buffers.

The Print Job Definition's File Contents must be set to Byte Stream; otherwise, NetWare tries to interpret and print control characters in the print job, rather than passing them to the printer for interpretation.

The CAPTURE or NPRINT command must use the NT (No Tabs) and NB (No Banner) parameters. NT tells NetWare's print spooler that the job is a Byte Stream file. (The default is TABS=8, which NetWare interprets as a text file.) NB is required because NetWare, not the application, generates the banner. The application's printer driver embeds the Postscript codes needed for the data portion of the print job, but the application does not know about the banner. It's impossible to generate the proper Postscript code for the banner.

When the buffers NetWare uses for control codes are full, the codes can cause problems with certain Postscript printers. You can increase these buffers at the workstation by changing the workstation's SHELL.CFG or NET.CFG file to include the following commands:

```
PRINT HEADER = 255
PRINT TAIL = 64
```

IBM 3816 Page Printer Not Printing Properly
Keywords: printing, RPRINTER, IBM

Scenario Using the IBM 3816 Page Printer with the NetWare print server has been a common problem. Jobs begin to print, stop, and appear to hang up. The problem is the interface between RPRINTER, the PC, and the printer.

Solution Follow the next three steps to resolve the problem.

Verify: the pin-outs on the printer cable.

The serial cable used to connect the Page Printer should have the following pin-out. Check it with a multimeter.

PC Pin	Printer Pin
2	3
3	2
4	5
5	20
6	4
7	7
8	4

Verify: that the printer, the COM port, and the print server are all configured for the same interface settings.

You configure the COM port on the workstation with the DOS MODE command. You configure the printer with DIP switches on the printer itself. You configure the print server with the PCONSOLE program. Make sure that all three are set the same for the speed, number of data bits, number of stop bits, parity, and XON/XOFF handshaking. XON/XOFF should be set to Yes or On.

Verify: the DIP switch setting on the printer.

DIP switches 1 to 3, the COM port, and the print server configuration should be set for the same speed. DIP switch 6 should be On. This sets DTR (Data Terminal Ready). All other switches should be Off.

Cannot Attach to Selected Server
Keywords: printing, PRINTCON, CAPTURE, NPRINT

Scenario   This problem is infrequent but baffling because the error message itself is too brief. It happens because the job definition specifies a file server that is not on the network. All NetWare print jobs use a print job definition established by the PRINTCON.DAT file created with the PRINTCON program. The print job definition includes a file server chosen from the list of file servers available at the time.

Solution   The more obvious of the two common causes of this message is found on networks with multiple file servers. When you create print job definitions with the PRINTCON program, you can specify any file server that is up on the network as the file server for the job. If the file server specified for a print job is no longer up when a user selects a print job definition, the error occurs. The solution is to make sure the file server is up or to change the print job definition so it includes another file server.

The second cause of this problem is similar, but happens in a different way. As LANs grow, it is normal to add new file servers and adjust the LAN's configuration as needed. One change might be renaming a file server with the NETGEN or ELSGEN program. The new name takes effect when the file server is booted. But, any print job definitions containing the old name for the file server must also be changed; otherwise, the error occurs.

Changes in PCONSOLE Not Taking Effect
Keywords: printing, print server, PCONSOLE, PSERVER

Scenario The arrival of the new NetWare print server software means you must define many new print server items with the PCONSOLE program. As the network evolves, you often change the configuration of the print server, also with PCONSOLE. Users often complain that these changes do not take effect until the print server is rebooted—a major annoyance if the print server runs on the file server.

Solution This problem results from poor documentation of how to effect your changes. The steps to follow depend on where you run the PSERVER software. Before you begin, make sure no jobs are printing on shared printers.

Take the next steps if the file server is also the print server (it runs PSERVER.VAP when the file server boots up) and you use NetWare 286.

Issue the PSERVER STOP command at the file server's console.

Issue: the PSERVER START command.

If the file server is also the print server and you use NetWare 386,

Issue: the command UNLOAD PSERVER at the console.

Issue: the LOAD PSERVER command.

A workstation becomes a file server when you run the PSERVER.EXE program at the workstation. Here, you initiate your changes through the PCONSOLE program, run from another workstation. Take the next steps if the print server is a dedicated workstation.

Select: Print Server Information from the Available Topics menu.

Select: the print server from the list of available print servers.

Select: Print Server Status/Control.
Select: Server Info from the Print Server Status and Control menu.
Press: ENTER.
Select: Down. This downs the print server.
Reboot: the print server workstation.
Reload: PSERVER.EXE.

Volume Names Corrupted when PSERVER.VAP Is Used
Keywords: PSERVER, VAP, volume names, server name

Scenario

The PSERVER.VAP print server software seems to corrupt volume names on the file server. This disastrous problem can render all your data useless! It happens when the file server volume name is exactly six characters long. This is obviously a bug that Novell needs to fix.

Solution

Use the NETGEN or ELSGEN program to change the volume name so it does not have six characters. To begin, you need your working copies of the installation diskettes labelled NETGEN and SUPPORT and a bootable DOS diskette. Follow the next steps to rename a volume on the file server. (You must be a network supervisor to undertake this procedure.)

Make sure:	everyone is logged off the file server.
Shut down:	the file server.
Issue:	the DOWN command at the server console or run the FCONSOLE program from a workstation.
Turn off:	the file server.
Insert:	a bootable DOS diskette in the server's floppy drive.
Turn on:	the file server.

The file server should boot up. You will see the DOS A> prompt.

Insert:	the diskette labelled NETGEN in drive A.
Type:	NETGEN and press ENTER.
Insert:	the SUPPORT diskette when prompted.
Select:	Custom Configuration from the menu.

To select a menu item, highlight it and press ENTER.

Select:	Installation Option.

The next menu lists four ways you can run the NETGEN program: Standard (floppy disk), RAM Disk, Hard Disk, and Network Drive.

Select: Standard.

You must select Standard because you use only the NETGEN and SUPPORT floppy diskettes for this procedure.

Select: Install NetWare from the NetWare Installation menu.

This option should already be highlighted if you are using your working copies of the NetWare installation diskettes. If it is not, you are not using the right diskettes. After you select this option, you will swap the diskettes about four times, following the prompts.

Confirm: the Disk Drive list.

After you swap the diskettes as prompted, a window appears. It lists the type of disk drive interface installed when your version of NetWare was initially configured. No changes should be needed. Respond to prompts by pressing ESCAPE and then select the option Drive List Is Correct from the following menu.

Select: Custom Configuration from the System Configuration menu.

This necessary but redundant step reflects poor programming by Novell. Although you have already chosen Custom, the parameter is not passed to this point, so select Custom again.

Select: Miscellaneous Maintenance from the Installation menu.

This is the only selection you make from this menu. Volume information is accessed through the Miscellaneous Maintenance menu.

Select: Volume Information from the Miscellaneous Maintenance menu.

NETGEN lists the volumes installed on the file server.

Select: the volume name you want to change.

Press: F3 (Edit).

F3 is the Edit or Modify key in NetWare. You can now change the name of the volume. All its data will be intact because changing a volume name does not affect data.

Press: ESCAPE after you change the name.

You return to the Miscellaneous Maintenance menu.

Volume Names Corrupted when PSERVER.VAP Is Used

Change: the Load Operating System option to No.

At the top of the Miscellaneous Maintenance menu is the choice Load Operating System. Changing a volume name does not affect the operating system, so set this option to No. The default is Yes.

Change: the Load System and Public Files option to No.

The second choice on the Miscellaneous Maintenance menu is Load System and Public Files. Changing a volume name does not affect the files loaded in the SYSTEM or PUBLIC directories, so set this option to No. The default is Yes.

Select: Return to Previous Menu from the Miscellaneous Maintenance menu.

Select: Return to Previous Menu from the Installation Options menu.

Select: Continue Installation from the Configuration Options menu.

Select: Yes from the Install Networking Software on File Server menu.

This may be the most misleading, misnamed option in the entire NETGEN/ELSGEN program. It really means, "Do you want to save your changes?" Of course, the answer is Yes. The system prompts for the NETGEN and SUPPORT diskettes and then returns to the NetWare Installation menu.

Select: Exit NETGEN from the Installation menu.

Reboot: the file server.

Slow Printing on PC and XT Class Remote Printer Workstations
Keywords: printing, RPRINTER

Scenario   When you use the RPRINTER program on a PC or XT (8086/8088 CPU) machine, printing to the shared workstation printer can be very slow. This is because many of these machines use **polled** communications ports, not interrupt-driven LPT or COM ports. The RPRINTER program works very slowly with polled communications ports because DOS must constantly survey the various hardware devices to determine if they need service. Interrupt-driven devices interrupt the CPU when they need service, eliminating the overhead of polling.

Solution   Replace the polled port with an interrupt-driven LPT or COM port. Make sure the interrupt value for the port matches the one defined in PCONSOLE for the remote printer.

Copying the Print Job Database to Other Users

Copying the Print Job Database to Other Users
Keywords: printing, print jobs, PRINTCON, MAIL

Scenario NetWare's PRINTCON (Print Job Configuration) program creates a database file called PRINTCON.DAT in the mail directory of the user who runs the PRINTCON program. (This user usually is a supervisor.) One of the tasks required is to copy the database to the other network users' mail directories. This is a problem for several reasons. First, the PRINTCON program only lets you copy the database to one user at a time, making the task very time consuming and requiring a list of all valid user names. Second, you must repeat this process every time you change the print job configuration database. Finally, having one database accessible to all users would be much more convenient and reduce the network's maintenance requirements.

Solution I have two solutions for this problem. The first makes the task of copying the print job configuration database to each user easier. The second presents a method of establishing shared print job configuration databases.

The diskette included with this book contains three programs that let you easily copy the PRINTCON.DAT file to multiple users. The first program is NETPRINT. It copies the PRINTCON.DAT file from the supervisor's mail directory (SYS:MAIL\1) to *all* other user mail directories on the server. The second program, PRINTCOP, is a $15.00 shareware program for selecting the user mail directories you copy the PRINTCON.DAT file to. The last program, GMCOPY, lets you copy not only the PRINTCON.DAT but also Login Scripts and other configuration files from user to user. Like all the programs on the diskette, the programs must be "unzipped" before you can use them.

In my discussions with network administrators, I have learned that they usually want shared print configuration databases rather than a database for each user. This preference stems largely from the maintenance required for separate databases for each user. Creating a shared database is easier than you might think. You only need to consider a couple of items and learn about an underutilized NetWare feature.

First consider how many print job configuration databases you need and where (in which directories) they should reside. In some environments, one universal database suffices for all users. This works when you only need one default job definition, which is assigned to a specific queue on a specific server, with a specific printer assigned. In other words, this solution works best in small networks with a limited number of printers. The obvious directory for the PRINTCON.DAT file is the SYS:PUBLIC directory. You can copy the master PRINTCON.DAT file into this directory:

```
NCOPY SYS:MAIL\1\PRINTCON.DAT SYS:PUBLIC
```

Then flag the file as a shareable, read-only file:

```
FLAG SYS:PUBLIC\PRINTCON.DAT SRO
```

In many environments, the best solution is to have different PRINTCON.DAT files for different departments or organizational units. These groups usually need their default jobs printed on a printer in their department, rather than on some centralized printer located elsewhere in the building. In this situation, you copy a department-specific PRINTCON.DAT file into a directory shared by all users in the department. For example, if the network serves the group MFG (short for manufacturing), there may be a directory for this group's shared files on the file server (SYS:MFG). Copy the print configuration database into this directory and flag it as a shareable, read-only file:

```
NCOPY SYS:MAIL\1\PRINTCON.DAT SYS:MFG
FLAG SYS:MFG\PRINTCON.DAT SRO
```

The second part of setting up these shared print job configuration databases is to alter the way that certain programs search for their data files. Four NetWare programs use the PRINTCON.DAT file: PCONSOLE.EXE, NPRINT.EXE, CAPTURE.EXE, and PRINTCON.EXE. These programs are in the SYS:PUBLIC directory. Normally, NetWare searches for programs the same way DOS does.

Copying the Print Job Database to Other Users

The search path locates only executable files (with .COM and .EXE file name extensions) or batch files (with .BAT file name extensions). The search path does not locate data files like PRINTCON.DAT.

The NetWare SMODE command changes the way programs search for their data files. SMODE changes an extended attribute that is associated with executable files. The default setting for the SMODE attribute, 0, instructs the program to search in the same manner DOS does. Changing the attribute to 5 tells the program to search the directories in the search path for data files. Using this technique affects the four NetWare programs that use the PRINTCON.DAT file:

```
SMODE SYS:PUBLIC\CAPTURE.EXE 5
SMODE SYS:PUBLIC\NPRINT.EXE 5
SMODE SYS:PUBLIC\PCONSOLE.EXE 5
SMODE SYS:PUBLIC\PRINTCON.EXE 5
```

Because these commands set a file attribute, the SMODE command is only performed once. The attribute stays set until you issue another SMODE command to change it. The SMODE attribute is not affected when users log in or out or when the file server is shut down or rebooted.

The final step is to make sure the directory containing the PRINTCON.DAT file is in the user's search path. To do so, map a search drive to the appropriate directory. For example, if the PRINTCON.DAT file is in SYS:PUBLIC, then users probably have this directory in their search drive lists already. If the PRINTCON.DAT file resides in SYS:MFG, then the MAP command might be similar to the following:

```
MAP SEARCH16:=SYS:MFG
```

SUMMARY

This chapter's objective was to solve some of the common problems in the NetWare printing environment. You will need to study the information carefully in this chapter and apply it to your installation. Ninety percent of all printing problems I have seen relate to problems setting up the printing options. Properly configured, NetWare should enhance your user's environment by making more printers available and by queueing jobs that need to be printed. A print job may not print as quickly as it would on a stand-alone workstation if it is put into a queue, but the user remains free to do other things while waiting.

12
Remote Printing

Remote printing refers to the concept of using printers attached to workstations as shared network printers. Although other network operating systems have always supported this concept, it is new to NetWare. Until recently, remote printing in NetWare required using a third-party software package. The term **print server** usually refers to the programs used to implement shared printing in a network environment. Many vendors jumped into the print server arena before Novell finally shipped their version in 1990. In this chapter, I investigate aspects of using various third-party print servers in a NetWare LAN.

THIRD-PARTY PRINT SERVERS

It is difficult to discuss every vendor's products in this arena, so I will limit the discussion to those products that I have personally installed and used. The three vendors and products I have selected (in no particular order) are PS-Print and Queue-It, (Brightworks Development, (800) 552-9876); LAN Spool, (LAN Systems, (800) 827-LANS); and Printer Assist and Queue Assist, (Fresh Technology, (602) 497-4200).

I selected these products for a variety of reasons, the most important of which is that they all work. All understand Novell's bindery files and security systems. Well integrated into the NetWare environment, they permit you to use their programs or Novell's programs for many management tasks. All are reasonably priced and offer better than average customer support.

PS-Print and Queue-It

These products provide a bundle of print server features for NetWare and a memory-resident queue manager. PS-Print lets you share any printer on the network. Designed for NetWare 286 and NetWare 386 versions 2.1x and above, they support operator notification when the printer is off line or out of paper. They use the NetWare standard programs, CAPTURE, NPRINT, PRINTCON, PRINTDEF, and PCONSOLE. These products have five major components.

PSP-CFG.EXE	Configures PS-Print and Queue-It for shared printers. It creates, edits, or deletes queues; assigns queues to printers at various priorities; and creates queue users, queue operators, and printer configuration files. The printer configuration file contains the name of the printer, type of printer port used, start-up font file, user message option, queue scan interval, and service mode. Service mode determines how PS-Print and Queue-It handle form change requests.
PSP.EXE	Loads on a workstation that is going to share its printer with the network. It requires about 8K RAM on the workstation.
PSP-CON.EXE	Brightwork's version of a PCONSOLE program that lets you monitor and control the print jobs in the queue. NetWare's PCONSOLE can also be used.
QIT.EXE	A memory-resident program that lets the user use a "hot key" to access a list of job definitions that have been created with NetWare's PRINTCON. It also lets the user change printer definitions used for the user's print job.

Third-party Print Servers

QSLIM.EXE — Memory-resident software that allows the user to use a "hot key" to access a list of print job definitions that have been created with NetWare's PRINTCON. This program does not allow the user to change print job definitions.

PS-Print and Queue-It use the standard NetWare CAPTURE and NPRINT commands to send jobs to shared printers. You can manage queues created by PS-Print and Queue-It from NetWare's PCONSOLE program. Any software that is aware of NetWare queues can use PS-Print and Queue-It with no changes.

LAN Spool

LAN Spool's approach is different from PS-Print's and Queue-It's but similar to NetWare's own print server. LAN Spool runs as a VAP or NLM on the file server, depending on the NetWare version you are using. It lets any workstation on the network share its attached printer. The workstation software requires 2.5K RAM. The VAP on the file server uses about 120K RAM. (The NetWare 386 NLM size was not definite at press time.)

LAN Spool uses NetWare's PCONSOLE program to define print server names, queue names, queue users, and queue operators. The LAN Spool system consists of four major modules.

ACCTGIVE — Only used when NetWare's accounting features are being used. The print server is an object with an account balance like any other NetWare object. This program updates the balance of the print server.

SETNAME — Updates the VAP for the name of the print server created in PCONSOLE.

NODE — Runs at workstations that share their printer with the network. It is configured for the type of port being used and allows queues to be assigned to the printer. In addition, it establishes operator notification options for actions associated with printers that are off line or out of paper.

LANPRINT   A memory-resident module that allows the user to select different print job definitions and modify print job parameters from within the user's application.

LAN Spool uses the standard NetWare CAPTURE and NPRINT commands to send jobs to shared printers. You can manage queues created by LAN Spool from NetWare's PCONSOLE program. Any software that is aware of NetWare queues can use LAN Spool with no changes.

I am pleased with the most recent version of LAN Spool. Older versions used more workstation RAM and seemed slower than the other products. The newer versions have solved these problems and put LAN Spool's performance on par with the others.

Printer Assist and Queue Assist

Printer Assist runs on any LAN using NetWare 286 version 2.0 or above and NetWare 386 version 3.0 and above. The software requires 3K to 5K RAM and runs on the workstations that are going to share their printers. Printer Assist uses NetWare's PCONSOLE program to define print server names, queue names, queue users, and queue operators. The major components of Printer Assist are listed next.

PAINSTALL   The installation program for Printer Assist. It copies the necessary files to the file server.

PACONFIG   Creates configuration files for each workstation's use when it shares its printer. It determines the type of output port, and the names of the queues that will be assigned to the printer. In addition, it establishes user and operator notification options. A unique feature (not shared by the other print servers mentioned) is the ability to load into high memory. Printer Assist also supports banner pages on PostScript printers, a feature needed in many environments.

PA		The resident program that loads at a non-dedicated workstation that is sharing its printer.
PAD		A version of the PA program for a workstation that will function as a dedicated print server.
PAREPORT		Prints a usage report summarizing how the printers were used. Various selection parameters limit the report to only the information you need.
PAPC		A memory-resident module that lets the user who is printing a job customize job parameters and execute printer commands without leaving their application.

Fresh Technology's companion product to Printer Assist is Queue Assist. This program allows the user to display and control print queue contents from within an application, reassign queues to different printers, send print jobs to a print file, and send escape sequences to the printer selected from a pop-up definition window.

SUMMARY

I hope that one of these products suits your needs if the NetWare print server doesn't. While it is hard to recommend just one, if I had to choose, I would lean toward Fresh Technology's Print Assist and Queue Assist pair for a couple of reasons. First, Print Assist and Queue Assist have more features for queue management from within the application than any of the others. The support for PostScript printers and banner pages is welcome. Finally, being able to load into high memory without any other software like Quarterdeck's QEMM or QRAM is a nice feature.

All three products are nicely implemented. You need to understand NetWare queues, queue users, and queue operators to set up these products.

Part V
User Accounts and Security

A major activity of managing a NetWare LAN is setting up users' accounts and establishing users' privileges. Securing a NetWare LAN involves three tasks. The first task is keeping unauthorized people out of the network. The second is establishing login restrictions for each user. The final task is granting users' rights to network directories and files. An outstanding aspect of NetWare's security system is its **cafeteria plan**, which allows the network supervisor to choose those features best suited to the organization's security needs. This part investigates these tasks and illustrates how to create a secure climate for your network.

13
Controlling the LOGIN Process

Controlling how people log into the network involves two distinctly different requirements. The first is to keep unauthorized people from logging into the network. The second is to establish conditions that permit the authorized users to log in. This chapter discusses NetWare features you can implement to control these aspects of the network.

KEEPING UNAUTHORIZED PEOPLE OUT OF THE NETWORK

In some environments, keeping unauthorized people out of the network is a major concern. Fortunately, NetWare has four good defenses against people who try to gain unauthorized access. I do not include the fact that the PC must be connected to the network and the workstation shell programs must be loaded in these defenses. If a workstation has no connection to the LAN, the workstation cannot access it. Because the workstation shell programs are usually loaded via a batch file on the workstation, I assume that the potential violator could find the files and load the programs.

NetWare controls unauthorized access to the network in four ways:

- It prevents file access directly at the server.
- It requires a valid account name.
- It offers passwords to protect valid accounts.
- It locks valid accounts in the event of unauthorized attempts to log in.

Accessing Files at the File Server

No one can access files stored on the file server except through a workstation logged into the network. Even on a non-dedicated file server running ELS I, ELS II, or Advanced NetWare, the files on the server's volumes cannot be accessed unless the user logs into the server at the console. Logging in at the server console has the same requirements as logging in at a workstation.

Another way someone could attempt to access information stored on the file server is to attempt to avoid the NetWare operating system. This is impossible at a workstation, but could be achieved at the file server itself. It would be simple to boot the file server with a bootable DOS diskette and prevent the NetWare operating system from loading. Of course, this would be detected by any one logged into the LAN.

NetWare uses non-DOS disk partitions on the file server to prevent surreptitious DOS access. DOS cannot read or write to non-DOS partitions; therefore, files are inaccessible to someone trying this approach. This feature also prevents DOS utility programs such as Norton Utilities or PC Tools from directly accessing files stored on the file server.

Invalid Account Names

Another way people try to enter the network is to run the LOGIN program. A person who does not know a valid account name tries to guess an account name. If the guess is incorrect, NetWare does not permit access to the LAN, nor tell the person that the account name is invalid.

In addition, NetWare always asks for a password after an invalid account name. This is good psychology. If the invalid account name represents an attempt to break into the LAN, the person has no clue that the name is invalid. Also, by prompting for a password, NetWare encourages the user to keep trying to use the invalid account. Some would like an audit trail of invalid attempts but, since invalid account name log in attempts pose no threat to security, NetWare does not track them.

Keeping Unauthorized People Out of the Network

Passwords

The best defense against someone using a valid account in an unauthorized attempt to enter the LAN is passwords. If you do not use passwords, anyone who knows a valid account name can log into the network. Passwords can be from 1 to 47 characters long.

NetWare's password features are flexible. The supervisor establishes password requirements for each user when the supervisor adds the account name to the network's bindery files through the SYSCON, MAKEUSER, or ADDUSER programs. The operating system keeps all security information for the file server in the NetWare bindery files. Passwords are encrypted in the file to prevent someone from finding the passwords if they should happen to discover the bindery files and have sufficient rights (they are a supervisor) to edit them through a program such as DOS DEBUG. The supervisor can change password requirements as needed.

Intruder Detection

The final barrier against unauthorized persons accessing the LAN protects valid account/password combinations. It is likely that someone who is not a valid user of the LAN can learn the name of a valid account on the file server. All NetWare LANs contain two accounts that always have the same name: SUPERVISOR and GUEST. You need to take steps to prevent someone from repeatedly trying to log in using a valid account name and guessing a password. Given enough time and luck, the intruder could find a valid combination. Some would-be intruders write small programs that repeatedly try to log in using different passwords.

Intruder detection helps prevent this breech. This feature can determine a set of circumstances that cause NetWare to lock an account that someone is attempting to break into. It's activated by a supervisor using the SYSCON program. NetWare defines an intruder as someone who is attempting to log in using a valid account name and incorrect passwords. Since everyone mistypes their password occasionally, NetWare lets the supervisor define an intruder by answering the question: How many failed log in attempts on a given account over a given time period constitute an intrusion?

After a supervisor sets it up, intruder detection applies to all accounts that have passwords. You cannot selectively enable or disable it based on users' account names. After NetWare detects an intruder, it can lock the account so that additional attempts to use the account are automatically denied access to the file server. The supervisor establishes the duration of the lock when setting up intruder detection; it is the same for all accounts. After NetWare locks the account, the account cannot be logged into, even with the valid account name/password combination. The account remains locked for the duration of the lockout unless a supervisor (all NetWare versions), workgroup manager (NetWare 386), or manager (NetWare 386) uses the SYSCON program to unlock the account.

Locked Supervisor Account; No Other Supervisors
Keywords: intruder, lockout, supervisor, password

Scenario
To protect valid accounts, the supervisor enables the intruder detection feature with the SYSCON program. The file server has the SUPERVISOR account set up as the only supervisor. Someone attempts to use the SUPERVISOR account without knowing its password, and the account is locked. Because no other supervisors are established for the file server, the supervisor cannot log in nor unlock the account.

Solution
This scenario illustrates one reason why I advise clients to establish at least two supervisor accounts, even if there is only one supervisor. The supervisor could log in using the other supervisor account and use the SYSCON program to unlock the SUPERVISOR account. But, when there is a single supervisor, the supervisor can unlock the SUPERVISOR account from the file server's console with the command:

```
ENABLE LOGIN
```

This command usually reverses the effect of a DISABLE LOGIN command. However, if no DISABLE LOGIN is in effect, the ENABLE LOGIN command unlocks only the SUPERVISOR account. It does not unlock other accounts that may also be locked. After unlocking the account, the supervisor can log in at a workstation using the SUPERVISOR account name and its valid password.

CONTROLLING VALID USER'S LOG IN

The next aspect of NetWare's security is controlling how valid users log into the LAN. Certain restrictions commonly govern when a user can log in and use the LAN. This section explores the NetWare features that control how a valid user logs in. Four user-specific features govern the user's LOGIN process:

- Account restrictions
- Station restrictions
- Time restrictions
- Account balance restrictions

You impose these restrictions as you add users to the file server with the SYSCON, MAKEUSER, or ADDUSER programs. You can modify them with the SYSCON program. An item on the User Information menu corresponds to each restriction.

Account Restrictions

Account Restrictions let the supervisor or manager establish certain login restrictions for the user. The restrictions are discussed in the next four sections.

Account Disabled

You can disable the user account, preventing the user from logging in at all. This conveniently protects an account when someone is absent for an extended period. Disabling the account does not delete it.

Account Expiration Date

With this feature, you can establish a date when the account is automatically disabled. On that date, NetWare disables the account, preventing the user from logging in. This useful feature helps to manage users who need temporary access to the LAN.

Limit Concurrent Connections

NetWare lets users log in concurrently, based on the number of workstations set up to use this feature. This feature can force the user to log out from one station before logging in on another.

Controlling Valid User's Log In

Passwords Required

You determine if a user must have a password to use the LAN. If you require passwords, you also can establish a minimum password length, how often the user must change the password, whether the user can reuse an old password, and how many times the user can log in using an expired password.

Station Restrictions

The supervisor can establish a list of workstations that the user is permitted to use. The items on the list are the network number and the workstation's node number. You must type these numbers: NetWare does not display a menu to choose from, nor does it check the numbers you type to verify their existence. NetWare prohibits the user from logging in on an unlisted workstation.

Time Restrictions

The supervisor can restrict each user's access to the file server according to time of day and day of the week. NetWare's calendar week is segmented into half-hour increments for each day. You can establish the times the user can access the file server and thereby control the user's ability to log in and how long the user can use the file server. When users reach a period during which they are not permitted to use the file server, NetWare automatically logs them out.

Account Balance Restrictions

I saved this restriction for last because it is the least implemented login access control. An accounting feature that can be activated for the file server lets NetWare track the user's activities by five different measures:

Disk blocks read

Disk blocks written

Disk storage

Connect time

Service requests

You may track any or all measures according to management needs. For each activity type, you can establish different charge rates that can vary according to day of the week and time of day. Charges are assessed against the user's account according to use.

When you add a user to the network, you establish an account balance for the user's account. Then NetWare deducts usage charges from the user's account balance. When users reach their low balance limits, they cannot log in. Also, NetWare automatically logs users out when their accounts reach this limit.

I believe that the reason so few network supervisors take advantage of this feature is Novell's failure to address two critical needs and its omission of features necessary for a functional accounting system. The first need is to reset users' account balances to a predetermined level. This process would usually be done at regular intervals, probably for all file server users. A batch process of some sort would work well. Right now, the only way to update the account balance is to use the SYSCON program to change users' balances manually—a very time-consuming process with potential for errors in posting the wrong balance or missing accounts altogether.

The second critical need is for reports. The major reason for management to implement usage tracking of this kind is to analyze file server usage. This analysis could be useful for making a variety of decisions, for example, to allocate costs associated with the network to various departments based on each department's actual use or to project future LAN expansion needs based on use. NetWare has only one provision for this: the PAUDIT program which is run by a supervisor to list transactions that NetWare has posted. You must redirect this program's output into a file using the DOS redirection feature. The file you create can be processed by any software or database application that the client creates for the task. NetWare provides no analytical reports for this data.

Unfortunately, because Novell failed to address these needs, most network supervisors ignore NetWare's accounting features. They feel that the feature is more trouble than it is worth. I am amazed that the third-party NetWare utility vendors have not developed a generalized application package that optimizes this NetWare feature.

Supervisor Needs to Update Multiple Users with Same Restrictions
Keywords: restrictions, SYSCON, groups

Scenario   Often access restrictions apply the same criteria to groups of users. When these restrictions change, criteria for everyone in the group needs updating. Unfortunately, account restrictions do not apply to NetWare groups. Using the SYSCON program to change one user's restrictions at a time is a time-consuming task.

Solution   When supervisors update restrictions applying to more than one user, they overlook the SYSCON feature for marking multiple users on the User Information User list using the F5 function key. After you mark multiple users this way, press ENTER to see a SYSCON menu that permits you to change the four areas of access control. The defaults shown for each area are determined by the system defaults the supervisor sets up. After you make changes, SYSCON asks you to confirm that the changes are to be applied to all marked users.

User Account Restrictions Working Improperly
Keywords: restrictions, LOGIN, bindery, BINDFIX, VREPAIR

Scenario Now and then, a user account's behavior is inconsistent with the parameters that the supervisor established for the account when it was created. Verifying the user's information in SYSCON shows no unusual settings. Still, the account behaves inconsistently when the user attempts to log in.

Solution This problem is a symptom of a corrupted bindery. **Bindery files** are hidden system files located in the SYS:SYSTEM directory. They contain the file server's security information, including all user account information, group information, trustee assignments, print server information, and queue information.

> **WARNING:** Before you attempt to repair damaged bindery files, you must completely back up the file server.

You can fix corrupted bindery files a couple of ways. First, if no one has changed the network's security features recently, you may be able to restore a copy of the bindery files from a backup. The second way to cure this problem is to rebuild the bindery files with the NetWare BINDFIX program. It builds new bindery files from old. While it rebuilds the binderies, BINDFIX tries to correct any errors it finds. The program renames the existing bindery files and then builds the new ones. A supervisor must run this program, and should do so only when no one else is logged into the file server.

> **WARNING:** After you run BINDFIX, do not log out of the supervisor station where you ran BINDFIX. Log in from another workstation and test the account that experienced the problems.

User Account Restrictions Working Improperly

On the rare occasions when bindery files are extremely corrupt, BINDFIX makes the problem worse. If this happens, return to the workstation where you originally ran BINDFIX and run the BINDREST program. BINDREST restores the old, albeit corrupt, bindery files. The only other option Novell supplies to repair bindery files is the VREPAIR program on the NetWare UTILEXE-2 diskette. You must run VREPAIR from the file server. To do so,

Boot the file server with a DOS diskette.

Run VREPAIR from a floppy disk.

> **WARNING:** Make sure that the VREPAIR program is the one from your *current* version of NetWare. Different NetWare versions require different VREPAIR versions. Using the wrong version causes data corruption.

If all these attempts fail to repair your bindery files, a third-party utility program named NETUTILS lets you edit the bindery files directly. It's available from Ontrack Computer Systems Inc., (612) 937-1107.

> **WARNING:** This program can be dangerous. Don't use it unless you know exactly what you are doing. If you do choose to use NETUTILS, closely follow the instructions that come with it.

Because the bindery files are so important to NetWare's well-being, I advise you to run BINDFIX often. My general practice is to run it every week on our LAN. Because BINDFIX does not hide the old renamed bindery files, I can easily copy them onto a floppy disk. To minimize the possibility of having an unrecoverable or corrupted set of bindery files, I keep three diskettes in rotation.

SUMMARY

This chapter discussed NetWare features that control how users log onto the network. NetWare's options permit you to implement a flexible security scheme for your network that is neither cumbersome nor intrusive. Although most networks need some security provisions, you may not need to use every defense that NetWare offers. The next chapter discusses how NetWare controls users' abilities to access files on the file server. After a user logs into the network, you need to determine what the user can access.

14
Solving the Rights Puzzle

NetWare Rights are one of the most important security features of the operating system. After the user logs in, Rights determine what files the user can access and the type of activities permitted. Establishing user Rights can be time-consuming and frustrating for the network administrator. In this chapter I discuss how to set up Rights and solve common problems related to this topic.

RIGHTS DEFINITIONS

Eight categories of Rights in NetWare 286 and NetWare 386 govern the type of activity the user is permitted. Novell has changed some categories between the NetWare 286 versions and NetWare 386. Table 14–1 lists categories of Rights for both versions.

Table 14-1. NetWare Rights

NetWare 286 Right	NetWare 386 Right	Use
Create	Create	This Right allows the creation of files or directories. Files created by an application can be written to at the time of creation without Write, Search, or Open Rights. Future writing to the file would require additional Rights.
Delete	Erase	When used in conjunction with Search Right or File Scan, this Right allows deletion of files or directories.
Modify	Modify	When used in conjunction with Search Right or File Scan, this Right allows changing the file's or directory's name or attributes.
Open		When used in conjunction with Search Right, this Right permits you to open the file on the file server.
Parental	Access Control	This Right permits a trustee to grant Rights to someone else or remove Rights from someone else. The trustee may only grant those Rights that the trustee possesses.
Read	Read	When used in conjunction with Search and Open Rights (NetWare 286) or File Scan (NetWare 386), this Right allows the file to be read by a workstation.
Search	File Scan	This Right allows the file names to be viewed within a directory. This Right must accompany several other Rights for them to work properly.
Write	Write	When used in conjunction with Search and Open Rights (NetWare 286) or File Scan (NetWare 386), this Right permits writing to a file by a workstation.
	Supervisory	This Right gives the user all Rights in the directory and overrides any other restrictions. This Right also permits the user to override any disk space limitations set up for the user in the volume.

BASIC RIGHTS CONCEPTS FOR NETWARE 286

Fundamentally, NetWare Rights are granted at two levels. The first is Rights associated with the directory itself, regardless of the user. These Rights are called **Maximum Rights Mask**. The default Maximum Rights Mask for a newly created directory is all eight Rights. You can only change the Rights contained in the Maximum Rights Mask using the NetWare FILER program.

The second level where Rights are granted is the Rights granted to users or groups. Called **Trustee Assignments**, these Rights can be made using the NetWare FILER, SYSCON, GRANT, REVOKE, and REMOVE programs.

NetWare lets users perform various activities based upon the user's **Effective Rights**. For a Right to be effective, it must be present in the directory's Maximum Rights Mask and the user's or group's Trustee Assignment. If a Right exists in one place but not the other, the Right will not be effective. Table 14-2 illustrates the relationship between Maximum Rights Mask, Trustee Assignments, and Effective Rights.

Table 14-2. Effective Rights

Type of Right	Granted to	Create	Delete/ Erase	Modify	Open	Parental/ Access Control	Read	File Scan/ Search	Write
Maximum Rights Mask	Directory	1	0	0	1	0	1	1	1
Trustee Assignment	User or group	0	1	0	1	1	1	1	1
Effective Rights		1	1	0	2	1	2	2	2

In Table 14-2, Rights assigned to the Maximum Rights Mask and the Trustee Assignment have the value 1. Rights not assigned have the value 0. Adding the Maximum Rights Mask and Trustee Assignment values results in the Effective Rights value. If the Effective Rights value equals 2, the Right is effective. If the value is 0 or 1, the Right is not effective. Supervisory Rights were not included in Table 14-2 since this Right does not apply to NetWare 286.

Setting the Maximum Rights Mask for a Directory

The way Maximum Rights Mask is used depends upon how the directory is used. If you consider the directories on the file server, you can generally classify them into two groups. Some directories hold programs and files related to an application package, such as help files, overlays, and so on. Other directories hold data files. In data directories, the general practice is to have all eight rights in the Maximum Rights Mask. Then Rights granted to the user or group will be Effective Rights also. Table 14-3 illustrates this concept.

Table 14-3. Effective Rights if All Rights in Maximum Rights Mask

Type of Right	Granted to	Create	Delete/ Erase	Modify	Open	Parental/ Access Control	Read	Search	Write
Maximum Rights Mask	Directory	1	1	1	1	1	1	1	1
Trustee Assignment	User or group	0	1	0	1	1	1	1	1
Effective Rights		1	2	1	2	2	2	2	2

In program directories I am concerned about users performing undesirable tasks. As a safety mechanism, you should remove from the Maximum Rights Mask the Rights that you do not want the user to use. Then, even if a Trustee Assignment is made to the user or group, the Right assigned does not become an Effective Right. I also use the Maximum Rights Mask on a temporary basis when I want to keep everyone out of a directory while I update software. An easy way to keep everyone out of a directory is to remove the Search Right from the Maximum Rights Mask.

THREE WAYS TO GAIN IMPLICIT RIGHTS

Two entities can have Trustee Assignments: users and groups. I call user Trustee Assignments **Explicit Rights**. Yet, having a Trustee Assignment in a directory is not the only way to have Rights in a directory. There are three ways that users can possess

Three Ways to Gain Implicit Rights

Rights in a directory that were not assigned as a Trustee Assignment. I call these **Implicit Rights**. Usually, when network supervisors try to diagnose Rights problems, they look at Trustee Assignments, using either the NetWare SYSCON or FILER programs. Unfortunately, Implicit Rights do not appear in the user's Trustee Assignments in either of these programs. This makes Implicit Rights difficult to manage and document. In this section, I look at the three sources of Implicit Rights: group membership, downline directories, and security equivalences.

Group Membership

Groups are the key to easy NetWare Rights management. If Rights are assigned to a group, the members of the group implicitly have the same Rights. If network groups are well designed, maintaining the network and adding new users is simple.

Downline Directories

If a user or group has Rights in a directory and downline directories exist beneath it, the user inherits the same Rights in the downline directory. This can be a convenient way to set up Rights when the user or group can create new directories. No new Trustee Assignments are needed for the user or group in the downline directories. If it is undesirable to have the Rights passed to the downline directories, then you must block them with a Trustee Assignment of no Rights in the downline directory.

Security Equivalences

The final way to give a user Implicit Rights is with a NetWare feature called security equivalence. The supervisor can make any user a security equivalent of any other user on the file server using the SYSCON program. After one user is security equivalent to another user, the user inherits the other user's Explicit Rights (Trustee Assignments to the other user) as Implicit Rights. The user does not inherit the other user's implicit rights, however.

For security equivalences to be a useful Rights management technique, the Trustee Assignments must be assigned to individual users rather than groups. This is an extremely tedious way to manage the file server. Although security equivalences can be used for Rights, they are not a very effective way to manage this aspect of NetWare.

The only useful purpose of security equivalences is to create other supervisors. To become a supervisor, the user must become security equivalent to the SUPERVISOR account. If a new user becomes security equivalent to another user who is a supervisor, the new user is not a supervisor.

CLARIFICATION OF RIGHTS GAINED FROM MULTIPLE SOURCES

Determining users' Rights can be a difficult business, especially when Novell's documentation of the topic is incomplete. I want to clarify a couple of principles that impact the user whose Rights come from multiple sources. These two principles help to clarify Rights behavior when there are multiple Rights assignments, possibly to different entities and in different directories. These two principles and the rules covered earlier in this chapter should give you a solid foundation for understanding NetWare Rights.

Principle #1

If a user or group has Implicit Rights in a directory and the same user or group has Explicit Rights (a Trustee Assignment) in the same directory, the Explicit Rights prevail and the Implicit Rights are ignored. In addition, Explicit Rights become Implicit Rights in any downline directories.

This generally happens when Rights in the downline directories need to differ from Rights in the upline directory. For example, suppose a group has the Trustee Assignments Read, Open, Search, Create, and Delete in a directory called SYS:MFG. Suppose, also, that there is a downline directory called SYS:MFG/STAFF. The group would have the Implicit Rights Read, Open, Search, Create, and Delete in the SYS:MFG/STAFF directory. If you make

Clarification of Rights Gained from Multiple Sources

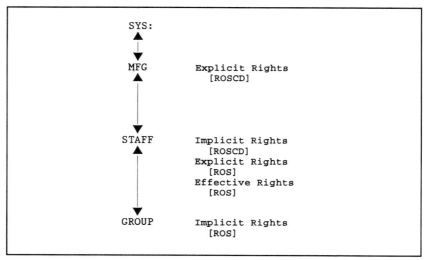

Figure 14-1. Principle #1

the Trustee Assignments Read, Open, and Search to the group in the SYS:MFG/STAFF directory, these are the group's Effective Rights. The Implicit Rights Create and Delete are not effective. Furthermore, suppose there is a directory called SYS:MFG/STAFF/GROUP. The group has Read, Open, and Search Rights only in that directory. Figure 14-1 illustrates this principle.

Principle #2

If a user has Rights in a directory because the user is a trustee or a member of a group with Rights in the directory and the same user is a member of another group that has Rights in the same directory, the user's Effective Rights encompass both sets of Rights in that directory and any downline directories.

This principle addresses the issue of multiple Rights coming from different entities. A user is an entity and so is a group. If a user gets Rights from more than one entity for a given directory, the Rights combine. Since Rights are implicit in any downline directories, the user has the combined Rights in all downline directories, too. Suppose a group called DEPT__A had Read, Open, Search, Create, and Write Rights in a directory called SYS:BUDGET. A group called DEPT_B has Read, Open, Search, Delete, and Modify Rights in the SYS:BUDGET directory. If user JAN belongs to both groups, then JAN's Effective Rights will be Read, Open, Search, Delete, Modify, Create, and Write.

NETWARE 386 DIFFERENCES

NetWare 386 makes a few significant changes to the Rights mechanisms NetWare 286 offers. Some changes are in the Rights categories themselves. Other changes affect the way Rights are inherited or granted. Finally, there is a new level of Rights—the file level. In the next sections, I discuss these changes.

Changes to Rights Categories

There are a few changes in the Rights categories. One NetWare 286 Right is gone and two are renamed. NetWare 386 also has one Right that doesn't exist in NetWare 286.

The Open Right from NetWare 286 is gone. The Open Right was always used with the Read or Write Right, so NetWare 386 automatically opens the file based upon the Read or Write Rights.

The NetWare 286 Delete Right has been renamed Erase. This change is a nuisance! Many people have multiple file servers, some running NetWare 286 and some running NetWare 386. Now network supervisors must remember which Right applies to which file server. Because NetWare 286 servers probably outnumber NetWare 386 servers 100 to 1, I think Novell should have left this Right's name alone.

The NetWare 286 Parental Right has also been renamed Access Control. This Right governs the user's ability to grant Rights in a directory he or she has Rights in to someone else.

The NetWare 286 Search Right has been renamed File Scan. This Right governs the user's ability to view a file name in a directory list. This Right is needed to erase or write to a file.

NetWare 386 Differences

The new NetWare 386 Right is Supervisory. It makes the user a "supervisor" in the directory where the Right was granted. Supervisory Rights let the user perform any activity in the directory without having each individual Right. The other unusual aspect of this Right is that it overrides any volume disk space limitations placed on the user.

Table 14-4 summarizes the differences between NetWare 386 Rights and NetWare 286 Rights.

Table 14-4. NetWare Rights Changes

NetWare 286 Right	NetWare 386 Right	Status
Create	Create	Same in both versions
Delete	Erase	Renamed in NetWare 386
Modify	Modify	Same in both versions
Open		Does not exist in NetWare 386
Parental	Access Control	Renamed in NetWare 386
Read	Read	Same in both versions
Search	File Scan	Renamed in NetWare 386
Write	Write	Same in both versions
	Supervisory	New in NetWare 386

For definitions of Rights, see Table 14-1 earlier in this chapter.

Differences in Effective Rights

NetWare 386 changes some key elements in how Effective Rights behave. First, NetWare 286's Maximum Rights Mask (the rights assigned to the directory itself) has been replaced with NetWare 386's Inherited Rights Mask. You change this mask using the NetWare FILER program.

The Inherited Rights Mask operates entirely differently from NetWare 286's Maximum Rights Mask. In NetWare 286, a Right needs to exist in both the Maximum Rights Mask and the user or group Trustee Assignment to be an Effective Right. In NetWare

386, Trustee Assignments are automatically Effective Rights. Trustee Assignments override the Inherited Rights Mask associated with the directory. In addition, the Trustee Rights assigned become the Inherited Rights Mask in any downline directory.

These changes make NetWare 386 easier to manage. Now, when you make Trustee Assignments to a user or group, you can count on those Rights being the Effective Rights. You could not make this assumption in NetWare 286 due to the Maximum Rights Mask.

File-level Rights

Perhaps the most significant change in NetWare 386 is its ability to assign Rights at the file level, in addition to the directory level. File-level Rights solve certain exceptional conditions. Table 14-5 summarizes file-level Rights.

Table 14-5. NetWare 386 file Rights

Right	Use
Access Control	Allows changes in the file's Trustee Assignments and Inherited Rights Mask.
Create	Allows the file to be salvaged after it has been deleted.
Erase	Allows deletion of the file.
File Scan	Allows files to be seen in the directory.
Modify	Permits changes to the file's directory information. This Right is needed to change the file attributes or the file name.
Read	Grants the ability to open the file on the server and read its contents or run it on the workstation.
Supervisory	Grants all Rights to the file. Also allows the user to grant Rights to the file to others and modify the Inherited Rights Mask.
Write	Grants the ability to open the file on the server and write to it.

Addressing Rights at the file level is necessary because application software creates temporary files in the directory where the software resides. For the software to create these temporary files, the user must have Create, Write, and Delete Rights in addition to the Rights needed to run a program—Search, Open, and Read. A user who has delete Rights can delete any file in the directory that is not flagged as a read-only file. This potentially dangerous situation can be avoided by assigning Rights at the file level that prevent the user from deleting necessary files.

Another important advantage of file-level Rights is when data directories are shared. In a shared directory, you sometimes need to give different users Rights to different files within the directory. You cannot do this with NetWare 286. In NetWare 286, you can only handle this problem by creating different directories for different sets of files. With NetWare 386, you can make separate Trustee Assignments to different users or groups, giving them the access Rights they need to the applicable files.

File-level Rights assignments solve a variety of specific Rights problems. You do not need to assign file-level Rights to all files on the server. In fact, this would be much too tedious. For the most part, you will manage Rights at the directory level whenever possible.

User's Directory Rights Are Not Appropriate
Keywords: Rights, WHOAMI, SYSCON, Trustee Assignments, FILER, groups

Scenario

One challenge of managing a network is managing users' Rights. Sometimes users have Rights in directories where they should not have Rights. Unfortunately, figuring out the source of the Rights is difficult because in NetWare there's no single place to look for a complete picture of the users' Rights and their sources.

Solution

To solve this problem, you must take a series of steps that clarify users' Rights. Users' Rights come from four primary sources: Trustee Assignments, group membership, security equivalences, and downline directories.

1. The users' own Trustee Assignments give them Rights in specific directories. You can find these Rights with the NetWare SYSCON program. When you do, write a list of the directories where the user has been assigned Rights.

2. Users can gain Rights by belonging to groups. You can determine a user's group memberships with the SYSCON program by looking at the User Information section. Again you need to write a list of the groups the user belongs to. You can then find each group's Trustee Assignments. You also need to write a list of directories where each group has Rights.

3. A user can gain Rights by being security equivalent to other users. You can determine a user's security equivalences with the User Information section of the SYSCON program. You need to write the name of anyone that the user is a security equivalent to. Now look at each of these users' Trustee Assignments. List the directories where they have Rights.

4. After you write down all directories where the user has Rights because of Trustee Assignments, group memberships, and security equivalences, you are almost finished. The final way a user gains Rights is through downline

User's Directory Rights Are Not Appropriate

directories. Now that you have listed every directory where the user has Rights, you must determine if there are directories beneath each of these directories. The utility program on the diskette called VTREE is a handy way to do so. VTREE lists your server's directory structure for the current default volume. If you have multiple volumes, you must run VTREE for each. You can also redirect the output to your printer using DOS redirection:

`VTREE >LPT1:`

To create an ASCII file containing the VTREE information, redirect the information to a file with the command:

`VTREE >[d:][\directory path\]filename.ext`

You should be able to figure out from all the information you collect how the user got Rights in the directory. You should also review the Rights principles covered earlier in this chapter for further clarification on how NetWare Rights behave.

User's Rights Are Insufficient for Logging In
Keywords: Rights, LOGIN, SLIST

Scenario A user attempts to log in and cannot. The user has loaded the correct version of IPX for the NIC, has successfully loaded the re-director program, NETx, EMSNETx, or XMSNETx, and has been attached to the file server without difficulty.

Solution It's likely that the LOGIN.EXE file is corrupted. When this happens, no one can log in. Follow these steps to correct the problem:

- **Copy:** a version of the LOGIN program from the NetWare installation diskette labelled SYSTEM or PUBLIC-6 to the user's local hard disk.
- **Load:** the network shell files as usual, but run the LOGIN program from the user's local disk.
- **Log in:** as a supervisor.
- **Flag:** the LOGIN.EXE file in the LOGIN directory as read-write.
- **Copy:** the LOGIN.EXE file from the local hard disk to the LOGIN directory.
- **Flag:** the LOGIN.EXE file as read-only.

User Can Create Directories Without Parental Rights
Keywords: Rights, directories, Parental, Create

Scenario The user's Effective Rights in the parent directory do not include the Parental Right. Without this Right, the user cannot create or remove parent directories. Yet, the user can create downline directories.

Solution There are two probable explanations for this scenario. First, NetWare's Parental Right was modified in NetWare versions 2.15 and later. Prior to version 2.15, the Parental Right governed the user's ability to create, rename, or remove directories. This Right had to exist in conjunction with the Create, Modify, or Delete Rights to perform these activities. However, giving a user Parental Rights also gave the user the right to grant Rights to another user. In NetWare versions 2.15 and later, users don't need the Parental Right to perform these functions. Users need only Create, Modify, or Delete Rights to create, rename, or delete a downline directory. This is a change in NetWare, not an anomaly.

If you use a version of NetWare older than version 2.15, this problem probably occurs due to an Implicit Rights problem. A user's total Rights is a combination of Explicit Rights (Trustee Assignments) and Implicit Rights. Implicit Rights are gained through group memberships, security equivalences, and downline directories. You must follow the next steps to make sure the user is not gaining the Parental Right through one of these sources.

1. You determine a user's group memberships with the SYSCON program by looking at the User Information section. You need to write a list of the groups the user belongs to. You can then find each group's Trustee Assignments. You also need to write a list of directories where each group has Rights.

2. You can determine a user's security equivalences with the User Information section of the SYSCON program. You need to write down the name of anyone that the user is a security equivalent to. Now look at each of these users' Trustee Assignments. List the directories where they have Rights.

3. After you write down all directories where the user has Rights because of group memberships and security equivalences, you are almost finished. The final way a user gains Rights is through downline directories. Now that you have listed every directory where the user has Rights, you must determine if there are directories beneath each of these directories. The utility program on the diskette called VTREE is a handy way to do so. VTREE lists your server's directory structure for the current default volume. If you have multiple volumes, you must run VTREE for each. You also can redirect the output to your printer using DOS redirection:

   `VTREE >LPT1:`

   To create an ASCII file containing the VTREE information, redirect the information to a file with the command:

   `VTREE >[d:][\directory path\]filename.ext`

You should be able to determine from all the information you collect how the user got the Parental Right in the directory. You should also review the Rights principles covered earlier in this chapter for further clarification on how NetWare Rights behave.

SUMMARY

This chapter covered one of the most important aspects of NetWare security: directory and file Rights. Rights govern which directories users can access and give them the ability to run programs and create, update, and delete data files. Due to the varied needs of different network environments, complex rules and principles govern the operation of NetWare Rights. It is essential that network supervisors understand these issues. The objective of the NetWare Rights system is to prevent unauthorized access to files while making the network easy to use. Only the network administrator who understands the rules can accomplish this. The next chapter expands on these Rights principles, giving specific examples of how to set up NetWare groups in an effective manner for managing a network.

15
Using Groups to Manage Rights

As I mentioned in Chapter 14, managing NetWare Rights at the group level is the key to making NetWare directory and file security easy to manage. In this chapter I discuss how to develop a plan for effectively implementing the group concept. Actually, the usefulness of groups in NetWare extends beyond the topic of directory or file Rights. Groups can be used to establish print queue users and print queue operators, too.

In discussing the issue of establishing groups to make the file server easier to manage, it is important to understand that a central part of the discussion is the topic of hard disk organization. The plan for user Rights and group Rights must be combined with a plan for organizing the file server's disk volumes. I integrated these ideas so that the details of both will be apparent.

TWO WAYS TO SET UP GROUPS

There are two popular opinions on how to set up user groups for managing NetWare Rights. One is to establish groups corresponding to the application software being used—a word processing group, a spreadsheet group, a graphics group, etc. Each application's files would reside in its own directory on the file server. The group would be assigned Trustee Rights in the directory on the file server where the software resides. Any user who belongs to the group would have the Rights necessary to run the programs. Figure 15-1 shows an example of the server directory structure and the group concept.

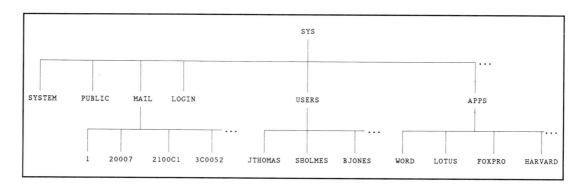

Group Name	Directory	Trustee Rights Assignment	Group Members
Word	SYS:APPS/WORD	Read, Open, Search	JTHOMAS, SHOLMES, BJONES
Lotus	SYS:APPS/LOTUS	Read, Open, Search	JTHOMAS, BJONES
Foxpro	SYS:APPS/FOXPRO	Read, Open, Search	SHOLMES, BJONES
Harvard	SYS:APPS/HARVARD	Read, Open, Search	JTHOMAS, SHOLMES

Figure 15-1. Application group model

The disk organization illustrated in Figure 15-1 is typical of most file servers. NetWare establishes the directories called SYSTEM, PUBLIC, MAIL, and LOGIN. NetWare also adds directories beneath MAIL for each user according to the user's NetWare-assigned ID number. It's up to the network administrator to organize and maintain the rest of the volume.

The plan illustrated in Figure 15-1 works well when the file server is used to share programs and to store the user's work in a directory belonging to the user. Users would have an appropriate Trustee Assignment in their home directories that would permit them to store and manage their files. This organization is typical for some NetWare LANs. As new software is added to the file server in its own directory, new groups are created and given Rights in the software directory. Users are added to groups based on the application packages each user is permitted to use.

The model presented in Figure 15-1 has a major shortcoming. It does not address the need to share data files, a critical need

Two Ways to Set Up Groups

of many network users. Nor does the plan provide any logical place to store these shared files. It makes no sense to store shared files in the application directory. Doing so complicates other tasks such as back up. Obviously, putting the files in a user's home directory would be unworkable also.

This problem emphasizes the need for the other type of group that is often used with NetWare. I call these groups **organizational groups**. Most shared data files belong to groups that are already established according to their roles in the organization. The best way to handle the need for shared files in the network is to establish groups that correspond to these needs. Figure 15-2 illustrates a model for using organizational groups.

This illustration uses an example based on two major groups being served by the file server and needing to share files—accounting and personnel (ACCTG and PERS). Also, each group has two subgroups. The ACCTG group has an accounts payable group (AP) and an accounts receivable group (AR). The PERS group has two subgroups, administration (ADMIN) and plant (PLANT).

Figure 15-2 gives each organizational group Trustee Rights in the directory that corresponds to the group's name. These directories contain the data files that all group members share. As users are added to the network, the supervisor decides which organizational groups they will belong to. This gives the user the Rights necessary to access the shared files. In most organizations, it's easy to decide where someone belongs on the organizational chart and it's equally easy to decide which groups the user needs to belong to.

However, there is a problem that is not obvious in Figure 15-2. The next section covers this problem. Before you set up your network this way, make sure you have read and understand the next section.

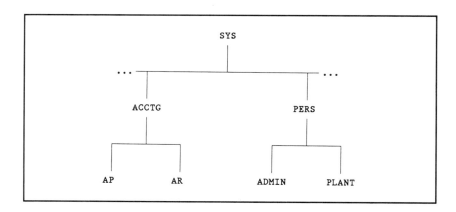

Group Name	Directory Name	Trustee Rights Assigned
ACCTG	SYS:ACCTG	Read, Open, Search, Create, Write, Delete, Modify
ACCTG__AP	SYS:ACCTG/AP	Read, Open, Search, Create, Write, Delete, Modify
ACCTG__AR	SYS:ACCTG/AR	Read, Open, Search, Create, Write, Delete, Modify
PERS	SYS:PERS	Read, Open, Search, Create, Write, Delete, Modify
PERS__ADMIN	SYS:PERS/ADMIN	Read, Open, Search, Create, Write, Delete, Modify
PERS__PLANT	SYS:PERS/PLANT	Read, Open, Search, Create, Write, Delete, Modify

Figure 15-2. Organizational group model

RIGHTS IN DOWNLINE DIRECTORIES

One principle of NetWare Rights is that users or groups who have Rights in a directory inherit the same Rights to downline directories. Figure 15-3 illustrates how this principle works for user directories.

Figure 15-3 illustrates that JTHOMAS has created downline directories. These directories need no Trustee Assignments because

Rights in Downline Directories

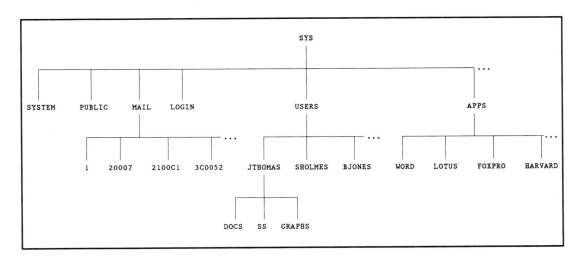

User Name	Directory	Trustee Rights Assignment
JTHOMAS	SYS:USERS/JTHOMAS	Read, Open, Search, Create, Delete, Write, Modify
	SYS:USERS/JTHOMAS/DOCS	None
	SYS:USERS/JTHOMAS/SS	None
	SYS:USERS/JTHOMAS/GRAPHS	None
SHOLMES	SYS:USERS/SHOLMES	Read, Open, Search, Create, Delete, Write, Modify
BJONES	SYS:USERS/BJONES	Read, Open, Search, Create, Delete, Write, Modify

Figure 15-3. Application group model with downline directories

JTHOMAS automatically inherits Rights in these directories. This works well because users are usually allowed to create directories downline from their home directory; the network supervisor does not need to bother making Trustee Assignments every time this happens.

However, there is a problem when users or groups should not have Rights to downline directories. Figure 15-4 helps to illustrate this problem.

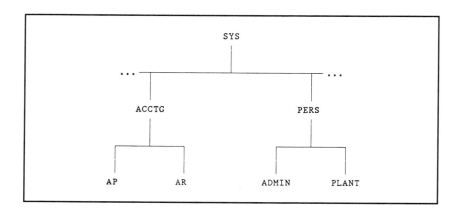

Group Name	Directory Name	Trustee Rights Assigned
ACCTG	SYS:ACCTG	Read, Open, Search, Create, Write, Delete, Modify
	SYS:ACCTG/AP (Implicit)	Read, Open, Search, Create, Write, Delete, Modify
	SYS:ACCTG/AR (Implicit)	Read, Open, Search, Create, Write, Delete, Modify
ACCTG_AP	SYS:ACCTG/AP	Read, Open, Search, Create, Write, Delete, Modify
ACCTG_AR	SYS:ACCTG/AR	Read, Open, Search, Create, Write, Delete, Modify
PERS	SYS:PERS	Read, Open, Search, Create, Write, Delete, Modify
	SYS:PERS/ADMIN (Implicit)	Read, Open, Search, Create, Write, Delete, Modify
	SYS:PERS/PLANT (Implicit)	Read, Open, Search, Create, Write, Delete, Modify
PERS_ADMIN	SYS:PERS/ADMIN	Read, Open, Search, Create, Write, Delete, Modify
PERS_PLANT	SYS:PERS/PLANT	Read, Open, Search, Create, Write, Delete, Modify

Figure 15-4. Organizational group model with downline directories

Rights in Downline Directories

You may not want the group ACCTG or PERS to have Rights to the downline directories. If so, you have to know how to block access to these directories and protect the files stored in them. This is why you never give users or groups a Trustee Assignment in the root directory. If they have Trustee Rights in the root directory, they have Rights everywhere. In the next scenario I discuss how to prevent user or group Rights from passing to downline directories.

Blocking Implicit Rights
Keywords: Rights, directory, downline

Scenario Often, it's undesirable to permit a user's or group's Trustee Rights to pass downline to directories. Figure 15-4 showed that anyone who belongs to the ACCTG group inherits Rights in SYS:ACCTG/AR and SYS:ACCTG/AP. Likewise, anyone who belongs to the PERS group inherits the Rights in SYS:PERS/ADMIN and SYS:PERS/PLANT. These Rights have nothing to do with the Rights that the subgroups ACCTG_AR, ACCTG_AP, PERS_ADMIN, or PERS_PLANT have in the directories illustrated in Figure 15-4. If you study the problem, you'll discover that you cannot change the Trustee Assignments given to the ACCTG group for the SYS:ACCTG directory or to the PERS group for the SYS:PERS directory because a group can have but one Trustee Assignment per directory.

Solution To prevent groups from inheriting Rights to downline directories, make a new Trustee Assignment for those groups (ACCTG and PERS in Figure 15-4). Because these groups already have Trustee Assignments in their home directories, you must make the new Trustee Assignments in the downline directories. Because our concern is preventing these groups from using the downline directories, the Rights we will assign are NO RIGHTS! Table 15-1 lists the new Trustee Assignments.

You assign no Rights by making the group a trustee of the directory and deleting all Rights listed for the Trustee Assignment in either the SYSCON or FILER program or with the NetWare GRANT command. This technique is called **blocking rights**. By creating a Trustee Assignment with no Rights, you have blocked the Implicit Rights inherited from the upline directory.

It is important to note that the explicit Trustee Assignment of no Rights becomes the group's implicit Rights in any directories further downline. For example, the ACCTG group would have no Rights in the new directory SYS:ACCTG/AP/JOB_1. The

Blocking Implicit Rights

Table 15–1. Blocking Implicit Rights from Passing to Downline Directories

Group Name	Directory Name	Trustee Rights Assigned
ACCTG	SYS:ACCTG	Read, Open, Search, Create, Write, Delete, Modify
	SYS:ACCTG/AP	NO RIGHTS
	SYS:ACCTG/AR	NO RIGHTS
ACCTG__AP	SYS:ACCTG/AP	Read, Open, Search, Create, Write, Delete, Modify
ACCTG__AR	SYS:ACCTG/AR	Read, Open, Search, Create, Write, Delete, Modify
PERS	SYS:PERS	Read, Open, Search, Create, Write, Delete, Modify
	SYS:PERS/ADMIN	NO RIGHTS
	SYS:PERS/PLANT	NO RIGHTS
PERS__ADMIN	SYS:PERS/ADMIN	Read, Open, Search, Create, Write, Delete, Modify
PERS__PLANT	SYS:PERS/PLANT	Read, Open, Search, Create, Write, Delete, Modify

ACCTG__AP group would have Rights in the directory. If this is undesirable, you can block these Rights by making a Trustee Assignment of no Rights to the ACCTG__AP group in the SYS:ACCTG/AP/JOB__1 directory.

If you plan to use hierarchical directory structures for shared data directories, it is vital that you fully understand this technique of blocking Rights. If you do not, users will have Rights in directories where you did not intend them to have Rights. This example also shows why you must avoid giving anyone Rights in the root directory. Because every directory is downline from the root directory, a user with Rights in the root directory has those Rights in all downline directories, unless those Rights are explicitly blocked.

SUMMARY

This short chapter covered one of the most important topics in NetWare—Rights management. NetWare Rights, when properly set up, require little management, or they can be an ongoing source of problems and frustration. Which situation occurs largely depends on the supervisor's ability to grasp the rules that govern NetWare Rights and to develop an implementation plan that suits the needs of users. If there is one area that new supervisors should spend time studying and planning, this is it. When I hear excessive NetWare administration woes, the problem is usually lack of understanding about how Rights work or lack of a solid organizational plan for the network.

Designing a good network administration plan is much like designing a good program. You start by determining the organization's needs or goals. You translate these into general design criteria for how different aspects of the network need to work. After you establish criteria, you map out the details of the plan. Next, you take detailed steps to set up the network. Finally, you test everything to make sure that it works the way you planned it. If it does, great! If it doesn't, retrace your steps and find out what went awry.

Part VI
Managing the LAN

This part explores aspects of managing a NetWare LAN that have not been discussed earlier. If you are reading this book chapter by chapter, you have gained valuable insights into various NetWare components. Now it's time to address the topics that pull all the pieces tightly together into an integrated LAN offering optimal performance and easy maintenance.

In this part I discuss some new supervisory functions that have been added to NetWare 386 and may be added to NetWare 286 in the future. These new features make your network easier and safer to manage. I also explore FCONSOLE, an important NetWare program for monitoring the file server's performance. Finally, I make suggestions for documenting the LAN.

16

NetWare Supervisors, Workgroup Managers, and User Account Managers

One of the most significant changes Novell made to NetWare 386 is better management capabilities. In the past, NetWare 286 only had two types of users: supervisors and non-supervisors or users. All supervisors had the same capabilities. They were all-powerful in managing the LAN. Their authority included the ability to create and delete users and other supervisors and to change the password of any user. Supervisors did not need any Trustee Assignments because they had all Rights in all directories.

This carte blanche power for all supervisors has always been somewhat dangerous. It has been one of the deciding factors in many network administrators' decisions to have only one supervisor. Yet, in most networks, it is preferable to distribute administrative tasks among several individuals. This is particularly true of large networks where one person cannot keep up with the demands and needs of users.

NetWare 386 changes all this with two new classes of users: workgroup managers and user account managers.

NETWARE 386 WORKGROUP MANAGERS

A network supervisor can designate workgroup managers with the SYSCON program's Supervisor Options menu. The workgroup manager can add new users to the manager's list of managed users and groups. (The supervisor must add users who existed prior to the creation of the workgroup manager.) The workgroup manager's capabilities are outlined in Table 16-1.

Table 16-1. Workgroup Manager Abilities	
Supervisor options in SYSCON	NO
Delete any user at large	NO
Add/Delete users to their user domain	YES
Add/Delete users to other groups or domains	NO
Assign Rights in all directories	NO
Assign Rights in supervised directories	YES
Change user information at large	NO
Change user information for managed users or groups	YES
Change their own user login restrictions	NO

As you see, because their capabilities are restricted, creating workgroup managers is safer than creating other supervisors. Simply stated, workgroup managers can add or delete users in their domain only. I use the word **domain** to refer to those users and groups that the workgroup managers supervise. The workgroup manager can manage any user information about their users. They can assign Rights only in directories where a supervisor has given the workgroup manager Rights.

These abilities allow the supervisor to design the file server's security so that it can be managed on a group basis. Each workgroup manager would have their own domain to manage. Although workgroup managers can see a list of every user of the file server, they cannot query user information or change it unless the user belongs to their managed groups.

The supervisor assigns directory access privileges to the workgroup manager. The workgroup manager can assign Rights to other managed users in the directory where the workgroup manager has supervisory or access control Rights. The workgroup manager has no Rights in any directories other than those the supervisor designates.

NETWARE 386 USER ACCOUNT MANAGERS

A user account manager differs from a workgroup manager. I wish Novell had given this group a name that reflects the difference. Workgroup managers or supervisors can create user account managers. A NetWare 386 user account manager cannot create users. User account managers can change information about the users that they manage. They can make Trustee Assignments in directories where they possess Rights, but not in other directories. User account managers may delete users that belong to the user group manager's domain. In a sense, a user account manager is like a workgroup manager without the ability to create users.

In some network designs, shared data files reside in directories shared by organizational groups that use these files. This often leads to hierarchical directory structures like the one illustrated in Figure 16–1.

The benefit of having workgroup managers and user account managers in this type of structure is obvious. Having workgroup managers and user account managers at various levels distributes network management tasks. As users are added to the LAN, they become part of the workgroup manager's or user account manager's group(s).

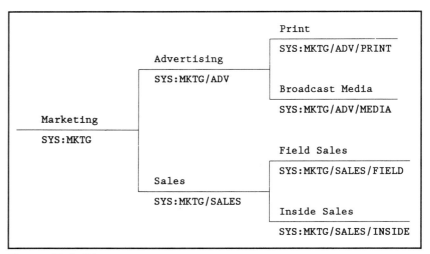

Figure 16-1. Directory structures

CREATING GROUPS

Group management is different in a network with workgroup managers and user account managers. The next three sections outline the differences.

Users Created by Supervisors

The supervisor creates managed groups with the Group Information menu in SYSCON. The supervisor also may create group members. To put a user account or group that the supervisor creates under the care of either a workgroup manager or user account manager, the supervisor adds the user or the group as a managed user while in the Workgroup Manager's User Information menu or User Account Manager's User Information menu. After a group is in a workgroup manager's or user account manager's domain, the workgroup manager or user account manager may change the group member's user information.

Users Created by Workgroup Managers

Users created by workgroup managers are automatically in their domain and may be added to any other group that the workgroup manager manages. If the workgroup manager wishes to place a user under a user group manager's care, the workgroup manager must update the Managers option in the user's User Information menu. Or the workgroup manager may add the user by updating the Managed Users and Groups option in the Manager's User Information menu.

Users Who Have More Than One Manager

A user can be managed by multiple workgroup managers or user account managers. If this is the case, any of the user's managers can update the user's information. In addition, any of the user's managers could delete the user's account. I believe that Novell should change this risky feature so that only a supervisor can delete users who have more than one manager. If a workgroup manager or user account manager stops managing a particular user, the manager can remove the user from their Managed Users list in SYSCON.

CREATING INDEPENDENT FILE SERVER DOMAINS

Earlier in this chapter I discussed the functions of the new workgroup managers and user account managers in NetWare 386. Now I want to complete the picture by explaining how to implement the workgroup manager and user account manager features so one file server appears to be many independent file servers. This will help the many network administrators I talk with who want to distribute administrative activities to managers.

Allocating Space on File Servers
Keywords: disk space, users, groups

Scenario Now that users, groups, and directory rights can be managed by workgroup managers and user account managers, the remaining task is allocating space on the file servers, if needed. One concern some network administrators voice is the need to limit how much disk space a group can occupy. Historically, NetWare let you limit disk space only on a user basis. This is still true in NetWare 386.

Solution If you need to control disk space on a group basis, the best solution is to establish separate volumes for each group. Volumes are created when NetWare is installed and their size is fixed. If workgroup managers have Rights at the root directory of volumes, they have complete control over the volumes. Their managed user's files cannot grow beyond the volume's capacity. Using this technique, the network administrator can allocate independent disk space for different groups without worrying about one's group's use being inequitable.

You need to be careful when changing disk volume sizes, however. You can safely increase volume size without losing data, if the volume starts on the same cylinder. You cannot decrease volume size. If you do, you lose all files stored on the volume. If possible, determine volume size before setting up the file server to avoid reallocating volumes later.

> **WARNING:** You should always back up the entire drive before attempting to modify volume sizes!

MIXED NETWARE 286 AND NETWARE 386 ENVIRONMENTS

The last issue for discussion is mixed environments with multiple file servers, some running NetWare 286 and some running NetWare 386.

Management Techniques for Different File Servers
Keywords: SYSCON, management, administration

Scenario The workgroup manager and user account manager feature implies that different management techniques must be used for different file servers because these features do not yet exist in NetWare 286. This can be a big problem.

Solution Right now, Novell's unofficial solution to this problem is to copy your NetWare 386 SYSCON.EXE and SYSCON.HLP files to your NetWare 286 file servers. Novell has not widely publicized this procedure but has recommended it on their bulletin board on an "at your own risk" basis. You can access the bulletin board via CompuServe. To date, I have not heard of any problems with the procedure. We have tried it in our office and it works fine.

One User Group Is Using All the Disk Space
Keywords: disk, volumes, files

Scenario

This scenario evolved not long ago from a client need. The company involved was a data processing service that had begun as a batch service bureau. This means that our client used to pick up the customer's work, process it on their mainframe, and then return finished reports and other output to the customer. This service eventually became an on-line service: customers had terminals hooked up over telephone lines to do their data entry and inquiry. The telephone lines were expensive, and the customers could only perform the functions that had been set up. The customers could not use the terminals for anything else. Now our client is installing NetWare LANs in their customer's offices. These LANs have specialized software for processing the customer's work in conjunction with a mainframe connection (distributed processing).

The problem arose because the customers want to add their software to the LAN for other activities such as word processing and spreadsheets. Our client faced a dilemma on two fronts. The first is supervisory. Who is going to manage the LAN? If our client assumes this role, the client is going to have to install other software, as well as troubleshoot problems with this software when they arise. If the customer assumes the supervisor's role, our client risks having the customer make improper changes to the file server that could make a mess out of our client's software and data files. In addition, who would train all the customer's supervisors?

The other problem is controlling how much disk space the customer uses for other application software. The customer could potentially use so much disk space that our client's software would no longer run.

Solution

The solution for this case is actually pretty simple. Our client divided the file server disk into separate volumes. One volume (SYS:) contained all NetWare files and default directories and our client's software and data file directories. Another volume contained the software and data files that the customer wanted to add to the LAN. With separate volumes, the customer's files cannot grow too large, nor prevent our client's software from running.

Next, our client created a workgroup manager for their customer. The workgroup manager was given a Trustee Assignment in the root directory of the second volume, allowing the workgroup manager to set up and use this volume for the other software applications.

Each network user has two different account names. One account name lets the user access our client's software applications and all files associated with it. Our client created these accounts, and the workgroup manager could not change them. The other account name lets the user access the customer-installed software. The customer's workgroup manager created and managed these accounts.

Using these procedures, our client was able to distribute the network's administrative tasks. The customer was able to add new software to the second volume and give users access to these applications. Our client retained control over the portion of the file server that contained their software and did not need to worry about the customer's causing a problem by changing or deleting something.

SUMMARY

NetWare 386's workgroup manager and user group manager features offer some definite advantages in creating a more manageable network environment. For a long time, I have felt that Novell should make these features available for all NetWare versions. The present NetWare 286 user types of supervisors and users are hard to manage and inherently dangerous. Novell is likely to address this problem in two ways. First, they may add the new capabilities to NetWare 286, officially upgrading the product. This would be wise and appreciated by the supervisors of hundreds of thousands of NetWare 286 installations. Second, Novell may try to encourage everyone to buy NetWare 386 and abandon NetWare 286. To accomplish this, Novell must reduce the price of NetWare 386 to make it more reasonable in comparison with NetWare 286 prices.

17
Monitoring the File Server

An important activity of the network administrator is to monitor the file server to determine how well it is performing. The network administrator must occasionally adjust the file server to meet the changing needs of network users. NetWare provides a tool for monitoring the file server, a supervisor's program called FCONSOLE. The Statistics option of the program reports various file server performance factors. In this chapter I discuss this program and how to interpret the data that it presents.

FILE SERVER STATISTICS SUMMARY

This on-screen page of information recaps several key components of the file server's memory configuration and CPU utilization. It is a logical place to start investigating when you suspect a performance problem. Figure 17-1 shows a sample of this screen. The next several sections describe the type of information the summary provides.

File Server Up Time

This value tells how long the server has been running since it was last booted. All cumulative statistics for the FCONSOLE program are totals based on the time the file server has been up. This piece of information can be useful for estimating certain load factors.

```
NetWare File Server Console  V1.00b                    February 1x, 199x  5:24 pm
              User HADER On File Server ATRIUM Connection 1

                         File Server Statistics Summary

File Server Up Time:    0 Days  9 Hours 37 Minutes  2 Seconds
Number Of File Service Processes:     5  Current Server Utilization:        1%
Disk Requests Serviced From Cache:  96%  Packets Routed:                     0
Total Packets Received:       3,150,926  File Service Packets:              86
Total Number Of Cache Buffers:      125  Dirty Cache Buffers:               14
Total Server Memory:          2,097,152  Unused Server Memory:           9,216

                          Maximum      Peak Used    Currently In Use
Routing Buffers:              150             42                  22
Open Files:                 1,000            348                 119
Indexed Files:                 40             11                   0
Transactions:                  90              4                   0
Bindery Objects:              500            329                 145
Connections:                  100             12                   2
Dynamic Memory 1:          17,272          1,858                 842
Dynamic Memory 2:          65,436          6,636               4,676
Dynamic Memory 3:          47,104            712                 120
```

Figure 17-1. FCONSOLE statistics summary

Number of File Service Processes

This value represents the number of file service processes (FSPs) the file server can handle simultaneously. When no FSPs are available, NetWare queues file requests for processing until an FSP becomes available. When a server runs out of FSPs, performance is degraded. A shortage of FSPs contributes to the communication or routing buffers filling up. Packets may eventually be lost because no buffers are available. This causes the workstations to resend data and results in further performance degradation. The number of FSPs is a complex calculation based on many factors. Later in this chapter, I discuss FSPs in more detail and present some ideas on how you can increase the number available.

Current Server Utilization

This value constantly fluctuates because it shows the percentage of time that the file server's CPU is in use. A value of 80% or more may mean that you should investigate having a faster file server or spread the workload among multiple file servers.

File Server Statistics Summary

Disk Requests Serviced from Cache

This percentage reflects how often the file server serviced disk requests from the cache memory of the file server. NetWare calculates this figure by taking the total cache hits and dividing them by the sum of the disk read requests plus the total disk write requests. If this number consistently drops below 80%, it is probably time to add more RAM to the file server. NetWare's excellent caching algorithms should result in a hit rate of over 90%.

Packets Routed

This value represents the number of packets routed. These packets are received from one physical network and routed to another physical network. The packet's destination could be a workstation or another file server located on another network. This file server received the packet because it was in the logical path the packet traveled from its origin to its destination.

Total Packets Received

This number reflects the total number of packets the file server received since it was brought up. This value can be useful in assessing the rate at which the file server receives packets. Also, for each packet received, a packet is usually sent. Using this information with the packet size (determined by the protocol), you can roughly estimate the number of bytes or bits transmitted over your LAN channel during a given period. This is useful in determining if a performance bottleneck is occurring at the physical channel.

File Service Packets

This value represents the number of packets that requested file services during the last second. These packets use file service processes on the file server. A file service request is any packet that needs any file-related processing. The packet is not limited to user files, but includes file server files such as binderies and directories.

Total Number of Cache Buffers

This value is important in determining how much RAM your server has available for file caching activities. Cache buffers are 4096 bytes each. Multiply the value shown by 4K to determine the amount of RAM available for caching. You can use this value to determine how much RAM a VAP requires on the file server. Bring up the file server without loading the VAP and record this value. Then bring up the file server, loading the VAP. The difference between these two values is the number of 4K blocks of RAM the VAP uses.

Dirty Cache Buffers

This value represents the number of cache buffers that contain data that must be written to the disk but has not yet been written. This number increases and decreases as file server conditions change dynamically. All disk writes are made from cache, not directly based on a packet received. The server sends the workstation an acknowledgement that the data has been written, even if it is still in the cache. Writes wait in the cache for two reasons. First, NetWare compares data being written to data originally received. If the data has not changed, NetWare does not perform the write. This is a cache write hit. Second, NetWare sorts disk reads and writes them in a logical sequence based on their disk location, rather than the order in which they are received. The result is better performance and less wear and tear on the disk drive. The maximum amount of time a write waits in the cache is three seconds. If your server looses power, you can loose the data waiting in the cache. This is why you always down the file server. It's also why an uninterruptable power supply is recommended for the file server. Dirty cache buffers are the same as "Disk I/Os Pending" that is displayed on the file server monitor.

Total Server Memory

On a dedicated file server, this value represents the total RAM installed in the file server. On a non-dedicated file server, this value represents the total RAM available for the file server's

File Server Statistics Summary

network tasks, exclusive of the RAM used for supporting a DOS session. Non-dedicated file servers use between 800K to 1500K for the DOS session, although the user has only 640K available.

Unused Server Memory

This value represents fragmented memory that the file server is unable to use. Memory fragments during the file server boot up process as NetWare allocates RAM to its various needs. Sometimes leftover pieces of logical RAM blocks result in this number. If this number is over 1Mb, you may have VAPs in your SYS:SYSTEM directory and the file server is still waiting for a response to the question, "Value added processes have been defined. Do you wish to load them?"

Routing Buffers

Routing buffers are the same as communication buffers. NetWare calls them different names in different places. These buffers hold incoming requests until the file server can process them. Routing buffers also hold outgoing requests until they can be transmitted. Too few routing buffers result in reduced performance if your server repeatedly reaches the maximum in the Peak Used column or Currently In Use column.

Open Files

This number indicates how many files the file server can have open simultaneously. When the server reaches the maximum, no more files can be opened until others are closed. The maximum value is 1000.

Indexed Files

The maximum value for this entry determines the number of indexed files that may be open simultaneously on the file server. An indexed file is a file that has been flagged with the FLAG command. You should flag any file that is 2Mb or larger. When an indexed file is opened, NetWare builds a RAM index of the file's entries in the FAT so that NetWare can work more efficiently with the file. Indexing large files can have a dramatic and positive impact on performance as NetWare accesses the file.

Transactions

This entry only applies to SFT NetWare. SFT NetWare and "SFT-aware" applications use this feature to record in a log file changes made to data files during a transaction update process. If the transaction fails to complete for some reason, the log file can be used to restore the original data files.

Bindery Objects

This entry only applies when you select the option to limit disk space occupied during the NETGEN process. Because NetWare must track the disk space used by bindery objects, you establish a maximum value when the Limit Disk Space option is turned on. These values represent the status of the bindery object count.

Connections

The number of connections to the file server depends on the NetWare version being used. ELS I permits 4, ELS II permits 8, Advanced NetWare, and SFT NetWare permit 100 simultaneous connections.

Dynamic Memory 1

This value represents the amount of RAM available for NetWare's DGroup memory pool. DGroup memory is used for mapped drive tracking and temporary buffers. Each mapped directory uses 16 bytes of DGroup memory. Each print queue uses 56 bytes. Each NIC installed in the file server also uses DGroup memory. The buffer size of the NIC driver determines the amount of memory used. Ethernet cards use 1024 bytes, standard ARCnet uses 512 bytes, and token ring is configurable from 1024 to 4096 bytes. Each disk volume installed in the file server uses 3K of DGroup RAM. Remaining DGroup memory is allocated to FSPs.

Cache Statistics

Dynamic Memory 2

The file server uses this memory region to track open files, file locks, and record locks. The amount of memory available is configured when the maximum number of open files is configured for the file server.

Dynamic Memory 3

The server uses this final region of dynamic memory to keep routing tables for internal packet routing and for other server information. This value is not configurable.

CACHE STATISTICS

Cache statistics report on memory activities within the file server. These statistics can be useful in evaluating how well the server's cache is performing and when it might be prudent to install more RAM on the file server. Figure 17-2 is a sample screen showing the cache statistics. The next several sections describe the types of statistics included on the screen.

```
       NetWare File Server Console   V1.00b        February 1x, 199x  7:15 pm
              User HADER On File Server ATRIUM Connection 1

                              Cache Statistics

File Server Up Time:    0 Days  1 Hours 28 Minutes 10 Seconds
Number Of Cache Buffers:           125  Cache Buffer Size:          4,096
Dirty Cache Buffers:                 0
Cache Read Requests:            69,247  Cache Write Requests:       7,792
Cache Hits:                     74,278  Cache Misses:               3,241
Physical Read Requests:          2,931  Physical Write Requests:      947
Physical Read Errors:                0  Physical Write Errors:          0
Cache Get Requests:             73,521
Full Write Requests:             3,518  Partial Write Requests:     4,274
Background Dirty Writes:           311  Background Aged Writes:       605
Total Cache Writes:                929  Cache Allocations:          3,236
Thrashing Count:                     0  LRU Block Was Dirty:            5
Read Beyond Write:                 103  Fragmented Writes:             18
Hit On Unavailable Block:           70  Cache Blocks Scrapped:          0
```

Figure 17-2. Cache statistics

File Server Up Time

This entry tells how long the server has run since it was last booted. All cumulative statistics for the FCONSOLE program are totals based on the time the file server has been up. This can be a useful piece of information when trying to estimate certain load factors.

Number of Cache Buffers

This is an important value for determining how much RAM your server has available for file caching activities. Cache buffers are 4096 bytes each. Multiply the value shown by 4K to determine the amount of RAM available for caching. You can use the result to determine how much RAM a VAP requires on the file server. Bring up the file server without loading the VAP and record this value. Then bring up the file server, loading the VAP. The difference between these two values is the number of 4K blocks of RAM the VAP uses.

Cache Buffer Size

This value represents the size of each cache buffer. In NetWare 286 version 2.1x, the value is always 4096 bytes. Multiply this value by the number of cache buffers to calculate how much memory in the file server is available for file caching.

Dirty Cache Buffers

This value represents the number of cache buffers that contain data that must be written to the disk but has not yet been written. This number increases and decreases as file server conditions change dynamically. All disk writes are made from cache, not directly based on a packet received. The server sends the workstation an acknowledgement that the data has been written, even if it is still in the cache. Dirty cache buffers are the same as "Disk I/Os Pending" that is displayed on the file server monitor.

Cache Statistics

Cache Read Requests

This is the total number of read requests issued that have resulted in an actual read to the disk. When a read is serviced from the cache during a partial write request that requires a read request, that read is not recorded here. The read is not counted in the Cache Hits value.

Cache Write Requests

This value tallies the number of times that NetWare was asked to write to the disk. NetWare always holds data being written to the disk in cache memory before writing. Writes wait in the cache for two reasons. First, NetWare compares data being written to the data originally received. If the data has not changed, NetWare does not perform the write. This is a cache write hit. Second, NetWare sorts disk reads and writes them in a logical sequence based on their disk location, rather than the order in which they are received. The result is better performance and less wear and tear on the disk drive. The maximum amount of time a write waits in the cache is three seconds. If your server loses power, you can lose the data waiting in the cache. This is why you always down the file server. It's also why an uninterruptable power supply is recommended for the file server. The Cache Writes Requests value includes the values for both Full Write Requests and Partial Write Requests.

Cache Hits

This value represents the sum of the number of Cache Write Requests where the data being written is the same as the data already in the cache buffer, plus the number of Cache Read Requests when the data requested is already in the cache buffer, plus the number of Partial Write Requests when the data is already in the cache buffer, minus the number of Cache Misses.

Cache Misses

This value represents the number of times the data requested for a read or write was not in the cache. Since all reads and writes are cached, you might think that this value could be 0; this is not true. You can determine this value by adding the Cache Allocations value and the LRU Block Was Dirty value, because these values determine where the cache gets new cache blocks to use for reading and writing data that was not in the cache.

Physical Read Requests

This value represents the number of times that a read request was issued to the disk controller. This happens when the data is not in the cache.

Physical Write Requests

This value is the sum of the Total Cache Writes and Fragmented Writes values. These are the write requests issued to the disk controller.

Physical Read Errors

This value represents the number of times that the disk controller reported an error when attempting to read from the disk. Check this value periodically: it can signal you that your drive or controller is developing a problem.

Physical Write Errors

This value represents the number of times that the disk controller was unable to write to the disk successfully. Physical write errors use the Hot Fix Table and, if excessive, indicate potential disk problems.

Cache Statistics

Cache Get Requests

This value represents the number of times that the disk controller was instructed to retrieve data from the disk whether the data was in the cache or not.

Full Write Requests

This value represents the number of times the disk controller could write an entire disk sector because the entire sector had been changed. In this case, the data could be written without having the disk controller read the disk sector first.

Partial Write Requests

This value represents the number of times the disk controller was instructed to write the partial contents of a sector. When this happens, the controller must read the sector into the cache before performing the write.

Background Dirty Writes

This value represents the accumulated total of Dirty Cache Buffers. These are writes that were not made immediately to the disk, but waited in the cache for a period of up to three seconds. A low value suggests that most writes are being made immediately.

Background Aged Writes

This value represents the number of Dirty Cache Buffers written to the disk when the data waited in the cache for the maximum time of three seconds.

Total Cache Writes

This value represents the number of cache buffers written to the disk when the entire buffer was full and then written to a single disk block. For more information, see the later section, "Fragmented Writes."

Cache Allocations

This value represents the number of times a new cache block was allocated from a free pool of cache blocks. This happens when a cache block is needed for new data being retrieved from or written to the disk. For more information, see the later section, "LRU Block Was Dirty."

Thrashing Count

This value represents the number of times **thrashing** occurred. Thrashing happens when a cache block is needed but not available because the operating system is using all cache blocks. This means cache block requests wait while the operating system tries to free some cache blocks. Thrashing seriously degrades performance. You can stop it by adding RAM to the file server.

LRU Block Was Dirty

This value represents the number of cache blocks allocated from a pool of dirty cache blocks waiting to be written to the disk. The data in the dirty cache block must be written to the disk before the block can be allocated for other uses. NetWare uses the Least Recently Used (LRU) algorithm to decide which block to reallocate. Therefore, cache blocks that are hit more often are allocated last.

Read Beyond Write

This value represents the number of times that a read request for data from the cache exceeds the amount of data in the cache available for the read so that the remainder of the read must be issued to the disk controller. In other words, part of the data was in the cache and part of the data was not.

Fragmented Writes

This value represents the number of times that a partially filled cache buffer is written to the disk. Each group of sectors must be written as a separate request.

Hit On Unavailable Block

This value represents the number of times the data requested was in the cache but unavailable because the cache block was being read from the disk or written to the disk. The request must wait until the block is available and the disk read or write is finished.

Cache Blocks Scrapped

This value represents the number of times that a cache block requested was allocated from the dirty cache buffers and, while the process waited for the dirty cache block to be written to disk, another process read the data the first process needed into a different cache block. The first process stops waiting for the original block and gets the data from the second block. After the first block is written to the disk, it is returned to the free cache block pool.

CHANNEL STATISTICS

The second option on the FCONSOLE Statistics menu is Channel Statistics. It lets you see information about a selected disk channel. Other than verifying driver and controller data, this screen does not provide any useful analytical statistics. Figure 17-3 displays an example of this screen. The next several sections describe the types of statistics the screen provides.

```
NetWare File Server Console   V1.00b            February 1x, 199x  8:49 pm
              User HADER On File Server ATRIUM Connection 1


                              Disk Channel 0
File Server Up Time:   0 Days 13 Hours  2 Minutes 15 Seconds
Status: Channel is running.
Synchronization: No one is using the channel.
Driver Type: 116. TMC 880 Future Domain SCSI
Driver Version: 117.114
IO Addresses:
Shared Memory Addresses: CA0000:0000h to CA0000:FFFFFFFFh
Interrupts Used: 0Eh
DMA Channels Used:
Channel Configuration: INT 14 TMC-880
```

Figure 17-3. Channel statistics

File Server Up Time

This value tells how long the server has run since it was last booted. All cumulative statistics for the FCONSOLE program are totals based on the time the file server has been up. This piece of information can be useful for estimating certain load factors.

Status

This entry states the status of the disk channel:

`Channel is running.`	This is the normal status, indicating that the disk channel is working properly.
`Channel is being stopped.`	A disk read or write failed. The operating system's recovery processes have taken over the channel to attempt to recover from the failure. All other disk access to this channel is blocked.
`Channel is stopped.`	The operating system's recovery processes have taken over the channel to attempt to recover from a disk failure.
`Channel is non-functional.`	No disk drives on this channel are accessible due to a non-recoverable failure.

Synchronization

On non-dedicated file servers, NetWare and DOS can share the disk channel. On a dedicated server, only NetWare accesses the channel. Use of the shared channel must be synchronized to permit only one operating system to use the channel at a time. This entry shows the status of the synchronization. If the channel is not shared, the status is

`No one is using the channel.`

Channel Statistics

If the channel is shared, the status may be

```
No one is using the channel.
NetWare is using the channel.
NetWare is using the channel, someone else wants it.
Someone else is using the channel.
Someone else is using the channel, NetWare needs it.
The channel has been released, NetWare should use it.
```

Driver Type

This entry shows the Novell-assigned numeric driver type and also the driver name used for the disk controller. This information is useful for verifying which driver was selected when the operating system was linked during NETGEN or ELSGEN.

Driver Version

This displays the version number of the driver.

I/O Addresses

This entry lists any I/O addresses the controller uses to communicate with the CPU. Not all controllers use I/O addresses.

Shared Memory Addresses

If the driver uses shared memory addresses to communicate with the disk controller, those addresses are listed here.

Interrupts Used

If the disk controller uses interrupt channels to communicate with the CPU, the hex value of the interrupt used is displayed here.

DMA Channels Used

If the disk controller uses DMA channels for communicating with the CPU for memory transfers, the channels are listed here.

Channel Configuration

This entry shows the hardware configuration selected for the driver when NETGEN or ELSGEN was run. This line summarizes the I/O addresses, shared memory addresses, interrupts, and DMA channels used.

DISK MAPPING INFORMATION

Used only in SFT NetWare, this option shows the status of any mirrored or duplexed disk drives. To minimize the impact of a disk failure, SFT NetWare lets data be written redundantly to separate physical drives. This screen displays the status of mirrored drives, if installed, and tells which disk channels are in use. Figure 17-4 is a sample of this screen.

File Server Up Time

This value tells how long the server has run since it was last booted. All cumulative statistics for the FCONSOLE program are totals based on the time the file server has been up. This piece of information can be useful when trying to estimate certain load factors.

```
NetWare File Server Console   V1.00b              February 1x, 199x   9:50 pm
              User HADER On File Server ATRIUM Connection 1

                        Disk Mapping Information

File Server Up Time:    0 Days  4 Hours  2 Minutes 47 Seconds
SFT Support Level:      2           Pending I/O Commands:    0
Logical Disk Count:     1           Physical Disk Count:     2
Disk Channels  0) Active    1) Unused   2) Unused   3) Unused   4) Unused
              Logical Disk To Physical Disk Mappings
      Primary  Mirror              Primary  Mirror              Primary  Mirror
   0)    0       1            11)                           22)
   1)                         12)                           23)
   2)                         13)                           24)
   3)                         14)                           25)
   4)                         15)                           26)
   5)                         16)                           27)
   6)                         17)                           28)
   7)                         18)                           29)
   8)                         19)                           30)
   9)                         20)                           31)
  10)                         21)
```

Figure 17-4. Disk mapping information

Disk Mapping Information

SFT Support Level

This value represents the level of SFT support that the file server operating system supports.

- Level 0   Duplicate copies of File Allocation Tables and directories stored on the disk.
- Level 1   All features of Level 0, plus Hot Fix Redirection Tables for recovery from bad disk block errors.
- Level 2   All Level 1 features, plus mirrored or duplexed disk drives to recover from disk drive failures.

Pending I/O Commands

This value represents the number of disk requests waiting in the cache due to **elevator seeking**. Elevator seeking means that NetWare arranges disk reads and writes in logical order according to their disk location rather than the order in which the requests were received. This improves performance and reduces wear and tear on the drive.

Logical Disk Count

This value represents the number of disk drives that "appear" to users logged into the file server. A mirrored drive pair appears as only one drive to the user.

Physical Disk Count

This value represents the number of disk drives actually installed on the file server.

Disk Channels

These entries show the status of the disk channels available on the file server. A NetWare file server has up to five disk channels (0 to 4). Channels can be Active, Inactive, or Failed.

Active   Disk drives are installed on these channels.
Inactive   No disk drives are installed.
Failed   These channels suffered a severe failure of some sort. No drives attached to a failed channel are accessible.

Logical Disk To Physical Disk Mappings

This table shows how physical drives are mapped to logical drives. It also can show the status of mirrors. For a mirrored disk with normal status, the primary drive and mirror drive numbers are listed opposite the logical disk number. If the drive is mirrored, the primary drive is always listed, but if the status is not normal, a status message replaces the mirror drive number:

`Disabled`   The drive has been "un-mirrored" because of a console command or a disk failure.

`Remirroring` The drive is being remirrored. All data from the primary drive is being recopied to the mirror drive. This can happen during boot up if the server detects that the mirror is different. The REMIRROR console command can initiate it also.

`None`   There is no mirror drive.

`Dead`   A failed drive has been shut down by the file server.

DISK STATISTICS

Disk statistics are related to the physical disks installed on the file server. Some file server installation and configuration information is shown. Figure 17-5 shows an example of this screen. The next sections describe the several useful pieces of information contained on this screen.

Disk Statistics

```
NetWare File Server Console  V1.00b      Sunday  February 17, 1991  10:18 pm
              User HADER On File Server ATRIUM Connection 1


                              Physical Disk  0

    File Server Up Time:    0 Days 14 Hours 31 Minutes 16 Seconds
    Disk Type:   81. Future Domain SCSI (830/840/880) V1.4
    Non-Removable Drive
    Disk Channel:     0     Controller Number:   0    Drive Number: 0
    Controller Type: 81.
    Drive Size (less hot fix area): 229,376,000 bytes
    Drive Cylinders:    999  Drive Heads:  27   Sectors Per Track:  17
    IO Error Count:       0
    Hot Fix Table Start: 56,000          Hot Fix Enabled
    Hot Fix Table Size:  1,317 blocks    Hot Fix Remaining: 1,279 blocks
```

Figure 17–5. Disk statistics

File Server Up Time

This value tells how long the server has run since it was last booted. All cumulative statistics for the FCONSOLE program are totals based on the time the file server has been up. This piece of information can be useful for estimating certain load factors.

Disk Type

This entry shows the disk type that corresponds to the drive type in the file server's ROM BIOS or in the disk driver linked with the NetWare operating system.

Disk Channel

This entry tells which disk channel the drive is running on, as well as the controller number and the drive's number.

Controller Type

This value represents the numeric disk controller type assigned to the controller running this disk drive.

Drive Size

This value represents total drive size in bytes. It does not include the size of the area set aside for the Hot Fix Redirection Table.

Drive Cylinders

This value represents the number of cylinders on the disk drive, the number of drive heads for the disk drive, and the number of sectors per track or cylinder. To calculate the size of the drive, including the Hot Fix Redirection Table, multiply the number of drive cylinders times the number of drive heads, times the number of sectors per track, times 512.

I/O Error Count

This value represents the number of I/O errors this drive experienced since the file server was brought up.

Hot Fix Table Start

This value represents the block number on the disk where the Hot Fix Redirection Table begins.

Hot Fix Status

The next piece of information is a message indicating the status of the hot fix redirection feature.

Hot Fix Enabled	Hot fix is functional.
Hot Fix Disabled	Hot fix is available but the file server has shut it down because of repeated disk failures on the disk drive or controller.
Hot Fix Not Available	This file server's operating system does not support the hot fix feature.

Hot Fix Table Size

This value represents the size of the Hot Fix Redirection Table when the file server was configured using NETGEN or ELSGEN. The size reflects the number of 4K disk blocks.

Hot Fix Remaining

This value represents the number of unused blocks in the Hot Fix Redirection Table. Six blocks are pointers that track which blocks have been redirected into the hot fix area. The remainder hold the redirected data.

FILE SYSTEM STATISTICS

File system statistics report on file activities performed at the file server. You can use these statistics to analyze how many files have been opened and how many read and write requests have been made. Figure 17-6 shows a sample File System Statistics screen. The next several sections describe the information the screen provides.

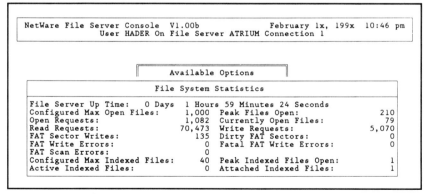

Figure 17-6. File system statistics

File Server Up Time

This value tells how long the server has run since it was last booted. All cumulative statistics for the FCONSOLE program are totals based on the time the file server has been up. This piece of information can be useful for estimating certain load factors.

Configured Max Open Files

This value represents the number of files the file server can have open simultaneously. When the server reaches the maximum, no more files can be opened until others are closed. The maximum value is 1000.

Peak Files Open

This value represents the largest number of files that have been open simultaneously on the file server since it was brought up.

Open Requests

This value represents how often a file open request has been processed by the file server.

Currently Open Files

This value represents the number of files currently open on the file server.

Read Requests

This value represents the number of read requests for a file that the file server has processed.

Write Requests

This value represents the number of write requests that the file server has processed since it was brought up.

File System Statistics

FAT Sector Writes

This value represents the number of times the file server has written a sector to the disk that was part of the File Allocation Table. Although NetWare caches the FAT into RAM, the FAT changes when files are added, extended, or shortened. These changes must be written to the disk.

Dirty FAT Sectors

This value represents the number of FAT sectors that have changed since they were last written to the disk. Until these changes are made, the integrity of the FAT is susceptible to a power loss at the file server.

FAT Write Errors

This value is worth watching. It represents the number of failed attempts to write to a FAT sector. The hot fix redirection features of NetWare automatically handle most errors.

Fatal FAT Write Errors

This value represents the number of fatal FAT write errors. These errors occur when updated FAT information cannot be successfully written to the disk in either copy of the FAT. If this happens, you should immediately back up the file server and then shut it down. The server would continue to operate from the copy of the FAT in its memory. However, any changes to the FAT will be lost, possibly causing major data corruption.

FAT Scan Errors

This value represents the number of FAT scan errors. These errors occur when the FAT in the file server's RAM differs from the FAT stored on the disk.

Configured Max Indexed Files

The maximum value for this entry determines the number of indexed files that may be open simultaneously on the file server. An indexed file is a file that has been flagged with the FLAG command. You should flag any file that is 2Mb or larger. When an indexed file is opened, NetWare builds a RAM index of the file's entries in the FAT so that NetWare can work more efficiently with the file. Indexing large files can have a dramatic and positive impact on performance as NetWare accesses the file.

Peak Indexed Files Open

This value represents the number of indexed files that have been open on the file server simultaneously. If this value nears the Max Indexed Files value, you should reconfigure the file server to permit more open indexed files.

Active Indexed Files

This value represents the number of indexed files currently open on the file server.

Attached Indexed Files

When a file with a corresponding FAT index is closed, the RAM occupied by the FAT index can be reallocated to another FAT index by the operating system. This value represents dormant FAT indexes that have not been released from RAM. The indexes have not been released because the operating system has not needed to use the RAM for another indexed file.

LAN I/O STATISTICS

LAN I/O statistics are one of the most helpful FCONSOLE features for troubleshooting network problems. These statistics can help you diagnose problems related to the packets transmitted on the network. Figure 17-7 shows a sample LAN I/O statistics screen. The next several sections describe the information the screen provides.

LAN I/O Statistics

```
NetWare File Server Console  V1.00b              February 1x, 199x  6:43 am
              User HADER On File Server ATRIUM Connection 1

                             LAN I/O Statistics

File Server Up Time:   0 Days  0 Hours 13 Minutes 56 Seconds
Total Packets Received:              36,212  Packets Routed:               144
File Service Packets:                35,886  NetBIOS Broadcasts:             0
Packets With Invalid Slots:               0  Invalid Connections:            0
Invalid Sequence Numbers:                 0  Invalid Request Types:          0
Detach With Invalid Slot:                 0  Forged Detach Requests:         0
New Request During Processing:            0
New Attach During Processing:             0  Ignored Duplicate Attach:       0
Reply Canceled By New Attach:             0
Detach During Processing Ignored:         0
Reexecuted Requests:                      1  Duplicate Replies Sent:         1
Positive Acknowledges Sent:               9  File Service Used Route:        0
Packets Discarded Because They Crossed More Than 16 Bridges:        0
Packets Discarded Because Destination Network Is Unknown:           0
Incoming Packets Lost Because Of No Available Buffers:              0
Outgoing Packets Lost Because Of No Available Buffers:              0
```

Figure 17-7. LAN I/O statistics

File Server Up Time

This value tells how long the server has run since it was last booted. All cumulative statistics for the FCONSOLE program are totals based on the time the file server has been up. This piece of information can be useful for estimating certain load factors.

Total Packets Received

This value represents the number of packets the file server received since it was brought up. This value can be useful in assessing the rate at which packets have been received. Also, a packet is usually sent for each packet received. Using this information with the packet size (determined by the protocol), you can roughly estimate the number of bytes or bits transmitted over your LAN channel during a given period. This is useful in determining if a performance bottleneck is occurring at the physical channel.

Packets Routed

This value represents the number of packets routed. These packets are received from one physical network and routed to another physical network. The packet's destination could be a workstation or another file server located on another network. This file server received the packet because it was in the logical path the packet traveled from its origin to its destination.

File Service Packets

This value represents the total number of file service packets the file server received. A file service request is any packet that needs file-related processing. A file service packet is not limited to user files, but includes file server files, such as binderies and directories. The FCONSOLE statistics summary displays the number of packets received in the last second.

NETBIOS Broadcasts

NetWare versions 2.1 and later support the IBM-developed NETBIOS protocols in addition to NetWare's IPX/SPX protocols. Some software applications only run with NETBIOS protocols. When you bring a workstation up and the NETBIOS emulator is loaded, the workstation "broadcasts" its name to the network. **Broadcast** means that the destination address of the packet is all hex F—the packet is addressed to all stations. The workstation wants to know if any other station in the network has the same name. The file server picks up the broadcast and transmits it to any other physical networks connected to the file server via an internal bridge. This value represents the number of times this transmission of the packet to another network was done.

Packets With Invalid Slots

This value represents the number of packets with invalid slots the file server received. A **slot** is a connection number the file server assigns to a workstation. When a workstation transmits a packet to the file server, the packet includes the connection number or slot. This number is between 1 and the maximum number of connections the NetWare version running on the file server permits. Invalid slot numbers suggest a software problem at the workstation, a faulty cable or cable connector, a defective NIC

LAN I/O Statistics

in the workstation, or excessive electrical interference. Unfortunately NetWare doesn't tell which workstation sent the packet. This would be very helpful troubleshooting information.

Invalid Connections

This value represents the number of packets with invalid connection (slot) numbers the file server received. An invalid connection happens when the file server receives a packet from a workstation that uses a connection number that is no longer assigned to the workstation. This can happen if the file server is brought down and then back up without the workstation being reinitialized. It also can happen if the file server has cleared the workstation's connection.

Invalid Sequence Numbers

This value represents the number of invalid packet sequence numbers the file server receives. The workstation shell assigns a sequence number to every frame the workstation transmits to the file server. Each successive packet should be assigned the next sequential number when it is transmitted. When the file server receives a packet with a number that is out of sequence, this value increases. Possible causes of invalid sequence numbers are a software problem at the workstation, a faulty cable or connector, a defective NIC, or excessive electrical noise. Again, it would be helpful if NetWare indicated which workstation sent the packets.

Invalid Request Type

This value represents the number of packets the file server received which contained requests the file server did not understand. Usually workstation software not fully compatible with NetWare causes this problem. Occasionally the problem is NIC drivers.

Detach With Invalid Slot

This value represents the total number of packets the file server received with a connection number that was invalid during a log out. This can happen if the file server is brought down and then back up without the workstation being reinitialized and the workstation attempts to log out. It also can happen if the file server has cleared the workstation's connection and the workstation attempts to log out.

Forged Detach Requests

This error differs slightly from Detach With Invalid Slots. It happens when the file server gets a detach (log out) packet from a workstation and the workstation number does not match the number assigned to the connection.

New Request During Processing

This value represents the number of times a certain sequence of events happens. A workstation sends a request to the file server. While waiting for the file server's response, the workstation times out. The workstation reissues the request to the file server (Same Request). The file server sends the response to the first request to the workstation and begins to process the second request (reprocessing the first request—Same Request). The workstation processes this response and issues a New Request to the file server while the file server is still processing the second request.

When this sequence of events occurs, the cause is usually heavy channel traffic or a heavily loaded file server.

New Attach During Processing

This infrequent error is the result of a specific sequence of events. A workstation sends a connection request to the file server. While the server is processing the request, the workstation is rebooted. The workstation sends a second connection request while the file server is still acting upon the first.

Ignored Duplicate Attach

This value represents the number of times the file server received an attach request from a workstation already attached to the file server. Generally application software running at the workstation causes this infrequent error.

Reply Canceled By New Attach

This value represents the number of times a workstation was being rebooted while the file server was processing a file service request. When the workstation is rebooted, it issues a new attach request to the file server. The file server cancels the reply to the previous file service request and responds to the attach request. This also increments the New Attach During Processing value.

Detach During Processing Ignored

This value represents the number of times the file server ignores a detach request. If the file server is processing a file service request from a workstation and receives a detach (log out) request, the request is ignored. Users are unlikely to cause the error. A program running improperly at the workstation is often the cause.

Reexecuted Requests

This value represents the number of times the file server receives a duplicate request from a workstation. Excessive traffic on the LAN channel, packets lost due to faulty cabling, or connector or electrical interference causes this problem. Packets with the same sequence number count as duplicate requests. This happens when a workstation times out waiting for the file server's response.

Duplicate Replies Sent

This item is related to Reexecuted Requests. Its value represents the number of times the file server can respond to a duplicate request from memory rather than reprocessing the request from scratch.

Positive Acknowledgments Sent

This value represents the number of positive acknowledgments sent. A high value can indicate a heavily loaded file server. This value is incremented when the file server takes a long time to process a request, due to load conditions on the file server. If the workstation sends a duplicate request to the file server, the server sends an acknowledgement to the workstation indicating that it knows about the request and is waiting to process it.

File Service Used Route

This value represents the number of times the file server could not act immediately on a file service request due to the lack of available file service processes (FSPs). As a result, the request is queued in a routing buffer until an FSP is available to process the request. This value is important in assessing the file server load. If the ratio of File Service Used Route packets to File Service Packets exceeds 10%, your server will benefit from more FSPs.

Packets Discarded Because They Crossed More Than 16 Bridges

This infrequent error only occurs in internets. NetWare assumes any packet that crosses more than 16 bridges is either lost or traveling in circles without being removed from the network. The file server removes the packet and discards it.

Packets Discarded Because Destination Address Is Unknown

This error only occurs in internets. The value represents the number of packets the file server received to route that included unknown destination network addresses. The network address is the address assigned to the physical network, not the node address of a workstation.

Incoming Packets Lost Because Of No Available Buffers

This error indicates a shortage of communication/routing buffers at the file server. The value represents the number of times the file server could not receive a packet because no routing buffers were available to hold the packet's contents. The workstation has to retransmit the packet, and the network's performance is degraded.

Outgoing Packets Lost Because Of No Available Buffers

This error suggests a shortage of communication/routing buffers at the file server. The value represents the number of times the file server could not send a packet because no routing buffers were available to hold the packet's contents. The file server has to reprocess the packet, and the network's performance is degraded.

TRANSACTION TRACKING STATISTICS

These statistics track the performance of SFT NetWare's Transaction Tracking System (TTS). If your LAN has software that uses TTS, these values are important in assessing the status of the transactions.

File Server Up Time

This value tells how long the server has run since it was last booted. All cumulative statistics for the FCONSOLE program are totals based on the time the file server has been up. This piece of information can be useful for estimating certain load factors.

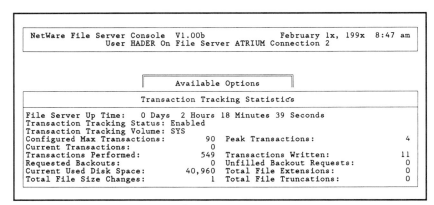

Figure 17-8. Transaction tracking statistics

Transaction Tracking Status

This line tells whether TTS is enabled or disabled. TTS can be disabled with the file server console command, TTS OFF.

Transaction Tracking Volume

This entry shows which file server volume TTS log files use.

Configured Max Transactions

This value represents the maximum number of transactions that can be active simultaneously. Each transaction requires a separate log file. SFT NetWare permits a maximum of 100 simultaneous TTS transactions.

Peak Transactions

This value represents the peak number of transactions that have been active simultaneously since the server was brought up. If the peak number approaches the value for configured maximum transactions, you should increase the maximum unless it is 100, the maximum NetWare allows.

Current Transactions

This value represents the number of transactions currently active.

Transactions Performed

This value represents the number of transactions the file server has processed since it was brought up.

Transactions Written

This value represents the number of transactions that have updated data files since the file server was brought up.

Transaction Tracking Statistics

Requested Backouts

This value represents the number of times that TTS has performed a rollback, backing out changes made during a TTS transaction.

Unfilled Backout Requests

This is probably the most important statistic on the screen because it suggests a problem. The value represents the number of times the file server was unable to perform a requested rollback.

Current Disk Space Used

This value represents the amount of disk space TTS log files are using. If the volume where the log files reside runs out of space, TTS is disabled.

Total File Extensions

This value represents the number of times that a TTS transaction increased a file's size, requiring new disk blocks to be allocated. If the file server performed a rollback, these blocks would be released.

Total File Size Changes

This value represents the number of times that a TTS transaction changed a file's size, regardless of new disk block allocation. This value is typically larger than the value for Total File Extensions.

Total File Truncations

This value represents the number of times a file was truncated during a TTS transaction. The log file must record all data in the truncated part of the file in case a rollback is required.

VOLUME INFORMATION

Volume information pertains to the status of the file server's disk volumes. A volume can be selected if multiple volumes exist on the file server. This information is useful for tracking directory entries and free space on the file server. Figure 17-9 shows a sample Volume Information screen.

File Server Up Time

This value tells how long the server has run since it was last booted. All cumulative statistics for the FCONSOLE program are totals based on the time the file server has been up. This piece of information can be useful for estimating certain load factors.

Volume Name

This entry displays the name of the volume this screen describes.

Volume Number

This is the volume number the file server assigned when it mounted the volume.

```
NetWare File Server Console  V1.00b              February 1x, 199x  9:23 am
            User HADER On File Server ATRIUM Connection 2


                              Volume Information

     File Server Up Time:    0 Days  2 Hours 54 Minutes 37 Seconds
     Volume Name:       SYS              Volume Number:            0
   C Volume Mounted:    Yes              Volume Removable:  No
   C Volume Hashed:     Yes              Volume Cached:     Yes
   D Block Size:        4,096            Starting Block:           4
   D Total Blocks:      55,996           Free Blocks:          5,191
   F Maximum Directory Entries:          10,112
   L Peak Directory Entries Used:         6,604
   S Current Free Directory Entries:      4,186
   T Logical Drive Number:     0
   V Volume Mirrored:         Yes
     Primary Disk Number:       0        Mirror Disk Number: 1
```

Figure 17-9. Volume information

Volume Information

Volume Removable

The entry is Yes if the volume is a removable disk pack, such as a Bernoulli disk cartridge. You can use file server console commands to mount and dismount removable volumes as needed.

Volume Hashed

This entry should always be Yes. If it is No, your file server is extremely short of memory and its performance seriously degraded. A **volume hash** is a RAM index to the directory of the volume that NetWare uses to locate directory entries quickly.

Volume Cached

This entry tells the status of the volume cache. Volume caching is defined when the file server is configured. If the file server is short of RAM, the volume will not be cached, even though the option was turned on when the file server was set up.

Block Size

This value represents the block size for the disk blocks on this volume. In NetWare versions 2.1x, the value is 4096 bytes.

Starting Block

This value represents the number of the block where this volume begins on the disk drive.

Total Blocks

This value represents the total number of 4K blocks in the volume. To calculate disk space for the volume, multiply the block size by the total blocks.

Free Blocks

This value represents the number of disk blocks available on the volume.

Maximum Directory Entries

This value represents the maximum number of files and directories that the volume can store. You can configure this number using the NETGEN or ELSGEN program.

Peak Directory Entries Used

Unlike most peak use entries in the FCONSOLE statistics, this value is not based on data collected since the file server was last booted. The value represents the largest number of directory entries ever used on the volume.

Current Free Directory Entries

This value represents the number of free directory entries available on the volume. When no directory entries are free, users get

```
disk full
```

error messages, although many megabytes of disk space may be free.

Logical Drive Number

This value represents the number of the logical drive containing the volume.

Volume Mirrored

This message shows that status of SFT NetWare mirrored drives and other volume conditions for all NetWare versions. It shows the status of any volume mirror. Valid status messages are

Yes	The volume is mirrored and the mirror is active.
No	The volume is not configured to be mirrored.

Comments on FCONSOLE

`Warning: Mirroring is disabled.`	The volume is not being mirrored because of a drive failure.
`Warning: Volume is shut down.`	The volume is not available. It has been shut down because the drive where the volume is has failed.
`Volume Dismounted`	The volume has been dismounted because the drive where the volume is has failed or because a file server console command dismounted the volume.

Primary Disk Number

On SFT NetWare with mirrored drives, this value represents the disk number of the drive designated as the primary drive.

Mirror Disk Number

On SFT NetWare with mirrored drives, this value represents the disk number of the drive designated as the mirror drive.

COMMENTS ON FCONSOLE

FCONSOLE is an important component of NetWare for the network administrator because it reflects how many aspects of the file server are performing. As a troubleshooting aid, however, it is limited. FCONSOLE is good for determining RAM needs, the number of routing buffers used, and disk-related information.

It's not very useful for diagnosing packet transmission problems. LAN I/O statistics can tell you if the file server is experiencing packet-related problems, but it does not help you identify which workstations sent the packets. If you experience packet problems frequently, you must use third-party software or hardware to diagnose and solve the problems.

DIAGNOSTIC AIDS

Check three major components if network packet problems persist. First, check the cable plant and its related components, such as connectors, repeaters, and hubs. Second, check the NIC itself. Third, check the software. In the rest of this chapter, I discuss tools that are available to help you diagnose and solve these problems.

Cable and Physical Network Problems

When troubleshooting a packet transmission problem, I always start with cables and the associated hardware that accompanies the physical wiring aspects of the network. After all, how far can you go to diagnose a problem if you are not sure that the cable plant is solid? I doubt you can get very far at all. The steps listed next may help you to isolate cable problems.

Check: cable distances.

It is critical that you follow the manufacturer's specifications regarding cable distances. The problem with doing so is that you may not have documentation that shows where the cables run and how long they are. A TDR (Time Domain Reflectometer) such as Microtest's Cable Scanner or Pair Scanner can help tremendously. (Microtest is based in Phoenix, Arizona.) These devices use sonar to send a signal down a cable and time its reflection. From this the devices calculate the cable's length. On bus topology LANs, testing is done from one end of the bus. Star and ring topology LANs are tested from the hub, wire center, or MAU. If you use twisted-pair cable, it is possible to approximate

Diagnostic Aids

distances if you know the gauge of the wire. Short the wire at one end and use a multimeter to measure the resistance. You can calculate the length using Table 17-1. The factors shown are based on the round-trip resistance of the wire to the multimeter.

Table 17-1. Wire Resistance for Common LAN Wire Gauges

Wire Gauge	Resistance per 1000 Feet of Wire	Multiply Meter Reading by the Following Factor to Determine Cable Length
26	41 ohms	12.2
24	26 ohms	19.2
22	16 ohms	31.3

Check: Terminators on Ethernet.

Use the multimeter to measure the terminator's DC resistance. It should be 50 ohms. Make sure a terminator is properly installed on the end of each bus segment.

Check: Terminators on ARCnet.

Use the multimeter to check the resistance of any ARCnet terminators. It should be 93 ohms. Make sure unused ports of passive hubs are terminated. Make sure all cables coming off passive hubs have PCs attached; otherwise, you have an unterminated port on a passive hub.

Check: all connectors.

Loose or damaged connectors constitute over 50% of cable problems that I find. Tug firmly but not too hard on each cable going into the connector to make sure that someone didn't pull the cable loose from the connector and then jam it back into the connector. Make sure the connectors are fastened securely.

Check: power supplies.

Any active hub, wire center, MAU, concentrator, or repeater may require a separate power supply, usually a simple AC/DC adapter. Check to make sure that all power supplies are plugged in and the outlet is receiving power. Also, check for blown fuses on the hub, wire center, MAU, concentrator, or repeater.

Make sure: that the right type of cable was used.

It is critical that the cable specified by the NIC manufacturer was used. All too often, cable problems result from the wrong type of cable or wire.

Check: Ring-In and Ring-Out Status on token ring wire centers.

You can check the IBM token ring MAU with the initialization tool that comes with it. (Check to make sure the battery in the tool is good.) Other vendors use solid state MAUs (wire centers) that have LEDs to show the status of each port.

Check: for excessive electrical interference if you are using an unshielded, twisted-pair cable.

Without a TDR, this test can be difficult to perform. Unshielded cable is particularly susceptible to electrical interference caused by AC wiring close to the LAN cable. Try moving or rerouting the cables to see if there is any change.

Make sure: that ground wires or straps are intact if the cable requires grounding.

Here again, it is difficult to test the integrity of the ground itself. Many utility companies will test grounds for you. I know that grounds made to water pipes have been disrupted because a plumber fixed a damaged pipe using plastic pipe, rather than lead, copper, or iron.

Inspect: the cable visually for damage.

I save this step for last because it is the most difficult and time-consuming. When all else fails, you may have to inspect all exposed cable. I have seen cables crushed and nicked by furniture, filing cabinets, and office equipment.

NIC Problems

Usually, when a NIC fails, it dies altogether. Now and then, a NIC can develop intermittent problems. If this happens, follow these steps to diagnose the problem.

Run: any vendor-supplied diagnostics that come with the NIC.

Diagnostic Aids

Swap: the card for another NIC known to be good to see if the PC or the card is the problem.

Run: the NetWare COMCHECK program to test communication between any two stations on the LAN. COMCHECK runs after the IPX and NETx program is loaded at the workstation. COMCHECK can run while the network is up. It does not interfere with other work on the network.

Channel Diagnostics

When all else fails to remedy a packet transmission problem, it's time to turn to an outside diagnostic/testing package. Several are available in the marketplace. The premier LAN diagnostic tools are protocol analyzers. These are the most capable and the most costly. The reason protocol analyzers are best is that they read and physically display data transmissions. If you can "see" the data as it is being sent around the network in its most basic form, you can analyze exactly what is happening. The problem is that this sort of analysis requires that you understand the protocols being used. Because most people are not very experienced in this area, the task is more difficult. Several protocol analyzers are available from various vendors, including the Novell/Excelan LANalyzer, Spider Systems' Spider Analyzer, and Network General's Sniffer.

I much prefer Sniffer for several reasons. I think it has the widest protocol support. This means Sniffer can work with many different types of networks. This may help justify its cost. More importantly, Sniffer software is superb. It allows you to work at the protocol level where you are most comfortable. In fact, you do not need to know much about protocols because the software does the work for you. Sniffer has excellent filtering capabilities that let you view packets originating from or going to specific nodes, excluding all the other traffic. It also lets you set up triggers where the device waits passively for a specific event to happen. If you are installing lots of LANs, I think that you will recover the cost of Sniffer easily. If you are trying to troubleshoot a single LAN, Network General will rent you a Sniffer on a short-term basis. You also can call them for a free demo diskette.

A step down from protocol analyzers in both capabilities and cost are software monitoring and diagnostic tools. I recommend Network General's Watchdog, Thomas Conrad's TXD, Cheyenne Software's Monitrix, Brightwork's E-Monitor and ArcMonitor, and Novell's NetCare. Not as capable as protocol analyzers, these products are still better than FCONSOLE for diagnosing problems. They collect and analyze data on a station-by-station basis, helping you determine the problem's source. Each product works differently and has different options, so investigate each in terms of your specific needs. Any of these tools pay for themselves the first time you trace a packet transmission problem.

FILE SERVICE PROCESSES (FSP)

An important component of NetWare 286 is File Service Processes (FSP). These can best be described as processes within NetWare 286 that are used to process file service request packets. These packets are also called NetWare Core Protocol (NCP) requests. When a workstation reads data from a file stored on the file server, the network shell creates an NCP packet and sends it to the file server.

FSPs are used to service NCP requests. Each FSP can only process one NCP at a time. The FSP will either process the NCP request immediately or it will schedule other disk request processes that the FSP will use to handle the request. While the FSP is waiting for these other processes, it becomes dormant. While dormant, the FSP cannot be used for any other NCP request.

When all FSPs are in use, no additional NCP requests can be serviced, resulting in degradation. NCP requests wait in a queued buffer for a free FSP to process them. When the buffer gets full, additional NCP requests from workstations are ignored. The workstation will have to retransmit the NCP request to the file server, resulting in additional degradation.

Determining If You Have FSP Problems
Keywords: FCONSOLE, FSP, degradation, statistics

Scenario One of the problems with FSPs in NetWare is determining when they are causing degradation. Due to the limited number of FSPs and the limited size of the queue for NCP requests, it is important to figure out when your LAN may experience degradation due to a shortage of these resources.

Solution There are two statistics that can be used to determine if lack of FSPs are causing degradation on your LAN. These statistics can be found in the FCONSOLE program. The first statistic is File Service Used Route, which is found on the FCONSOLE, Statistics, LAN I/O Statistics screen. The second statistic is File Service Packets and can be found on the same screen. You will need to measure both of these by taking two readings. The first reading should be done before a heavy I/O application runs. The second should be taken after a heavy utilization period. The File Service Used Route counter will rollover at 65,536, so if your second reading is less than the first, add 65,536 to the value to get the actual value.

The goal is to determine the ratio of File Service Used Route packets to File Service Packets. This ratio should not exceed 10 percent.

Finally, this test will not work with RACAL-INTERLAN NP6000 NICs installed in the file server using the most recent drivers. These drivers cause the File Service Used Route statistic to be incremented for every NCP request. If your number is a very high percentage and you are using these NICs, you cannot perform this calculation.

Obtaining More FSPs
Keywords: FSP, dynamic memory, DGroup, memory, map

Scenario When the LAN experiences a high I/O activity load at the file server, degradation takes place because there are too few FSPs available to process file requests. Also, too few FSPs can result from configuration choices. Gaining additional FSPs will improve LAN performance.

Solution The major component in determining the number of FSPs is the file server memory segment known as DGroup. The amount of memory used by DGroup is 64K. This value cannot be changed. DGroup is used for many processes at the file server. These areas and how much RAM is occupied by each are discussed next.

Global Static Data This contains all the global variables defined by NetWare 286, the NIC drivers and disk drivers installed in the file server. This area comprises 28-39.3K, depending on the number of NIC and disk drivers installed. The amount used can be determined for a given file server by using the NetWare NLINK utility found on the diskette labelled AUXGEN. The syntax for using this program is:

```
NLINK -m <output filename> <object filename>
```

This will create a linker map in the output file for the object file specified. You will have to run this program for each object that was part of your operating system. A list of the modules can be obtained from the file called NET$OS.LNK on your AUXGEN diskette. Figure 17-10 lists a sample NET$OS.LNK file.

All objects in this file need to be analyzed, except for NET$OS, which is the operating system code file, and the NULLB, NULLC, and NULLD files, which represent NIC drivers not installed. You will need a DOS path to the directory where you have copied the NLINK program. The following command could be used to create a map file for the ISADISK disk driver:

```
NLINK -m ISADISK.MAP ISADISK
```

The resulting map file would look similar to Figure 17-11.

Obtaining More FSPs

```
OSEXE-1:NET$OS
TTSOBJ:TTS_1
OSOBJ:TTS_2
GENDATA:CACHE
lan_drv_002:ane2000
LAN_DRV_001:NULLB
LAN_DRV_001:NULLC
LAN_DRV_001:NULLD
DSK_DRV_001:ISADISK
```

Figure 17-10. Sample NET$OS.LNK file

```
Segment Table
Start      Len                        Name              Class
0000:0000  0124  WORD  PUBLIC         DATA              DATA
0012:0004  0D0E  WORD  PUBLIC         ASSEMBLY
Groups
0000:0000  DGROUP
    DATA

Publics by name
0000:0000  ADDLOGICALDRIVE                              UNDEFINED
0000:0000  ALLOCSEG                                     UNDEFINED
0000:0000  ASSEMBLYABEND                                UNDEFINED
0000:0000  ASSEMBLYASDATASEGMENT                        UNDEFINED
0000:0000  DECLARESEGMENT                               UNDEFINED
0000:0000  FINISHOPERATION                              UNDEFINED
0000:0000  INTERNALFLAG                                 UNDEFINED
0000:0000  KILLCHANNEL                                  UNDEFINED
0000:0000  NETWARELOCKCHANNEL                           UNDEFINED
0000:0000  NETWARERELEASECHANNEL                        UNDEFINED
0000:0000  REALINTERRUPTSEGMENT                         UNDEFINED
0000:0000  RESTOREINTERRUPTVECTOR                       UNDEFINED
0000:0000  SETCHANNEL                                   UNDEFINED
0000:0000  SETINTERRUPTVECTOR                           UNDEFINED
0000:0000  SETTIMEOUT                                   UNDEFINED

Publics by address
0000:0000  ADDLOGICALDRIVE                              UNDEFINED
0000:0000  NETWARELOCKCHANNEL                           UNDEFINED
0000:0000  DECLARESEGMENT                               UNDEFINED
0000:0000  SETCHANNEL                                   UNDEFINED
0000:0000  ASSEMBLYABEND                                UNDEFINED
0000:0000  INTERNALFLAG                                 UNDEFINED
0000:0000  REALINTERRUPTSEGMENT                         UNDEFINED
```

Figure 7-11. NLINK map listing

```
0000:0000  SETTIMEOUT                              UNDEFINED
0000:0000  ALLOCSEG                                UNDEFINED
0000:0000  ASSEMBLYASDATASEGMENT                   UNDEFINED
0000:0000  FINISHOPERATION                         UNDEFINED
0000:0000  KILLCHANNEL                             UNDEFINED
0000:0000  NETWARERELEASECHANNEL                   UNDEFINED
0000:0000  RESTOREINTERRUPTVECTOR                  UNDEFINED
0000:0000  SETINTERRUPTVECTOR                      UNDEFINED

Module ISADISK.OBJ(isadisk.ASM)
  Segments:
    DATA                    ASSEMBLY
  Groups:
    DGROUP
  Externals:
    ASSEMBLYABEND           SETINTERRUPTVECTOR
DECLARESEGMENT
    ALLOCSEG                ADDLOGICALDRIVE
REALINTERRUPTSEGMENT
    NETWARERELEASECHANNEL   ASSEMBLYASDATASEGMENT
FINISHOPERATION
    SETCHANNEL              SETTIMEOUT           KILLCHANNEL
    RESTOREINTERRUPTVECTOR  NETWARELOCKCHANNEL
INTERNALFLAG

Relocation Items
    0012:0C05

No stack segment.
No starting address specified.  Using 0000:0000.

0 Error(s).
15 Warning(s).
```

Figure 17-11. NLINK map listing, continued

The important part of this listing is the Segment Table. The line where the word DATA occurs under both the name and class column is the critical element, as follows.

```
Start       Len                   Name           Class
0000:0000   0124  WORD PUBLIC     DATA           DATA
```

The length shown (0124) is the amount of RAM occupied by this driver's Global Static Data in hexadecimal. The number of bytes should be converted into its decimal equivalent, 292 bytes. For the sample NET$OS.LNK file displayed in Figure 17-10, the sizes were determined for each module using the NLINK program, as shown in Table 17-2.

Obtaining More FSPs

Table 17-2. Global Static Data Allocations

Module Name	Size—Hexadecimal	Size—Decimal
ISADISK Driver	124	292
NE2000 Driver	196	406
TTS__1 OS Object File	530B	21259
TTS__2 OS Object File	1C87	7303
CACHE Object File	28	40
Total Bytes Used for Global Static Data		29300

Process Stacks This area is used for stack space for the operating system. The Process Stack area is between 7–10.5K. This space is allocated as follows:

Operating System Processes	7136 bytes total
Print Spooler Port Stack	688 bytes for each printer installed in NETGEN. A maximum of five printer ports may be installed. (688 × 5 = 3440 bytes) If you are using the new NetWare print server, shared printer ports are not installed in NETGEN, thereby freeing this memory.

Volume Tables This area contains information about each volume mounted on the file server. The amount of RAM required depends on the sizes of the volumes. This requirement can be calculated as follows:

Each volume mounted	84 bytes
Each Mb of disk space	1.75 bytes
Each unit of 18 directory entries	1 byte

The final result is rounded to the nearest integer. One of the servers in my office has the following specifications: 1–224Mb disk drive with 10,112 directory entries. The amount of RAM required for the volume tables is 1037.77 bytes, which, when rounded up to the nearest integer is 1038 bytes.

Monitor Tables This area contains information used for the monitor screen on the file server console. This area is 84 bytes, and it is not configurable.

Dynamic Memory Pool 1 This pool is used by various operating system processes and is used for both temporary and static work areas. Its size ranges from 16K to 20.9K. Workspace is allocated to NetWare processes and then reclaimed upon completion.

File Service Process Buffers This is the area where incoming NCP requests or File Service Request packets are queued. The number of FSP buffers available determines the number of FSPs your server will have. For each FSP buffer, you will have one FSP. The maximum number of FSPs you may have is 10. The following items are used to calculate the memory requirements of an FSP buffer:

Reply buffer	94 bytes
Workspace	106 bytes
Stack space	768 bytes
Receive buffer	512–4096 bytes

The receive buffer size corresponds to the largest packet size permitted by any installed NIC driver. For example, if the file server has both an Ethernet driver, which uses 1024 byte packets, and a token ring driver, which uses 4096 bytes, the FSP buffer size would be 5064 bytes (94 + 106 + 768 + 4096). A typical ARCnet uses 1480 bytes. A typical Ethernet uses 1992 bytes.

In addition, NetWare will allocate 94 bytes to a single additional reply buffer. This does not affect the FSP buffer size but is allocated from this memory space. Finally, if the NIC uses DMA channels, NetWare will allocate up to 4096 bytes based on the size of the receive buffer.

A Sample Calculation for DGroup RAM The following summarizes a calculation for DGroup RAM based on the examples given earlier:

Obtaining More FSPs

Global Static Data	29,300 bytes
Process Stacks (3 printers installed)	9140 bytes
Volume Table (earlier example)	1038 bytes
Monitor Table	84 bytes
Dynamic Memory Pool 1	16,384 bytes
File Service Process Buffers	
Extra Reply Buffer	94 bytes
DMA Ethernet NIC Card Used	1024 bytes
SUBTOTAL	57,064 bytes

Subtract the subtotal from the total amount of DGroup memory of 65,536 bytes, leaving 8472 bytes. This number is divided by the size of the FSP buffer. I'll use 1992 bytes for Ethernet (8472 / 1992 = 4.253). This results in four FSP buffers of 1992 bytes or 7968 bytes. The remainder of 504 bytes is added to Dynamic Memory Pool 1. This file server will have four FSPs.

Getting the Additional FSP

To gain another FSP, you will have to gain 1488 bytes (1992–504). Now that you know the long way to calculate FSPs, you can determine quickly how close you are by looking at the amount of memory allocated to Dynamic Memory Pool 1 in the FCONSOLE Statistics Summary. Subtract the Maximum from 16,384 bytes. This results in the amount left over after calculating FSP requirements. Subtract this value from your FSP buffer size.

The final question is, "Where can I get additional RAM for another FSP?" There are several items you can investigate:

- Reduce the packet size used by your NIC driver. These have the most impact since this calculation is at the very end of the process. For example, if the above illustration could use 512-byte packets instead of 1024, the FSP buffer size would be 1480 bytes. 8472 divided by 1480 results in 5.72. This means one more FSP and puts you 408 bytes away from another FSP.
- Change a DMA-driven NIC for a NIC that does not use DMA memory transfers.

- Reduce the number of entries permitted on the volume, if you determine that you have a large number of free directory entries. Use the NetWare VOLINFO program to assess this possibility.
- Reduce the number of spooled ports in NETGEN. Attach shared printers using the NetWare print server or some third-party print server which does not require shared ports to be indicated in NETGEN.
- On SFT NetWare, you could decide to regenerate the operating system without TTS, thereby freeing Global Static Data space.

SUMMARY

This chapter covered so many details of file server performance, monitoring, and troubleshooting that it requires study and analysis. More importantly, it's a good reference that you can use whenever you need. It should give you insights that make the FCONSOLE statistics much more useful. Among a network administrator's primary concerns is keeping the network running optimally. I hope that this chapter allows you to accomplish this goal. The next chapter covers the topic of documentation, also one of the network administrator's main duties.

18
Documentation

Documentation plays an important role in solving most network problems. Problem solving without documentation is like trying to drive a car from Los Angeles to New York in the dark with no headlights and no road map. People in my seminars snicker when I talk about LAN documentation. Everyone knows they need it and no one wants to do it. Documentation helps you solve problems more efficiently. The trade-off is the time spent documenting the LAN up front against the extra time spent later trying to figure out what is causing problems. It reminds me of a commercial that used the line, "You can pay me now or you can pay me later." The inference was that it costs a whole lot more to pay later. I feel the same way about LAN documentation.

To put you at ease, I can tell you that some aspects of the documentation project can be done via software. This dramatically reduces the time required. You have to do other parts of the task manually. For many of these parts, I have included sample forms on your diskette. You can print them with WordPerfect and a laser printer set to condensed mode.

This chapter has two sections. The first outlines the documentation tasks that must be done manually. The second covers a couple of third-party software packages which do many of the remaining tasks automatically.

MANUAL DOCUMENTATION TASKS

Several parts of the network environment must be documented by designing forms and recording the needed information. Some people create databases for this information, but hard copy is always useful because you can carry it with you and use it when no computer is available. No standard set of documentation items is complete for every LAN. You may have components in your LAN that I do not address. Here is a list of the items that I feel should be included for all LANs.

- Workstation configuration worksheets
- File server memory worksheet
- File server configuration worksheet
- Node ID and location lists
- Network number lists
- Wiring floor diagrams
- Wire lists for wire closets
- LAN and print server diagrams
- Software documentation

Workstation Configuration Worksheets

Every PC in the LAN, and perhaps in the organization, should have a configuration worksheet that is a record of the salient information about the workstation's hardware components. It can also include the settings needed for CONFIG.SYS, AUTOEXEC.BAT, and SHELL.CFG or NET.CFG. This information is needed to reduce the time spent when configuring a new hardware component, such as a NIC, for the PC and to make sure there are no conflicts between the devices installed in the PC.

This worksheet should include the following information:

- Workstation type, serial number, and date of purchase.
- Types and amount of RAM installed (e.g., base, expanded, and extended).
- Types and number of floppy disk drives installed.

Manual Documentation Tasks

> Types, size, and interface (e.g. ST506, ESDI, SCSI, IDE) of any hard disks.
>
> Type of disk controller, including manufacturer.
>
> Information on all peripherals, including the NIC:
>> Device type
>> Serial number
>> Date of purchase
>> IRQ setting
>> DMA setting
>> I/O address setting
>> RAM or ROM addresses
>
> Node ID for this workstation.
>
> Network number this workstation is connected to.
>
> Required CONFIG.SYS settings and drivers.
>
> Required SHELL.CFG or NET.CFG settings.
>
> Figure 18-1 illustrates the sample workstation configuration worksheet that is included on the diskette.

File Server Memory Worksheet

Although this piece of documentation is easily calculated if you have the material covered in Chapter 1, it's handy to have a worksheet that shows how the file server's memory requirements were calculated. Figure 18-2 shows the worksheet that is provided on the diskette for this purpose.

File Server Configuration Worksheet

You can create this worksheet by adapting the workstation configuration worksheet. It should have all the same information plus the following items:

> Configuration information for each NIC installed
>
> Volume names, number of directory entries permitted, and if the volume is cached

Workstation Configuration Worksheet

Workstation Model:		Installed by:
Serial Number:	Network Number:	Date:

MEMORY	Base ______k Expanded ______k Extended ______k	DRIVES	Type / Number 360K ______ 1.2M ______ 720k ______ 1.4M ______	FIXED DISKS	Size ______ Brand ______ Interface Type IDE ST506 ESDI SCSI Size ______ Brand ______ Interface Type IDE ST506 ESDI SCSI

LAN ADAPTER INFORMATION Manufacturer/Model	IRQ USED	DMA USED	I/O ADDRESS	Remote Boot ROM Installed Yes No	ROM Address	Station ID Number

OTHER PERIPHERALS INSTALLED	IRQ USED	DMA USED	I/O ADDRESS	NOTES
1. Disk Controller				
2. Video Adapter				MONO CGA HERCULES EGA VGA 8514
3. LPT1: Port				
4.				
5.				
6.				
7.				
8.				
9.				

SHELL.CFG Options	Notes:

CONFIG.SYS

Designed by: Micheal Hader Atrium Learning Center Duplicate Without Restriction

Figure 18–1. Workstation configuration worksheet

Manual Documentation Tasks

	File Server Memory Configuration Worksheet					
1.	Operating System					400 k
2.	Directory Mapping & Temporary Buffers (Dynamic Memory 2)					64 k
3.	File Allocation Tables	Total Disk Space on Server (Mb) including Mirrored or Duplexed Drives:			Multiply by 1k	
4.	Transaction Tracking Work Area (SFT NetWare Only)	0 k if not using SFT NetWare 22 k if installed in SFT NetWare 0 k if not installed				
5.	Non-Dedicated Server (Advanced NetWare Only)	640 k if installed in NetWare 0 k if not installed 0 k if using SFT NetWare				
6.	Communication Buffers	Number of Network Cards in Server	x 10	Total	Multiply by .6	
		Number of Shared Printers	x 2			
		Number of Users	x 1			
		Number of NetBios Users	x 10			
7.	NIC Drivers	Number of NIC Cards Installed		Multiply by 20 k		
8.	Directory Hashing	Number of Directory Entries		Multiply by .004		
9.	Directory Caching	Number of Directory Entries		Multiply by .03		
10.	Open Files	Number of Users x	Average Open Files =	Total Files	Multiply by .04	
11.	FAT Indexes	Number of Open Indexed Files		Multiply by 1 k		
12.	Shared Printers	Number of Shared Printers Installed		Multiply by 15 k		

Minimum Memory Requirements (File server will boot up.)								
Item 1	Item 2	Item 3	Item 4	Item 5	Item 6	Item 7	Item 8	Memory Needed to Boot Server
								Total 1:

Remaining Memory Needs As Configured						Cache Memory	Total RAM
Item 6	Item 9	Item 10	Item 11	Item 12	Other Memory (VAPS)	Min. 512Kb	

Developed by: Micheal Hader, Atrium Learning Center, (714) 544-9010
Reproduction Permitted.

Figure 18-2. File server memory worksheet

Server name

Maximum number of open files

Maximum number of indexed files

Hot Fix Table size

Number of transactions permitted

TTS volume name

Shared printer port numbers and type (e.g., LPT, COM)

Limit disk space option and number of bindery objects permitted

Node ID and Location Lists

I did not include a sample of this form because it is so straightforward. You use it to compile a list of your node IDs and locations and possibly the make and serial number of the PC for each. Certain NetWare screens like USERLIST /A display the user's node ID. Intruder Detection displays which node caused the lockout. This list is useful for finding out where these nodes are.

Network Number Lists

If you install multiple LANs, compile a list of network numbers used. If you plan to interconnect these LANs, each must have a unique network number.

Wiring Floor Diagrams

Part of your LAN documentation should include a floor plan that shows how the cables run and their respective lengths. This can be the most difficult piece of documentation to generate if the wiring is in place. In a new building, it should be part of the blueprints. This is one of the most useful pieces of documentation for solving a problem related to cable faults.

Manual Documentation Tasks

Wire Lists for Wire Closets

If you use unshielded, twisted-pair wiring, you are probably terminating cable runs at a punch-down block in a wire closet. One piece of documentation should show how these are jumpered. Figure 18-3 is a sample of a twisted-pair wire list.

LAN and Print Server Diagrams

The LAN and print server diagrams should show the location of your file servers, print servers, and shared printers. In addition, they should show the number assigned to each printer and the type of interface used (e.g., LPT or COM). If possible, show which queues are assigned to each printer. This document makes managing the print server much easier. For a sample, look at Figure 10-9 in Chapter 10. As a separate item, you may want to record your queue names, queue operators, and queue users for each print queue established. Figure 18-4 shows a sample form for this information.

Software Documentation

The last piece of manual documentation concerns the software installed on the file server. This documentation is not about how the software works, but how it was installed on your file server. Figure 18-5 shows a sample of the items you need to record. These include

   Serial numbers

   Support phone numbers

   File names used and directories where they were installed

   File attributes assigned to each file

   Configuration file names and locations

   Other installation notes relevant to the application

Documentation

Twisted-Pair Wiring Documentation								
Node I.D.	Physical Location	Origin				Destination			Connected To
		Pair Type	Wire Closet	Block Number	Cable Pair	Wire Closet	Block Number	Cable Pair	
		TX RX							

Designed by Micheal L. Hader - Atrium Learning Center - (714) 544-9010   Duplicate without restriction

Figure 18-3. Twisted-pair wiring documentation

Manual Documentation Tasks

```
                    File Server Printer and Queue Assignments
File Server Name                    Location              Network ID
Port        NetWare Printer Number  Type of Printer Attached
COM1        0   1   2   3   4
COM2        0   1   2   3   4
LPT1        0   1   2   3   4
LPT2        0   1   2   3   4
LPT3        0   1   2   3   4
```

Queue Name		Assigned to Printer:	P0	P1	P2	P3	P4	Print Server
		Priority:						
Queue Operators								
Queue Users								

Queue Name		Assigned to Printer:	P0	P1	P2	P3	P4	Print Server
		Priority:						
Queue Operators								
Queue Users								

Queue Name		Assigned to Printer:	P0	P1	P2	P3	P4	Print Server
		Priority:						
Queue Operators								
Queue Users								

Designed by Micheal L. Hader - Atrium Learning Center - (714) 544-9010   Duplicate Without Restriction

Figure 18-4. File server printer and queue assignments

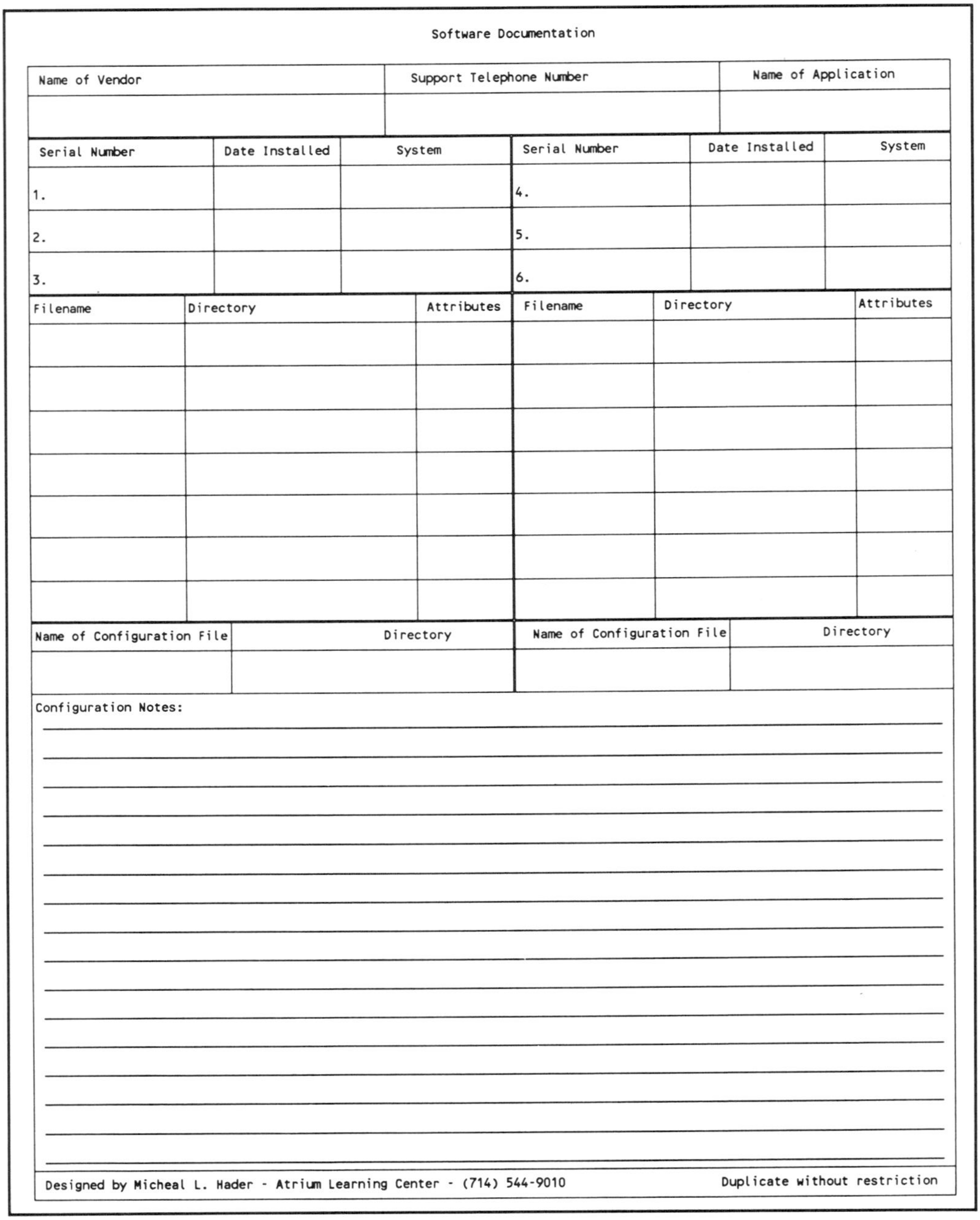

Software Documentation

Name of Vendor	Support Telephone Number	Name of Application

Serial Number	Date Installed	System	Serial Number	Date Installed	System
1.			4.		
2.			5.		
3.			6.		

Filename	Directory	Attributes	Filename	Directory	Attributes

Name of Configuration File	Directory	Name of Configuration File	Directory

Configuration Notes:

Designed by Micheal L. Hader - Atrium Learning Center - (714) 544-9010　　Duplicate without restriction

Figure 18-5. Software documentation

FILE SERVER DOCUMENTATION

The rest of the task is documenting your users, their Trustee Assignments, their security restrictions, groups, group members, group Trustee Assignments, etc. Unfortunately, although this data all resides within NetWare's own security files, NetWare has no reporting features for any of it. I know people who have attempted to get all this data on paper using SHIFT PRTSC. This is no solution. You need a way to create reports periodically because this information changes.

The best overall product that I have seen for this job is Lomax Utilities from J.A. Lomax and Associates, Novato, CA. This utility prints practically everything you could possibly want to know about your server. I affectionately call these reports the "missing NetWare reports" that everyone thinks should be a part of NetWare. Included in this utility are excellent user and disk reports. Anyone who has ever had to free disk space will appreciate the reports generated by this software. A nice new feature of the software is its ability to export any data you want so that you can bring it into your own database or report generator and create custom reports.

Another fine product is Bindview+ from LAN Support Group, Houston, TX. Some of the reports it produces are more attractive than Lomax Utilities's, but it does not offer the excellent disk utilization reports that Lomax does.

I highly recommend that you give one of these products serious consideration as an add-on to your administrative tool kit. They pay for themselves the first time you use them to solve a Rights or security problem.

The final topic in this section is user documentation. Usually, the users have nothing on their desks to help them cope with LAN problems. One of the more useful books published in the past year is *The NetWare 286 Manual Maker*, written by Christine Milligan and published by M & T Books. This gem comes with WordPerfect and ASCII templates that you can customize and print for your users. You will have a nice little manual about the LAN and NetWare to give your users. I think that this book is a great investment. There is also a NetWare 386 version.

SUMMARY

This chapter could possibly be the first in this book. Documenting the LAN is an important task you must do to make your LAN easy to manage. If you have ever had to modify a program without documentation, you know how difficult it can be. Your network's configuration can be just as difficult to comprehend as that undocumented program. Good documentation makes life in the LAN much more pleasant.

Appendix A

NetWare 286 Command Summary

This appendix is a quick summary of the NetWare 286 commands you can issue after the system prompt. In many cases, you can use several commands to accomplish similar or related tasks or you can reverse the effect of one command with another command. Often you may need to study similar commands to learn their differences and nuances. Yet, having an alphabetical list of these commands can be convenient to a new NetWare user.

The format for the command descriptions in this appendix is:

COMMAND   The command's name in capital letters.

Syntax   The command's format, including its arguments and parameters. Square brackets ([ ]) enclose optional parameters. The term directory path refers to the complete description of the location of a specific directory:

server_name/volume:
/directory_name/directory_name/...

As is always true with NetWare, if the LAN has only one server, then you can omit server name/. In addition, if the sole server only has one volume, then you can omit volume: when specifying a directory path.

	The term filespec refers to a full file name including its file name extension:
	filename.ext
Example	Actual ways to use the command, following the correct format.
Default	The default parameter for the command.
Related commands	A list of similar commands.
Description	An explanation of how to use the command, including, if appropriate, lists of possible parameters, arguments, and keywords.

ATTACH

Syntax	`ATTACH [server_name[/account_name]]`
Example	`ATTACH ATRIUM2/BILL`
Default	None. You must specify a server with this command.
Related command	LOGIN

Description—Use the ATTACH command to attach your workstation to another server, when you are working in a multiple server LAN. A unique name identifies each server on the network. You must log into the LAN before you can use ATTACH. Also, to attach to another file server, your account must be valid on the other file server. After you successfully attach, you can access directories and files on the other server according to the Rights the supervisor granted to you. Now you must use the appropriate server and volume names with commands that refer to the other server or its volumes.

If you use the ATTACH command and do not specify a server name, the system prompts:

```
Enter server name:
Enter user name:
Enter your password:
```

If you specify the server name and the account name in the ATTACH command, NetWare only prompts for your password. The password is not part of the ATTACH command syntax.

CAPTURE

This command is often used in Login Script files in a multiple server environment so that other servers can be attached during the LOGIN process.

CAPTURE

Syntax	CAPTURE [parameter] [parameter] [parameter] ...
Example	CAPTURE J=Standard TI=30 Q=Hot_Queue C=2
Default	See the list of parameters in the next section.
Related commands	ENDCAP, NPRINT

Description—CAPTURE has many optional parameters that control how the job will be printed. A space separates each option on the command line. These options let you control the number of copies, the banner page, and other important printing features.

Parameters	Use
J=*jobname*	Jobname. Specifies a job name that has been created with the PRINTCON program which defines many print job specifications, including the form name, the queue, the number of copies, etc. The supervisor establishes the default job in the PRINTCON program.
Q=*queue*	Queue. Directs output to a specific queue that is managed by the PCONSOLE program. The default queue is the one specified by the Jobname parameter if a job name is specified; otherwise it is the queue specified for the default jobs in PRINTCON.
L=*n*	Local Printer. Specifies which of the workstation's local parallel (LPT) printer ports is being "captured" and rerouted to a shared network printer. The default for this parameter is 1.
Notify	Notify causes the NetWare 386 and NetWare 286 version 2.15 Rev. C versions of the CAPTURE command to send a message to the user when the job is finished printing.

Parameters	Use
S=*server*	Server. Specifies which server should receive this output in a multiple server environment. The default is the server that was initially logged into.
P=*n*	Printer. Used to select a specific shared printer. Shared printers are assigned numbers from 0 through 4 during installation. The default value is 0.
C=*n*	Copies. Instructs the server to print multiple copies of the print job. The default value is 1.
F=*n* F=*name*	Form. This numeric value specifies which form should be used for this print job. You define a form with the PRINTDEF program and give it a name and numeric value from 0 through 255. The form can be specified by its name or its number. The default value is 0.
NAM=*user*	Name. Specifies which user name is printed on the top of the banner page. The default is the user name used to log in.
B=*text*	Banner. Specifies any text up to 12 characters that will be printed at the bottom of the banner page at the beginning of a print job. Spaces are not permitted, so use a hyphen (-) or an underscore (__) to connect multiple words. The default is LST:.
NB	No Banner. Omits the banner page from the beginning of a report. However, when used in conjunction with a multiple copy report and the B (Banner) option, this parameter prints a banner at the beginning of the first copy of the report but not at the beginning of subsequent copies. The default prints a banner page at the beginning of the report.
TI=*n*	Timeout. Used with software that is not designed for network printing. Often, these packages do not send an end-of-file character when printing is complete. NetWare needs the end-of-file

CAPTURE

Parameters	Use
	character to detect the end of a print job. When an application does not send an end-of-file character, NetWare assumes the print job has more data to send and does not close the print file. Enabling the Timeout parameter sets a period of time from 1 second to 1000 seconds. If NetWare does not receive more data after the timeout period, NetWare assumes the print job is finished and closes the print file. If NetWare receives more data after the timeout period, NetWare opens a new print job. The default is no timeout.
A	Autoendcap. Tells NetWare to close an open print file upon exiting from the current application program or upon starting a new application. This parameter is also generally used with software that is not designed for network printers. It forces an automatic end-of-file character. See TI=n (Timeout) and NA (No Autoendcap).
NA	No Autoendcap. Prevents NetWare from closing an open print file when exiting from or entering a new application. This parameter is useful for gathering several pieces of output from different programs.
CR=[*directory_path*]*filespec*	Create Filespec. Captures output to a disk file rather than sending it directly to the print queue. You can later send this print file to the printer via the NPRINT command. The advantage of printing this way is that it is often much faster. The print file contains any special formatting characters that would go to the printer to control special printing features.
FF	Form Feed. Instructs NetWare to perform a form feed when printing is complete. This parameter is generally required for laser printers because they often hold the last page if the page is not full.

Parameters	Use
NFF	No Form Feed. Prevents NetWare from performing a form feed at the end of the print job. This is the default setting.
T=n	Tabs. Instructs NetWare to replace tab characters in the print job with the number of spaces indicated. The value of n can be from 0 through 18. Most applications do not require this parameter. The exceptions are applications that do not have good print format control, for example, applications that print reports with misaligned spacing between data items.
NT	No Tabs. Overrides the TABS option, if set for a default print job. It passes tab characters to the printer intact. This setting should be used whenever there are special formatting control codes in the print job or when printing graphics.
K	Keep. Lets NetWare close a print file when the connection between the file server and the workstation is interrupted. This could occur when the job hangs, the workstation is accidentally reset, power is lost at the workstation, or the workstation is off. NetWare closes the print file 15 minutes after the interruption occurs. If you do not use this parameter, the server discards the print file when these events occur.
SH	Show. Shows the current status of your local printer ports. It lists "captured" ports and any CAPTURE command options in effect. The data displayed looks similar to this:

CAPTURE DEFAULT SETTINGS SUMMARY

The default parameters of the CAPTURE command are listed next.

- If you specify a print job with the J=parameter, NetWare uses the setting established for that job.
- If you did not specify a print job and you used no other parameters with the CAPTURE command, the default parameters in effect are

CASTON

Parameters	Use
L=1	Capture LPT1: printer port
Q=PRINTQ_0	Send output to queue PRINTQ_0
C=1	Print only one copy
NAM=*account_name*	Print the user account at the top of the banner
B=LST:	Print LST: on the bottom of the banner
A	Enable Autoendcap
T=8	Convert tab characters to 8 spaces
FF	Perform a form feed at the end of the job

CASTOFF

Syntax   CASTOFF [ALL]
Default   CASTON
Related commands SEND, CASTON

Description—The CASTOFF command prevents your workstation from receiving messages sent by other workstations. Messages sent from other workstations interrupt the processing of your current application until you press CTRL ENTER. If the receiving station is unattended, then the station's application is suspended until someone presses the appropriate keys. The ALL parameter disables the workstation from receiving messages from other users and also from the file server console. When you issue the CASTOFF command, NetWare displays this message at your workstation:

```
Broadcast messages from other stations will now
be rejected.
```

CASTON

Syntax   CASTON
Default   CASTON
Related commands SEND, CASTOFF

Description—This command reverses the effect of the CASTOFF command by enabling the workstation to receive messages other users and the file server console send. When you issue the CASTON command, NetWare displays this message at your workstation:

```
Broadcast messages from other stations or the
console will now be accepted.
```

CHKVOL

Syntax	CHKVOL [*server_name/volume:*]
	CHKVOL [*drive:*]
	CHKVOL *wildcards/wildcards*
Examples	CHKVOL ATRIUM/SYS:
	CHKVOL F:
	CHKVOL */*
	CHKVOL */SY*
Default	CHKVOL *current_server/volume:*

Description—This command displays information about file server disk volumes. The data displayed looks similar to this:

```
Statistics for fixed volume ATRIUM/SYS:
  69885952 bytes total volume space,
  45158400 bytes in 1783 files,
  24727552 bytes remaining on volume,
  24727552 bytes available to user HADER,
     2953 directory entries available.
```

The statistics CHKVOL provides are

- Name of the server and the volume for this report.
- Total size of the volume in bytes.
- Number of bytes and files presently used on the volume.
- Number of bytes available for use on the volume.
- Number of bytes available to this user on the volume.
- Number of unused directory entries available for new file names or directory names.

You can use the wildcards * and ? as you do in DOS to specify a pattern for the server name or volume name. Using wildcards prints multiple portions of the CHKVOL report. This is useful in multiple volume and/or multiple server environments as an indication of how disk space is used across the servers and volumes. Do not use the DOS CHKDSK program on a network drive. It does not work! If you use CHKDSK to check available RAM memory, specify a local drive on the workstation as the object of the CHKDSK program.

ENDCAP

Syntax	ENDCAP [parameter] [parameter] [...]
Examples	ENDCAP ALL
	ENDCAP L=1
	ENDCAP C ALL
Default	ENDCAP ALL
Related command	CAPTURE

Description—The ENDCAP command disables all or a portion of any active CAPTURE commands. The ENDCAP program has several optional parameters:

Parameter	Use
C	Stop capturing LPT1 and cancel any data waiting to be sent to a network printer or file.
L=n	Stop capturing the workstation's LPT port n, where n is a number from 1 through 3.
CL=n	Stop capturing the LPT port n and cancel any data waiting to be sent to a network printer or file. n is a number from 1 through 3.
ALL	Stop capturing on all LPT ports which are presently captured.
C ALL	Stop capturing on all LPT ports and cancel any data waiting to be sent to a network printer or file.

FLAG

Syntax	FLAG [directory_path]filespec [parameter][parameter]...
Examples	FLAG *.*
	FLAG ATRIUM/SYS:/MFG/*.DAT SRO
Default	FLAG *.* (no attributes)
Related commands	HOLDON, HOLDOFF

Description—The FLAG command is an important NetWare command for changing a file's attributes in a directory where the user has Modify and Search Rights. File attributes control the type of access a user has to a file. File attributes also indicate special file types. Normal DOS wildcards can be used in the filespec. Used without parameters, the FLAG command displays the current file attributes for the file(s) specified. If no server or volume is indicated, FLAG uses the default. If no directory path is used, FLAG uses the current default directory. If no filespec is entered, FLAG uses all files in the current directory. The attributes available for the FLAG command are listed next.

Attribute	Use
S	Shareable. Marks a file so more than one user can open it at a time, permitting concurrent access to its data. Read-only files are generally shareable files.
NS	Non-shareable. Indicates that only one user can open a file at one time. Many files are not held open after they are sent to the user's workstation. For example, when a program runs, the program file is open while NetWare transmits the program to the user's PC. After that has been accomplished, the server closes the file. Because the file is no longer open, another user can access it, even though the file has the NS attribute. The HOLDON and HOLDOFF commands for data files can affect this attribute.

FLAGDIR

Attribute	Use
RO	Read-only. Indicates that this file cannot be updated, but it can be read. NetWare assumes that read-only files are program files and therefore shareable even though the Shareable attribute has not been set.
RW	Read/Write. Tells NetWare that the file is a data file which can be updated. Read/write files are assumed to be non-shareable unless the Shareable attribute is on. When marked non-shareable, these files are affected by the settings of HOLDON and HOLDOFF.
N	Normal. A non-shareable, Read/write file.
T	Transactional. (SFT NetWare only.) Indicates that this file can have flagged transactions against it that SFT NetWare monitors.
I	Indexed. Indicates a large data file (over 2 Mb). A special NetWare feature causes this file's FAT entries to be indexed for faster data retrieval.

FLAGDIR

Syntax `FLAGDIR [directory path[parameter]]`

Examples `FLAGDIR ATRIUM/SYS:USERS/HADER P`
`FLAGDIR ATRIUM/SYS:USERS/ANN N`

Default `FLAGDIR`

Related commands None

Description—This command is used to change the status of a directory. You must have Parental and Modify Rights in the parental directory to use this command. The parameters that can be used with this command are:

Parameter	Use
N	Normal. This setting cancels any other status that had been set for the directory and returns the directory to normal status.

Parameter	Use
H	Hidden. This makes the directory invisible to other users when they perform a directory list using NDIR or DIR. It does not prevent the user from changing to the directory, however.
S	System. This setting makes the directory invisible to other users so that it will not appear in a directory list. It does not prevent the user from changing to the directory.
P	Private. Prevents users from viewing the contents of the directory unless they have the Search Right. They may see the directory in a directory list.

GRANT

Syntax

GRANT rights FOR [directory_path] TO [USER] account_name

GRANT rights FOR [directory_path] TO [GROUP] group_name

GRANT rights [BUT rights] FOR [directory_path] TO [USER] account_name or [GROUP] group_name

GRANT [ONLY] rights FOR [directory_path] TO [USER] account_name or [GROUP] group_name

GRANT NO RIGHTS FOR [directory_path] TO [USER] account_name or [GROUP] group_name

Examples

GRANT ROS FOR ATRIUM/SYS:/LOTUS TO EVERYONE
GRANT ALL FOR /MFG/PROD/BILL TO USER BILL
GRANT ALL BUT P FOR /MFG/PROD TO GROUP MFG_PROD

Default

None. You cannot use this command without specific options.

Related commands   REVOKE, REMOVE

Description—Use the GRANT command to make Trustee Assignments in directories where the user has Parental Rights. This command makes an entry in the user's or group's Trustee Assignments list. Type the appropriate Rights letters where indicated in the command syntax.

- S   Search. The user or group can view the file names in a directory.
- O   Open. The user or group can open existing files.

R	Read. The user or group can read an open file.
W	Write. The user or group can write to an open file.
C	Create. The user or group can create a new file.
D	Delete. The user or group can delete an existing file.
M	Modify. The user or group can change existing file attributes and file names.
P	Parental. The user or group can create new subdirectories and remove existing subdirectories.

The Rights indicated in the command line are added to the user's or group's existing Rights for the directory specified. You can use keywords to modify the result of the GRANT command.

Keywords	Use
ONLY	Grants specific Rights while revoking any others the user or group possesses in the directory.
ALL BUT	Grants all but specific Rights to a user or group.
NO RIGHTS	Removes any Rights from the group or user, but the user or group will remain a trustee.

HOLDOFF

Syntax	HOLDOFF
Default	HOLDOFF
Related command	HOLDON

Description—The HOLDOFF command allows access to files after another user has accessed them through the server. You must use this command only in conjunction with the HOLDON command. It reverses the effect of the HOLDON command.

HOLDON

Syntax	HOLDON
Default	HOLDOFF
Related command	HOLDOFF

Description—Use the HOLDON command with software applications which are not properly designed for a LAN environment. Some applications do not place a hold on open data files which are not designed to be shared. Other users can open and update these files and possibly cause data corruption. The HOLDON command holds open any files accessed from your application and prevents other users from updating the file until you exit from the application. Well designed LAN applications do this for you so you do not need to use the HOLDON command. You can reverse the effect of HOLDON with the HOLDOFF command.

LARCHIVE

Syntax	LARCHIVE [directory_path]
	LARCHIVE [SYSTEM]
Example	LARCHIVE SYS:
Default	LARCHIVE
Related command	LRESTORE

Description—The LARCHIVE command starts a program that backs up data files from the server to a local drive. The program's prompts guide you through the several options explained next. To archive data files from a directory, you must possess the Effective Rights of Read, Open, Search, and Modify in the directory. Only a supervisor can archive the file server security files. The diskettes you use must be formatted and empty.

Type: LARCHIVE SYS:/MFG.

Type: A, the letter of the local drive on which to archive files.

The LARCHIVE program prompts

Do you wish to print a log report of this session? (Y/N)

Type: Y

The log report creates the file ARCHIVE.LOG which NetWare stores on the drive where the files are being archived. It contains the date and time of the archive's creation, as well as the directory path and names of all files archived. When you type Y, NetWare prints the ARCHIVE.LOG file immediately after the archive session. You can print the log file

LARCHIVE

at any time, however, using either NPRINT to print it on a network printer or DOS PRINT to print it on a local printer.

The LARCHIVE program prompts

```
Do you want to save directory rights and trustee lists? (Y/N)
```

Type: Y

LARCHIVE backs up the Maximum Rights Mask and Trustee Assignments list with the data. Only if you are logged in as SUPERVISOR does the next prompt appear.

```
Do you want to archive the user and group definitions? (Y/N)
```

Type: Y

NetWare archives the hidden system security files from the server.

The LARCHIVE program prompts

```
Select specific directories to be backed up?
(N = Back up all directories)
```

Type: Y

LARCHIVE prompts for each downline directory from the one where you started the archive session.

Select: one of the first two back-up modes listed for this directory:

```
Back up ALL qualified files in each directory
Back up ONLY qualified files that have been
  modified since last backup
Choose specific files to be backed up
```

If you choose one of the first two options another prompt appears:

```
Do you want to:
    Select specific files
    Ignore specific files
    Back up all files
```

Select: one of the first two options.

The first two options let you use wildcards in a file specification and use as many file specifications as you need. Enter each file specification on a separate line. When you finish,

Press: ENTER on the next blank line.

The LARCHIVE utility now backs up all the files specified, prompting you to change diskettes whenever needed. Steps 5 through 9 are repeated for each directory to be archived.

LISTDIR

Syntax　　　　　　　　LISTDIR [directory_path]
　　　　　　　　　　　[parameter][parameter][...]

Examples　　　　　　　LISTDIR ATRIUM/SYS:/ACCTG
　　　　　　　　　　　LISTDIR SYS:/S

Default　　　　　　　 LISTDIR current_server/volume:

Related command　　　 NDIR

Description—Use this command to list the directories of a given volume on the server. With the optional parameters, you can obtain other data about the volume.

Parameter	Use
/D	Date. Display the date when the directory was created.
/T	Time. Display the time when the directory was created.
/R	Rights. Display the Maximum Rights Mask for the directory.
/S	Subdirectories. Display any subdirectories and their information as specified.
/A	All. Display all information for the directory and its subdirectories.

This command gives you quick access to the names of directories located on a file server volume because you do not need to change the default directory. Here's some sample output from the LISTDIR command.

LOGIN

```
F>LISTDIR ATRIUM/SYS:/MAIL /A
The sub-directory structure of ATRIUM/SYS:MAIL
     1        11-01-88    8:44a  [RWOCD SM]
     20007    11-01-88    8:44a  [RWOCD SM]
     5001D    11-01-88    8:44a  [RWOCD SM]
     7002F    11-14-88    9:30a  [RWOCD SM]
     2F00A3   5-20-89     3:04p  [RWOCD SM]
     2E0037   5-20-89     3:04p  [RWOCD SM]
     3100AD   5-20-89     3:04p  [RWOCD SM]
7 sub-directories found
```

LOGIN

Syntax	LOGIN [*server_name*[/*account_name* [*parameters*...]]]
Examples	LOGIN LOGIN ATRIUM/ LOGIN ATRIUM/MIKE MAIL
Default	LOGIN server attached. When you run the NETx.COM program, your workstation broadcasts a message indicating that the station is looking for a server. This message is not visible. The first server to respond is the one that is displayed with the "attach" message. If you do not specify a server, NetWare tries to log into the "attached" server.
Related commands	ATTACH, LOGOUT

Description—The LOGIN program validates the user account and password and lets the user into the system. If a user cannot successfully log in, then the user is denied access to the server. If you only type LOGIN, the program prompts for the account name. If the account uses a password, then LOGIN prompts for the password. To log into a specific server, you must type a slash (/) after the server name.

NetWare treats other parameters that follow the user name in the command line as parameters during Login Script processing. NetWare assigns each parameter a sequential variable number, just as DOS does. The user name is %1, the next parameter is %2, etc. The Login Script can process these parameters. For instance, the example

```
LOGIN ATRIUM/MIKE MAIL
```

might indicate that the user wants to access the electronic mail application immediately after LOGIN. The Login Script might contain the command:

```
IF ''%2'' = "MAIL" THEN EXIT "MAIL"
```

LOGOUT

Syntax	LOGOUT [server_name]
Default	LOGOUT current_server
Related command	LOGIN

Description—The LOGOUT command logs the user out of the server and releases any network mappings that the user has attached except for the /LOGIN directory. If the user was logged into multiple file servers, the user can log out of a specific server by entering the server name with the LOGOUT command; otherwise, LOGOUT logs the user out of all servers.

LRESTORE

Syntax	LRESTORE
Example	LRESTORE
Default	LRESTORE
Related command	LARCHIVE

Description—The LRESTORE program restores files back onto the server from diskettes created with the LARCHIVE program. The program's prompts guide you through the necessary steps.

Type: LRESTORE.

Type: A, the letter of the local drive from which to restore files.

The LRESTORE program prompts

```
Do you wish to restore security information with
the directories? (Y/N)
```

Type: N.

The LRESTORE program prompts

```
Select specific directories to be considered
   for restoration? (Y/N)
(N = Consider all archived directories)
```

Type: N to restore all directories contained on your archive disks, or Y to be able to restore directories selectively.

The LRESTORE program prompts

```
Specify files to restore to each selected directory? (Y/N)
(N = Restore all selected directories)
```

Type: N to restore all files from your archive diskette for this directory, or Y to select which files to restore. The system now begins to restore files from the local drive to the network drive. If a file already exists on the network, the system asks if you wish to replace it with the version from the local archive disk:

```
File already exists. Recreate? (Y/N)
```

MAP

Syntax	MAP [ROOT] [*drive:*]=*directory_path*
	MAP [INSERT] SEARCH*n*:=*directory_path*
	MAP DEL *drive:*
	MAP
Examples	MAP P:=ATRIUM/SYS:USERS
	MAP INS SEARCH1=\APPS\WP
Default	MAP. This command displays the current status of all logical drive letters and search paths.

Description—The MAP command is one of the most important commands in NetWare. Use it to create or remove logical drive assignments or search paths. MAP lets you reference directories on the network disk easily. Because network disk drives and volumes tend to be larger than their DOS counterparts due to the number of users sharing data on the network, Novell's Advanced

NetWare uses names for servers, volumes, and directories. Typing the entire reference every time you refer to a file or directory can be quite tedious.

```
server_name/volume:/directory_path/filename.ext
```

The longer the data string a user must type, the greater the chances for error. Retyping these long references is very annoying. The MAP command simplifies the process.

The MAP command has four uses in NetWare:

- Allows the substitution of a logical drive letter for referencing a server, volume, and directory path.
- Creates a search path for NetWare to use when files with the file name extension .COM, .EXE, or .BAT are not in the user's current default directory.
- Removes logical drive letter assignments and search paths.
- Displays information about the current assignments of logical drive letters and search paths.

The syntax of the MAP command for assigning *logical* drive letters is

```
MAP [ROOT] d:=[server_name/][volume:]\directory_path
```

Examples of the MAP command used this way are

```
MAP G:=ATRIUM/SYS:\WORD
MAP G:=\WORD
MAP ROOT G:=\WORD
```

The square brackets ([ ]) in the command syntax denote optional parts of the command. If you only have one server and one volume, NetWare automatically refers to them. In the examples, I show both ways. In the example, we created the *logical* drive, G:, and assigned it to the directory WORD. In this context, *logical* describes an abstract. The *physical* drive G: does not exist. However, I can now use G: to refer to the disk area formerly known as ATRIUM:SYS:\WORD. This logical assignment is a shorthand way to refer to network disk directories.

MAP

NetWare can assign all twenty-six letters, A–Z, to logical drives using the MAP command. Drive letters A through E are assumed to be local physical drives on the user's workstation. If you use the MAP command to assign these drive letters, NetWare asks if you wish to assign these letters:

```
Drive D: currently maps to a local disk
Do you want to assign it as a network drive? (Y/N) Y
```

Drive D: would be one of the drives A to E that the user specified in the MAP command. If you respond Y, NetWare performs the MAP specified. This can be a problem. If the drive letter corresponds to a real physical drive, NetWare asks the same question again. If you respond Y, then NetWare executes the MAP command as specified. Now the physical drive D: is not available until logical drive D: is removed!

Usually the MAP command is used in this way to create logical drive letters for the data directories for the user's work. Logical drive mappings are not permanent. They terminate when the user logs out of the network. When the user logs into the network, any needed logical drive mapping must be redone unless the MAP command is part of the User Login Script or part of a batch file which is processed when the user logs in.

You can use the MAP command to set search routes to both local and network directories. The syntax for the MAP command used this way is

```
MAP [INSERT] SEARCHx:=server_name/volume:\directory_path
```

The letter x in the command line sets the priority or sequence number for this MAP SEARCH command. x can have a value from 1 through 16. In both the DOS PATH command and the NetWare MAP SEARCH command, the specified search path only applies to the named directory. Any downline directories are not searched. To search a downline directory, you must stipulate a separate PATH segment or MAP SEARCH command.

Several rules are associated with the MAP SEARCH command.

- There can be no more than 16 MAP SEARCH commands, SEARCH1: through SEARCH16:. NetWare permits 26 search directories, but SEARCH17 through SEARCH26 are created by inserting search directories resulting in other searches being pushed down past SEARCH16.
- No gaps can exist between successive search priority numbers. NetWare automatically renumbers any search priorities to avoid this. For example, if you issue these two MAP SEARCH commands

    MAP SEARCH1:=*server_name/volume*:PUBLIC
    MAP SEARCH5:=*server_name/volume*:DATABASE

    and no other MAP SEARCH commands had been issued, NetWare *automatically* transforms the second MAP SEARCH to

    MAP SEARCH2:=*server_name/volume*:DATABASE

- NetWare assigns MAP SEARCH segments a logical drive letter starting with the letter Z and then works back toward the beginning of the alphabet.
- If an existing DOS PATH statement exists, NetWare maps the DOS segments to SEARCH segments in the order that they were in the DOS PATH statement. The first segment becomes SEARCH1, the second becomes SEARCH2, and so on. The NetWare MAP SEARCH command *replaces* the segment of the DOS PATH statement with the corresponding MAP SEARCH drive letter assignment. This replacement is done on a equivalence basis. That is, SEARCH1 replaces the first segment, SEARCH3 replaces the third segment, SEARCH5 replaces the fifth segment, and so on.
- The optional INSERT parameter places a SEARCH segment before existing segments. SEARCH segment priorities shift up one number starting where the insert was made. For example, assume these MAP SEARCH segments already exist:

    MAP SEARCH1:=*server_name/volume*:\PUBLIC
    MAP SEARCH2:=*server_name/volume*:\DOS
    MAP SEARCH3:=*server_name/volume*:\DATABASE

    Now a new MAP SEARCH command is issued:

    MAP INSERT SEARCH2:=*server_name/volume*:\WORDPROC

The MAP SEARCH segments are now:

    MAP SEARCH1:=*server_name/volume*:\PUBLIC
    MAP SEARCH2:=*server_name/volume*:\WORDPROC
    MAP SEARCH3:=*server_name/volume*:\DOS
    MAP SEARCH4:=*server_name/volume*:\DATABASE

A MAP INSERT SEARCH *does not* replace DOS PATH segments.

- Upon logout, NetWare automatically releases the network segments of the PATH, leaving only any local drive segments in the DOS PATH statement.
- Unless otherwise specified, NetWare automatically executes these MAP commands:

    MAP SEARCH1:=*server_name/volume*:\PUBLIC
    MAP Y=:*server_name/volume*:\PUBLIC
    MAP F:=*server_name/volume*:*user_name*

In other words, NetWare sets up the first search segment to the directory containing the NetWare utilities and assigns this area logical drive Z:. It also sets up logical drive letter Y:, mapped to this same area. NetWare looks in the root directory for a directory corresponding to the user's name and, if one exists, NetWare maps this area to logical drive F:.

NCOPY

Syntax	NCOPY [*directory_path*]*filespec* [TO] *filespec*
	NCOPY [*directory_path*]*filespec* [TO] *directory_path*
	NCOPY [*directory_path*]*filespec* [TO] *directory_path*/*filespec*
Examples	NCOPY *.* TO H:
	NCOPY ATRIUM/SYS:/ACCTG/*.DAT TO /NEW
	NCOPY *.DAT TO /MFG/*.ORG
Default	None. The NCOPY command must be used with specifications for both source and destination files.

Description—The NCOPY command is a network version of the DOS COPY command with a few changes. You should always use it in place of the DOS COPY command for a couple of reasons. First, NCOPY does an automatic read-after-write verification of the data to insure its integrity. Second, NCOPY copies files from one place to another on the file server disk volumes more quickly. DOS COPY causes the network server to send the file to the workstation, which, in turn, sends it back to the file server for rewriting to the new location. The NCOPY command, when used to copy files on the server to other directories or names on the same server, performs the copy strictly within the server, reducing LAN traffic significantly.

The earlier example

```
NCOPY *.* TO H:
```

copies all files in the current default directory to the directory mapped logical drive H:. The example

```
NCOPY ATRIUM/SYS:/ACCTG/*.DAT TO /NEW
```

copies all files with the .DAT file extension that reside in the /ACCTG directory of the SYS volume in server ATRIUM to the directory /NEW on the current volume. The last example

```
NCOPY *.DAT TO /MFG/ *.ORG
```

copies all files in the current default directory with a .DAT file extension to a directory called /MFG and gives the files the new file name extension .ORG.

NDIR

Syntax

```
NDIR [directory_path]filespec
     [parameter][parameter][...]
NDIR directory_path[filespec]
     [parameter][parameter][...]
NDIR directory_path [filespec option]
```

NDIR

Examples	`NDIR *.WP`
	`N>NDIR *.* SIZE GREATER THAN 50K SUB`
	`N>NDIR *.* SIZE GREATER THAN 100K REVERSE SORT SIZE SUB`
	`N>NDIR *.* SIZE GREATER THAN 50K REVERSE SORT SIZE SUB BR`
Default	`NDIR *.* SUB`

Description—The NDIR command is a powerful network version of the DOS DIR command. Its power comes from all the flexibility that its filespec options and parameters offer. Filespec options define selection criteria and presentation order. Parameters control the amount of data displayed with the files. Filespec selection and sequence options and information parameters are listed next.

Filespec Selection Options	**Selects**

FILENAME = *filespec*
FILENAME NOT = *filespec*
	All files with related file names. The filespec usually includes wildcards ? and *. You can use this option without the =filespec statement just as you can issue the DOS DIR command without an argument. However, the FILENAME NOT option is not offered with the DOS DIR command. Here are two examples.
	`NDIR FILENAME = A*.?A?`
	`NDIR FILENAME NOT = A*.?A?`

ACCESS BEFORE = *mm-dd-yy*
ACCESS NOT BEFORE = *mm-dd-yy*
	Files last accessed before the date specified. With the NOT option, files are selected based upon the last access date not being before the date specified. Here are examples of each option.
	`NDIR /ACCTG ACCESS BEFORE =01-31-89`
	`NDIR /ACCTG ACCESS NOT BEFORE=01-31-89`

Filespec Selection Options	Selects

ACCESS AFTER = *mm-dd-yy*
ACCESS NOT AFTER = *mm-dd-yy*
	Files last accessed after the date specified. The NOT option selects files that were last accessed not after the date specified.
	`NDIR /ACCTG ACCESS AFTER= 12-31-89`
	`NDIR /ACCTG ACCESS NOT AFTER=12-31-89`

CREATE AFTER = *mm-dd-yy* CREATE NOT AFTER = *mm-dd-yy* CREATE BEFORE = *mm-dd-yy* CREATE NOT BEFORE = *mm-dd-yy*	Files based on their creation date.
E O NOT E O	Execute Only. Files based on whether the Execute-only attribute is set.
H NOT H	Hidden. Files based on the setting of the Hidden attribute.
I NOT I	Indexed. Files based on the setting of the Indexed file attribute.
M NOT M	Modified. Files based on the setting of the Modified attribute. Modified is On if the file has been updated or added to the system since the last back up.

OWNER = *user_name*
NOT = *user_name*
	Files based on who created the file. Using the Not option selects files not created by the user specified. Here are two examples.
	`NDIR OWNER = SUPERVISOR`
	`NDIR OWNER NOT = SUPERVISOR`

R O NOT R O	Read-only. Files based on the setting of the Read-only attribute.

NDIR

Filespec Selection Options	Selects
R W NOT R W	Read/Write. Files based on the setting for the Read/Write attribute.
S NOT S	Shareable. Files based on the setting for the Shareable attribute of the file.
SIZE = n SIZE GREATER n SIZE LESS n	Files based on the file size in bytes. You can use the letter K to specify kilobytes (1024 bytes) and the letter M to specify megabytes (1024 × 1024).
SY NOT SY	System. Files based on the setting of the System attribute for the file. System files are those NetWare uses as part of the operating system environment.
T NOT T	Transactional. (SFT NetWare only.) Files based on the setting of the Transactional attribute.

Filespec Sequence Options	Sorts by (ascending by default)
[REVERSE] SORT ACCESS	Access date—oldest first
[REVERSE] SORT CREATE	Creation date—oldest first
[REVERSE] SORT FILENAME	Filename—alphabetical order
[REVERSE] SORT OWNER	File owner—alphabetical order
[REVERSE] SORT SIZE	File size—smallest first
[REVERSE] SORT UPDATE	Update date—oldest first

Information Parameters	Use
BR	Brief. Displays file name, size, and last update.
D O	Directories Only. Displays only directory names within a directory.
HELP	Help. Displays help on the NDIR command syntax.
SUB	Subdirectories. Displays data for all downline directories.

NPRINT

Syntax	NPRINT [directory_path]filespec [parameter][parameter]...
Examples	NPRINT ATRIUM/SYS:/MFG/PROD/DAILY.RPT J=LASER C=2
	NPRINT MYFILE.DOC Q=HOT_QUEUE D
Default	None. You must enter a filespec for a specific file.
Related commands	CAPTURE, ENDCAP

Description—Use the NPRINT command to print a file on a network printer. Many software applications let you print to a file rather than directly to the printer. In most cases, it is faster to print to a file and then use the NPRINT command to print the file than it is to print directly to the network printer from within your application. The NPRINT command has several parameters which control printing.

Parameters	Use
J=*jobname*	Jobname. Specifies a job name that has been created with the PRINTCON program which defines many print job specifications, including the form name, the queue, the number of copies, etc. The supervisor establishes the default job in the PRINTCON program.
Notify	Notify causes the NetWare 386 and NetWare 286 version 2.15 Rev. C versions of the NPRINT command to send a message to the user when the job is finished printing.
Q=*queue*	Queue. Directs output to a specific queue that is managed by the PCONSOLE program. The default queue is the one the job name parameter specifies if a job name is specified; otherwise, it is the queue specified for the default jobs in PRINTCON.

NPRINT

Parameters	Use
S=*server*	Server. Specifies which server should receive this output in a multiple server environment. The default is the server that was initially logged into.
P=*n*	Printer. Used to select a specific shared printer. Shared printers are assigned numbers from 0 through 4 during installation. The default value is 0.
C=*n*	Copies. Instructs the server to print multiple copies of the print job. The default value is 1.
F=*n* F=*form_name*	Form. This numeric value specifies which form should be used for this print job. You define a form with the PRINTDEF program and give it a name and a numeric value from 0 through 255. The default value is 0.
NAM=*user*	Name. Specifies which user name prints on the top of the banner page. The default is the user name used to log in.
B=*text*	Banner. Specifies any text up to 12 characters that will be printed at the bottom of the banner page at the beginning of a print job. Spaces are not permitted, so use a hyphen (-) or an underscore (_) to connect multiple words. The default is LST:.
NB	No Banner. Omits the banner page from the beginning of a report. However, when used in conjunction with a multiple copy report and the B (Banner) option, this parameter prints a banner at the beginning of the first copy of the report but not at the beginning of subsequent copies. The default prints a banner page at the beginning of the report.
FF	Form Feed. Instructs NetWare to perform a form feed when printing is complete. This parameter is generally required for laser printers because they often hold the last page if the page is not full.

Parameters	Use
NFF	No Form Feed. Prevents NetWare from performing a form feed at the end of the print job. This is the default setting.
T=*n*	Tabs. Instructs NetWare to replace tab characters in the print job with the number of spaces indicated. The value of n can be from 0 through 18. Most applications do not require this parameter. The exceptions are applications that do not have good print format control, for example, applications that print reports with misaligned spacing between data items.
NT	No Tabs. Overrides the TABS option, if set for a default print job. It passes tab characters to the printer intact. This setting should be used when printing graphics or files containing special formatting characters.
D	Delete. Deletes the original file automatically after the print job has been successfully queued and printed. This keeps unnecessary print files from accumulating on the disk.

> **NOTE:** The only files that NetWare automatically deletes are those stored on the network volume. It cannot delete a print file stored on a local workstation disk.

NVER

Syntax	NVER
Example	NVER
Default	NVER
Related commands	None

Description—This command is used to display the workstation shell and DOS version information for the particular workstation. When it runs, it displays information similar to the following:

PURGE

```
The NetWare NetBIOS module is not loaded,
    unable to provide version information.
IPX Version: 3.01
SPX Version: 3.01
LAN Driver:   NetWare Ethernet NE2000  V1.02EC (890309) V1.00
         IRQ = 3, I/O Base = 300h, no DMA or RAM
Shell:        V3.01 Rev. A
DOS:          MSDOS V4.00 on VGA_LJ
FileServer:   ATRIUM
    Novell    SFT NetWare 286 TTS V2.15 Rev. A    12/11/88
```

PSTAT

Syntax	PSTAT [S=*server_name*] [P=*printer*]
Example	PSTAT
Default	PSTAT *current_server*

Description—The PSTAT program tells you the status of any of the five network printers. Specifying the server name lets you see the status of a server other than your current default server. Printers are numbered 0 through 4. The information displayed will look something like this.

```
Server ATRIUM: Network Printer Information
Printer     Ready        Status     Form: number, name
-------     ---------    --------   --------------------
   0        Off-Line     Active     0, SHEET_PAPER
   1        On-Line      Active     1, CONTINUOUS
   2        On-Line      Stopped    1, CONTINUOUS
```

In the sample status report, printer 0 is either turned off or off-line. Printer 1 is printing and the file server console deactivated Printer 2. Printers 1 and 2 are using a form named CONTINUOUS defined as form 0 in PRINTDEF. Printer 0 is using a form named SHEET__PAPER defined as form number 1 in PRINTDEF.

PURGE

Syntax	PURGE
Example	PURGE
Default	PURGE

Description—The PURGE command releases the file space being held in suspense by the file server for the user's last delete command. When the FILER, DEL, or ERASE command removes files from the file server, NetWare does not immediately free the space the files occupied. To free this space immediately, use the PURGE command. It makes previously deleted files unrecoverable. Purge only affects files that users deleted from their workstation. It does not affect files other users deleted.

REMOVE

Syntax	REMOVE [USER] *account_name* FROM *directory_path*
	REMOVE [GROUP] *group_name* FROM *directory_path*
Examples	REMOVE GROUP EVERYONE FROM /MFG
	REMOVE USER TOM FROM ATRIUM/SYS:/MFG/QA
	REMOVE JILL
Default	None. You must use this command with other parameters.
Related commands	GRANT, REVOKE, TLIST

Description—The REMOVE command removes all Trustee Assignments that a user or group may have had in the directory specified or the current default directory.

RENDIR

Syntax	RENDIR *directory_path* TO *directory_name*
Examples	RENDIR ATRIUM/SYS:/MFG/PRD TO PROD
	RENDIR /ACCTG TO ACCOUNTG
Default	None. You must use this command with parameters.

Description—The RENDIR command renames directories. Only a user with both Parental and Modify Rights for a directory can rename it. This command does not affect any Trustee Assignments in the directory. However, you must change the Login Script files that referenced the old directory name to reflect the new name.

REVOKE

Syntax	REVOKE *rights* FOR [*directory_path*] FROM [USER] *account_name*
	REVOKE *rights* FOR [*directory_path*] FROM [GROUP] *group_name*
Examples	REVOKE ROS FOR ATRIUM/SYS:/LOTUS FROM EVERYONE
	REVOKE ALL FOR /MFG/PROD/BILL FROM USER BILL
Default	None. You must use this command with other parameters.
Related commands	GRANT, REMOVE, TLIST

Description—The REVOKE command eliminates Trustee Assignments in directories where the user has Parental Rights. This command makes an entry into the user's or group's Trustee Assignments list. Type the appropriate Rights letters where indicated in the command syntax.

- S   Search. The user or group can view the file names in a directory.
- O   Open. The user or group can open existing files.
- R   Read. The user or group can read an open file.
- W   Write. The user or group can write to an open file.
- C   Create. The user or group can create a new file.
- D   Delete. A user or group can delete an existing file.
- M   Modify. A user or group can change existing file attributes and file names.
- P   Parental. The user or group can create new subdirectories and remove existing subdirectories.

The Rights indicated in the command line are removed from the user's or group's existing Rights for the directory specified.

RIGHTS

Syntax	RIGHTS [*directory_path*]
Example	RIGHTS ATRIUM/SYS:USERS
Default	RIGHTS *current_directory*
Related commands	GRANT, LISTDIR, REMOVE, REVOKE

Description—This command starts the RIGHTS program which displays your Effective Rights in a specified directory or in the current default directory. Effective Rights are those that you can actually exercise. To have an Effective Right, the Right must exist in the directory's Maximum Rights Mask *and* you must have either an explicit Trustee Assignment in the directory or an implicit Trustee Assignment as a result of group membership or security equivalence.

SALVAGE

Syntax	SALVAGE [*server_name/volume*:]
Example	SALVAGE
Default	SALVAGE *current_server/volume*:
Related command	PURGE

Description—This command starts the SALVAGE program which recovers files that have been deleted from a network volume. The directory path you specify must be the network volume where the files were erased. Several conditions govern the activity of the SALVAGE command and program:

- The same user who performed the delete activity must run the SALVAGE program. Only files the user issuing the SALVAGE command deleted are recovered.
- SALVAGE recovers all files deleted during the most recent delete activity. If you perform another delete activity using DOS DEL, DOS ERASE, or NetWare FILER, you cannot recover any files previously deleted. SALVAGE also recovers all files deleted with a wildcard filespec. In addition, do not create any new files until the SALVAGE program is finished running. After you create a new file, you cannot recover deleted files.

- You must execute the SALVAGE program during the same session as the delete file activity. After you log out of the network, you can no longer recover deleted files. (Executing a LOGIN without a LOGOUT performs an automatic LOGOUT even if the LOGIN specifies the same user account.)
- You must issue the SALVAGE command at the same workstation on which you performed the delete activity. You cannot log in at another workstation and recover files you deleted from another station.
- After you issue a PURGE command, you cannot recover deleted files. PURGE releases the space the files occupied to the network server to be used by any user.

The server holds files deleted on the network in suspense until the user who performed the delete activity either creates a new file, issues another delete command, purges the files, or logs out. After one of these activities occurs, NetWare releases the space the files formerly used for use by any other user. The network disk is a shared pool of space for all users. No partitions or fences separate one user's data from another's. The physical location of data on the disk bears no relation to the user or the directories the user owns.

SEND

Syntax

SEND "*message*" [TO] [USER] [*server_name*/] *user_name* [*server_name*/][*user_name*]

SEND "*message*" [TO] [GROUP] [*server_name*/] [*group_name*] [*server_name*/][*group_name*]

Examples

SEND "Can you help me?" TO Supervisor

SEND "Meeting starts in 15 minutes." TO GROUP Prod

SEND "Can I see you in my office?" TO John Bill

SEND "Meeting delayed to 2:30." TO Mfg_Prod Mfg_Qa

SEND "New software is on-line." TO Atrium/Mike Atrium2/Sales

Default	None. A message and a destination must accompany the SEND command.
Related commands	CASTOFF, CASTON

Description—Use the SEND command to send short messages (45 characters or less) to other users or groups on the network. You only need to use the identifiers USER or GROUP when both a user and a group have the same name. You can specify multiple users and/or groups by separating their names each with a space. You can specify users or groups on other servers by preceding the user or group name with the server name which the other users or groups are on. However, you must already be attached to the other file server. You must enclose the message in quotation marks (" "). To send a message to everyone on the LAN, use the EVERYONE group.

SETPASS

Syntax	`SETPASS [server_name]`
Examples	`SETPASS ATRIUM`
	`SETPASS ATRIUM2`
	`SETPASS`
Default	`SETPASS current_server`

Description—This command starts the SETPASS program that changes your password on the default server or any other server you are currently attached to. After you type the SETPASS command, NetWare prompts:

`Enter your old password:`

Type your old password. The server verifies it before letting you continue. This prevents intruders from changing your password if they have access to a machine that you logged into and left unattended. NetWare then prompts:

`Enter your new password:`

After you do so, the system prompts:

`Retype your new password:`

SLIST

You must verify that you know the password you are entering, because you cannot see the password as you type it on the screen. After you verify the password, the server responds

    Your password has been changed.

> **NOTE:** Spaces are not allowed in passwords in all NetWare versions 2.1 and higher. If you type a space as part of a password, NetWare converts it to an underscore character (__). Then you must type the underscore character as part of the password, not the space. If you do not type the underscore, the result is an invalid password.

SETTTS

Syntax	SETTTS [logical_numeric_value [physical_numeric_value]]
Example	SETTTS 2 2
Default	SETTTS 1 1

Description—This advanced feature for SFT NetWare sets the number of logical or physical locks that NetWare ignores before beginning to track a transaction. For network supervisors' use only, this feature is documented in the Novell *SFT/Advanced NetWare 286 Maintenance* manual.

SLIST

Syntax	SLIST
Default	None. There are no parameters.

Description—This command starts the NetWare program you can use to find the names of servers currently active on your network. This program and LOGIN are the only programs that you can run if you are attached to, but not yet logged into, the file server. The SLIST program displays information similar to:

```
Known NetWare File Servers    Network     Node Address
--------------------------    --------    ------------
ATRIUM                        00000001    0008D0047164
ATRIUM2                       00000002    0000004F3226
```

The network address was established during the NetWare NETGEN configuration and the server name was established during the NETGEN installation process. The LAN Adapter card installed in the server determines the node address.

SMODE

Syntax	SMODE [directory_path] [parameter]
	SMODE [filespec] [parameter]
Examples	SMODE ATRIUM/SYS:/MFG 2
	SMODE ACCTG.COM 5
Default	Files not changed with the SMODE command have default SMODE 0.

Description—SMODE is an important NetWare command. It is somewhat related to the DOS PATH command and the NetWare MAP SEARCH command. Normally, PATH and MAP SEARCH instruct the system to search directories other than the current default directory when trying to locate executable files with the file name extension (.COM or .EXE) or batch files with the file name extension (.BAT). The system looks for the file with the .COM extension in the current directory first. If the search fails, then the system searches the current directory for an .EXE file. If the search fails again, the system checks the current directory for a .BAT file. If all three searches fail, the system moves to the first directory specified in the PATH statement and repeats the process. This continues until the system finds and executes the program or batch file or the system notifies the user that the command or file name is bad.

SMODE expands on the default method of searching for files. One reason for this is that the normal procedure only searches for either executable files (.COM or .EXE) or batch files (.BAT), totally ignoring data files and other files such as program overlays. SMODE sets options that change the default means of searching for files. The SMODE parameter determines how the system searches. Only one parameter can be issued with the SMODE command. If you omit the parameter, SMODE displays the current setting.

A major feature of SMODE is that it assigns an SMODE parameter to the executable file itself. This means that SMODE settings are a fixed parameter stored in the NetWare directory information along with the file's other pertinent data. You can change the parameter after you set it for a given file by using another SMODE command. SMODE parameters are listed next. A bug in the current version of SMODE in NetWare 386 prevents it from working if the file name exceeds five characters.

Parameter	Use
0	The default mode uses the standard procedure described earlier for locating files; that is, it only searches for executable or batch files.
1	If you specified a path to search for an executable file, then the system searches that directory for data files. If it does not find the data file, then the system searches the directories specified in the PATH statement, for example:

```
F>SYS:\APPS\DBASE\DBASE
```

This command tells the system to run a program called DBASE located in the SYS volume, in a directory path known as \APPS\DBASE. When it searches for a data file, the system searches the current default directory. Then it searches the SYS:\APPS\DBASE directory. If the file is not there, the system searches according to the PATH statement in effect.

2	The search is limited to the current default directory.
3	If you specified a path to search for an executable file, then the system searches that directory for data files. It does not search other directories unless the data file is to be opened in

Parameter	Use
	Read-only mode. If the system does not find the data file and the data file is to be opened as a Read-only file, then the system searches the directories specified in the PATH statement.
5	The system searches the specified directory path where the program was found. Then the system searches the current default directory and all directories in the PATH statement for data files.
7	If files opened by the executable program are Read-only, the system searches the default directory and all directories in the search path.

SYSTIME

Syntax	SYSTIME [*server_name*]
Examples	SYSTIME ATRIUM
	SYSTIME ATRIUM2
Default	SYSTIME *current_server*

Description—This command displays the current date and time on the server specified and synchronizes your workstation's date and time with that server's. When you issue the command, the server responds with a message similar to

```
Current System Time: Thursday, February 2, 1989 10:15 am
```

TLIST

Syntax	TLIST [*directory_path*] USERS
	TLIST [*directory_path*] GROUPS
	TLIST [*directory_path*]
	TLIST *logical_drive*: USERS
	TLIST *logical_drive*: GROUPS
	TLIST *logical_drive*:
Examples	TLIST ATRIUM/SYS:/MFG
	TLIST /MFG/PROD USERS
Default	TLIST *current_directory*

Description—This command stands for "Trustee List," a list of the users or groups who currently possess Trustee Assignments for the directory specified and the Rights assigned to that user or group. If you specify the keyword USERS or GROUPS, TLIST lists users or groups exclusively. Without a USERS or GROUPS keyword, TLIST lists both users and groups that have Trustee Assignments.

USERLIST

Syntax	USERLIST [server_name/][user_name][/A]
Examples	USERLIST ATRIUM2
	USERLIST /A
Default	USERLIST current_server

Description—The USERLIST command gives you information about users logged into the specified server. If you specify a user, the program shows the user's connection number and login time. The /A option lists the network number and physical station number.

WHOAMI

Syntax	WHOAMI [server_name][/G][/S][/R][/ALL]
Examples	WHOAMI
	WHOAMI /ALL
	WHOAMI ATRIUM
	WHOAMI ATRIUM2 /ALL
Default	WHOAMI [current_server] no options

Description—The WHOAMI command displays information about your account on the network. You can include a server specification in the command for those situations in which a user can log into multiple servers. The parameters you can include in the WHOAMI command are listed next.

Parameter	Use
/G	Displays the groups that you belong to on the server.
/R	Lists your Effective Rights in any directory on the server in which you have either Explicit or Implicit Rights.
/S	Displays any security equivalences that you have on the server.
/ALL	Displays combined information for the /G, /R, and /S options.

Appendix B
NetWare 386 Command Additions

NetWare 386 uses all the NetWare 286 commands and a few new ones. This appendix highlights the new commands. The format for the command descriptions in this appendix is:

COMMAND
: The command's name in capital letters.

Syntax
: The command's format, including its arguments and parameters. Square brackets ([ ]) enclose optional parameters. The term directory path refers to the complete description of the location of a specific directory:

    *server_name/volume:
    /directory_name/directory_name/...*

    As is always true with NetWare, if the LAN has only one server, you can omit server name/. In addition, if the sole server only has one volume, then you can omit volume: when specifying a directory path. The term filespec refers to a full file name including its file name extension:

    filename.ext

Example
: Actual ways to use the command, following the correct format.

Default
: The default parameter for the command.

Related commands	A list of similar commands.
Description	An explanation of how to use the command, including, if appropriate, lists of possible parameters, arguments, and keywords.

ALLOW

Syntax	`ALLOW server_name/volume:directory_name [TO INHERIT] rights`

Examples	`ALLOW ATRIUM/SYS:USERS/HADER/DOCS TO INHERIT ALL`
	`ALLOW \MFG R W C E F`
	`ALLOW SYS:APPS`

Default	`ALLOW`
Related commands	GRANT, REVOKE, REMOVE, TLIST

Description—This command lets you view, modify, or set the Inherited Rights Mask of a directory or file. Used without a target directory path or file, it displays the current values of the Inherited Rights Mask for all files in the current default directory. You can specify Rights by their first letter or the entire word. The values that you use for the Rights are listed next:

Parameter	Use
ALL	Includes all Rights in the Inherited Rights Mask.
A	Access Control. Lets users grant Rights to others and change the Inherited Rights Mask.
C	Create. Lets users create files and directories.
E	Erase. Lets users erase files and empty directories.
F	File Scan. Lets users view a directory list for the directory. This Right is used with other Rights.
M	Modify. Lets users change directory information and file attributes, and rename files and directories.
N	Nothing. Revokes all Rights from the Inherited Rights Mask except Supervisory.

CHKDIR

Parameter	Use
R	Read. Lets users open and read files. This Right is required to run programs.
S	Supervisory. Gives users all Rights to the directory and the files it contains. Also grants all Rights in any downline directories regardless of the Inherited Rights Mask settings in the downline directories.
W	Write. Lets users open and write to files in the directory.

CHKDIR

Syntax   CHKDIR *directory_path*

Examples   CHKDIR SYS:MFG
CHKDIR ATRIUM/SYS:USERS/HADER

Default   CHKDIR *current_default_directory*

Related commands   DSPACE, CHKVOL, VOLINFO

Description—Use CHKDIR to determine the disk space available on a given volume or directory. After you issue this command, you see a list of the overall volume space, the space available in the directory, and the amount available to you as a user. The list also includes the maximum amount of disk space permitted for the volume, directory, and user. Here is an example of a CHKDIR display.

```
Directory Space Limitation Information For:
ATRIUM\SYS:MFG
     Maximum    In Use    Available
     40,664 K   16,800 K   23,784 K    Volume Size
      4,000 K      120 K    3,880 K    User Volume Limit
      8,192 K      120 K    3,880 K    \MFG
```

Note that the example lists 3880K as available for both the User Volume Limit and the \MFG directory. This is caused by the user's disk space limitations. Even though 8072K is available (8192 − 120), this user only has 3880K available.

DSPACE

Syntax	DSPACE
Example	DSPACE
Default	DSPACE
Related commands	None

Description—This command starts the program that assigns disk space limits for directories and users. It is one of the NetWare menu utilities and has no command line options. All users can use this program to determine their disk space limits. Supervisors, workgroup managers, and user group managers can use this program to assign limits to users.

Appendix C

NetWare 286 Console Commands

You must issue console commands at the file server while the server is in Console mode. Console commands have a variety of uses, including printer operations, form management, and session control. These commands affect various resources in the file server itself.

PUTTING A NON-DEDICATED SERVER IN CONSOLE MODE

The file server indicates it is in Console mode by displaying a colon prompt (:). If your file server is non-dedicated, then it can be in either Console mode or DOS mode. In DOS mode the server can run normal DOS programs. To return the file server to Console mode, finish your application and type CONSOLE after the system prompt.

The format for the console commands in this appendix is:

COMMAND	The command's name in capital letters.
Syntax	The command's format including its arguments and parameters. Square brackets ([ ]) enclose optional parameters.
Example	Actual ways to use the command, following the correct format.

Default	The default parameter for the command.
Related commands	A list of similar commands.
Description	An explanation of how to use the command, including, if appropriate, lists of possible parameters, arguments, and keywords.

BROADCAST

Syntax	BROADCAST *message*
Example	BROADCAST Please logout as soon as possible.
Default	None
Related command	User Command → SEND

Description—The BROADCAST command sends messages from the server to all users currently logged into the LAN, usually to notify all users of some important situation. Messages are displayed on the 25th row on the user's monitor. The message interrupts the station's job until the user clears the message by pressing CTRL ENTER. Messages can contain up to 60 characters on a single line. It is not necessary to enclose BROADCAST messages in quotation marks (" ").

CLEAR MESSAGE

Syntax	CLEAR MESSAGE

Description—This command clears messages displayed on the file server while the server is in Console mode.

CLEAR STATION

Syntax	CLEAR STATION *x*
Example	CLEAR STATION 5
Default	None. You must enter a station number.
Related commands	DISABLE LOGIN, ENABLE LOGIN

Description—This command detaches a workstation from the file server's resources, closing any files open for the specified workstation.

> **WARNING:** Use this command with extreme care. If the user's station is executing a process, the process terminates immediately. Even though the server closes open files, aborting an updating process can corrupt data files because the files may be only partially updated.

CONFIG

Syntax	CONFIG
Example	CONFIG<ENTER>
	Hardware Configuration Information for Server ATRIUM
	Number of Service Processes: 6
	LAN A Configuration Information:
	Network Address: [00000001] [0020D13A0012]
	Hardware Type: NetWare Ethernet
	Hardware Settings: IRQ = 3, I/O Base = 300h,
	RAM Buffer at D000:
Default	None

Description—This console command displays the file server's hardware configuration.

CONSOLE

Syntax	CONSOLE
Default	None
Related command	DOS

Description—Use the CONSOLE command only with Advanced NetWare servers configured as non-dedicated file servers. Issue it when the server is in DOS mode to put the server into Console mode so you can issue console commands.

DISABLE LOGIN

Syntax	DISABLE LOGIN
Default	None
Related command	ENABLE LOGIN

Description—This console command keeps users from logging into the LAN. This feature is often necessary when you prepare to down the file server for routine maintenance or when you do not want additional users logging in for other reasons. Disabling LOGIN lets users logged into the LAN continue to work until they log out. After users log out, they cannot log back in.

DISMOUNT

Syntax	DISMOUNT [PACK] [*volume*]
Default	None
Related command	MOUNT

Description—This command is used only when the file server has removable disk packs or drives such as a Bernoulli Box. It instructs NetWare to remove the physical disk media, close any files on the volume, and write any data resident in cache memory that has not been written to disk. Some removable media contain removable diskette packs, a set of diskettes that are loaded as a unit. You must use the PACK keyword whenever you refer to this type of removable media. The volume indicates which volume when more than one removable drive is attached to the file server.

> **WARNING:** For obvious reasons, you should never remove a pack while it is still being accessed. Most systems do not permit this, but make sure first. Also never remove a volume that is still being accessed by a user. This causes data loss and possible physical damage to the drive and disk media. The server warns you if you attempt to DISMOUNT a volume currently in use.

DOS

Syntax	DOS
Default	None
Related command	CONSOLE

Description—This command applies only to NetWare systems configured to allow a non-dedicated file server. Non-dedicated file servers let a user use the file server as a workstation while it is also in use as the file server. The DOS command puts the server into DOS mode so that it can be used for an end-user application.

DOWN

Syntax	DOWN
Example	DOWN
Default	None
Related command	MONITOR

Description—DOWN is a very important NetWare console command used to prepare the file server to be turned off. Part of this preparation involves the file server making sure that any data waiting in the cache to be written to the disk gets written. It also makes sure that the File Allocation Table (FAT) is updated and that the disk directory is up to date. Another important function of the DOWN command is that it warns you if other users still have files open. Turning off a server when files are open can cause data corruption. To see if other users are still logged into the LAN before issuing the DOWN command, use the MONITOR command.

ENABLE LOGIN

Syntax	ENABLE LOGIN
Example	ENABLE LOGIN
Default	None
Related command	DISABLE LOGIN

Description—The ENABLE LOGIN command reverses the action of the DISABLE LOGIN command, allowing users to log into the LAN. You only need to use this command when you issue a DISABLE LOGIN command, but have not turned off the file server. You do not need to issue this command if you turned off the file server since you issued the DISABLE LOGIN command.

ENABLE LOGIN will unlock the supervisor account if it has been locked due to intruder detection.

MONITOR

Syntax	MONITOR *station*
Examples	MONITOR 12
	MONITOR 1
Default	MONITOR 1

Description—The MONITOR command puts the file server in a mode in which workstation activity can be monitored. It divides the screen into six activity panels, so six sessions can be monitored simultaneously. The station number entered sets the first session that will be displayed in the upper-left portion.

The display is similar to that shown in Figure C-1.

The top line of the monitor displays file server status information you can use to roughly monitor the load on the network.

NetWare Version	The level and version of NetWare being used.
Utilization	This value is updated every second and represents the percentage of time that the processor spent on network requests during the last second.
Disk I/O Pending	This number represents the number of cache buffers in memory waiting to be written to the disk. The server holds data in memory and schedules writes to disk during idle moments, thereby improving performance. Each cache buffer is 4096 bytes.

The six panels display various information about the session in progress. The first line of data displays the type of activity or request that the file server is handling for the workstation. There are forty-four different activities that the file server may be processing for the station.

MONITOR

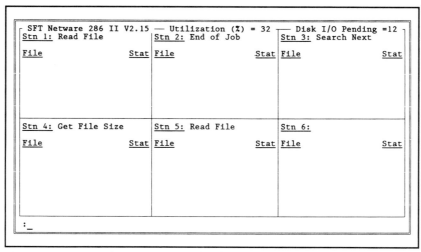

Figure C-1. Sample MONITOR display

1 Alloc Resource	12 End of Job	23 Log Record	34 Rename File
2 Begin Trans	13 End Trans	24 Open File	35 Search Next
3 Clear File	14 Erase File	25 Pass File	36 Semaphore
4 Clear File Set	15 Floppy Config	26 Read File	37 Set File Atts
5 Clear Record Set	16 Get File Size	27 Rel Phy Rec	38 Start Search
6 Close File	17 Lock File	28 Rel Phy Rec Set	39 Sys Log
7 Clr Phy Rec	18 Lock Phy Rec Set	29 Rel Record Set	40 Unlock Record
8 Clr Phy Rec Set	19 Lock Record	30 Rel Resource	41 Win Format
9 Copy File	20 Log Out	31 Release File	42 Win Read
10 Create File	21 Log Pers File	32 Release File Set	43 Win Write
11 Dir Search	22 Log Phy Rec	33 Release Record	44 Write File

The server uses the File and Stat areas to display the files in use by each workstation. Beneath the File heading each file the workstation has open is listed along with the logical drive letter where the file is located. A question mark (?) in the drive letter space indicates that the server is still searching for the file. Beneath the Stat heading is a single digit representing the DOS task being used with the file. Following the DOS task are up to four characters that describe the type of access granted to the file. The access types are listed next.

Column 1	2	3	4	Access
P				Other workstations cannot read the file.
	R			The file is open for a read operation.
		P		Other workstations cannot write to the file.
			W	The file is open for a write operation.
T				The file is a transaction-tracked file with a transaction in process (SFT NetWare only).
	H			The file is a transaction-tracked file which is on hold until a transaction is completed (SFT NetWare only).
P	e	r	s	The file is logged but not locked. Others can use it.
L	o	c	k	The file is locked.

MOUNT

Syntax	`MOUNT [PACK] [volume]`
Example	`MOUNT SYS:`
Default	None
Related command	DISMOUNT

Description—This command is used only when the file server has removable disk packs or drives such as a Bernoulli Box. It instructs NetWare that you wish to access the physical disk media that has been changed after a DISMOUNT command. Some removable media contain removable diskette packs, a set of diskettes that are loaded as a unit. You must use the PACK keyword whenever you refer to this type of removable media. The volume indicates which volume when more than one removable drive is attached to the file server.

NAME

Syntax	`NAME`
Example	`NAME<ENTER>` *This is server ATRIUM.*

PRINTER ADD QUEUE

Description—Use this command to determine the name assigned to the file server during installation. It is useful when there are multiple file servers in a LAN, especially when those servers are close to one another.

OFF

Syntax	OFF
Example	OFF
Default	None

Description—This command clears the file server's screen when in the Console mode. It is also used to clear Monitor mode.

PRINTER

Syntax	P[rinter[s]]

Example	PRINTER
	 PRINTER 0
	 ATRIUM is configured for 2 printers:
	 Printer 0: Running On-Line Form 0 mounted
	                     Servicing 2 Queues.
	 Printer 1: Halted at Console Off-Line
	                     Form 5 mounted Servicing 1 Queues.

Default	Printer

Description—This console command displays the status of shared printers. It provides information about the shared printer's number (0 through 4), its current status, the current form number mounted on the printer, and the number of queues currently attached to the printer.

PRINTER ADD QUEUE

Syntax	P[rinter] n ADD [QUEUE] queue_name [[AT] [PRIORITY] p] P[rinter] n = [QUEUE] queue_name [[AT] [PRIORITY] p]
Examples	Printer 1 Add Queue MFL P2 Add Q_Prod AT 3
Default	None
Related command	PRINTER DELETE QUEUE

Description—This command attaches a queue to a given printer at a specific priority level. The keywords QUEUE, AT, and PRIORITY are not required. The value for *n* is 0 through 4, a number corresponding to the number defined for the shared printer port when the file server was installed. If you do not specify a priority (p), the priority is automatically set to 1. Priorities are 1 through 9; 1 is the highest priority. You can attach multiple queues to a single printer. If the queues have different priorities, the jobs in the highest priority queue print before any jobs in the queue with the next highest priority. Multiple queues facilitate management of print jobs that have different priorities. Without multiple queues, you must manage print jobs via the PCONSOLE program by changing the print job's sequence number to move it to a different position in the queue. This means that queue operators have to exit from any applications that they are using, run the PCONSOLE program, change the sequence number, exit from the PCONSOLE program, and then return to their other work.

If multiple queues attached to a printer have equal priorities, jobs are printed according to the date and time they were placed in the queue because each queue maintains its own series of print job numbers.

You can also attach the same queue to more than one printer. This is useful when more than one identical printer is attached to the file server as a shared printer. Print jobs are sent to the printer that is available first according to their normal sequence. The key to attaching a queue to multiple printers is that the printers must be the same type. This is because different printers use different internal codes to initiate special features such as bold or underlined print. Because the software used to print the job was configured for a specific printer, attaching dissimilar printers to a queue results in jobs printing improperly on one of the printers. NetWare cannot convert print jobs that were issued for one printer style to the format of another printer style.

PRINTER DELETE QUEUE

Syntax	P[rinter] n DEL[ete] [QUEUE] queue_name
Examples	PRINTER 1 DELETE QUEUE MFG
	P 2 DEL Q_PROD
Default	None
Related command	PRINTER ADD QUEUE

Description—This console command is used to detach a queue from a specific printer. It *does not* remove or delete the actual queue or the print jobs that the queue contains. The keyword QUEUE is optional.

This command is commonly used when a queue needs to be detached from one printer and attached to another. This commonly occurs when a printer goes down for some reason and must be taken off line for repairs. You may still place jobs in the queue while it is detached from the printer.

PRINTER FORM FEED

Syntax	P[rinter] n FORM FEED
	P[rinter] n FF
Examples	PRINTER 1 FORM FEED
	P 2 FF
Default	None
Related command	PRINTER FORM MARK

Description—This command sends a form feed to the printer the number n specifies. n is a physical printer numbered 0 through 4, corresponding to the installation of shared printers during the NETGEN process. This command advances the printer to the top of the next page. The printer must be on line for this command to work.

PRINTER FORM MARK

Syntax	P[rinter] n FORM MARK
	P[rinter] n MARK [[TOP OF] FORM]
Examples	Printer 1 FORM MARK
	P 2 MARK

Default	None
Related commands	PRINTER FORM FEED, REWIND PRINTER, PRINTER START, PRINTER STOP

Description—This console command helps align continuous forms and paper on a printer. It directs NetWare to print a row of asterisks (*) showing where printing on the page will begin. You can use these asterisks as a reference for adjusting the vertical position of the form. After you do so, issue a PRINTER FORM FEED command to position for the next form.

PRINTER MOUNT FORM

Syntax	P[rinter] n MOUNT [FORM] nnn P[rinter] n FORM [MOUNT] nnn P[rinter] n FORM nnn [MOUNT[ED]]
Examples	PRINTER 1 MOUNT FORM 4 P 2 FORM 5 P 3 FORM 3 MOUNT
Default	None
Related commands	PRINTER FORM FEED, PRINTER FORM MARK, PRINTER, QUEUE

Description—Each print job created with the PRINTCON program can have a specific form associated with it. You define forms in the PRINTDEF program by name and number. To mount a specific form, refer to it by the number (nnn) defined in PRINTDEF. The commands CAPTURE and NPRINT and the F= parameter can also specify a form for the print job. You must specify the printer (n = 0 through 4) for which you are mounting the form and the form number.

PRINTER QUEUES

Syntax   P[rinter] n [Q[ueue[s]]]

Example

```
PRINTER 1 QUEUES
P 2 Q
PRINTER 0
Printer 0:  Running  On-line  Form 0 mounted
            Servicing 2 Queues
Servicing HOT                          at priority 1
Servicing PRINTQ_0                     at priority 3
```

Default   None

Related commands   QUEUE, PRINTER

Description—This command lists the status of a given printer (0 through 4). The status information includes the printer's status, the current form number mounted, and the number of queues attached. In addition, it includes the name and priority of each attached queue.

PRINTER REWIND

Syntax   P[rinter] n REWIND [xx] [PAGES]

Examples   PRINTER 1 REWIND 5 PAGES
P 2 REWIND 3

Rewind back 5 pages:

P 0 REWIND 5

Rewind back to the beginning of the current page:

P 0 REWIND 0

Rewind to the beginning of the print job:

P 0 REWIND

Default   None

Related commands   PRINTER FORM FEED, PRINTER MARK FORM

Description—This command is an essential. It "rewinds" a print job that is currently being printed. It interrupts the printer (n = 0 through 4) and backs up the print job the number of pages specified by xx (xx = 0 through 10). If you need to back up more than ten pages, you must rewind the entire job. Omit the xx parameter to rewind to the beginning of the print job; use the parameter 0 to rewind to the beginning of the current page.

PRINTER START

Syntax	P[rinter] n START
Examples	PRINTER 1 START
	P 2 START
Default	None
Related commands	PRINTER, PRINTER STOP

Description—This console command restarts a printer that the PRINTER STOP command has stopped. The value for n is 0 through 4, corresponding to the number assigned to the shared printer port during NETGEN.

PRINTER STOP

Syntax	P[rinter] n STOP
Examples	PRINTER 1 STOP
	P 2 STOP
Default	None
Related commands	PRINTER MOUNT FORM, PRINTER REWIND, PRINTER START

Description—This command stops the specified printer. You often need to do this to change the form that is mounted, to change a printer ribbon or cartridge, or to issue other printer commands that affect the current print job.

QUEUE

Syntax	Q[ueue] [queue_name]
Example	QUEUE
	Q Q_MFG
	QUEUE<ENTER>
	ATRIUM Print Queues:
	PRINTQ_0 4 queue jobs serviced by 1 printers.
	PRINTQ_1 3 queue jobs serviced by 1 printers.
	HOT 2 queue jobs services by 1 printers.
	QUEUE HOT<ENTER>

QUEUE CREATE

```
                    Jobs currently in Print Queue HOT:
                    Priority  User    File         Job   Copies
                        1     HADER   MIKE.TXT     711   1
                        2     JOHN_S  USERRPT.DOC  712   1
```

Default — None

Description—The QUEUE command lists the queues that have been created on the file server and their current status. If you specify the queue name, the jobs within the queue are listed.

QUEUE CHANGE PRIORITY

Syntax — Q[ueue] queue_name C[hange] [JOB] xxx [TO][PRIORITY] xxx

Examples — QUEUE Q_MFG CHANGE JOB 14 TO PRIORITY 2
Q Q_MFG C 21 3

Move a print job that is currently number 12 in the PRINTQ_0 queue so it prints as soon as the job currently printing is finished:

QUEUE PRINTQ_0 CHANGE JOB 12 TO PRIORITY 2
Q PRINTQ_0 C 12 2

Default — None

Related commands — PRINTER ADD QUEUE, QUEUE DELETE JOB

Description—This console command moves a job in a queue to a different position within the queue. It can only move jobs within a given print queue. If the priority number given exceeds the number of jobs in the queue, the job is automatically placed at the end of the list of print jobs.

QUEUE CREATE

Syntax — Q[ueue] queue_name CREATE

Examples — QUEUE Q_MFG CREATE
Q Q_MFG CREATE

Default — None

Related commands — PRINTER ADD QUEUE, QUEUE DESTROY

Description—This command creates a new print queue on the file server. Queue names can be up to 47 characters long; no spaces are permitted. You can also create queues with the PCONSOLE program described in Chapter 11. After you create the queue, you must attach it to the appropriate printer with the PRINTER ADD QUEUE console command. The default users for the queue are the EVERYONE group. The default queue operator will be SUPERVISOR.

QUEUE DELETE JOB

Syntax	Q[ueue] queue_name D[el[ete]] [JOB] nn
	Q[ueue] queue_name D[el[ete]] [JOB] *
Examples	QUEUE Q_MFG DELETE JOB 14
	Q Q_MFG D 14
Default	None
Related commands	QUEUE DESTROY, PRINTER START, PRINTER STOP, PRINTER REWIND

Description—This command deletes jobs from the queue specified. The keyword JOB is optional. The value for nn is the job sequence number in the queue. If you enter an asterisk (*) for the job number, NetWare deletes all jobs in the print queue. Jobs below the one deleted automatically advance one number. Deleting the current job stops printing after the buffer is emptied. Then the next job in line begins to print automatically.

QUEUE DESTROY

Syntax	Q[ueue] queue_name DESTROY
Examples	QUEUE Q_MFG DESTROY
	Q Q_MFG DESTROY
Default	None

Description—This console command removes the queue completely from the server. Any jobs in the queue are also removed.

> **WARNING:** Be careful with this command. It does not warn you if you are destroying a queue that contains print jobs waiting to be printed! Before using this command, verify the queue's status with the QUEUE command.

REMIRROR

Syntax	`REMIRROR`
Example	`REMIRROR`
Default	None
Related command	UNMIRROR

Description—This command applies to SFT NetWare only. SFT supports mirrored or duplexed disk drives which "mirror" all activity on the disk in a second identical drive. The objective is to have redundant data in case of a drive failure. If a drive has to be replaced, the REMIRROR command copies the contents of the operating drive to the new drive, thereby re-creating a new mirror drive.

SEND

Syntax	`SEND "message" [TO [station] stationlist]`
Examples	`SEND "Please Log Out" TO 5`
	`SEND "Please Log Out" TO 5, 3, 14`
Default	None
Related command	BROADCAST

Description—This command sends a message of up to 40 characters to other LAN users. You must enclose the message in quotation marks (" "). The stationlist is a list of workstation numbers separated by commas (,) or spaces. If you do not specify a stationlist, the message is sent to all users currently logged into the LAN.

SET TIME

Syntax	SET TIME [mm/dd/yy] [hh:[mm:[ss]] [AM/PM]]
Example	SET TIME 04/01/91 08:15 AM
Default	None

Description—This console command sets the time at the file server. You can enter the time in either a 12-hour or 24-hour format. Separate hours, minutes, and seconds with a colon (:). If you do not enter the date or time, the server displays the current date and time it has in its clock.

SPOOL TO QUEUE

Syntax	S[pool] n [TO] [QUEUE] queue_name S[pool] n [=] queue_name
Examples	SPOOL 0 TO QUEUE Q_MFG S 1 = Q_MFG
Default	None

Description—This command is designed for those who are upgrading from a NetWare 2.0x version to a 2.1x version. On-line printing with 2.0x was initiated with the SPOOL command and terminated with the ENDSPOOL command. There was a single 2.0x spool for each printer shared on the file server. In 2.1x, NetWare offers print queues and you can create more or less queues than the number of shared printers. On-line printing is initiated using the CAPTURE and ENDCAP commands in 2.1x. Upgrading to 2.1x involves both installing the new software and changing any batch files or menus that had the 2.0x SPOOL command so they include the newer 2.1x CAPTURE command. This job can be very time-consuming.

This command reroutes print jobs initiated with a 2.0x SPOOL command to a 2.1x print queue, where it is managed just like any other 2.1x print job.

> **TIP:** The SPOOL and ENDSPOOL programs do not come with the 2.1x diskettes even though SPOOL and ENDSPOOL can still be used. To use them, you must copy them from the 2.0x diskettes to the server's /PUBLIC directory. These programs are on the diskettes marked PUBLIC in version 2.0x.

TIME

Syntax	TIME
Example	TIME
Default	None

Description—This command displays the current date and time from the file server's clock.

UNMIRROR

Syntax	UNMIRROR nn
Example	UNMIRROR 01
Default	None
Related command	REMIRROR

Description—This command, used with SFT NetWare only, turns off a drive's mirroring and shuts down the drive. The parameter nn refers to the drive number. The drive(s) that you do not shut down continue to operate normally.

Appendix D

NetWare 386 Console Commands

NetWare 386 has an entirely different set of commands for the file server console than NetWare 286. This appendix acquaints you with these commands. For your convenience, the commands are listed alphabetically. The format for the console commands in this appendix is:

COMMAND	The command's name in capital letters.
Syntax	The command's format, including its arguments and parameters. Square brackets ([ ]) enclose optional parameters. The bar symbol (¦) means that you can choose one of the values on either side of the symbol.
Example	Actual ways to use the command, following the correct format.
Range or Values	The values allowed for various NetWare 386 console commands are indicated. Some of the values require Yes or No; others are numeric and some are periods of time.
Default	The default parameter for the command.
Related commands	A list of similar commands.
Description	An explanation of how to use the command, including, if appropriate, lists of possible parameters, arguments, and keywords.

ADD NAME SPACE

Syntax	ADD NAME SPACE *name_type* [TO VOLUME *volume*]
Example	ADD NAME SPACE MACINTOSH TO VOLUME SYS
Default	None
Related command	LOAD

Description—This command adds NetWare 386 support for non-DOS file-naming conventions. This means you can store files with DOS file names and files from other non-DOS systems on the NetWare 386 file server. The most common of these is support for Macintosh file names. NetWare 386 version 3.11 added support for Sun Microsystem's NFS. After you add name support to the volume, you cannot remove it without deleting the volume.

BIND

Syntax	BIND *protocol* [TO] *lan_driver* [*driver parameters*] [*protocol parameters*]
Example	BIND IPX TO NE2000 INT=3 PORT=300 NET=10000001 FRAME=Ethernet_802.3
Default	None
Related commands	LOAD, PROTOCOL, UNBIND

Description—This NetWare 386 command attaches (binds) a network protocol to a NIC driver and sets various operating parameters for the NIC driver and NetWare. You can issue this command many times for a single NIC that will receive or transmit many frame types. NetWare most commonly uses the IPX protocol. NetWare 386 version 3.11 has added support for TCP/IP protocols. The lan__driver parameter is the name of the NIC driver software that was loaded (MACINTOSH in the example) or the name assigned to the NIC driver when it was loaded. The driver parameters you use depend on the NIC driver installed: refer to the NIC vendor's documentation for these values. The only protocol parameter is NET=, which establishes an eight-character hexadecimal value for the physical network address.

BROADCAST

Syntax	BROADCAST "*message*" [[TO] *user_name¦connection_number*][[and¦,] *user_name¦connection_number*]...
Examples	BROADCAST "Server will be down at 7PM for maintenance."
	BROADCAST "Please log off immediately!" TO Joe
	BROADCAST "Meeting today at 4PM. Conference room." TO 5, 11, and Ann
Default	None. Default recipient is all users.
Related commands	SEND, CASTOFF (user command)

Description—This command sends a message containing up to 55 characters to all users, a list of users, or a specific user. You select the users by typing their user names or their connection numbers on the file server. You can determine connection numbers with the USERLIST user command or by running the MONITOR program at the file server.

CLEAR STATION

Syntax	CLEAR STATION *number*
Example	CLEAR STATION 5
Range or Values	1 to 250
Default	None

Description—This command releases a connection that a file server has established for a given workstation. It closes all open files and releases any other network resources the connection is using. You can determine connection numbers with the USERLIST user command or by running the MONITOR program at the file server. Use this command to clear the connection when a workstation crashes and leaves files open on the file server. After you do so, be sure to check the files for accuracy. If the workstation attempts to access the file server after a CLEAR STATION command, the user receives a message similar to

```
Network error on server ATRIUM: Connection no longer valid.
Abort? Retry?
```

The user must reboot the workstation to reconnect to the file server.

CLS

Syntax	CLS
Example	CLS
Default	None
Related command	OFF

Description   This command clears the file server's monitor.

CONFIG

Syntax	CONFIG
Example	CONFIG
Default	None
Related command	DISPLAY NETWORKS

Description   This command displays configuration data about the current settings on the file server:

- File server name
- IPX internal network number
- NIC driver(s) installed
    I/O port used
    Interrupt used
    DMA channel used
    ROM/RAM addresses
    Frame type
    Board name
    Network number assigned
- Protocols bound to NIC drivers

Here is an example of a list from a file server.

```
:CONFIG
File server name: ATRIUM
IPX internal network number: 00000033
```

```
NE-2000 LAN Driver V3.10 (900517)
  Hardware setting: I/O Port 300h to 31Fh, Interrupt 2h
  Node Address: 00001B31236A
  Frame type: Ethernet_802.3
  Board name: Backbone_A
  LAN protocol: IPX network 19910115
NE-2000 LAN Driver V3.10 (900517)
  Hardware setting: I/O Port 320h to 35Eh, Interrupt 3h
  Node Address: 00001B31252B
  Frame type: Ethernet_802.3
  Board name: Backbone_B
  LAN protocol: IPX network 19890719
```

DISABLE LOGIN

Syntax	DISABLE LOGIN
Example	DISABLE LOGIN
Default	None
Related command	ENABLE LOGIN

Description—This command prevents users from logging into the file server. Users already logged in are not affected unless they log out. This command is useful when you are getting ready to down the server.

DISABLE TTS

Syntax	DISABLE TTS
Example	DISABLE TTS
Default	None
Related command	ENABLE TTS

Description—This command disables the NetWare 386 Transaction Tracking System. NetWare uses TTS to track update processes and make sure they complete successfully and also to track updates to its bindery files. Application software may also use TTS to improve reliability.

DISMOUNT

Syntax	DISMOUNT volume
Examples	DISMOUNT SYS
	DISMOUNT ALL
Default	None
Related command	MOUNT

Description—This command makes disk volumes unavailable to those users logged into the file server. Use this command when you need to shut the volume down for maintenance or removal.

DISPLAY NETWORKS

Syntax	DISPLAY NETWORKS
Example	DISPLAY NETWORKS
Default	None
Related commands	CONFIG, DISPLAY SERVERS

Description—This command lists the networks that the file server knows about. On NetWare 386 file servers, at least two networks are listed, the physical network and the internal IPX network the file server uses for internal routing of packets. As the sample display shows, next to each network number listed are two values. The first value is the number of hops (or networks traveled) that a packet takes to reach the network. The second value is the estimated time, in clock ticks, a packet takes to reach the network. A clock tick is about 1/18th of a second.

```
:DISPLAY NETWORKS
    00000033  0/1      19910115  0/1      19890719  0/1
There are 3 known networks
```

DISPLAY SERVERS

Syntax	DISPLAY SERVERS
Example	DISPLAY SERVERS
Default	None
Related commands	DISPLAY NETWORKS, CONFIG

Description—This command lists file servers that the file server knows about. As the sample display shows, the list includes the names of the file servers and how many hops a packet takes to get to other file servers.

```
:DISPLAY SERVERS
    ATRIUM386    0    ATRIUM386    1    ATRIUM286    1
There are 3 known servers
```

DOWN

Syntax	DOWN
Example	DOWN
Default	None
Related command	EXIT

Description—This command prepares a file server to be turned off, checking that the contents of all cache buffers are written to the disk, open files are closed, and File Allocation Tables and directories are updated and closed. All NetWare file servers should be downed before you turn them off. If you do not do so, you risk losing some of the data in the cache. Do not down the file server until all users have logged out of the file server. If the server reports that files are open and no one is logged in, a user has probably turned off a PC without logging out. In this case, you can usually shut down the file server without damaging the files. This often happens when users have menu files open and turn their machine off. The server would have eventually closed the files anyway.

ENABLE LOGIN

Syntax	ENABLE LOGIN
Example	ENABLE LOGIN
Default	None
Related command	DISABLE LOGIN

Description—This command reverses the status of a DISABLE LOGIN command that prevented users from logging into the file server. After you issue the ENABLE LOGIN command, users can log into the file server once again. You only need to use this command when you have not downed the server after you issued a DISABLE LOGIN command. Downing a file server and bringing it up again automatically enables login.

This command also unlocks the SUPERVISOR account if NetWare's Intruder Detection feature has locked it. It does not unlock any other supervisor or user accounts.

ENABLE TTS

Syntax	ENABLE TTS
Example	ENABLE TTS
Default	None
Related command	DISABLE TTS

Description—To reactivate NetWare's Transaction Tracking System after you issue a DISABLE TTS command, use ENABLE TTS. NetWare automatically disables TTS if either of these conditions exists:

- The SYS volume is full. TTS uses the SYS volume for its log files.
- The file server has insufficient RAM to operate TTS.

ENABLE TTS reactivates TTS after NetWare automatically disables it because of one of these conditions. You will see an error message after you issue ENABLE TTS if one of these conditions exists:

- The SYS volume is not mounted.
- The SYS volume is out of disk space.
- Memory is insufficient for TTS to operate properly.

EXIT

Syntax	EXIT
Example	EXIT
Default	None
Related commands	DOWN, REMOVE DOS

LOAD

Description—Use this command after downing the file server to exit NetWare's operating system and return to DOS at the file server. You return to the directory where you originally booted the file server. You cannot use this command to return to DOS while the file server is running NetWare 386 or if you have issued a REMOVE DOS command.

LOAD

Syntax	LOAD module_name [parameters]
Examples	LOAD INSTALL
	LOAD PSERVER ATRIUM_PS
	LOAD NE2000 Port=300 Int=3 Frame=Ethernet_802.2
Default	None
Related commands	UNLOAD, MODULES

Description—This command loads programs called NetWare Loadable Modules (NLMs) into the file server's RAM. NetWare 386's multitasking modular design lets you load individual programs while other modules are also in RAM. NetWare 386 NLMs fall into four categories:

Disk drivers

NIC drivers

Name space modules

Utility modules

Each module may have unique parameters which should be listed in the vendor's documentation. NetWare 386 comes with various modules. Consult your NetWare 386 documentation for information about these modules.

MEMORY

Syntax	MEMORY
Example	MEMORY
Default	None
Related command	REGISTER MEMORY

Description—This command directs the file server to display the amount of memory installed.

MODULES

Syntax	MODULES
Example	MODULES
Default	None
Related commands	LOAD, UNLOAD

Description—This command displays the modules that have been loaded into RAM at the file server. Here is a sample display.

```
:MODULES
MONITOR.NLM    NetWare 386 Console Monitor
PSERVER.NLM    NetWare 386 Print Server v1.2 (900611)
CLIB.NLM       NetWare 386 C Runtime Library 3.1 Jun 08 1990
STREAMS.NLM    NetWare STREAMS v3.10
RSPX.NLM       NetWare 386 Remote Console SPX Driver
REMOTE.NLM     NetWare 386 Remote Console
MAC.NAM        NetWare 386 Macintosh Finder Name Space Support
NE2000.LAN     NE-2000 LAN Driver v3.10 (900517)
NMAGENT.NLM    Network Management NLM V1.02
ISADISK.DSK    NetWare 386 ISA Device Driver V3.10 (900611)
```

MOUNT

Syntax	MOUNT volume¦ALL
Examples	MOUNT SYS
	MOUNT ALL
Default	MOUNT ALL
Related command	DISMOUNT

PROTOCOL

Description—This command mounts a disk volume that is not currently mounted so that the volume becomes accessible to users logged into the file server. If NetWare cannot find all segments belonging to a volume, it does not mount the volume. NetWare 386 allows a single volume to span multiple partitions and physical drives.

NAME

Syntax	NAME
Example	NAME
Default	None
Related command	CONFIG

Description—This command displays the name assigned to the file server. You can change this name by editing the AUTOEXEC.NCF file using the SYSCON program.

OFF

Syntax	OFF
Example	OFF
Default	None
Related command	CLS

Description—This command clears the display on the file server's monitor.

PROTOCOL

Syntax	PROTOCOL
Example	PROTOCOL
Default	None
Related commands	CONFIG, PROTOCOL REGISTER

Description—Use this command to display the protocols currently in use on your file server. As the sample display shows, the information includes the type of protocol, the type of data frame, and the protocol's ID.

Protocol: IPX   Frame type: VIRTUAL_LAN Protocol ID: 0
Protocol: IPX   Frame type: ETHERNET_802.3 Protocol ID: 0

PROTOCOL REGISTER

Syntax	PROTOCOL REGISTER *protocol frame id_number*
Example	PROTOCOL REGISTER IPX ETHERNET_II 8137
Default	None
Related commands	LOAD, BIND, PROTOCOL

Description—This command registers another protocol with the file server. As additional NLMs for using protocols other than IPX become available, Novell and other vendors will supply them. You load these modules into the file server's RAM using the LOAD command. After you load them, you must register them with the file server using the PROTOCOL REGISTER command. After doing so, you use the NetWare BIND command to bind the protocol to the NIC driver.

REGISTER MEMORY

Syntax	REGISTER MEMORY *starting_address length*
Examples	REGISTER MEMORY 1000000 400000
	REGISTER MEMORY 1000000 1000000
Default	None
Related command	MEMORY

Description—This command registers memory in excess of 16Mb when the file server does not automatically recognize the memory. You must indicate the starting address for the RAM and how much RAM exists beyond 16Mb (length). Both values are entered as hexadecimals. Hex value 1000000 is 16Mb (16,777,216). Common values for RAM increments are listed next.

1Mb	100000h
2Mb	200000h
4Mb	400000h
6Mb	600000h

8Mb	800000h
10Mb	A00000h
12Mb	C00000h
14Mb	E00000h
16Mb	1000000h
32Mb	2000000h

REMOVE DOS

Syntax	REMOVE DOS
Example	REMOVE DOS
Default	None
Related commands	EXIT, SECURE CONSOLE

Description—This command removes DOS from the file server's RAM, freeing memory for NetWare 386 to use for file caching and other activities. After you use this command, NetWare cannot load modules located on the file server's DOS partition or floppy drives. If you remove DOS, the file server EXIT command causes a warm boot.

RESET ROUTER

Syntax	RESET ROUTER
Example	RESET ROUTER
Default	None

Description—NetWare 386 maintains an internal table called the Router table to track the servers on the network. The file server uses this information to route packets to the other networks and file servers. This command rebuilds the Router table. You will not need to use this command very often because NetWare 386 updates its Router table every two minutes to track servers that have been added or removed from the network.

SEARCH

Syntax	SEARCH
	SEARCH ADD [*number*] *directory_path*
	SEARCH DEL *number*
Examples	SEARCH ADD 1 SYS:NLMS
	SEARCH ADD 2 C:\NW386
	SEARCH DEL 2
	SEARCH
Range or Values	1 to 26
Default	No parameters
	SEARCH 1: SYS:SYSTEM

Description—Use this command to view and change the paths where the server searches for loadable modules, STARTUP.NCF, and AUTOEXEC.NCF. In some situations, you might want to keep third-party NLMs in separate directories. (They might have the same file name.) You can add other directories for NetWare 386 to search with this command. The NetWare defaults cause the system to use the SYS:SYSTEM directory when looking for these modules.

The optional number in the SEARCH ADD statement inserts the path at that place in the current list. If you omit the number, NetWare adds the path to the end of the current list. Deleting a search number decrements higher value search segments by 1.

SECURE CONSOLE

Syntax	SECURE CONSOLE
Example	SECURE CONSOLE
Default	None
Related commands	REMOVE DOS, EXIT

Description—This command removes DOS from the file server's RAM and prevents loadable modules from being loaded from any directory other than SYS:SYSTEM. Novell also designed this command so it would prevent users other than console operators from changing the date and time on the file server. This works

SET Allow Unencrypted Passwords

when someone attempts to change the date or time at the file server console. However, anyone can still change the date and time with FCONSOLE.

SEND

Syntax	SEND "*message*" [TO] *user_name¦number* [,][*user¦number*]...
Examples	SEND "Please log out." TO Joe
	SEND "Meeting today at 3PM in conference room." TO 17, 4, ANN
Default	None
Related command	BROADCAST

Description—This command sends a message containing up to 55 characters to all users, a list of users, or a specific user. You select the users by typing their user names or their connection numbers on the file server. You can determine connection numbers with the USERLIST user command or by running the MONITOR program at the file server.

SET

Syntax	SET *file_server_option* = *number*

Description—SET commands configure and manage the NetWare 386 file server. So many different parameters can be adjusted through these commands that I will discuss each SET command individually.

SET Allow Unencrypted Passwords

Syntax	SET Allow Unencrypted Passwords = On¦Off
Example	SET Allow Unencrypted Passwords = On
Values	On or Off
Default	Off

Description—NetWare 386 workstation shells encrypt the user password before sending it in a packet to the server. NetWare 286 workstation shells do not. NetWare 286 versions 2.1 and above can use the NetWare 386 shells, and public and login files. This setting should be On when you are using both NetWare 386 and NetWare 286 in an interconnected LAN environment and

- Your version of NetWare 286 is below 2.1 OR
- You do not wish to upgrade your NetWare 286 shells, and public and login files.

This setting should be Off when

- You are using only NetWare 386 on the file servers of a network.
- You are using both NetWare 386 and NetWare 286 file servers, you have updated the NetWare 286 file server's public and login files, and you have updated the workstation shells.

SET Auto Register Memory Above 16 Megabytes

Syntax	`SET Auto Register Memory Above 16 Megabytes = number`
Example	`SET Auto Register Memory Above 16 Megabytes = ON`
Values	On or Off
Default	On
Related commands	SET Cache Buffer Size SET Maximum Alloc Short Term Memory

Description—You can use this command to instruct the server what kind of memory and bus architecture your file server has.

You should set this parameter to Off if your machine uses an industry standard bus architecture (ISA). Most clone PCs use this architecture. This type of machine cannot address more than 16Mb of RAM. Memory over 16Mb will be useless in this type of machine.

If your machine uses extended industry standard architecture (EISA) or micro channel architecture (MCA), then set this parameter to on. This will register memory over 16Mb with the NetWare 386 operating system.

You must place this command in the STARTUP.CNF file.

SET Auto TTS Backout Flag

Syntax	SET Auto TTS Backout Flag = On¦Off
Example	SET Auto TTS Backout Flag = On
Values	Off or On
Default	Off
Related commands	SET Maximum Transactions
	SET TTS Abort Dump Flag
	SET TTS Backout File Truncation Wait Time
	SET TTS Unwritten Cache Wait Time

Description—This version of the SET command determines whether the file server *automatically* backs out incomplete transactions that it finds during boot-up or waits for your response to the message:

```
Incomplete transaction(s) found. Do you wish to back them out?
```

You cannot change this parameter using the console SET command. You must place the SET Auto TTS Backout Flag = Off/On command in the STARTUP.NCF file.

SET Cache Buffer Size

Syntax	SET Cache Buffer Size = *number*
Example	SET Cache Buffer Size = 4096
Values	4096, 8192, or 16384
Default	4096
Related commands	SET Auto Register Memory Above 16 Megabytes
	SET Maximum Alloc Short Term Memory

Description—This setting should correspond to the block size set up for the server volume. If you have multiple volumes with different block sizes, set this entry to the smallest block size used for the volumes.

You cannot change this parameter using the console SET command. You must place the SET Cache Buffer Size = *number* command in the STARTUP.NCF file.

SET Console Display Watchdog Logouts

Syntax	SET Console Display Watchdog Logouts = On¦Off
Example	SET Console Display Watchdog Logouts = On
Values	On or Off
Default	Off
Related commands	SET Maximum Packet Receive Buffers SET Maximum Physical Receive Packet Size SET Minimum Packet Receive Buffers SET New Packet Receive Buffer Wait Time

Description—This version of the SET command determines whether the console displays a message when the server loses contact with a workstation and clears the connection. Losing contact can indicate a problem or a user turning off a workstation without logging out first.

SET Directory Cache Allocation Wait Time

Syntax	SET Directory Cache Allocation Wait Time = *number*
Example	SET Directory Cache Allocation Wait Time = 2 seconds
Range	.5 seconds–2 minutes
Default	1.1 seconds
Related commands	SET Directory Cache Buffer Nonreferenced Delay SET Dirty Directory Cache Delay Time SET Maximum Concurrent Directory Cache Writes SET Maximum Directory Cache Buffers SET Minimum Directory Cache Buffers

Description—This setting determines how long the file server waits before allocating an additional directory cache buffer after allocating a directory cache buffer. Decreasing this value can cause too many buffers to be allocated during a peak load situation. Increasing this value can cause the file server to search directories slowly.

SET Directory Cache Buffer Nonreferenced Delay

Syntax	SET Directory Cache Buffer Nonreferenced Delay = *number*
Example	SET Directory Cache Buffer Nonreferenced Delay = 5.5 seconds
Range	1 second–5 minutes
Default	33 seconds
Related commands	SET Directory Cache Allocation Wait Time SET Dirty Directory Cache Delay Time SET Maximum Concurrent Directory Cache Writes SET Maximum Directory Cache Buffers SET Minimum Directory Cache Buffers

Description—This version of the SET command determines how much time a directory entry must remain in the cache when not being accessed. After an entry has been in the cache for this period and has not been accessed, the server can release this information and use the memory for another entry.

SET Dirty Directory Cache Delay Time

Syntax	SET Dirty Directory Cache Delay Time = *number*
Example	SET Dirty Directory Cache Delay Time = 2 seconds
Range	0–10 seconds
Default	.5 seconds
Related commands	SET Directory Cache Allocation Wait Time SET Directory Cache Buffer Nonreferenced Delay SET Maximum Concurrent Directory Cache Writes SET Maximum Directory Cache Buffers SET Minimum Directory Cache Buffers

Description—This parameter determines how long the file server keeps a directory write request in memory. Decreasing this value impedes file server performance, while increasing it can increase the potential for corrupted directory information in the event of a power failure, unless an uninterruptible power supply (UPS) is used on the file server.

SET Dirty Disk Cache Delay Time

Syntax	SET Dirty Disk Cache Delay Time = *number*
Example	SET Dirty Disk Cache Delay Time = 10
Range	.1–10 seconds
Default	3.3 seconds
Related commands	SET Minimum File Cache Buffers
	SET Minimum File Cache Buffer Report Threshold

Description—This setting controls how long the server waits before writing new data or data changed since it was read into the cache to the disk. Decreasing this value forces the server to write more often and can reduce overall performance. If your server runs on a UPS, you might be able to increase this value to reduce file I/O demands and take better advantage of NetWare's elevator seeking technology.

SET Enable Disk Read After Write Verify

Syntax	SET Enable Disk Read After Write Verify = On¦Off
Example	SET Enable Disk Read After Write Verify = On
Values	On or Off
Default	On

Description—This disk parameter controls the read-after-write verification aspect of Hot Fix Redirection (the last item in the bulleted list). NetWare redirects information to the hot fix area under any one of three conditions:

- Write requests. When the disk controller reports an error during a write operation, the system redirects the data to a different block and marks the original block bad.
- Read requests. When the disk controller reports an error during a read operation and the drive *is not mirrored*, the data is lost but the block is marked bad. If the drive *is mirrored*, the data is retrieved from the mirrored drive and is redirected on the primary drive. The block on the primary drive is marked bad.
- Read-after-write verification. After a write operation, the data on the disk is read and compared to the data in the cache buffer. If they do not match, the data is redirected to another block and the original block is marked bad.

SET File Delete Wait Time

Syntax	SET File Delete Wait Time = *number*
Example	SET File Delete Wait Time = 7 days
Range	0 seconds–7 days
Default	5 minutes 29.6 seconds
Related commands	SET Immediate Purge Of Deleted Files SET Maximum Subdirectory Tree Depth SET Minimum File Delete Wait Time SET Turbo FAT Re-use Wait Time SET Volume Low Warn All Users SET Volume Low Warning Reset Threshold SET Volume Low Warning Threshold

Description—This version of the SET command controls when a salvageable file can be purged from the server volume. When a volume is full, NetWare purges files beginning with the oldest first. It continues to purge files until it releases disk space equal to at least 1/32 of the volume size.

SET Immediate Purge of Deleted Files

Syntax	SET Immediate Purge of Deleted Files = On¦Off
Example	SET Immediate Purge of Deleted Files = Off
Values	On or Off

Default	Off
Related commands	SET File Delete Wait Time
	SET Maximum Subdirectory Tree Depth
	SET Minimum File Delete Wait Time
	SET Turbo FAT Re-use Wait Time
	SET Volume Low Warn All Users
	SET Volume Low Warning Reset Threshold
	SET Volume Low Warning Threshold

Description—When set to On, NetWare immediately purges deleted files from the server volume. As a result, the SALVAGE command is ineffective. When set to Off, you can use the SALVAGE command to recover deleted files.

SET Maximum Alloc Short Term Memory

Syntax	SET Maximum Alloc Short Term Memory = *number*
Example	SET Maximum Alloc Short Term Memory = 3145725
Range	50000–16777216
Default	2097152 (recommended by Novell for 250 users)
Related commands	SET Auto Register Memory Above 16 Megabytes
	SET Cache Buffer Size

Description—This version of the SET command allocates memory to the short term memory pool. This pool is used for many processes in a NetWare 386 server:

- Drive mappings—all MAP commands active for all users are stored on the server.
- NetWare Loadable Modules (NLMs)
- Service requests
- Open and locked file handles
- Queue Operator tables
- User connection information
- Messages waiting to be sent or broadcast
- Server advertising

SET Maximum Concurrent Directory Cache Writes

Syntax	`SET Maximum Concurrent Directory Cache Writes = number`
Example	`SET Maximum Concurrent Directory Cache Writes = 25`
Range	5–50
Default	10
Related commands	SET Directory Cache Allocation Wait Time SET Directory Cache Buffer Nonreferenced Delay SET Dirty Directory Cache Delay Time SET Maximum Directory Cache Buffers SET Minimum Directory Cache Buffers

Description—This version of the SET command determines the number of directory cache entries that can be written to the disk at one time. Increasing this number permits more simultaneous writes, but reduces the server's efficiency in servicing disk reads.

SET Maximum Concurrent Disk Cache Writes

Syntax	`SET Maximum Concurrent Disk Cache Writes = number`
Example	`SET Maximum Concurrent Disk Cache Writes = 50`
Range	10–100
Default	50
Related commands	SET Dirty Disk Cache Delay Time SET Minimum File Cache Buffers SET Minimum File Cache Buffer Report Threshold

Description—This sets the number of cache buffers that can be written to the disk simultaneously. Increasing this number permits more simultaneous writes, but reduces the server's efficiency in servicing disk reads. If the number of dirty cache buffers exceeds 70% of the total cache buffers, increasing this setting may improve the server's performance.

SET Maximum Directory Cache Buffers

Syntax	SET Maximum Directory Cache Buffers = *number*
Example	SET Maximum Directory Cache Buffers = 1000
Range	20–4000
Default	500
Related commands	SET Directory Cache Allocation Wait Time SET Directory Cache Buffer Nonreferenced Delay SET Dirty Directory Cache Delay Time SET Maximum Concurrent Directory Cache Writes SET Minimum Directory Cache Buffers

Description—This setting determines the maximum number of buffers used for directory caching. Reducing this number frees file server RAM for other duties. Increase this setting if directory searches seem sluggish.

SET Maximum File Locks

Syntax	SET Maximum File Locks = *number*
Example	SET Maximum File Locks = 10000
Range	100–100,000
Default	10,000
Related commands	SET Maximum File Locks Per Connection SET Maximum Record Locks SET Maximum Record Locks Per Connection

Description—This setting controls the number of open and/or locked files permitted on the server.

SET Maximum File Locks Per Connection

Syntax	SET Maximum File Locks Per Connection = *number*
Example	SET Maximum File Locks Per Connection = 250
Range	10–1000
Default	250

SET Maximum Physical Receive Packet Size

Related commands   SET Maximum File Locks
SET Maximum Record Locks
SET Maximum Record Locks Per Connection

Description—This entry determines how many open and/or locked files a connection can have at one time. Stations using multitasking operating systems such as OS/2 require more file locks than stations running DOS.

SET Maximum Outstanding NCP Searches

Syntax   SET Maximum Outstanding NCP Searches = *number*
Example   SET Maximum Outstanding NCP Searches = 51
Range   10–1000
Default   51

Description—This parameter controls how many Network Core Protocol (NCP) directory searches NetWare can perform simultaneously.

SET Maximum Packet Receive Buffers

Syntax   SET Maximum Packet Receive Buffers = *number*
Example   SET Maximum Packet Receive Buffers = 200
Range   50–2000
Default   100
Related commands   SET Console Display Watchdog Logouts
SET Maximum Physical Receive Packet Size
SET Minimum Packet Receive Buffers
SET New Packet Receive Buffer Wait Time

Description—This setting determines the maximum number of buffers the file server can establish for incoming data packets.

SET Maximum Physical Receive Packet Size

Syntax   SET Maximum Physical Receive Packet Size = *number*
Example   SET Maximum Physical Receive Packet Size = 1130

Range	618–4202
Default	1130
Related commands	SET Console Display Watchdog Logouts SET Maximum Packet Receive Buffers SET Minimum Packet Receive Buffers SET New Packet Receive Buffer Wait Time

Description—This setting controls how many bytes the data packets transmitted on the network can contain. The default size permits 1024 data bytes and 106 bytes of header. Here are some guidelines for choosing a setting:

If your network uses ARCnet, use 618.

If your network uses 1K packets, use the default.

If your network uses Ethernet, use 1518.

If your network uses Token Ring, use 4202.

You cannot change this parameter using the console SET command. You must place the SET Maximum Physical Packet Size = *number* command in the STARTUP.NCF file.

SET Maximum Record Locks

Syntax	SET Maximum Record Locks = *number*
Example	SET Maximum Record Locks = 20000
Range	100–200,000
Default	20,000
Related commands	SET Maximum File Locks SET Maximum File Locks Per Connection SET Maximum Record Locks Per Connection

Description—This setting controls the number of record locks permitted on the file server at one time.

SET Maximum Record Locks Per Connection

Syntax	SET Maximum Record Locks Per Connection = *number*
Example	SET Maximum Record Locks Per Connection = 500
Range	10–10,000

Default	500
Related commands	SET Maximum File Locks
	SET Maximum File Locks Per Connection
	SET Maximum Record Locks

Description—This sets the number of simultaneous record locks permitted by a connection.

SET Maximum Service Processes

Syntax	SET Maximum Service Processes = *number*
Example	SET Maximum Service Processes = 20
Range	5–40
Default	20

Description—This setting controls how many service processes the operating system can create. Increase the number if the file server frequently uses the maximum file service processes.

SET Maximum Subdirectory Tree Depth

Syntax	SET Maximum Subdirectory Tree Depth = *number*
Example	SET Maximum Subdirectory Tree Depth = 25
Range	10–100
Default	25
Related commands	SET File Delete Wait Time
	SET Immediate Purge of Deleted Files
	SET Minimum File Delete Wait Time
	SET Turbo FAT Re-use Wait Time
	SET Volume Low Warn All Users
	SET Volume Low Warning Reset Threshold
	SET Volume Low Warning Threshold

Description—This setting controls how many levels of subdirectory nesting the operating system permits.

SET Maximum Transactions

Syntax	SET Maximum Transactions = *number*
Example	SET Maximum Transactions = 10000

Range	100–10,000
Default	10,000
Related commands	SET Auto TTS Backout Flag
	SET TTS Abort Dump Flag
	SET TTS Backout File Truncation Wait Time
	SET TTS Unwritten Cache Wait Time

Description—This parameter sets the maximum number of transaction processes that can be logged simultaneously.

SET Minimum Directory Cache Buffers

Syntax	SET Minimum Directory Cache Buffers = *number*
Example	SET Minimum Directory Cache Buffers = 20
Range	10–2000
Default	20
Related commands	SET Directory Cache Allocation Wait Time
	SET Directory Cache Buffer Nonreferenced Delay
	SET Dirty Directory Cache Delay Time
	SET Maximum Concurrent Directory Cache Writes
	SET Maximum Directory Cache Buffers

Description—This parameter instructs the operating system on the minimum amount of RAM that *must* be set aside for the directory cache. The operating system cannot re-allocate this memory, even if it is not in use.

SET Minimum File Cache Buffers

Syntax	SET Minimum Cache Buffers = *number*
Example	SET Minimum Cache Buffers = 100
Range	20–1,000
Default	20
Related commands	SET Dirty Disk Cache Delay Time
	SET Maximum Concurrent Disk Cache Writes
	SET Minimum File Cache Buffer Report Threshold

Description—This sets the minimum number of cache buffers that the file server must allocate in RAM. After all other memory requirements are met, including the Minimum File Cache Buffers parameter, the server uses all remaining RAM for file cache buffers.

SET Minimum File Cache Buffer Report Threshold

Syntax	SET Minimum File Cache Buffer Report Threshold = *number*
Example	SET Minimum File Cache Buffer Report Threshold = 20
Range	0–1000
Default	20
Related commands	SET Dirty Disk Cache Delay Time SET Minimum File Cache Buffers SET Maximum Concurrent Report Threshold

Description—This parameter sets a value used to determine, in part, when the file server should issue a warning of too few cache buffers. The value of this setting is added to the value for the Minimum File Cache Buffers parameter. When the file server has allocated the RAM it needs for all other processes and the remaining RAM available for file caching is less than this sum, a warning message will be displayed on the file server console.

SET Minimum File Delete Wait Time

Syntax	SET Minimum File Delete Wait Time = *number*
Examples	SET Minimum File Delete Wait Time = 3 days SET Minimum File Delete Wait Time = 2 days 3 hours 12 minutes
Range	0 seconds–7 days
Default	1 minute 5.9 seconds
Related commands	SET File Delete Wait Time SET Immediate Purge of Deleted Files SET Maximum Subdirectory Tree Depth SET Turbo FAT Re-use Wait Time SET Volume Low Warn All Users

SET Volume Low Warning Reset Threshold
SET Volume Low Warning Threshold

Description—This setting determines how long a deleted file can remain on the server and be recovered with the SALVAGE command. Files on the server for less time will remain on the server, even if the volume becomes full.

SET Minimum Packet Receive Buffers

Syntax	SET Minimum Packet Receive Buffers = number
Example	SET Minimum Packet Receive Buffers = 25
Range	10–1000
Default	10
Related commands	SET Console Display Watchdog Logouts SET Maximum Packet Receive Buffers SET Maximum Physical Receive Packet Size SET New Packet Receive Buffer Wait Time

Description—This option controls how many communication buffers the operating system must allocate for incoming packets. This memory cannot be re-allocated even if the buffers are not in use.

SET New Packet Receive Buffer Wait Time

Syntax	SET New Packet Receive Buffer Wait Time = number
Example	SET New Packet Receive Buffer Wait Time = .1 second
Range	.1–20 seconds
Default	.1 second
Related commands	SET Console Display Watchdog Logouts SET Maximum Packet Receive Buffers SET Maximum Physical Receive Packet Size SET Minimum Packet Receive Buffers

Description—The setting for this parameter determines how long NetWare 386 waits after receiving a request for another packet receive buffer before granting the request.

SET New Service Process Wait Time

Syntax	SET New Service Process Wait Time = *number*
Example	SET New Service Process Wait Time = 2.2 seconds
Range	.3–20 seconds
Default	2.2 seconds
Related commands	None

Description—This entry controls how long the operating system waits after receiving a request for another service process before granting it.

SET Time

Syntax	SET Time [*mm/dd/yy*] [*hh:mm:ss*]
Examples	SET Time 03/11/91 13:13
	SET Time March 11, 1991 2:00 PM
	SET Time 11 March 1991 14:15
	SET Time 3:15 PM
	SET Time 3/11/91
Value	Any valid date or time
Related command	SECURE CONSOLE

Description—This command sets the time and date on the file server if the SECURE CONSOLE command has not been issued. You can set only the date or the time by omitting the other parameter.

SET TTS Abort Dump Flag

Syntax	SET TTS Abort Dump Flag = On¦Off
Example	SET TTS Abort Dump Flag = On
Value	Off or On
Default	Off
Related commands	SET Auto TTS Backout Flag
	SET Maximum Transactions
	SET TTS Backout File Truncation Wait Time
	SET TTS Unwritten Cache Wait Time

Description—This setting determines what happens in the event of a failure on the file server during a write to a file that is marked transactional.

If set to On, the information backed out is written to a file called TTS$LOG.ERR on the SYS volume. You can view this file with a text editor or print it.

If set to Off, the data backed out is not saved.

SET TTS Backout File Truncation Wait Time

Syntax	SET TTS Backout File Truncation Wait Time = *number*
Example	SET TTS Backout File Truncation Wait Time = 30 minutes
Range	1 minute 5.9 seconds–1 day 2 hours 21 minutes 51.3 seconds
Default	59 minutes 19.2 seconds
Related commands	SET Auto TTS Backout Flag SET Maximum Transactions SET TTS Abort Dump Flag SET TTS Unwritten Cache Wait Time

Description—This setting determines how long the operating system holds allocated blocks for the backout file when these blocks are not currently in use.

SET TTS Unwritten Cache Wait Time

Syntax	SET TTS Unwritten Cache Wait Time = *number*
Example	SET TTS Unwritten Cache Wait Time = 2 minutes
Range	11 seconds–10 minutes 59 seconds
Default	1 minute 59 seconds
Related commands	SET Auto TTS Backout Flag SET Maximum Transactions SET TTS Abort Dump Flag SET TTS Backout File Truncation Wait Time

Description—This entry determines how long an updated cache block can be held in RAM before it's written to the disk.

SET Turbo FAT Re-use Wait Time

Syntax	SET Turbo FAT Re-use Wait Time = *number*
Example	SET Turbo FAT Re-use Wait Time = 15 minutes
Range	.3 seconds–1 hour 5 minutes
Default	5 minutes 29.6 seconds
Related commands	SET File Delete Wait Time
	SET Immediate Purge of Deleted Files
	SET Maximum Subdirectory Tree Depth
	SET Minimum File Delete Wait Time
	SET Volume Low Warn All Users
	SET Volume Low Warning Reset Threshold
	SET Volume Low Warning Threshold

Description—This parameter determines how long a Turbo FAT buffer remains in RAM after the file corresponding to the Turbo FAT is closed.

SET Volume Low Warn All Users

Syntax	SET Volume Low Warn All Users = On¦Off
Example	SET Volume Low Warn All Users = On
Value	On or Off
Default	On
Related commands	SET File Delete Wait Time
	SET Immediate Purge of Deleted Files
	SET Maximum Subdirectory Tree Depth
	SET Minimum File Delete Wait Time
	SET Turbo FAT Re-use Wait Time
	SET Volume Low Warning Reset Threshold
	SET Volume Low Warning Threshold

Description—This setting determines whether NetWare warns users when the volume is nearly full.

SET Volume Low Warning Reset Threshold

Syntax	`SET Volume Low Warning Reset Threshold = number`
Example	`SET Volume Low Warning Reset Threshold = 1000`
Range	0–100,000
Default	256
Related commands	SET File Delete Wait Time SET Immediate Purge of Deleted Files SET Maximum Subdirectory Tree Depth SET Minimum File Delete Wait Time SET Turbo FAT Re-use Wait Time SET Volume Low Warn All Users SET Volume Low Warning Threshold

Description—This setting determines how much disk space must be free before NetWare resets the warning message. Values are expressed in disk blocks.

SET Volume Low Warning Threshold

Syntax	`SET Volume Low Warning Threshold = number`
Example	`SET Volume Low Warning Threshold = 1000`
Range	0–100,000
Default	256
Related commands	SET File Delete Wait Time SET Immediate Purge of Deleted Files SET Maximum Subdirectory Tree Depth SET Minimum File Delete Wait Time SET Turbo FAT Re-use Wait Time SET Volume Low Warn All Users SET Volume Low Warning Reset Threshold

Description—This entry determines when NetWare issues a Volume Low warning, if activated. Values represent the number of disk blocks. Block sizes in NetWare 386 can be 4096 (4K), 8192 (8K), 16384 (16K), 32768 (32K), or 65536 bytes (64K).

SPEED

Syntax	SPEED
Example	SPEED
Default	None
Related command	None

Description—Use this command to display the speed of your 80386 or 80486 CPU chip in the file server. The value 100 is based on a 16MHz 80386DX CPU.

SPOOL

Syntax	SPOOL number [TO] [queue] queue_name
Examples	SPOOL 0 To Queue MFG_Q
	SPOOL 1 MFG_0
Related command	None

Description—This command provides the compatibility necessary to support older versions of NetWare. NetWare versions prior to NetWare 286 version 2.1x used print "spools" to capture print jobs. Since NetWare 286 version 2.1x, NetWare has handled print jobs and print queues with the CAPTURE and NPRINT commands. This command redirects old NetWare print jobs that specify a spooler number to a NetWare 286 or 386 print queue.

TIME

Syntax	TIME
Example	TIME
Default	None
Related commands	SET Time, SECURE CONSOLE

Description—This command displays the current date and time on the file server.

TRACK

Syntax	TRACK On¦Off
Examples	TRACK ON
	TRACK OFF
Default	TRACK OFF

Description—With TRACK On, the file server displays information about packets received and transmitted on the LAN. It displays the network number, the node address, the time the packet was sent or received, the name of the sender, and the number of hops from the server to the sender or recipient.

UNBIND

Syntax	UNBIND *protocol* [FROM] *NIC_driver* [*parameters*]
Example	UNBIND IPX FROM NE-2000
Default	None
Related command	BIND

Description—This command removes a communication protocol from the NIC driver. Use it when there has been a mistake in the BIND command or to update the protocol bound to the NIC driver.

UNLOAD

Syntax	UNLOAD *module*
Examples	UNLOAD Monitor
	UNLOAD PSERVER PS_ATRIUM
Default	None
Related command	LOAD

Description—You can use this command to remove any NLM module from the file server's RAM. The file server can then allocate the free memory to other processes.

VERSION

Syntax	VERSION
Example	VERSION
Default	None
Related command	CONFIG

Description—Use this command to direct the file server to display the version of NetWare in use and the NetWare copyright notice.

VOLUMES

Syntax	VOLUMES
Example	VOLUMES
Default	None
Related commands	MOUNT, DISMOUNT

Description—You can use this command to display a list of the volumes mounted on the file server.

Glossary

A

Access method. A set of rules the LAN uses to govern network traffic. This determines the major classification of the LAN. Types of access methods are carrier sense multiple access collision detection or token passing.

Adapter card. A circuit card that plugs into one of the expansion slots in an IBM PC or PC-AT compatible computer. Adapter cards are used for most I/O functions of the PC, including the LAN interface.

Address. A set of numbers that identify something to the computer. The LAN adapters have node addresses. Devices inside the PC have I/O addresses.

Algorithm. A procedure for doing something, usually a complex calculation.

Alternate buffer. A memory area set aside to receive data when the primary buffer is full so that data transmission is not interrupted.

Amplifier. A device which boosts signal strength. Usually used in broadband networks to overcome loss in signal strength due to attenuation.

Amplitude. The distance between the low value and high value of a waveform or signal. Changes in the amplitude indicate data transmission.

Amplitude modulation. A method of changing the height of a wave to convey information. The wave height for a 0 bit is generally lower than the wave height for a 1 bit.

Analog signal. An electronic signal that varies continuously over a range of voltages or frequencies. Analog signals vary continuously as they are sent. Modems use analog signals. See also **Digital signal**.

ANSI. American National Standards Institute. An organization that helps set data processing and communications standards.

API. Application Programming Interface. Software that provides certain functions to application software and makes programming the application software easier. APIs help software to look and work in a consistent manner across various types of applications.

APPC. Advanced Peer-to-Peer Communications. A standard programming interface from IBM that allows applications running on different systems to communicate with one another. APPC builds programs whose various parts run on different machines simultaneously. APPC governs how these parts communicate with each other over a network.

AppleTalk. Apple Computer's LAN software for linking Macintosh computers over a network. It uses CSMA access protocols and transmits data at 230K bits per second. It supports up to 32 devices. See also **LocalTalk**.

Application. A program that performs work on the computer that is useful to the user. Application software differs from system software, which performs tasks for the application software.

Application layer. The seventh (and highest) layer of the Open Systems Interconnection (OSI) data communications model of the International Standards Organization. It supplies functions to applications or nodes allowing them to communicate with other applications or nodes. See also **OSI Model**.

ARCnet. Attached Resource Computer NETwork. One of the most popular local area networks, as well as one of the earliest. Developed by Datapoint, it transmits data at 2.5Mb per second and uses a token passing protocol, both coaxial and twisted-pair cable, and either the star or bus topology.

Glossary

ARPANET. Developed by Advanced Research Projects Agency, ARPANET was the first major packet-switched network in the U.S.

ASCII. American Standard Code for Information Interchange. A way of interpreting and encoding data into bits for binary storage. The ASCII standard uses 7 bits to represent a 128 character set ($2^7 = 128$). IBM uses 8 bits and therefore has a 256 character set ($2^8 = 256$).

Asynchronous communication. A method of sending data one bit at a time. To indicate the beginning and end of a character, start bits and stop bits are added to the character bits. This simple form of data communications does not require a clocking device at each end, like synchronous communications. However, more data bits have to be sent for each character than in synchronous communications.

Attenuation. A reduction in signal strength due to the distance the signal is traveling. Attenuation is measured in decibels.

Audit trail. A record of events that have taken place. In LANs it generally refers to tracking which users use which resources, programs, data files, etc.

B

Babbling. A LAN workstation is transmitting meaningless data into the network channel due to a defect. This condition can cause severe performance degradation.

Background task. A task that is being executed as a secondary task while some other task is being executed as the primary task. The background task usually receives fewer CPU cycles than the primary task. The primary task usually controls both the monitor and the keyboard.

Back-end. Usually refers to a database management application where several different user interfaces can communicate with a common database processor. The back-end is sometimes called an engine or server. It performs all storage and retrieval functions for the front-end.

Back up. Usually refers to making copies of hard disk information on another medium, such as diskettes or a magnetic tape cartridge.

Balun. A transformer that matches one impedance with another. In LANs these are generally used to interface between twisted-pair cabling and coaxial cabling so that the same signals can be transmitted over both.

Bandwidth. The difference between the lowest frequency and the highest frequency used for transmitting signals. The larger the bandwidth, the more data the channel can carry. Bandwidth is usually measured in hertz (cycles per second).

Baseband. Describes a LAN that uses its entire bandwidth to transmit data for the LAN. Therefore, it is a dedicated LAN.

Batch file. A text file that contains operating system commands and program commands. It is used for standard procedures that are used repetitiously.

Batch processing. A type of processing that once started runs without further operator intervention or input.

Baud. The measure of speed in transmitting over a communications device. It is the number of times that the amplitude of the channel can be changed per second. At low speeds, each change can represent a single bit and therefore the baud rate can be the same as the bits per second. At high speeds, more than one bit can be represented by a change in amplitude and then the baud rate is not the same as the bits per second.

Bell 103. The AT&T specification for asynchronous transmission at 300 baud.

Bell 201. The AT&T specification for asynchronous transmission at speeds up to 2400 baud.

Bell 212. The AT&T specification for asynchronous transmission at speeds up to 1200 baud.

Binary. A numbering system with only two values, 0 and 1. Computers store data in binary form. The storage unit for a binary value is a bit.

Bindery files. NetWare's security information is kept in special, hidden files in the SYS:SYSTEM directory. All of the user information, Trustee Assignments, group information, and print server information is stored in these files. NetWare 286 has two files: NET$BVAL.SYS and NET$BIND.SYS. NetWare 386 has three files: NET$OBJ:SYS, NET$PROP.SYS, and NET$VAL.SYS. Backup systems must be able to back up these files.

Bisync. **BI**nary **SYNC**hronous. A method of transmitting character data in a synchronous fashion developed by IBM in 1964.

Bit. **BI**nary digi**T**. The storage unit of a computer that contains a binary value. In RAM, 0–2vdc (volts direct current) equals 0, 3.5–5vdc equals 1. In data communications, a high amplitude signal equals 1 and a low amplitude signal equals 0.

Bit error rate. The number of incorrectly transmitted bits. Telephone lines have a bit error rate of 10^{-4} or one per ten thousand bits. LANs generally have a bit error rate of 10^{-9} or one per one billion.

Block. A group of data that is treated as an entity. In NetWare 286, a block is 4096 bytes. NetWare 386 uses 4096, 8192, 16384, 32768, or 65536 byte blocks. Instead of using the word cluster to refer to disk storage increments, NetWare uses the term block. Synchronous communications send data in blocks of 512 or 1024 bytes. XMODEM asynchronous file transfers use a 128-character block.

Blocking Rights. NetWare directory Rights cascade to downline directories. Blocking Rights are created by making a Trustee Assignment of no Rights in a downline directory. Assigning no Rights blocks the cascading Rights from applying to downline directories.

BNC. **B**ayonet-**N**eil-**C**oncelman. This type of connector uses a quick release type of mechanism rather than a threaded sleeve. This type of connector is widely used with coaxial cable in a LAN.

Boot. The process of loading the operating system into the computer's memory so that the computer can function. A specialized ROM (read-only memory) chip causes the PC to load the operating system (PC-DOS or MS-DOS) into RAM, thus booting the computer.

Boot disk. A diskette which contains the operating system that the PC uses to boot from. In LAN environments, this diskette also contains the programs needed by the PC to connect with the network.

Bps. **B**its **p**er **s**econd. A measure of the speed at which data is or can be transmitted.

Breakout box. A device connected to two computer devices, such as a PC and a printer, which allows signal lines to be monitored and changed. Signals coming in on one wire can be sent out on another. It is very useful when the interface on one side is not standard and therefore a normal cable won't work.

Bridge. A device that allows LANs to be interconnected with other LANs, host computers, or remote PCs. The bridge converts one device's access method to the other's. Bridges do not perform any protocol conversion. The devices must use the same protocol. See also **Gateway** and **Routing**.

Broadband. Describes a LAN that can transmit several different types of data on one physical set of cables by giving each signal type its own unique frequency and bandwidth, called a channel. This is also called frequency division multiplexing (FDM). Devices designed to use the same channel can talk to each other. Therefore, a broadband network can have several networks on it.

Broadcast message. A message sent from one station to all other stations on the network.

Broadcast packet. A packet that has a destination address that contains hex character F in the entire field. All LAN protocols use this to denote that this packet is addressed (broadcast) to all workstations. All workstations process the packet and respond accordingly.

Buffer. A memory area used to send or receive data. Buffers are generally used to compensate for varying transmission speeds. For example, most disk drives and their controllers can transfer data at a speed of 500K to 1.5Mb per second, but a serial printer can only receive 9600 data bits per second. With a print buffer, the computer does not have to slow down to compensate for the slow printer. In LANs, buffers are often places to store data while waiting for the channel to become free to transmit.

Bus. The interconnection device used to connect all devices within the PC. It contains physical wires for transmitting data, interrupt signals, and direct memory access signals, as well as other internal timing and identification signals. It is usually measured by two components, the number of data bits that can be transmitted simultaneously (8, 16, or 32) and the speed at which they are transmitted in megahertz (MHz).

Bus topology. A LAN in which all computers are connected to a single cable called a backbone. Data is transmitted in both directions simultaneously. All stations "hear" all data transmitted and respond only to data addressed to them or a broadcast message. A terminating device located at each end of the backbone keeps the signal from bouncing back. Only one message can be sent at a time.

Byte. Eight bits. Usually eight bits represent one character; therefore, a byte can be a character. Storage capacities are measured in bytes.

C

Cable loss. The amount of signal (amplitude) lost (attenuated) while it travels on a network.

Cabling. The medium that connects devices on a network.

Cache. Memory set aside in RAM for holding data that has been retrieved in anticipation of user needs. Data could be held because the user has used it earlier or because of an algorithm that predicts future needs based upon past use.

Cafeteria plan. A series of options that can be selected on an individual basis rather than as a whole.

Carrier. A continuous single-frequency signal transmitted on the channel that indicates an idle channel.

Carrier detection. Listening to the channel to determine if a carrier signal is present. Also called carrier sensing or carrier sense.

Carrier sense. See **Carrier detection**.

CATV. Community Antenna TeleVision. A method of delivering television by taking signals from a central antenna and delivering it to homes via a coaxial cable network. These same components can be used for a broadband LAN.

CCITT. Comite Consulatif International de Telegraphie et Telephonie. An international consulting committee headquartered in Geneva, Switzerland, that sets international communication standards.

Channel. A physical or logical path for transmitting data.

Channel bank. A device used by a broadband network to divide the bandwidth into separate channels and to control those channels.

Character-based interface. A visual interface for the video portion of a computer system that relies on a preset character set for displaying information.

Character set. The numbers, letters, and symbols that a computer can use.

Chat. Messages sent between users on a LAN using software that permits peer-to-peer communications.

Circuit. A communications or data path between two points.

Circuit switching. A type of network in which the communications path is a physical circuit. The circuit exists as long as the two devices are communicating. Each time a device talks to another device, the path or circuit may be different. Telephone systems use circuit switching.

Client/server model. A software model that distributes the processing load between a front-end processor (FEP) and a back-end processor (BEP). It is most commonly used for database applications, where the FEP runs on the user's PC and the BEP runs on a central server. The FEP provides the user interface and various functions, but the BEP handles data storage and retrieval, including sorts, indexes, and queries.

Client-server protocols. These protocols establish how workstation software will interact with software running on a server. Client-server applications require software modules that run at the workstation and the server that work together to provide an integrated application. The workstation and the server each perform a portion of the overall task.

Closed architecture. Describes the design of a computer system and its operating system whose vendor has limited the ability of other vendor's products to interface with it. The limits are imposed by using proprietary designs and by not disclosing technical information.

Coaxial cable. A type of cable used in LANs that has a solid conductor sheathed in an insulator. A solid or woven metal conductor called a shield surrounds the insulator. Finally, an insulating material covers the shield. Coaxial cable has a wide bandwidth and can carry up to 500Mb per second.

Collision. Occurs when two or more data packets collide on a LAN, ruining the data packets. The collision is caused by two or more stations sending data at the same time.

Collision avoidance. The process by which a station attempts to avoid collisions on a network. Avoidance techniques vary from protocol to protocol. In carrier sense multiple access LANs, this is done by listening to the channel to make sure it is idle before transmitting. If the channel is busy, the station waits for it to be free before transmitting. In token passing LANs, the station must wait for a free token before transmitting.

Collision detection. The process by which a station determines that a collision has occurred on the network. Generally, the receiving station acknowledges every data packet sent. When the sending station does not receive an acknowledgement within a few milliseconds, it assumes that there has been a collision.

Communication buffers. An area of the NetWare 286 file server's RAM where the file server receives incoming packets and where the file server builds outgoing packets. These are also called routing buffers by Novell.

Communications server. A type of LAN gateway that translates the packets of a LAN to the asynchronous signals a minicomputer or mainframe requires. It can also handle various protocol types and allow LAN workstations to share host connections or modems. This is generally a PC with specialized hardware or software for performing protocol conversions.

Compilation. The translation of a program written in a high-level language into a machine-readable binary file (object code).

Compression. A technique used to represent information with fewer bits, thereby saving disk space and communication time.

Concurrency. Multiple users accessing the same information at the same time.

Concurrency control. Programming methods that allow multiple users to access the same data simultaneously without data corruption or disruption to the other users. Record locking and file locking are common concurrency control techniques.

CONFIG.SYS. A file that contains commands that configure the DOS environment and/or load device drivers. It is found in the root directory of the disk drive where the PC is booted.

Connect time. The time that a station is logged into the network.

Connectionless packets. NetWare uses a suite of protocols known as IPX/SPX. IPX protocols (Internetwork Packet Exchange) do not require a response from the recipient. SPX packets do require a response and therefore establish a virtual connection with the recipient. As a result, IPX packets are sometimes referred to as connectionless packets.

Contention. A LAN access method in which each station tries to transmit whenever it needs to. If the channel is already busy, the station has to wait and then try again. If multiple stations try to transmit at the same time and the channel is busy, they all wait and then try again. There is no way of knowing which station will transmit next.

Control character. A character used to modify or initiate a function. Control characters cause data to be interpreted in a specific way for the network. Control characters are the first 32 ASCII codes (0–31).

Controller. A device that controls the flow of data between two devices. In LANs, controllers are usually I/O devices that control communications between the LAN and a host computer. Controllers can also control the communications between a host computer and the terminals attached to the host.

Co-processor. A device that assumes some of the processing load from the CPU. Usually in PCs it is a special IC chip that performs intensive calculations, a math co-processor. In the Intel CPU series, co-processors generally have the same numeric model number as their compatible CPU, except that the last digit is a 7, i.e., 8087, 80287, and 80387. A communications co-processor can perform formatting and protocol conversion functions in a network.

CPU. Central Processing Unit. The part of the computer that actually manipulates data. In PCs the CPU consists of a large-scale integrated circuit chip called a microprocessor.

CRC. See **Cyclic redundancy check**.

Crosstalk. Interference on a communication channel caused when a signal's bandwidth and frequency overlap. Crosstalk can occur on broadband networks.

CSMA/CD. Carrier Sense Multiple Access Collision Detection. This LAN access protocol controls communications on networks. In the LAN, all PCs have continuous access to the channel. When one wishes to transmit data, it "listens" to the channel to see if it is busy. If the channel is not busy, the PC transmits. If it is busy, the PC waits. The receiving computer acknowledges all transmissions. If the sender does not receive an acknowledgement within a preset period of time, the sender assumes that a collision has occurred because the channel is being used by another PC and retransmits the data after waiting for a period of time. The amount of time the PC waits is randomly established each time there is a collision.

Cyclic redundancy check. A method of processing a data block through an algorithm and generating a result called a checksum. The checksum is then transmitted with the data. The receiving system processes the data through the same algorithm and generates its own checksum. It then compares the two checksums to see if they agree. If they do, the data received is the same as the data sent. If they differ, the receiving system requests that the sender transmit the data again. CRC is 99.997% accurate in catching data errors.

D

Database. An organized collection of data. Computerized databases organize data into sets of related fields called records or tables. A database can be a single table or a group of related tables.

Database server. A computerized database system for a network in which the workstation does some of the processing and a host system does some of the processing. This technique distributes the processing load and eliminates parsing the entire database through the workstation when all records need to be evaluated. This greatly reduces the communication load on the network. If a database has no server, the entire database must be parsed through the workstation for operations that require all records. Typical operations that require all records are sorting, indexing, and selecting records according to a criterion.

Data integrity. A measurement of how reliably the computer system stores, maintains, and transmits data. Hardware failures can cause loss of data integrity. Multiple users accessing a data file without any method for locking the file or records within the file can cause a loss of data integrity.

Data link. A communications connection between two computing devices.

Glossary

Data link layer. The second layer in the Open Systems Interconnection (OSI) architectural model for data communications established by the International Standards Organization (ISO). This layer coordinates the flow of data and the structure of data messages.

Data PBX. A device that establishes and disconnects connections between computers and peripheral devices as needed.

DBMS. DataBase Management System. A set of programs that allows the creation, maintenance, and manipulation of databases on a computer system.

DCE. Data Communications Equipment. In modem communications, a signal line the computer uses to talk to the data terminal equipment (DTE). It establishes the connection between the DCE and the DTE devices.

DECnet. Digital Equipment Corporation's proprietary LAN operating system, which uses Ethernet protocols and derives from Microsoft's PC-Net OEM LAN operating system.

Demodulation. The process of converting an analog data signal to a digital data signal.

Destination address. The part of a data communication message that indicates the recipient of the data message. In a LAN the destination address consists of the network ID and the station ID.

Device dependence. DOS is a device dependent operating system, meaning that it relies on each device knowing how to interact with the applications. Due to device dependence, applications that need to use special features of a device must have software that interfaces with the device rather than the operating system, making the applications device dependent.

Device driver. A program that extends DOS capabilities. Drivers are loaded through appropriate instructions in the CONFIG.SYS file during booting. These programs stay resident in the PC's memory while the machine is on, just like DOS.

Device independence. OS/2 is a device independent operating system. The operating system has software drivers that instruct it how to work with various hardware devices. The application software uses standard function calls to work with the operating system regardless of the hardware configuration, making the software device independent.

Digital signal. A method of transmitting data using only two discreet values to represent data bits as On or Off. Inside a PC, voltages represent these values.

DIP switch. Dual In-line Package switch. A switch with only two positions, On and Off. DIP switches are used on circuit boards to configure various options. On LAN adapter cards, they often set the IRQ signal line, the DMA channel, the I/O address, and the node address.

Directory caching. A performance-enhancing technique in which a disk's directory information is loaded into RAM so the system will be able to locate files in the directory much faster.

Directory hashing. This is a performance-enhancing technique in which NetWare builds a special table in the file server's RAM used to locate files in the directory quickly, without having to read the entire directory until the file is located.

Disk. A digital medium for storing data. Disks come in various sizes and capacities. Most use magnetic fields to store the data. Optical disks store data using a laser to change the surface structure of the disk itself. Another laser can read these changes in the surface of the disk.

Diskless workstation. A PC which has no disk drives and is connected to the LAN. These are used in security-sensitive environments to prevent data from being copied. They are also popular in environments where there are a lot of air-borne contaminants such as dust, or where there is a great deal of vibration that would harm disk drives. A special ROM chip on the LAN adapter card allows the workstation to load DOS directly from the network file server.

Distributed data processing. A method of sharing the processing load on multiple computers with each one performing different functions. A communications channel connects the computers.

Glossary

Distributed database. A database stored on separate computers that users can access as if it resided on a single computer. The distributed nature of the data is transparent to the user.

DMA. Direct Memory Access. A PC uses DMA channels to transfer data to or from memory and various peripheral devices without constant CPU monitoring. This frees the CPU to perform other tasks during the memory transfer. When the process is complete, the peripheral device notifies the CPU via a DMA channel.

Domain. NetWare uses this term to describe users and groups managed by a User Group Manager or a Workgroup Manager. Other network operating systems, such as Banyan's VINES, use this term to describe all of the network resources a user is entitled to.

DOS/ODI workstation shells. These are workstation software modules that NetWare 386 users may use to connect their workstation to the LAN. These new modules have the potential of supporting multiple protocols simultaneously, such as IPX and TCP/IP, with one set of programs. ODI stands for Open Datalink Interface.

DOS workstation shells. These are the workstation software modules that NetWare has used in NetWare 286 and 386 to connect a workstation to the LAN. These programs only support NetWare's IPX/SPX protocols and IBM's NETBIOS protocols.

Driver. A special program that interfaces a hardware device with a software program.

Drop cable. A cable that connects a PC to the network's main cable, a trunk or backbone cable in a bus or tree topology LAN. Drop cables usually use either twisted-pair or coaxial media.

DTE. Data Terminal Equipment. To establish a link in data communications, a data terminal equipment signal must connect with a data communications equipment signal.

Dumb terminal. A terminal device that cannot do its own processing. The host to which it is connected must perform processing for the device. Dumb terminals may have internal memory to buffer I/O to and from the host system.

Duplex. A characteristic of data communications that determines which side of a communication link can be active at a given moment. Half duplex allows only one side to be active at a time. Full duplex allows both sides to be active simultaneously.

Dynamic memory. Memory whose contents can be updated by software. The contents of dynamic memory are lost when power is interrupted or turned off.

Dynamic routing. A process for routing data through a network that allows the data to be routed through a different path if the chosen path is busy. The network picks the best path automatically and then alters it as the need arises.

E

Echo. The transmission of a data signal back to the sender in modem communications. In a LAN, echo refers to a situation in which an improperly configured tree or bus trunk cable "bounces" a data packet back along the channel rather than absorbing it or removing it from the channel. This reflected data frame interferes with other packets on the network.

Effective Rights. The rights that a NetWare user has in a directory. Effective Rights are a combination of the user's Trustee Assignments, the Maximum Rights Mask, and any group membership Rights.

EIA. Electronics Industry Association. An organization that helps establish standards in the electronics industry.

EISA. Enhanced Industry Standard Architecture. A new architecture for PCs that allows them to use the larger data paths and capabilities of newer circuitry while maintaining compatibility with the architecture of the IBM PC/PC-AT bus.

Electronic mail. A system for electronically creating, transmitting, storing, and retrieving messages.

Elevator seeking. This NetWare term describes how the disk read/write heads move in relation to the disk drive on a NetWare file server. Rather than randomly moving back and forth based upon first-in, first-out disk access requests, NetWare sorts disk read and write requests into track order so that the movement of the read/write mechanism is in one direction until it reaches the innermost or outermost track.

ELS. Entry Level System. Novell uses this name for less expensive versions of NetWare, which are restricted in the number of users that can be logged into the file server. ELS Level I supports four users, and ELS Level II supports eight users logged into the file server.

Emulation. One device imitating another device. This is used often when a host system expects to find a specific terminal type connected to it and the device on the other end is not that terminal type. The device has to emulate the terminal type that the host wants. Emulation also occurs in printers. Each manufacturer's printers may use a different set of control codes to initiate different modes; however, many printers can emulate (or use) the same control codes as another printer. For example, many different laser printers can emulate the Hewlett Packard LaserJet II.

EPROM. Abbreviation for Erasable Programmable Read-Only Memory. Read-only memory chips store programs. A programmable chip is one that someone other than the manufacturer can program with a special device. Erasable means that the programs stored on this chip can be erased using an ultraviolet light. EEPROM is an abbreviation for Electronic Erasable Programmable Read-Only Memory. These programs can be erased electronically.

Error Detection. A method for determining if a transmission error occurred during data communications. The oldest form of this is parity checking which checks each character individually. In block communications (LANs and mainframes), the most common type is CRC. See **Cyclic redundancy check**.

Escape codes. A series of characters that begin with the Escape character. These commonly control the various modes of a device, such as a printer or a monitor.

Ethernet. A set of network communications standards and protocols Xerox originally developed to allow for the networking of their minicomputers. Ethernets are a baseband, CSMA CD/CA

LAN that uses a bus or tree topology. The current transmission speeds are 10Mb per second.

Extended character set. An ASCII character set that uses all the 256 different characters that can be defined in an 8-bit word (2^8 = 256). The standard ASCII character set used only 128 (2^7) characters. Different manufacturers use different extended character sets for printers and monitors—this is a major source of incompatibility. The IBM Extended Character set is becoming a de facto standard, however.

Extended Graphics Array (XGA). This is a video graphics specification promoted by IBM initially in their PS/2 Model 90 series of computers. It supports 1024 X 768 resolution.

External modem. A modem that has its own housing and is connected to the computer via one of the computer's serial ports. External modems typically have status lights to indicate what activity is occurring and they may also require their own power source. Modems connect computing devices over the telephone system network.

F

Fault tolerance. Fault tolerance is techniques that help make a computer system or network less vulnerable to failures caused by the various system components. Techniques include disk mirroring, bad data block lockout, and redundant hardware such as CPUs, disk drives, cables, etc. Novell sells a fault tolerant version of NetWare known as SFT (System Fault Tolerant) NetWare.

FDDI. Fiber Distributed Data Interface. A new set of standards for using fiber optic cable in networks. It is specified for transmission speeds of 100M bits per second using a token passing communications protocol and ring topology. It is compatible with the physical layer of the OSI model.

Fiber optic cable. A type of cable that uses either a glass or plastic fiber as the communication medium and light as the carrier instead of electricity. Light emitting diodes (LEDs) or lasers modulate the light source. The light travels through the fiber. Fiber optic cable has advantages over traditional copper wire in that its

Glossary

diameter is smaller, its data capacity (bandwidth) is larger, and it is not susceptible to electrical interference or inductance. As of this printing, it costs about the same as high grade coaxial cable.

File. A set of data stored on the computer system as a single entity. Each file has a file name that identifies it to the user and to the application software. File names vary from operating system to operating system.

File attribute. Determines the type of access that is permitted to a file, and is used to determine if a file has been changed or added to the disk since the last backup was performed. File attributes can also be used by software to invoke special features of the software in NetWare's Indexed and Transactional attribute settings.

File caching. Refers to the performance-enhancement technique of prereading data into RAM prior to receiving a request for the data. NetWare uses a predictive algorithm to decide what data to cache based on the user's past file activity. NetWare's cache usually has a "hit" rate exceeding 90%.

File locking. A technique a computer system uses to help ensure data integrity. When a user locks a file, other users cannot update the file until it is unlocked. This prevents two users from attempting to add records simultaneously.

File server. A computer that shares its disk resources (files) with the users of the LAN. A workstation connected to the LAN can open files on the file server. The file server performs the administrative tasks associated with multiple users sharing the same disk drive, but usually does not process any user applications. See also **Database server** and **Communications server**.

Firmware. Programs stored on ROM, PROM, or EPROM chips in the computer. These programs provide low-level interface between the operating system and the hardware devices. Firmware is also called microcode. The BIOS chip is the common firmware of a PC.

Flag. Bytes used in LAN data communications to indicate the beginning and end of a data packet or frame. In NetWare, the FLAG utility program alters a file's attributes, such as read-write, read-only, shareable, etc.

Floppy disk. A removable storage medium that uses a flexible mylar disk enclosed in flexible or semi-rigid housing. Floppy disks come in three primary sizes—8", 5¼", and 3½". There is also a new 2" floppy disk. The storage capacity of a floppy disk ranges from 160K to 5Mb. The amount of data a disk can store depends on the diskette drive and the operating system being used.

Flow control. A process of controlling the data stream being sent to a workstation when the workstation cannot store the data as fast as it can be sent. Data buffers are one element to control flow.

Frame. A data packet that is transmitted over a LAN. The frame contains protocol information as well as the data itself. Frames are also called packets. The size and format of the frame depends on the protocol being used.

Frequency. The number of cycles per increment of time, usually measured in millions per second. In CPU chips it is measured in megahertz (MHz) or millions of cycles per second. In RAM chips it is measured in nanoseconds (ns) or billionths of a second. In LANs data rates are measured in bits per second.

Frequency division multiplexing (FDM). A technique that permits multiple signals on a common medium by assigning each signal type its own frequency bandwidth. This technique is used on broadband networks, as well as on most recent telephone PBX systems.

Frequency modulation. Modulation is the process of conveying information by changing the signal on a communication medium. In analog communications, data is transmitted by changing either the frequency, phase, or the amplitude of the signal. The frequency is essentially the length of the analog sine wave. Data is transmitted by changing the length of the sine wave (frequency). Low speed modems use this technique.

Glossary

Frequency shift keying. A method of sending data on a communication medium using analog signals. This process changes data values by modulating the signal from a mean frequency.

Full duplex. Two-way simultaneous communications.

G

Gain. Increased signal power due to amplification.

Gateway. A hardware/software combination that permits computer systems to use different protocols to communicate with one another. For example, multiple users on a PC network can attach to an IBM mainframe through a common SNA gateway. Gateways usually require a PC dedicated to this purpose because of the processing that must take place for protocol conversion. Different gateway products offer different characteristics.

Graphical user interface (GUI). A user interface which uses bit-mapped or vector-graphic images on the screen rather than character-based images. GUIs require more processing overhead than character-based interfaces. As screen resolution increases, more bytes are needed to present the information on the screen.

Guard band. Unused frequency bandwidth between two communications channels on a broadband network. This area helps to reduce problems with crosstalk.

H

Half duplex. Two-way communications between two points where communications can only travel in one direction at a time.

Handshake. An initial protocol used to establish communications and conditions or parameters of the communications. For example, in a LAN, when an Ethernet workstation first connects to the server, they handshake to establish the size of the data packets that will be used.

Hardware. The physical components of a computer system.

HDLC. High-level Data Link Control. An ISO-established protocol for international communications across a wide area network (WAN).

Header. The preamble portion of a packet that contains the necessary routing information for the packet. This area contains the source and destination addresses, as well as other protocol information.

Hertz (Hz). A cycle of one per second. 16 megahertz is 16 million cycles per second.

Hex or hexadecimal. A numbering system based on 16 rather than 10 (decimal) that is more efficient for working with binary information. ASCII characters 0 through 9 and A through F represent 0–16.

Hit. Describes a condition in a NetWare file server where data resides in the cache that is the same as the data requested by the workstation or is the same as the data being written by the workstation. In either event, NetWare will not have to perform any disk I/O to service the request.

Home directory. Refers to a user's personal directory on the file server, in which he or she is permitted to store files. The term can also refer to a directory where software was installed.

Host. A central computer that performs processing for devices attached to it. Mainframes and minicomputers are considered hosts to the terminals connected to them. File servers in a network are sometimes erroneously called hosts.

Hot fix area. Also known as the Hot Fix Redirection Table. This is an area of a disk installed on a NetWare file server that the file server will use to keep track of bad blocks that have developed since the disk was formatted.

Hub. The common connection point for a group of PCs in a LAN. Star and ring topology LANs use hubs to interconnect the PCs. The hubs in a token ring are called Multiple Access Units (MAUs). In some LANs, the file server acts as a hub. Novell's SNet uses this configuration.

Glossary

I

IBM LAN Server. IBM's LAN operating system based on the IBM/Microsoft OEM LAN Manager software. The LAN Manager is based on OS/2 as the underlying operating system for the PC that acts as the file server. The LAN Server runs as a session on OS/2.

IBM OS/2 Extended Edition. IBM's proprietary version of OS/2. The standard edition of OS/2 is an OEM product licensed to many manufacturers. Extended edition includes features not found in the standard edition, such as an SQL database manager, a communication protocol manager, and a graphical user interface (GUI) called Presentation Manager.

Idle signal. A signal on a communication channel indicating that the channel is not busy. For modems, the high frequency tone is used. The high frequency correlates to a one or On bit. The idle modem sends a continuous stream of one bits. The idle signal indicates that the connection is still valid, even though no data is being sent. Otherwise, a communications device might think that the connection has been terminated.

IEEE. Institute of Electrical and Electronic Engineers. This organization establishes and publishes communications standards in the U.S.

IEEE 802.2. A standard that describes the data link control layer of a LAN and how the data connection is made over the physical cable media.

IEEE 802.3. A standard that describes the physical layer of a LAN using CSMA/CD access methods on a bus or tree topology. Both Ethernet and AT&T Starlan use a subset of this standard.

IEEE 802.4. A standard that describes the physical layer of a LAN using token passing access methods on a bus topology. ARCnet *does not* use this standard, even though it is a token passing, bus topology LAN.

IEEE 802.5. A standard that describes the physical layer of a LAN using token passing access methods on a ring topology. IBM uses this standard with their token ring products.

Image program. A .COM program, in that it uses the same addresses when loaded as those that appear in the program when viewed on the disk.

Implicit rights. Rights that a NetWare user has inherited from some other source, such as group membership, downline directories, or security equivalence.

Incremental backup. A method of backing up only those files that are new or have been changed since the disk was last backed up.

Indexed files. In NetWare, indexed files refer to large data files (over 2Mb) where the file server will build a RAM index of the file's FAT entries. This feature must be installed in NetWare 286 but is automatic in NetWare 386.

Intelligent terminal. A data terminal with some limited processing capability, for example, text editing or programmable features. Intelligent terminals are not PCs, however.

Interactive. A type of program that uses or needs user input during processing. See also **Batch processing**.

Interface. The point where two or more computing entities meet. Interfaces can be hardware, for example, the expansion slots in a PC. As long as the modules are designed according to the specifications for the slot and the software supports the module, they should interface correctly. Interfaces can also be based on software. Software interfaces allow programs to use functions that are a part of the interface, even if the programmer does not know how the function is written. This simplifies and standardizes the way a program works.

Interface card. See **Adapter card** or **NIC**.

Internal bridges. Created by installing more than one NIC in the file server to interconnect separate physical LANs.

Internal modem. A modem installed inside the system unit of a PC. Modems connect computing devices over the telephone system network.

Glossary

Internetwork. A network made up of more than one subnetwork. These subnetworks may be running different network operating systems, different sets of protocols, and different wiring topologies.

Inter-operable. One device can be exchanged for another device without any modifications to the software. Many hardware devices are compatible but not inter-operable. Most NICs or the same type, such as Ethernet, are compatible but not inter-operable. Different NICs require different software drivers even though they use the same transmission protocols.

Interprocess communications (IPC). Communications that occur between application programs running on the same CPU or running on separate CPUs via a communication link. The communications that occur are integral to program functioning. On LANs important protocols for this feature are APPC, NETBIOS, and Named Pipes.

Interrupt. In a LAN a special packet that lets a workstation PC interrupt the file server to get some sort of service. The file server suspends whatever it is doing, services the PC's request, and then resumes its task.

Interrupt lines. Part of the PC's internal bus that allows peripheral devices to interact with the CPU on an as-needed basis.

Interrupt request signal (IRQ). A hardware feature that lets a peripheral device interrupt the CPU when the peripheral device needs the CPU's attention. In the IBM PC and PC-AT architecture machines, each interrupt has its own signal trace in the motherboard to the expansion slots. No two devices plugged into these slots may use the same interrupt channel. In IBM PS/2 Microchannel machines, multiple devices can use interrupts because the device ID is also a part of the interrupt signal.

Intruder detection. Used to lock a NetWare user's account when someone attempts to access it with an incorrect password.

I/O. Input/Output. Generally refers to the process of getting data (input) from a device or sending data (output) to a device. Some I/O devices are printer ports, video display adapters, modems, etc.

I/O address. The address in memory where a CPU transfers data to or receives data from an I/O device. No two devices can have the same I/O address within a PC.

IPX. Internetwork Packet EXchange—This is one of the protocols used by NetWare. IPX packets do not require a response from the recipient. Most packets transmitted on a LAN will result in a response from the recipient due to the nature of the request. Even though IPX packets do not require a response, most will cause the recipient to respond to the request.

ISO. International Standards Organization.

IVDT. Integrated Voice Data Terminal. A device combining both a telephone and a data terminal or PC in one piece of equipment. IVDTs are not widely used yet.

J

Jabber. A stream of incoherent bits on a communications channel. Defective communications devices, such as LAN adapter cards, can jabber. The communication channel slows down while error-handling protocols sort the good data from the gibberish.

Job. Any task on the computer.

Jumper. A small plastic block that makes a connection between two adjacent pins on a circuit board, such as an adapter card. Jumpers are often used to configure an adapter card's IRQ, DMA, or I/O address.

K

K or **kilobyte.** 1024 bytes. A standard measurement of the amount of memory installed in a computer. For example, 640K, the maximum amount of memory DOS uses, is actually 655,360 bytes or 640 times 1024.

Kbps. Kilobytes per second. A standard measurement of how fast data can be transmitted between two devices.

Glossary

L

LAN. Local Area Network. A network within a limited geographical range consisting of interconnected personal computers that can share resources.

LAN adapter card. The circuit card that controls the workstation's access to the network. The LAN adapter card frames outgoing data into the format the network requires. It also performs checksum (CRC) functions.

LAN administrator. The person responsible for the ongoing maintenance of the network. The LAN administrator adds and removes users and application software. The LAN administrator in a NetWare environment is called a supervisor.

LAN Manager. An OEM LAN operating system developed by IBM, Microsoft, and 3Com. Microsoft licenses it to other vendors who add their own features. OS/2 is its underlying operating system on the file server. However, workstations do not have to use OS/2. Also sometimes called LAN MAN for short.

LAN Server. See **IBM LAN Server**.

Layer. A part of the hierarchy of computing functions defined by a system's architecture.

Line turnaround. The delay time on a communications channel between when one block is sent and the next block is sent.

Local area network. See **LAN**.

LocalNet. Sytek's broadband network product.

LocalTalk. Apple Computer's trademarked name for their communications hardware. Most Macintoshes have built-in LocalTalk ports for networking and printer connections.

Locking. A function that blocks access to all or part of a data file, even though the file is normally accessible by multiple users. Locking helps to ensure data integrity when two users on the network attempt to change the same data simultaneously.

Logical locks. These work by assigning names to sections of data in the file which can be locked when the application accesses the data. Logical locks are not enforced by the operating system, but by the application software itself.

Logical name. A logical name is a name that is assigned to a physical device to make accessing the device easier.

Logical unit. In the IBM communications protocol, defines devices that are available to software interfaces. Logical unit is also the device name for devices attached to an SCSI controller in a PC.

LOGIN. The process of identifying oneself to a computer system so that one can access the computer's resources. This process provides security for the system. This is also the name of the program used for this purpose in Novell's NetWare. The LOGIN.EXE program is located in the NetWare \LOGIN directory.

Loopback. A diagnostic technique for a communications channel where a transmitted signal is returned to the sending device so that the received message can be compared to the message originally transmitted.

LSI. Large Scale Integrated circuit. A technology for putting tens of thousands of transistors on a single silicon chip.

LU 6.2. A protocol for logical units performing peer-to-peer communications in an IBM environment. It describes the access protocol used for APPC.

M

Mail slots. An application interface that is part of the LAN Manager software and facilitates the development of electronic mail applications for the LAN Manager environment.

Mainframe. A host computer system capable of supporting multitasking and multiple users, as well as interactive and batch processing. At one time mainframes were described as 32-bit computers, a definition that is obsolete. Many mainframes use closed architecture.

Glossary

MAP. Manufacturing Automation Protocol. A specification for a network that uses token-passing access methods on a bus topology LAN. Also a NetWare command that makes directories available as logical drives.

Mapping. The process of assigning a logical name to a physical device. The same physical device can have many different logical names, but within an application, or for a given user, the same logical name cannot be assigned to multiple devices. NetWare maps logical drive letters (logical names) to subdirectories on a server volume (physical device).

Master station. A station which controls access of the stations on a LAN. The master station on a token ring LAN determines which PC transmits next.

MAU. See **Multiple Access Unit**.

Maximum Rights Mask. NetWare Rights granted at the directory level. These Rights govern what a user can do in a directory, regardless of the user's Trustee Assignments.

Mbps. Megabits per second. Measures the transmission rates on a local area network in millions of bits per second.

Mean time between failure (MTBF). A measurement of the reliability of equipment. It is usually expressed as hours.

Media protocols. These protocols govern the type of physical connection made on the network.

Medium. The physical link used to transmit data. In a LAN, the medium refers to the type of cable being used to connect the stations in the network. Common mediums are twisted-pair copper wire, coaxial cable, and fiber optic cable.

Megabyte (M or Mb). 1,048,576 bytes (2^{20}). The basic size measurement for disk storage and data transmission rates.

Memory window. As used in Chapter 1, this term is used to describe a portion of the file server's RAM set aside to run end-user DOS programs on a nondedicated file server. NetWare assigns 640K of the file server's RAM to this area.

Microprocessor. A CPU contained on a single integrated circuit chip. Microprocessors have varying specifications for speed, word size, and bus size, as well as various capabilities for memory support and multitasking.

Microsecond. One millionth of a second.

Millisecond. One thousandth of a second.

Minicomputer. A host computer system capable of supporting multiple users, as well as interactive and batch processing. Originally, minicomputers were 16-bit word size machines whereas mainframes were 32 bit, but these definitions are obsolete. Today it's difficult to differentiate a mainframe from a minicomputer without using some arbitrary performance feature.

MIPS. **M**illions of **I**nstructions **P**er **S**econd. A measurement of processing speed. Large mainframes can transmit hundreds of MIPS, minicomputers can transmit dozens of MIPS, and current top-end PCs can transmit 2 to 12 MIPS.

Modem. A word derived from **Mo**dulator and **dem**odulator. A modem converts the digital computer signal to an analog (frequency) signal and vice-versa to provide a communication connection over telephone lines. Modem's transmission speeds vary from 300K to 64K bits per second.

Modes. NetWare uses this command to refer to the settings a printer can use. Printer modes are defined using the NetWare PRINTDEF program.

Modulation. A change in a signal on an analog communication channel indicating a change in a data value. Modulation can affect the signal's frequency, amplitude, or phase. For example, in low speed modems, bits are represented by varying the frequency of the signal only. In higher speed modems, bits can be represented by changes in both the phase and the frequency.

Motherboard. The main circuit card in the PC. It contains the CPU chip and the related support chips, some RAM, and the connectors for the expansion boards which can be plugged into the system.

Multicast. The technique of sending messages to a defined group of users on the network.

Multidrop. A communication bus that supports several devices off of the bus. The drop is a branch off of the bus.

Multiplexing. A technique for sending multiple signals simultaneously over a communications channel. Multiplexing can be done by varying the frequency and bandwidth to set up separate channels, as in a broadband network. This is called frequency division multiplexing (FDM). Multiplexing can also be done by sending each signal with a time interval in between. This is called time division multiplexing (TDM).

Multistation access unit. This is the name IBM and other vendors use to refer to their hubs used to connect PCs in a token ring LAN.

Multitasking. A system's ability to process more than one job at a time. Multitasking is an operating system feature that the hardware can facilitate. The CPU multitasks by dividing its processing cycles among the various jobs that are running. In a multitasking environment, the CPU must protect memory areas in use by one program from any other program.

Multi-user. The ability of a computer to support multiple users simultaneously in an interactive mode.

N

Named pipes. An OS/2 application interface that allows for interprocess communications across a network. This interface makes the development of distributed processing applications easier.

Nanosecond. One billionth of a second.

NETBEUI. The protocol program used by IBM's PC Network LAN software for accessing the network.

NetBIOS. The IBM API which many software applications use to control communications on the network. Many software packages are written for NetBIOS. Novell NetWare does not normally use NetBIOS; however, NetWare can emulate NetBIOS for applications written to use it.

NETBIOS emulation program. One of the components of the NetWare workstation shell files is a program called NETBIOS.EXE. This program allows applications that use the IBM NETBIOS protocols to run with NetWare's IPX/SPX protocols.

Net/One. The family of LAN products from Ungermann-Bass.

NetWare. The LAN operating systems from Novell Inc. There are several versions of NetWare.

NetWare Loadable Module (NLM). A program that is loaded and run on a NetWare 386 file server. NLMs are used to provide utility, communication, and disk services to the file server.

Network access control. Components on the LAN adapter card that control when the workstation can access the LAN.

Network architecture. The structure and protocols a network uses.

Network interface controller (NIC). See **LAN adapter card**.

Network layer. The third layer of the OSI model for data communications. This layer determines how data is routed through the network.

Network Operating System (NOS). A set of programs that control a local area network. The NOS controls multiple users who are accessing shared resources. Shared resources can include disk drives and their files, printers, and other output devices. PCs that share their resources on a network are called servers. The NOS controls these servers. The servers may be used as a workstation in some NOS. A portion of the NOS, referred to as the LAN shell, runs on the workstations attached to the network. The shell interfaces the PC to the LAN adapter card and it also interfaces DOS to the NOS. The workstation shell is sometimes called a re-director because it passes some functions or commands to DOS for processing and routes others to the NOS for processing on the file server.

Network shell programs. A set of programs that provides the interface between the user's workstation PC and the rest of the network. The set is made up of various individual components which perform different tasks in the process of a workstation communicating with the file server or other workstations in the network.

Network topology. The physical wiring scheme used to connect workstations on a LAN. Common topologies are bus, tree, star, and ring.

NIC. Network Interface Card. See **LAN adapter card**.

Nodes. The points at which workstations can be attached to the network or the attached workstations themselves.

Noise. Interference on an electrical circuit caused by faulty components, RF signals, or inductance. Data frames that collide with one another also cause noise on a LAN channel.

Non-volatile. A term used to describe a data storage device that retains data when power is turned off. Disks and tape are non-volatile media for data storage; RAM memory is volatile.

Null modem cable. A serial cable that has pins 2 and 3 transposed so that a computer can be connected on each end. The computers can communicate with each as if they were using modems.

O

Object code. Binary programs that a computer can directly execute. Compilers create object code from source code. See **Compilation**.

Operating system. The set of programs that provides the interface between the application programs and the computer hardware and performs the management tasks of controlling the hardware devices.

Organizational groups. Groups that share common data files. Most data files that are shared belong to groups already established by their roles or functions in the organization. The best way to handle the need for shared files in the network is to establish groups that correspond to these needs.

OS/2. An operating system for PCs developed by Microsoft and IBM to take advantage of the features of the 80286 CPU. Key elements are its ability to use 16Mb of RAM and programs of up to 1Gb, multitasking, and a graphical user interface. It can also run DOS programs.

OS/2 Extended Edition. IBM's proprietary extension to OS/2. Included in this version are a built-in SQL database manager and a communications manager for terminal emulation for connections to IBM mainframes.

OSI. Open Systems Interconnection. A logical structure for network operations that was standardized by ISO.

OSI Model. The Open Systems Interconnection design for network operations that arranges groups of protocols into seven layers. Each layer provides a specific function. This model is the standard for LAN product design. The layers are

- Data Transmission and Routing
    Physical
    Data Link
    Network
- Interface between Physical and Application
    Transport
- Application
    Session
    Presentation
    Application

Out-of-band signalling. A signal on an analog communications channel that uses a frequency just outside the data channel frequencies. Sometimes called sideband, it is used for controlling communications parameters.

P

Packet. Also called a frame. A stream of data of a particular length that contains addressing information, control information, and data. The packet is the transmission entity on a LAN. The packet contains protocol information, as well as the data itself. Its size and format depend on the protocol being used.

Glossary

Packet buffer. A memory area reserved to receive incoming data packets or to hold outgoing data packets before they are sent. This area is generally on the LAN adapter card itself, but can be an area in the PC's normal RAM.

Packet switching. A data transmission method that uses packets to transmit data messages or files over a network that has multiple paths to a given destination. The packet switch sends the data along the best available route. Not all packets for a given transmission must be sent along the same route. The receiving node re-assembles the packets into the message or file.

PAD. **P**acket **A**ssembler/**D**isassembler. An interface device for connecting non-X.25 devices to an X.25 network.

Parallel transmission. A data transmission method in which each bit of a byte uses a separate wire or trace. In each cycle, a complete set of bits can be sent. A parallel printer interface uses eight wires to transmit an entire byte.

Parity bit. The eighth bit. Originally ASCII asynchronous data communications only used the standard 128 characters defined by the ASCII character set. This character set only uses 7 bits ($2^7 = 128$). The eighth bit was used for parity.

Parity checking. An error detection scheme that uses the parity bit. This technique can be set to check for odd or even parity. If set to even, the sending device sets the parity bit to binary 1 if the number of binary 1 data bits is odd, resulting in an even number of 1 bits. The receiving device checks for an even number of 1 bits. If this is not the case, the device asks the sending device to transmit the byte again. Because this technique is only 50% effective in detecting errors, it is not used much today; however, all serial ports have to be set for odd, even, or no parity.

PCM. See **Pulse code modulation**.

PC-Net. IBM's initial LAN operating system based on Microsoft's MS-NET OEM LAN operating system. This DOS-based operating system permits any station to be a nondedicated file server.

Peer-to-peer. Communication between two devices of the same general type.

Phase modulation. A method of transmitting data on an analog channel by shifting the phase of the signal. If a signal is constant, the duration or interval of the sine wave is constant also. Phase shifting doesn't change the signal's duration (frequency); instead it starts another signal in a slightly different time interval, causing a dip in the sine wave. This technique encodes more data in a given bandwidth and is used for 1200 and 2400 baud modems.

Physical lock. Locks a range of bytes on the file and is used to permit multiple users access to the file, but protects given records during an update process. Physical locks are enforced by the operating system.

Pipe. A facility used so one program can talk to another. It sends data to a pipe.

Polling. The access method used by star topology LANs. The central hub polls each attached device to see if it has data to transmit. Some intelligent printer sharing devices use polling to determine who has access to the printer.

Port. An input/output interface of a computer system. PCs have serial and parallel ports.

Presentation layer. The sixth layer of the OSI model. It determines the format of data files and how information is presented on the user's monitor. Character sets and graphical user interfaces are determined at this layer.

Primary task. A task that receives priority processing from the CPU. The primary task usually controls the monitor and keyboard.

Print server. Print servers allow multiple users to share printers. Jobs sent to the printer are written to disk files and then sent to the printer as the printer becomes available. Most print servers have software to control the order in which the jobs are queued. Several third-party print servers are available for the Novell NetWare environment. They allow shared printers to be attached to local workstations rather than the file server.

Program. A set of instructions that a computer system executes to perform a task.

PROM. Programmable Read-Only Memory. See **Remote boot ROM**.

ProNet. A family of LAN products from Proteon Corporation.

Proprietary LAN. A LAN environment which can only use the devices from one manufacturer.

Protected mode. A mode of the 80286 and 80386 CPU chips. In the 80286 CPU, this mode allows 16Mb of addressable RAM. In the 80386, the CPU can address 4Gb of RAM. In this mode, the CPU chip supports multitasking by protecting data segments in use by one program from access by another program. Hence, the memory is protected, so this mode is called Protected mode. The other 80286 CPU mode is Real mode.

Protocol. A set of rules for controlling data communications. Protocols establish the data format, the control information needed, and the type of error correction and error detection performed, and also determine who controls the communication channel. Several protocols may be used at once.

Protocol converter. A device which translates one protocol to another.

Pulse code modulation (PCM). A method of converting an analog signal to a digital signal. Analog signals use constantly varying frequencies to transmit data while digital signals use discreet values for data bits. PCM converts analog signals to digital signals by sampling the analog signal as many as 8000 times per second, and then assigning each sample an 8-bit code according to the sample characteristics. These 8-bit codes are transmitted to the receiving end of the channel where the signal may be converted back to analog. Digital voice communications work this way.

Q

Queue. A place where things wait for their turn.

R

RAM. Random Access Memory. Memory where the computer can read or write data in any location as needed. In PCs, RAM consists of LSI chips capable of storing up to 4 million bits of information apiece. These chips are volatile; they lose their contents when power is turned off.

RAM resident software. A type of software that stays in RAM until the computer is booted again or turned off. Some RAM-resident software is called TSR. It can be activated at any time, but can be put to "sleep" when not needed, even though it is RAM resident. Other RAM-resident software, such as a LAN shell, stays active all the time the PC is on.

Read-Only Memory (ROM). A type of memory that permanently stores data or programs. This data cannot be changed by the user or the computer.

Real mode. The processing mode of the 808x series of CPU chips from Intel that is one of the available modes for the 80286 and 80386 CPU chips. A CPU running in this mode can only address 1Mb of memory. Its name derives from the fact that for each memory address there is a physical or real byte of memory at that address. This is not the case in a virtual memory CPU like the 80286 and 80386, which can run programs that exceed the physical memory size in Protected mode.

Record locking. One scheme employed in multi-user systems and LANs to ensure data integrity when multiple users access a shared data file simultaneously. A user who locks a particular record in a data file can update it or prevent someone else from changing it. Different users may have record locks on different records and may change those records.

Redirection. An operating system technique for receiving or sending data from a device other than the device the program expected. DOS uses the > character to redirect output that usually is displayed on the monitor to a printer or file. Likewise, DOS programs can receive input from a file rather than the keyboard using redirection. In a LAN environment, part of the workstation's

Glossary

LAN shell is a re-director. It interprets all DOS calls and decides whether DOS or the file server should process them. LANs also redirect output from a local printer to a shared printer on the network.

Re-director program. Intercepts all commands and function calls issued by the user or the application and then decides who should process the command. If the re-director decides that the command or function required a resource located within the workstation, it passes it to DOS. If the re-director decides that the command or function requires network resources, it passes it to IPX.COM, which bundles it into a packet to be sent to the file server.

Relay. An electromechanical device which uses an electromagnet to open or close a switch. IBM's initial multiple access units for its token ring LAN use relays to open or close the ring to the workstation.

Remote boot ROM or PROM. ROM stands for Read-Only Memory. PROM stands for Programmable Read-Only Memory. These devices allow the workstation to boot up from the file server rather than finding DOS on the workstation's own disk drives. PROMs are very popular in PCs that have only floppy drives, because they eliminate the need for a boot diskette. PROMs are required for the class of PCs known as diskless workstations. Diskless workstations have no drives and therefore cannot find DOS locally. When PROMs are used, the NIC must be configured for both their presence and the memory addresses used by the PROM.

Remote reset ROM. See **Remote boot ROM**.

Remote station. A workstation not located at the LAN site that can access the LAN over a modem.

Repeater. A device that amplifies signals from one source and repeats them to another source. LANs use repeaters to rectify loss in signal strength due to attenuation caused by the cable and enable the LAN to carry the signal farther.

Resource set. This term is used in the NetWare ELSGEN and NETGEN programs when generating the NetWare operating system. A resource set is an item comprised of more than one resource item. Several items may be combined into a set for convenience purposes. When you want to use all of these devices, the entire set can be selected with the menu option Select Resource Sets.

Rights. Rights govern the activities a user can perform in a directory. NetWare 286 Rights are Read, Write, Create, Delete, Open, Search, Modify, and Parental. NetWare 386 Rights are Access Control, Create, Erase, Modify, Supervisory, File Scan, Read, and Write.

Ring. A network topology in which the cable configuration completes an electronic circle. Data is sent around the loop from station to station in one direction with each station acting as a repeater. LAN rings usually look like a star topology, however, because the stations are connected to a hub. The hub device makes the connections a ring. IBM's hub device is called a multiple access unit (MAU).

Rollback. A technique for restoring data files to their original condition after an update cycle does not complete successfully. SFT NetWare has a feature used for this purpose called Transaction Tracking System (TTS).

Routing. The process of choosing the best route to send data through a network.

RS-232. An interface for connecting data terminal equipment (DTE) and data communications equipment (DCE). It defines both the mechanical and electrical interfaces.

S

SAA. Systems Application Architecture, a set of standards for application design developed by IBM that permits these applications to run on a wide range of IBM systems.

SCSI. Small Computer System Interface. This is a specification for a type of peripheral controller. Apple Corporation was one of the first to use the SCSI disk controllers.

Glossary

SDLC. Synchronous Data Link Control. A protocol developed by IBM as a part of their SNA suite of protocols and standards. This protocol controls access to a single data line channel and can be used in direct or switched lines in either full or half duplex mode.

Semaphore. A message that records the opening of a file or activity in a file. It controls access to the file by multiple users.

Sequencing. A process for dividing data into packets and assigning a sequence number to each packet so that the data can be reassembled after it has been transmitted over a communications channel.

Serial interface. A data channel which transmits data one bit at a time. Serial devices must be synchronized to send and receive at the same rates. In addition, serial devices must be set for the number of data bits (7 or 8), the number of stop bits (1 or 2), and whether parity is being used.

Server. A device that provides a service to the LAN, such as a file server, print server, or communication server. File servers are often called servers. A server can be software only or combine hardware and software.

Server/client model. An application design in which the file server performs some application processing and the workstation performs some processing. The processes running in the server and the workstation communicate with one another over the network. Database servers use this model.

SFT. System Fault Tolerant, a version of NetWare that has special features for error recovery.

Simplex. Single-direction data transmission.

Sine wave. A mathematic equation which produces a uniformly oscillating set of values. Sine waves are a natural phenomena which can be explained mathematically and reproduced through a variety of electronic means.

Slot. A connection number assigned by the file server to a workstation. When a packet is transmitted from a workstation to the file server, it includes the connection number or slot number.

SNA (Systems Network Architecture). A layered communications protocol IBM uses for networking their computers.

Socket. A buffer where packets can be received by the workstation from the LAN. Generally, a process that is occurring between the file server and a workstation requires a socket. The more processes, the more sockets required.

Source address. The part of a data message that indicates the message's origin.

Spool. Simultaneous Peripheral Operation On Line. A hardware component that controls a data buffer for some peripheral devices, such as a printer or tape drive. This permits data transmission to the device even when the device is busy.

SPX. Sequenced Packet EXchange. Part of the NetWare protocols, an SPX packet requires a response from the recipient. The sender and the recipient establish a virtual connection with each other. This type of communication requires more overhead than IPX communications.

SQL. Structured Query Language. A database query language IBM developed for use with their mainframe databases. SQL is implemented in many PC database software applications which allow for a more standard method of accessing data across both mainframe and PC platforms.

SRPI. Server/Requestor Programming Interface. A programming interface that allows mainframe computers to be accessed like a file server on the network.

Star topology. A wiring topology in which all devices are connected to a central hub.

StarLan. AT&T's LAN family of hardware and software products.

Start bit. The first 0 bit in asynchronous communications. In these communications, an idle channel has a carrier signal. The carrier is a continuous stream of 1 bits. The first 0 bit is the start bit, and it signals the modem that data is being transmitted.

Glossary

Station. A node on the network that can be used to process user applications.

Stop bit. In asynchronous communications, the last one or two bits of a character.

Synchronous communication. Data communication that uses constant intervals between data bits and characters. Each end synchronizes itself to standard signals using clock timing to regulate data, rather than using start and stop bits. This results in fewer bits being transmitted and therefore less time used than by asynchronous transmission.

System fault tolerant (SFT). This term is used to describe computer systems that have special realiability features designed to minimize the downtime due to hardware or software faults. Novell has a version of NetWare called SFT NetWare which has special features designed to minimize file server downtime as well as time lost restoring data files when a transaction has been interrupted. See also **Transaction tracking system**.

T

T-1 carrier. A digital transmission carrier AT&T developed to transmit data across a wide area network at 1.544 million bits per second. A single T-1 channel can carry twenty-four simultaneous voice communications encoded at 64,000 bits per second.

Tap. The link connecting a backbone cable and a drop cable to a computing device.

TCP/IP. Transmission Control Protocol/Internet Protocol. Developed by the Department of Defense, this protocol allows communications between dissimilar computers under widely varying conditions and networks.

Terminal. A device used to communicate with a host system that generally lacks its own computing capabilities.

Terminal server. A device used to connect terminals to a network so they can communicate with a host over the LAN cabling.

Thrashing. Takes place when a cache block is needed and all are in use by the operating system. This results in cache block requests waiting while the operating system tries to free up some cache blocks.

Throughput. The rate at which data can be processed or transmitted over a communication channel.

Time division multiplexing. A technique used with digital signals that permits multiple signals to be transmitted on a common channel by dividing each message into packets and transmitting these packets at sequential time intervals. The receiving device reassembles the message from the correct packets.

Timesharing. A method of processing several applications simultaneously by slicing the CPU's available time. Each application receives a certain amount of processing from the CPU according to the time slice allocated.

Time slice. This term means that the PC spends very small amounts of time doing each task, thereby appearing to be doing several things at once. The issue in time slicing is how the time is allocated between the various activities.

Token. A combination of bits used in LAN communications as a header for a packet. To transmit on a network, the workstation must receive an available token.

Token bus. A bus topology network that uses a token-passing access method.

Token passing. A LAN access method in which a workstation must acquire an available token before it can transmit data. Only one message can be attached to the token at a time. After a message has been successfully transmitted, the token passes to the next station. Each station gets an equal opportunity to transmit data.

Token ring. A LAN topology that uses the token-passing access method in which the token travels around the LAN in one direction in a ring. The ring is not necessarily a physical ring with cables running from one station to the next, but rather the ring can be created electrically by a hub device. (IBM's hub is called a MAU or multiple access unit.)

Topology. The physical connection scheme used to wire a LAN. Common topologies are bus, tree, star, and ring.

Transaction tracking. A data integrity feature of NetWare 386. It ensures that a group of updates are made successfully and completely, or they are backed out completely in the event of a power loss, workstation failure, cable failure, or process corruption. As these updates are being made to the respective data files, the server keeps a log file of the changes to use to reverse the changes if needed.

Transaction tracking system. This is a component of SFT NetWare 286 and NetWare 386 that allows NetWare to perform a transaction file rollback in the event of a transaction failing to process properly.

Transients. Short duration signals usually created by electrical interference.

Transmission media. The physical carrier used for transmitting data. Usually describes the type of wiring or cabling used to connect a LAN.

Transport layer. The fourth layer of the OSI model used for error checking and routing.

Transport protocols. Provide rules for moving data packets from one node on the network to another.

Tree topology. An interconnection scheme used to connect stations on a LAN in which there can be more than one backbone cable and the backbone cables are interconnected in a treelike fashion.

Trustee assignment. Rights explicitly granted to a user or group in NetWare.

TSR (Terminate Stay Resident). This term is used to describe a type of DOS program that loads into RAM but does not unload when the program is terminated, as most programs do. The program can be reawakened by a special keyboard sequence or program event.

TTS. See **Transaction tracking system**.

Twisted pair cable. A type of cable that consists of a pair of insulated wires twisted around each other. The twists help to eliminate electrical inductance and noise. The pair of wires are usually encased in a PVC jacket sleeve.

U

UNIX. An operating system for multi-user systems developed by AT&T.

V

Value Added Programs (VAPs). Novell provides this feature in NetWare 286 to allow the features of the basic operating system to be extended beyond what is provided in the basic system. Novell, as well as other companies, develops extensions to NetWare that can be added to the environment through loading the appropriate VAP in the server. Examples of this feature are the NetWare for Macintosh VAP and the Btrieve VAP from Novell.

VDC. Voltage Direct Current. Voltages are either alternating current (AC) or direct current (DC). Standard power outlets are AC. Integrated circuits such as those in a computer run off DC. As a result, most computers have a power supply that converts AC to DC.

VINES. A LAN operating system developed by Banyan based on the UNIX operating system.

Virtual circuit. A communication channel that appears to be an end-to-end dedicated circuit, even though the circuit can be changed dynamically and data from the same source could possibly travel different routes.

Virtual device. A method of providing a device interface to an application even though the corresponding physical device may not be present. The virtual device appears as a real device to the application. The operating system directs input and output to a physical device that has been assigned to the virtual device. The Intel 80386 CPU chip can run programs in separate memory segments where each program "thinks" it is running in a separate physical machine.

Virtual memory. Lets a computer process programs whose requirements exceed the system's physical memory. This is done by swapping unneeded program segments out to a disk, freeing these segments for programs that need additional memory.

VLSI. Very Large Scale Integration. Describes the dense organization of hundreds of thousands of transistors on a single chip.

Volatile. A type of data storage medium that looses the data when power is lost. Computer RAM is volatile. Disk storage is non-volatile.

Volume hash. A RAM index to the directory of the volume NetWare uses to quickly locate directory entries.

W

WAN. Wide Area Network. WAN is the concept that the individual networks that make up the internetwork are not located at the same site.

Word length. The internal instruction size of a computer system. The longer the word, the more powerful instructions can be. Word size is a function of the CPU of the computer. The 8088, 8086, 80186, and 80286 Intel CPUs have a 16-bit word. The 80386 has a 32-bit word.

Workstation. A PC connected to a LAN or a powerful computer used for engineering and design applications.

X

X.25. A communication protocol standard developed by CCITT for accessing packet-switched networks.

XGA. See **Extended Graphics Array**.

XNS. Xerox Network Services. A network transport protocol developed by Xerox Corporation.

XON/XOFF. Transmitter On/Transmitter Off. A common method used for adjusting data transmission between a fast device and a slow device. When the slow device is loaded it sends an XOFF code—Ctrl-S (ASCII 19). The computer stops sending until the slow device sends an XON code—Ctrl-Q (ASCII 17).

Z

Zero wait states. A hardware configuration that permits data transfer between the CPU and memory every cycle.

Index

A

Account balance restrictions, security, 327–328
Account names, valid names for security, 322
Account restrictions, 326–327
    account disabled, 326
    account expiration date, 326
    improperly working user account restrictions, 330–331
    limit concurrent connections, 326
    passwords required, 326
    supervisor update of multiple users with same restrictions, 329
ADD NAME SPACE, NetWare 386 console command, 506
Advanced NetWare, 11
ALLOW, NetWare 386 command, 482–483
Apple File Protocol, 61
Application Program Interfaces, 58
Applications. *See* Software applications
ArcMonitor, 415
ARCnet, 132
ARCnet cards, inter-operability, 38
ASCII codes, 262, 263
AT-style disk controller, 8
ATTACH, 200–201
    NetWare 286 command, 440–441
Auto Endcap, 275, 276
AUTOEXEC.BAT, 191, 196
    settings for, 170–174
    and WordPerfect, 242
AUXGEN, 418

B

Backup, incremental backup, 91
BIND
    to link LAN drivers, 77–78
    meaning of elements of, 78
    NetWare 386 console command, 506
Bindery files
    repairing, 99, 330–331
BINDFIX, 99, 330, 331
Bindview +, 437
BREAK, 201–202
BROADCAST
    NetWare 286 console command, 486
    NetWare 386 console command, 507
Broadcast packet, 128
BTRIEVE.NLM, 58
BTRIEVE.VAP, 20
Byte Stream, 299
    setting for printer, 275

Index

C

Cable, troubleshooting problems, 412–414
Cache statistics. *See* File server monitoring
Caching
    directory caching, 17–18, 63–64
    file caching, 62–63
    meaning of cache, 93
    See also Directory caching; File caching
Cafeteria plan, 319
CAPTURE, 240, 250–251
    NetWare 286 command, 441–445
    printing problems related to, 286–287
CASTOFF, NetWare 286 command, 445–446
Channel diagnostics, troubleshooting, 415–416
Channel statistics. *See* File server monitoring
Checkit, 124
CHKDIR, NetWare 386 command, 483
CHKVOL, NetWare 286 command, 446–447
CLEAR MESSAGE, NetWare 286 console command, 486
CLEAR STATION
    NetWare 286 console command, 486
    NetWare 386 console command, 507
CLIB.NLM, 58
Client-server protocols, 131
    standards problem related to, 132
CLS, NetWare 386 console command, 508
COMMAND
    NetWare 286 command, 439–440
    NetWare 286 console command, 485–486
    NetWare 386 command, 481–482

NetWare 386 console command, 505
COMMAND.COM, 190
Communication buffers, 40
    calculation of buffers needed, 15–16
    and file server, 15
    importance of, 15
    maximum allotment, use of, 15–16
    memory usage, 15–16
Communication protocols
    client-server protocols, 131
    media protocols, 131
    NetWare support of, 132
    transport protocols, 131
Communications, setting for NetWare 386, 66–67
COMPSURF, and installation, 26
COMSPEC, 202–203
    function of, 195
    setting, 190, 195
CONFIG, NetWare 386 console command, 508
CONFIG.SYS, 196
    settings for, 169–170
    and WordPerfect, 242
Configuration file
    EMSNETx options, 158
    EMSNETx re-director program, 143
    hardware configuration, 221
        and Lotus 1-2-3, 222–223
    IPX options, 155–158
    LAN.BAT, 138–139
    LANSUP driver options, 155
    location of, 137–139
    mistake related to loading, 138
    NETBIOS options, 150–152, 165–167
    NET.CFG, 152–154
    NETx options, 144–150, 158–165
    SHELL.CFG, 140–143
    software configuration files, 220
Connectionless packets, 140
Connection-oriented protocol, 140

Index

Connectors, setting for, 53
Control codes
  ASCII codes, 262, 263
  formats for, 262
  and printer definition, 262
  printing, 275
Copy-protection
  Execute Only file attribute, 96
  flaws of, 95
  and LAN environment, 95–96
Custom configuration, 29
Custom installation, NetWare 286, 28

D

Data failure, and Transaction Tracking, 91
Data recovery, and Transaction Tracking System, 34–35
Decimal codes, 262
Dedicated file server
  nature of, 13
  versus non-dedicated file servers, memory usage, 13–14
  setting as option, 33
Default configuration, 29
Default drive, elimination of mappings, 188–189
Default installation, NetWare 286, 28
Device dependence, 258
DGroup, 418
  calculation of RAM for, 422–423
DGroup data segment
  areas of, 9
  memory usage, 9
Direct memory access
  assignments for IBM PC and PC/XT, 49
  purpose of, 48–49
Directories
  corrupted, repairing, 99
  mapping to logical drives, 214–216
Directory caching
  memory usage, 17–18
  purpose of, 17
  setting for NetWare 386, 63–64
  verification of, 17–18
Directory hashing
  Directory Hash Table, 16–17
  memory usage, 16–17
  purpose of, 16
DISABLE LOGIN
  NetWare 286 console command, 487–488
  NetWare 386 console command, 509
DISABLE TTS, NetWare 386 console command, 509
Disk co-processor board, 58
Disk drivers
  drivers supplied by Novell, 39
  installation of NetWare 286, 28–31
  NetWare 386 drivers, 60, 61
  selection of drivers, 39
Disk interface drivers
  memory usage, 8
  types of drivers, 8
  verification of installation, 8
Diskless workstations, 54
Disk mapping information. See File server monitoring
Disk parameter, setting for NetWare 386, 69–71
DISKSET.NLM, 58
Disk statistics. See File server monitoring
Disk volumes, creation of, 44
DISMOUNT
  NetWare 286 console command, 488
  NetWare 386 console command, 510
DISPLAY, 203
DISPLAY NETWORKS, NetWare 386 console command, 510
DISPLAY SERVERS, NetWare 386 console command, 510–511
Documentation
  file server, 437
  file server configuration worksheet, 429, 432

Index

file server memory worksheet, 429
LAN and print server diagrams, 433
network number lists, 432
node ID and location lists, 432
software documentation, 433
wire lists for wire closets, 432
wiring floor diagrams, 432
workstation configuration worksheet, 428–429
DOS
locating utilities, 191–194
NetWare 286 console command, 488–489
SET COMSPEC, 190
DOS applications, and non-dedicated file server, 14
DOS BREAK, 204
DOS/ODI workstation shells, 131–133
components of, 133
purpose of, 132
DOS partition, modify partition table, 42
DOS PATH
choosing search number, 180–181
disappearing segments of, 176–177
format for command, 218
logging in and, 175–177
long DOS PATH statements, 178–179
DOS SET, 204–205
DOS utilities, locating correct utility, 191–194
DOS VERIFY, 205
DOS workstation shells, 117–131
Internetwork Packet Exchange (IPX.COM), 118–124
DOWN
NetWare 286 console command, 489
NetWare 386 console command, 511

Downline directories, Rights in, 354–357
DRIVE, 205
Drive mappings, reducing number of, 99
Drivers, installation of NetWare 286, 28–31
Drives, mirrored drives, 44
DSPACE, NetWare 386 command, 484
Dynamic RAM, memory usage, 9

E

EEPROM chip, 58
Effective Rights, 88, 335
Modify Right, 88
NetWare 386 differences, 341–342
ELSGEN, 98, 295
installation program, 25, 27
E-Monitor, 415
EMSNETx options, 143, 158
EMSNETx re-director program, 143
ENABLE LOGIN
NetWare 286 console command, 489
NetWare 386 console command, 511–512
Enable Timeout, 276
ENABLE TTS, NetWare 386 console command, 512
Encryption, passwords, 71–72
ENDCAP, NetWare 286 command, 447
Entry Level System, 4
Entry Level System I, 11
Entry Level System II, 11
Error messages
causes/solutions, 98–99, 100, 101, 102
types of, 98, 100, 101, 102
Ethernet, 132
Execute Only
file attribute, 89
use of, 96

Index

EXIT, 196, 206
    NetWare 386 console command, 512–513
Explicit Rights, 336

F

FCONSOLE, 82, 94
    and troubleshooting, 411–412
FDISPLAY, 207
Fiber Distributed Data Interface, 85
File Allocation Tables
    function of, 9
    indexing clusters from, 90
    memory usage, 10–11
    size of, 9
File attributes
    Execute Only, 89
    hidden file, 90
    Indexed (I), 90
    and local drives, 100
    modification of, 89
    modified since last backup, 91
    nature of, 88
    Normal (N), 89
    Read Only (RO), 89, 92
    Read-Write (RW), 89, 92
    Search Mode, 103–105
    Shareable (S), 89
    system file, 89
    Transaction Tracked (T), 91
File-based applications, data file integrity, 229
File caching
    memory usage, 22–23
    nature of, 22
    setting for NetWare 386, 62–63
    verification of memory for, 23
File Contents, setting for printer, 275
File-level Rights, NetWare 386 differences, 342–343
File lock, 68–69
FILER utility, 88, 90, 97
File server
    and Communication buffers, 15
    configuration worksheet, 429, 432
    documentation, 437
    memory, 3–4
    memory worksheet, 429
    multiple servers, problem related to, 201
File server monitoring
    cache statistics
        background aged writes, 385
        background dirty writes, 385
        cache allocations, 386
        cache blocks scrapped, 387
        cache buffer size, 382
        cache get requests, 385
        cache hits, 383
        cache misses, 384
        cache write requests, 383
        dirty cache buffers, 382
        file server up time, 382
        fragmented writes, 386
        full write requests, 385
        hit on unavailable block, 387
        LRU block dirty, 386
        number of cache buffers, 382
        partial write requests, 385
        physical read errors, 384
        physical read requests, 384
        physical write errors, 384
        physical write requests, 384
        read beyond write, 386
        total cache writes, 385
        trashing count, 386
    channel statistics
        channel configuration, 390
        DMA channels used, 389
        driver type, 389
        driver version, 389
        file server up time, 388
        interrupts used, 389
        IO addresses, 389
        shared memory addresses, 389
        status, 388
        synchronization, 388–389

Index

disk mapping information
    disk channels, 391–392
    file server up time, 390
    logical disk count, 391
    logical disk to physical
      disk mappings, 392
    pending I/O commands, 391
    physical disk count, 391
    SFT support level, 391
disk statistics
    I/O error count, 394
    controller type, 393
    disk channel, 393
    disk type, 393
    drive cylinders, 394
    drive size, 394
    file server up time, 393
    hot fix remaining, 395
    hot fix status, 394
    hot fix table size, 394
    hot fix table start, 394
file server statistics summary
    bindery objects, 380
    connections, 380
    current server utilization, 376
    dirty cache buffers, 378
    disk requests serviced
      from cache, 377
    dynamic memory 1, 380
    dynamic memory 2, 381
    dynamic memory 3, 381
    file server up time, 375
    file service packets, 377
    indexed files, 379–380
    number of file service
      processes, 376
    open files, 379
    packets routed, 377
    routing buffers, 379
    total number of cache
      buffers, 378
    total packets received, 377
    total server memory, 378–379
    transactions, 380
    unused server memory, 379

file system statistics
    active indexed files, 398
    attached indexed files, 398
    configured max indexed
      files, 398
    configured max open files, 396
    currently open files, 396
    dirty FAT sectors, 397
    fatal FAT write errors, 397
    FAT scan errors, 397
    FAT sector writes, 397
    FAT write errors, 397
    file server up time, 396
    open requests, 396
    peak files open, 396
    peak indexed files open, 398
    read requests, 396
    write requests, 396
LAN I/O statistics
    detach with invalid slot, 401–402
    detach during processing
      ignored, 403
    duplicate replies sent, 403
    file server up time, 399
    file service packets, 400
    file service used route, 404
    forged detach requests, 402
    ignored duplicate attach, 403
    incoming packets lost
      because of no available
      buffers, 404
    invalid connections, 401
    invalid request type, 401
    invalid sequence numbers, 401
    NETBIOS broadcasts, 400
    new attach during
      processing, 402
    new request during
      processing, 402
    outgoing packets lost
      because of no available
      buffers, 405

Index

packets discarded because
destination address is
unknown, 404
packets discarded because
they crossed more than
16 bridges, 404
packets with invalid slots,
400
packets routed, 399–400
positive acknowledgements
sent, 404
reexecuted requests, 403
reply canceled by new
attach, 403
total packets received, 399
transaction tracking statistics
configured max transactions,
406
current disk space used,
407
current transactions, 406
file server up time, 405
peak transactions, 406
requested blackouts, 407
total file extensions, 407
total file size changes, 407
total file truncations, 407
transactions performed, 406
transactions written, 406
transaction tracking status,
406
transaction tracking
volume, 406
unfilled blackout requests,
407
volume information
block size, 409
current free directory
entries, 410
file server up time, 408
free blocks, 409
logical drive number, 410
maximum directory entries,
410
mirror disk number, 411
peak directory entries used,
410
primary disk number, 411
starting block, 409
total blocks, 409
volume cached, 409
volume hashed, 409
volume mirrored, 410–411
volume name, 408
volume number, 408
volume removable, 409
File server statistics. *See* File server
statistics summary
File Service Processes
nature, 416
obtaining more FSPs, 418–424
troubleshooting problems, 417
uses of, 416
File system, setting for NetWare
386, 65–66
File system statistics. *See* File server
monitoring
FIRE PHASERS, 207
FLAG, 88, 100, 101, 102, 228
NetWare 286 command, 448–449
FLAGDIR, NetWare 286 command,
449–450
Fonts, downloadable, print setting,
275

G

Global static data, 418, 420–421
GOTO, 207–208
GRANT, NetWare 286 command,
450–451
Graphics printing
problems
improperly configured
applications, 283–284
improper print job
definitions, 285
problem with CAPTURE
command, 286–287
print setting, 275

H

Hexadecimal codes, 262
Hidden files
　file attribute, 90
　finding files, 90
　recording names of, 97
　use for sensitive data, 97
　uses of, 90
Hit, meaning of, 93
HOLDOFF, 89
　NetWare 286 command, 451
HOLDON, 89, 230
　NetWare 286 command, 451-452
Home directory, 232
Hot fix area, 9
Hot Fix Redirection Table, 9
　modification of, 43

I

I/O address port, listing of device settings, 50-52
IBM 3816 page printer, not printing properly, 301
IBM PS/2 ESDI and MFM disk controllers, 8
Identifiers, for Login Scripts, 198-199
ID numbers, and installation, 26
IF Login Scripts, 185
IF...THEN, 208-209
Image problem, 217
Implicit Rights
　blocking Implicit Rights, 358-359
　downline directories, 337
　group membership, 337
　security equivalences, 337-338
INCLUDE, 209
Incremental backup, 91
Indexed (I), file attribute, 90
Indexed files
　memory usage, 18-19
　nature of, 19
Industry Standard Architecture ST506 disk controller, 8
Initialization, reinitialization of disk, 43

Installation programs, 25
　processes performed by, 25
Installation. *See* NetWare 286, file server reconfiguration; NetWare 386, file server reconfiguration
INSTALL.NLM, 58
Internal bridges, 6
　installation of, 86
　purpose of, 6
　usefulness of, 6
　uses of
　　bridging existing dissimilar LANs, 84
　　reduction of LAN channel load, 81-83
　　as upgrade technique, 85
Internal commands, 216-217
Internetwork Packet Exchange (IPX.COM), 118-124, 140
　device configuration options, 120-123
　failure to load, 119-120
　NETBIOS emulation program, 130-131
　re-director program, 124-129
　unloading, 134
　verification of configuration, 123
Internetwork Packet Exchange/ Sequenced Packet Exchange, 132
Internetworks
　and communication protocols, 131-132
　and DOS/ODI workstation shells, 132-133
　WAN as, 131
Inter-operability, ARCnet cards, 38
Interrupt request signal line
　assignment of interrupt channels, 46-48
　priority and number value, 48
　purpose of, 46
Interrupts, adapter cards with, 48
Intruder detection, 323-324
IPX options, 140-143, 155-158
IPXS.NLM, 58

Index

J
Jukeboxes, 39

K
Keywords, for Login Scripts, listing of, 198–199

L
LAN I/O statistics. *See* File server monitoring
LAN
   and internal bridges
      bridging existing dissimilar LANs, 84
      reduction of channel load, 81–83
      upgrading technique, 85
   LAN standards, 38
   and print server diagrams, documentation, 433
LAN.BAT, 138–139
LAN drivers
   installation of, 35–39
   listings of options, 73–76
   setting for NetWare 386, 73–77
      BIND command to link drivers, 77–78
      LOAD command, 73–77
LAN Spool, 315–316
LANSUP driver options, 155
LARCHIVE, NetWare 286 command, 452–454
Laser printing, problems, improper printing, 289
LED array printers, 288, 289
LISTDIR, NetWare 286 command, 454–455
LOAD
   to load LAN drivers, 73–77
   NetWare 386 console command, 513
Locks
   file lock, 68–69
   logical locks, 69
   physical lock, 68–69
   setting for NetWare 386, 69
Logical drives
   logging out, problem related to, 216
   mapping directories to, 214–216
Logical locks, 69
LOGIN
   directory, locating, 173–174
   NetWare 286 command, 455–456
   process in, 46
Login Script commands
   ATTACH, 200–201
   BREAK, 201–202
   COMSPEC, 202–203
   DISPLAY, 203
   DOS BREAK, 204
   DOS SET, 204–205
   DOS VERIFY, 205
   DRIVE, 205
   EXIT, 206
   FDISPLAY, 207
   FIRE PHASERS, 207
   GOTO, 207–208
   IF...THEN, 208–209
   INCLUDE, 209
   listing of, 197–199
   MACHINE NAME, 210–211
   MAP, 213–220
   PAUSE, 211
   # command, 200
   REMARK, 212
   WRITE, 212–213
Login Scripts
   IF in, 185
   listing of keywords/identifiers, 198–199
   % in, 193
   # in, 185–187
   System Login Script, 184
   User Login Script, 184–185
   WordPerfect user ID in, 248–249
LOGOUT, NetWare 286 command, 456
Lomax Utilities, 437
Long Machine Type, 146, 193, 212, 237

Lotus 1-2-3
  and hardware configuration, 222–223
  printing, 251–252
  printing problems, 283
LRESTORE, NetWare 286 command, 456–457

M

MACHINE NAME, 210–211
Management
  group management
    users created by supervisors, 366
    users created by workgroup managers, 366
    users with more than one manager, 366
  independent file server domains, 367
    allocation of space on file servers, 368
  mixed environments
    management for different file servers, 370
    one user group using all disk space, 371–372
  of Rights, 351–354
  user account managers, 365
  workgroup managers, 364–365
MAP, 213–220
  choosing search number, 180–181
  mapping directories to logical drives, 214–216
  NetWare 286 command, 457–461
  program locations, 182–183
  reducing number of, 99
  searching to find programs, 216–220
  use in Login Scripts, 213–220
  uses of, 214
Mappings
  default drive, elimination of mappings, 188–189
    elimination at default drive, 188–189
  search drives, 179
MAP SEARCH, 163–164, 237
  rules for use, 218–220
  and Search Mode, 103, 104
MARKNET, 134
Math co-processor, 58
MATHLIBC.NLM, 59
MATHLIB.NLM, 59
Maximum Rights Mask, 92, 335
  setting for directory, 336
Maximum service processes, 72
Media protocols, 131
MEMORY
  NetWare 386 console command, 514
  cache buffer size, 68
  file server, 3–4
  maximum dynamic memory, 68
  NetWare use of RAM, 3
  setting for NetWare 386, 67–68
Memory addresses, for ROM, 52
Memory resident programs
  PRINTER, 278–279
  problem with loading, 186
  start up, 206
  unloading, 134–135
Memory usage
  communication buffers, 15–16
  dedicated versus non-dedicated file servers, 13–14
  directory caching, 17–18
  directory hashing, 16–17
  disk interface drivers, 8
  dynamic RAM, 9
  file allocation tables, 10–11
  file caching, 22–23
  indexed files, 18–19
  network interface card drivers, 6
  open files, 18
  operating system, 5
  operating system options, 11–12
  shared printers, 19–20
  value added programs, 20–21
Memory window, 14

Index

Menu, start up of, 196
Mirrored drives, 44, 71
Modes
    building for printing, 263–264, 266
    Re-initialize Mode, 264
    setting for printer, 276
Modified since last backup, file attribute, 91
MODULES, NetWare 386 console command, 514
MONITOR, 94
    NetWare 286 console command, 490–492
MONITOR.NML, 59
Monitrix, 82, 415
MOUNT
    NetWare 286 console command, 492
    NetWare 386 console command, 514–515

N

NAME
    NetWare 286 console command, 492–493
    NetWare 386 console command, 515
Name space modules, 61
    writing of, 61
NCOPY, NetWare 286 command, 461–462
NDIR, NetWare 286 command, 462–468
NETBIOS emulation program, 130–131
    function of, 130–131
    unloading, 134
NETBIOS options, 150–152, 165–167
NetCare, 415
NET.CFG, 152–154, 237
    EMSNETx options, 158
    IPX options, 155–158
    LANSUP driver options, 155
    NETBIOS options, 165–167

NETx options, 158–165
protocol options, 152–154
NETGEN, 98, 295, 424
    installation program, 25, 27
NETUTILS, 331
NetWare 286
    file server reconfiguration
        I/O address port, 49–52
        cable/connector type, 53
        configuration of adapters, 45–46
        configure drivers/resources, 40
        create disk volumes, 44
        custom installation, 28
        default installation, 28
        direct memory access, 48–49
        edit resource list, 40
        edit resource sets, 40
        establish mirrored pair, 44
        installation programs, 25
        installing NetWare on file server, 27–28
        interrupt request signal line, 46–48
        linking NetWare with drivers, 28–31
        linking operating system, 26–27
        load operating system, 45
        load system and public files, 45
        memory address, 52
        modify hot fix redirection table, 42
        modify partition table, 42
        node address/node ID, 52–53
        reinitialize disk, 43
        remote boot ROMs, 54
        save selections and continue, 41
        select disk drivers, 39
        select LAN drivers, 35–39
        select other drivers, 39

Index

select resource sets, 35
setting operation system
  options, 31–35
shared printer ports, 45
System Configuration
  items, 44
printer server program, 255
RAM supported by, 3
Rights, 335–340
NetWare 286 commands
  ATTACH, 440–441
  CAPTURE, 441–445
  CASTOFF, 445–446
  CHKVOL, 446–447
  COMMAND, 439–440
  ENDCAP, 447
  FLAG, 448–449
  FLAGDIR, 449–450
  GRANT, 450–451
  HOLDOFF, 451
  HOLDON, 451–452
  LARCHIVE, 452–454
  LISTDIR, 454–455
  LOGIN, 455–456
  LOGOUT, 456
  LRESTORE, 456–457
  MAP, 457–461
  NCOPY, 461–462
  NDIR, 462–468
  NVER, 468–469
  PSTAT, 469
  PURGE, 469–470
  REMOVE, 470
  RENDIR, 470
  REVOKE, 471
  RIGHTS, 472
  SALVAGE, 472–473
  SEND, 473–474
  SETPASS, 474–475
  SETTTS, 475
  SLIST, 475–476
  SMODE, 476–478
  SYSTIME, 478
  TLIST, 478–479
  USERLIST, 479
  WHOAMI, 479–480

NetWare 286 console commands
  BROADCAST, 486
  CLEAR MESSAGE, 486
  CLEAR STATION, 486
  COMMAND, 485–486
  DISABLE LOGIN, 487–488
  DISMOUNT, 488
  DOS, 488–489
  DOWN, 489
  ENABLE LOGIN, 489
  MONITOR, 490–492
  MOUNT, 492
  NAME, 492–493
  OFF, 493
  PRINTER, 493
  PRINTER ADD QUEUE,
    493–494
  PRINTER DELETE QUEUE,
    495
  PRINTER FORM FEED, 495
  PRINTER FORM MARK,
    495–496
  PRINTER MOUNT FORM, 496
  PRINTER QUEUES, 497
  PRINTER REWIND, 497–498
  PRINTER START, 498
  PRINTER STOP, 498
  QUEUE, 498–499
  QUEUE CHANGE PRIORITY,
    499
  QUEUE CREATE, 499–500
  QUEUE DELETE JOB, 500
  QUEUE DESTROY, 500–501
  REMIRROR, 501
  SEND, 501
  SET TIME, 502
  SPOOL TO QUEUE, 502
  TIME, 503
  UNMIRROR, 503
NetWare 386 C RunTime Libraries,
  61
NetWare 386
  NetWare loadable modules,
    57–61
  printer server program, 255
  RAM supported by, 3

Index

reconfiguration of file server
    communications settings, 66–67
    directory caching, 63–66
    file caching, 62–63
    linking LAN drivers, 77–78
    loading LAN drivers, 73–77
    locks, 68–69
    maximum service processes, 72
    memory allocation, 67–68
    Network Core Protocol searches, 72
    new service process wait time, 72
    password settings, 71–72
    transaction tracking, 69–71
reconfiguration of file server, SET command, 62
Rights, 340–348
NetWare 386 commands
    ALLOW, 482–483
    CHKDIR, 483
    COMMAND, 481–482
    DSPACE, 484
NetWare 386 console commands
    ADD NAME SPACE, 506
    BIND, 506
    BROADCAST, 507
    CLEAR STATION, 507
    CLS, 508
    COMMAND, 505
    CONFIG, 508
    DISABLE LOGIN, 509
    DISABLE TTS, 509
    DISMOUNT, 510
    DISPLAY NETWORKS, 510
    DISPLAY SERVERS, 510–511
    DOWN, 511
    ENABLE LOGIN, 511–512
    ENABLE TTS, 512
    EXIT, 512–513
    LOAD, 513
    MEMORY, 514
    MODULES, 514
    MOUNT, 514–515
    NAME, 515
    OFF, 515
    PROTOCOL, 515
    PROTOCOL REGISTER, 516
    REGISTER MEMORY, 516–517
    REMOVE DOS, 517
    RESET ROUTER, 517
    SEARCH, 518
    SECURE CONSOLE, 518–519
    SEND, 519
    SET, 519–538
    SPEED, 539
    SPOOL, 539
    TIME, 539
    TRACK, 540
    UNBIND, 540
    UNLOAD, 540
    VERSION, 541
    VOLUMES, 541
NetWare, 20
    memory usage, 4–23
    verification of versions, 12
    versions of, 3
NetWare Core Protocol requests, 416
NETWARE directory, creation of, 30
NetWare loadable modules, 57–61
    purpose of, 57
    types of
        disk interface drivers, 60, 61
        name space modules, 61
        network interface drivers, 60
        utilities and application modules, 58–60
Network Core Protocol searches, 72
Network interface card drivers
    configuration of settings, 45–46
    configure drivers/resources, 40
    installation of NetWare 286, 28–31
    internal bridging, 6
    items configured on, 38
    memory addresses, 52
    memory usage, 6
    NetWare 386 drivers, 60, 61
    node address, 52–53
    not interchangeable nature of, 37

types supplied by Novell, 36-37
verification of installation, 6
Network number lists, 432
Network shell programs
    DOS/ODI workstation shells, 131-133
    DOS workstation shells, 117-131
    removing, 133-135
NETx options, 144-150, 158-165
New service process wait time, 72
NIC problems, troubleshooting, 414-415
NLINK, 418
NMAGENT.NLM, 59
Node addresses, and physical network, 53
Node ID and location lists, 432
Non-dedicated file server, 33-34
    drawbacks related to, 13-14, 33-34
    nature of, 13
Normal file, 228
Normal (N), file attribute, 89
Novell Disk Co-Processor, 8
NVER, NetWare 286 command, 468-469

O

OFF
    NetWare 286 console command, 493
    NetWare 386 console command, 515
Open files
    maximum number for file server, 18
    memory usage, 18
    nature of, 18
Open Systems Interconnection Reference Model, 132
Operating system
    internal commands, 216-217
    memory usage, 5
    NetWare 286
        linking to file server, 26-27
        setting options, 31-35

options
    Advanced NetWare, 11
    Entry Level System I, 11
    Entry Level System II, 11
    memory usage, 11-12
    and RAM requirements of file server, 12
    System Fault Tolerant, 11
    Transaction Tracking System, 11-12
    verification of size, 5
Organizational groups, to manage Rights, 351-354
Other drivers, 39
Overlay files, moving to speed applications, 109-110

P

Parental Rights, creating directories without, 347-348
Partitions
    DOS partition, 42
    modify partition table, 42
Passwords
    encryption, 71-72
    features of, 323
PATH, 235-236
    DOS PATH
        choosing search number, 180-181
        disappearing segments of, 176-177
        logging in and, 175-177
        long DOS PATH statements, 178-179
    program locations, 182-183
    search for, 217-218
    and Search Mode, 103, 104
    setting, 218
PAUDIT program, 328
PAUSE, 211
PCCOMPATIBLE, 237
PCONSOLE, 250, 251, 266-272
    changes not taking effect, 303-304

Index

design of printing environment before use, 266
printer configuration, 267, 269
queues, queue users, queue operators, 267, 270
%, in Login Scripts, 193
Physical drive, 215, 216
Physical lock, 68–69
Plotter, printing to shared plotter, 291
Postscript, jobs not printing properly, 299–300
Pound sign (#), 200
   Login Scripts, 185–187
PRINTCON, 272–276
   auto endcap, 275
   device, 275
   enable timeout, 275
   file contents, 275
   mode, 275
   opening menu, 273
   print queue, 276
   tab size, 275
PRINTCON.DAT, 105, 277
PRINTDEF, 258–266, 259–266
   assigning printer name, 259, 261
   device functions, 261–263
   device modes, 263–264, 266
PRINTER, NetWare 286 console command, 493
PRINTER ADD QUEUE, NetWare 286 console command, 493–494
Printer Assist, 316–317
Printer definition files
   from 2.15 version, 259
   PRINTDEF, 259–266
PRINTER DELETE QUEUE, NetWare 286 console command, 495
Printer drivers, software applications, 258–259
PRINTER FORM FEED, NetWare 286 console command, 495
PRINTER FORM MARK, NetWare 286 console command, 495–496
PRINTER MOUNT FORM, NetWare 286 console command, 496
PRINTER QUEUES, NetWare 286 console command, 497
PRINTER REWIND, NetWare 286 console command, 497–498
Printers
   maximum for file server, 20
   print queue, viewing, 20
   resetting to default settings, 259
   shared printers, memory usage, 19–20
Printer sharing. *See* Shared printing
PRINTER START, NetWare 286 console command, 498
PRINTER STOP, NetWare 286 console command, 498
Printing
   Lotus, 1-2-3, 251–252
   and software applications, 240
   WordPerfect, 250–251
Printing problems
   cannot attach to selected server, 302
   cannot create spool file error message, 295–297
   copying print job database to other users, 309–310
   and graphics printing, 283–287
   IBM 3816 page printer not printing properly, 301
   and laser printers, 289
   PCONSOLE changes not taking effect, 303–304
   Postscript jobs not printing properly, 299–300
   RPRINTER not loading properly at workstation, 293–294
   slow printing on PC and XT remote printer workstations, 308
   volume names corrupted and use of PSERVER.VAP, 305–307
Print server program, versions of, 255–256

Process stacks, 421
Program files, protection of, 95-96
Program locations, 182-183
Programmable read only memory (PROM), 54
PROTOCOL, NetWare 386 console command, 515
Protocol analyzers, 415-416
PROTOCOL REGISTER, NetWare 386 console command, 516
PSERVER, 278
    PSERVER.EXE, 278
    PSERVER.NLM, 59, 278
    PSERVER.VAP, 278
        use and corruption of volume names, 305-307
PS-Print, 314-315
PSTAT, NetWare 286 command, 469
Public files, loading, 45
PURGE, NetWare 286 command, 469-470

Q

QAPlus, 124
Queue
    choosing for job, 276
    PCONSOLE, 267, 270
    PRINTCON, 276
    queue operators, 270
    queue users, 270
Queue Assist, 317
QUEUE, NetWare 286 console command, 498-499
QUEUE CHANGE PRIORITY, NetWare 286 console command, 499
QUEUE CREATE, NetWare 286 console command, 499-500
QUEUE DELETE JOB, NetWare 286 console command, 500
QUEUE DESTROY, NetWare 286 console command, 500-501
Queue It, 314-315

R

RAM
    calculation for DGroup, 422-423
    dynamic RAM, 9
    Netware use of RAM, 3
RAM-based applications, data file integrity, 229-231
Read-after-write verification, 71
Read-only file, 228
Read Only (RO), file attribute, 89, 92
Read requests, 71
Read-write file, 228
Read-Write (RW), file attribute, 89, 92
Re-director program, 124-129
    choices for, 124, 125
    failure to load, 127
    file server not found, 128-129
    loading, 126
    unloading, 133-134
REGISTER MEMORY, NetWare 386 console command, 516-517
RELNET, 134
REMARK, 189, 212
REMIRROR, NetWare 286 console command, 501
Remote boot ROM, 54
REMOTE.NML, 59
Remote printing
    PRINTER, 278-279
    third-party print servers
        LAN Spool, 315-316
        Printer Assist, 316-317
        PS-Print, 314-315
        Queue Assist, 317
        Queue It, 314-315
REMOVE, NetWare 286 command, 470
REMOVE DOS, NetWare 386 console command, 517
RENDIR, NetWare 286 command, 470
RESET ROUTER, NetWare 386 console command, 517

Index

Resources
    edit resource list, 40
    edit resource sets, 40
    installation of NetWare 286, 28–31
Resource sets, selection of, 35
REVOKE, NetWare 286 command, 471
Rights, 333–349
    blocking Implicit Rights, 358–359
    categories of, 334
    clarification of, principles related to, 338–340
    creation of directories without Parental Rights, 347–348
    Effective Rights, 335
    Explicit Rights, 336
    Implicit Rights
        downline directories, 337
        group membership, 337
        security equivalences, 337–338
    Maximum Rights Mask, 335
        setting for directory, 336
    NetWare 386
        changes to Rights categories, 340–341
        differences in Effective Rights, 341–342
        file-level rights, 342–343
        rights in downline directories, 354–357
    Trustee Assignments, 335
    user groups for management of, 351–354
    user's directory Rights not appropriate, 344–345
    user's Rights insufficient for log in, 346
    NetWare 286 command, 472
ROM
    I/O address port, 52
    programmable read only memory (PROM), 54
ROUTE.NML, 59

Routing buffers. *See* Communication buffers
RPRINTER, 278–279
    not loading properly at workstation, 293–294
    removing from workstation RAM, 279
    warning about, 279
RSPX.NLM, 59

S

SALVAGE, 65
    NetWare 286 command, 472–473
SEARCH, NetWare 386 console command, 518
Searches
    searching to find programs, MAP, 216–220
    search number, choosing, 180–181
Search Mode
    file attribute, 103–5
        function of, 103
        parameters for, 104–5
        use of, 105
    length of file names and, 111
    moving overlay files to speed applications, 109–10
    NetWare 386 bug and, 111
SECURE CONSOLE, NetWare 386 console command, 518–519
Security
    account balance restrictions, 327–328
    account restrictions, 326–327
    control of unauthorized access to network
        accessing files at file server, 322
        intruder detection, 323–324
        invalid account names, 322
        passwords, 323
    improperly working user account restrictions, 330–331
    locked supervisor account, 325

Index

Rights, 333–349
station restrictions, 327
supervisor update of multiple users with same restrictions, 329
time restrictions, 327
Semaphores, 96
SEND
    NetWare 286 command, 473–474
    NetWare 286 console command, 501
    NetWare 386 console command, 519
Sequenced Packet Exchange (SPX), 140
Serial ports, configuration for printer sharing, 45
Service Diagnostics, 124
SET
    NetWare 386 console commands, 519–538
        allow unencrypted passwords, 519–520
        auto register memory above 16 megabytes, 520
        auto TTS backout flag, 521
        cache buffer size, 521
        console display watchdog logouts, 522
        directory cache allocation wait time, 522
        directory cache buffer nonreferenced delay, 523
        dirty directory cache delay time, 523–524
        dirty disk cache delay time, 524
        enable disk read after write verify, 524–525
        file delete wait time, 525
        immediate purge of deleted files, 525–526
        maximum alloc short term memory, 526
        maximum concurrent directory cache writes, 527
        maximum concurrent disk cache writes, 527
        maximum directory cache buffers, 528
        maximum file locks, 528
        maximum file locks per connection, 528–529
        maximum outstanding NCP searches, 529
        maximum packet receive buffers, 529
        maximum physical receive packet size, 529–530
        maximum record locks, 530
        maximum record locks per connection, 530–531
        maximum service processes, 531
        maximum subdirectory tree depth, 531
        maximum transactions, 531–532
        minimum directory cache buffers, 532
        minimum file cache buffer report threshold, 533
        minimum file cache buffers, 532–533
        minimum file delete wait time, 533–534
        minimum packet receive buffers, 534
        new packet receive buffer wait time, 534
        new service process wait time, 535
        reconfiguration of file server, 62
        time, 535
        TTS abort dump flag, 535–536
        TTS blackout file truncation wait time, 536
        TTS unwritten cache wait time, 536

Index

turbo FAT re-use wait time, 537
volume low warn all users, 537
volume low warning reset threshold, 538
volume low warning threshold, 538
SETPASS, NetWare 286 command, 474–475
SET TIME, NetWare 286 console command, 502
SETTTS, NetWare 286 command, 475
Shareable file, 228
Shareable (S), file attribute, 89, 92
  and network performance, 93–94
Shared printing
  configuration for, 45
  hook-up for printers, 255
  memory usage, 19–20
  set-up
    assigning printer name, 259, 261
    copying job definitions to other users, PRINTCON.DAT, 277
    creating print server, PCONSOLE, 266–272
    defining printers, PRINTDEF, 258–266
    device functions, 261–263
    device modes, 263–264–266
    listing of programs/tasks, 257
    loading and using PSERVER, 278
    print job definitions, PRINTCON, 272–276
    remote print servers, RPRINTER, 278–279
  and workstation files, 256
SHELL.CFG, 140–143, 212, 237
  EMSNETx options, 143
  IPX options, 140–143

NETBIOS options, 150–152
NETx options, 144–150
SHGEN program, 118
Short Machine Type, 146, 193, 279
SLIST, NetWare 286 command, 475–476
SMODE, 223, 235, 239
  NetWare 286 command, 476–478
Sniffer, 82, 415
Socket, IPX, 142
Software applications
  configuration files
    changing behavior of application, 234–236
    configuration directory in user PATH, 237–238
    configuration file summary, 239
    number needed, 232–233
    placement of files, 232–233
    purposes of, 106, 231
  data file integrity, 227–231
    file-based applications, 229
    RAM-based applications, 229–231
  file attribute settings, 228
  Lotus 1-2-3, 251–252
  printer drivers, 258–259
  and printing, 240
  problem solving for, 106–8
  and record locking, 228
  shareable files revert back to normal, 112
  speeding, moving overlay files, 109–110
  WordPerfect, 241–251
Software documentation, 433
SPEED, NetWare 386 console command, 539
SPOOL, NetWare 386 console command, 539
Spool file, cannot create spool file error message, 295–297
SPOOL TO QUEUE, NetWare 286 console command, 502
SPXS.NLM, 60

SRW.COM, use of, 112
Standards
    and inter-operability, 38
    LAN standards, 38
Station restrictions, security, 327
STREAMS-based IPX protocol, 58
STREAMS.NLM, 60
Supervisory Rights, 340
SUPPORT diskette, 28, 41
SYSCON, 328, 329, 330, 347, 348, 366, 367, 370
System configuration, NetWare 286, items related to, 44
System Fault Tolerant, 4, 11
System files
    caution about, 90
    file attribute, 90
System Login Script, 107, 184, 194
SYSTIME, NetWare 286 command, 478

T

Tab, size and print setting, 275
Text, setting for printer, 275
Thermal transfer printers, 288, 289
Third-party monitoring packages, 82
TIME
    NetWare 286 console command, 503
    NetWare 386 console command, 539
Time restrictions, security, 327
TLI.NLM, 60
TLIST, NetWare 286 command, 478-479
TOKENRPL.NLM, 60
TRACK, NetWare 386 console command, 540
Transaction Tracked (T), file attribute, 91
Transaction tracking statistics. *See* File server monitoring
Transaction Tracking System, 11-12
    drawback of, 35
    purpose of, 34, 69, 91
    setting for NetWare 386, 69-71, 70
Transport protocols, 131
Troubleshooting
    cable and physical network problems, 412-414
    channel diagnostics, 415-416
    NIC problems, 414-415
Trustee Assignments, 87, 92, 335, 338, 344
TXD, 82, 415

U

UNBIND, NetWare 386 console command, 540
UNLOAD, NetWare 386 console command, 540
UPS.NLM, 60
User account managers, 365
USERLIST, 211
    NetWare 286 command, 479
User Login Script, 184-185
UTIL.EXE, 99

V

Value added processes, reducing number of, 98
Value added programs
    memory usage, 20-21
    nature of, 20
    verification of size, 21
VERSION, NetWare 386 console command, 541
VOLINFO, 98, 295, 424
Volume
    information program, 295
    names corrupted and use of PSERVER.VAP, 305-307
    specified volume not found, 101
    volume low warning, 65
Volume information. *See* File server monitoring
VOLUMES, NetWare 386 console command, 541

Index

VREPAIR, 99, 331
    and installation, 26
VREPAIR.NLM, 60
VTREE, 345, 348

W

Watchdog, 82, 415
Wide area network (WAN), 131
Wire lists for wire closets, 432
Wiring floor diagrams, 432
WordPerfect, 241–251
    and AUTOEXEC.BAT, 242
    and CONFIG.SYS, 242
    default set-up file, 244–245
    installation on LAN, 241–243
    printer set-up, 250–251
    user ID in Login Script, 248–249
    user set-up files, 246–247
Workgroup managers, 364–365
Workstation configuration worksheet, 428–429
Workstation shell programs, loading, events related to, 173–174
WRITE, 212–213
Write requests, 71

X

Xerox Network Services (XNS) protocol, 130